Brexit

All You Need to Know

Compiled by

Bailee Skeen

Scribbles

Year of Publication 2018

ISBN : 9789352979592

Book Published by

Scribbles

(An Imprint of Alpha Editions)

email - alphaedis@gmail.com

Produced by: PediaPress GmbH
Limburg an der Lahn
Germany
http://pediapress.com/

Contents

Introduction

Brexit

<indicator name="pp-default"> 🔒 </indicator>

Part of a series of articles on the
United Kingdom in the European Union
Accession

- 1973 EC enlargement
- 1975 Referendum Act
- 1975 EC membership referendum
- 1972 EC Act
- UK rebate
- 2011 EU Act

Membership

- The Euro
- European Movement UK
- Nationality law
- UK Euroscepticism
  - Maastricht Rebels
- Black Wednesday
- **Officials and bodies**
- EU Committee
- European Scrutiny Committee
- Northern Ireland Executive in Brussels
- EU Representative in London
- Young European Movement UK
- UK European Commissioners
- Permanent EU Representatives

Legislation

- 1972 EC Act
- 1986 EC (Amendment) Act
- 1993 EC (Amendment) Act
- 1998 EC (Amendment) Act
- 2002 EC (Amendment) Act
- 2008 EU (Amendment) Act
- 2011 EU Act

European Parliament Elections

- 1979
- 1984
- 1989
- 1994
- 1999
- 2004
- 2009
- 2014

  - 1973 delegation
  - 1st
  - 2nd
  - 3rd
  - 4th
  - 5th
  - 6th
  - 7th
  - 8th

Withdrawal

- 2004–05 EU Bill
- 2013–14 EU (Referendum) Bill
- 2015–16 EU membership renegotiation
- 2015 EU Referendum Act
- 2016 EU (Referendum) Act (Gibraltar)
- **2016 EU membership referendum**
- Issues
- Endorsements
- Opinion polling
- Results
- Causes
- **Campaigns**
- **Organisations advocating and campaigning for a referendum**
- People's Pledge
- Labour for a Referendum
- **Leave**
- **Vote Leave** (official lead group)
    - Business for Britain
    - Conservatives for Britain
    - Students for Britain
- Labour Leave
- Leave.EU
    - Bpoplive
- Grassroots Out
- Get Britain Out
- The Freedom Association
    - Better Off Out
- **Other anti-EU advocacy organisations**
- Bruges Group
- Campaign for an Independent Britain
- **Remain**
- **Britain Stronger in Europe** (official lead group)
- Labour In for Britain
- European Movement UK
- **Other pro-EU advocacy organisations**
- Britain in Europe
- British Influence
- Business for New Europe
- Nucleus
- **Pejorative term for pro-EU advocacy**
- Project Fear
- **Media coverage**
- *Brexit: The Movie*
- *In or Out*
- **Aftermath**
- International reactions
- Terms of Withdrawal from EU (Referendum) Bills
- 2016 Conservative Party election
- 2016 Labour Party election
- 2017 Liberal Democrats Party election
- Proposed second Scottish independence referendum
- Proposed London independence
- *The New European*
- European Union (Withdrawal) Act 2018 (including meaningful vote)
- European Union (Withdrawal Agreement) Bill 2017-19
- Gibraltar
- 2017 General Election
- EU Withdrawal Agreement (Public Vote) Bill 2017-19
- UK's relations with EU after 2019
- **Triggering of Article 50 & Negotiations**
- *R (Miller) v Secretary of State for Exiting the European Union*'
- EU (Notification of Withdrawal) Act 2017
- UK invocation of Article 50
- Brexit negotiations
- Department for Exiting the EU (Brexit Department)
- Department for International Trade
- Post referendum organisations

Calls for second vote

- European Union Withdrawal Agreement (Public Vote) Bill 2017-19
- **Organisations campaigning for a second vote via People's Vote**
- Britain for Europe
- European Movement UK
- For our Future's Sake
- Healthier IN the EU
- Open Britain
- Our Future Our Choice
- Scientists for EU
- **Other organisations campaigning for a second vote**
- Best for Britain
- **See also**
- Opposition to Brexit in the United Kingdom

- v
- t
- e[1]

Part of **a series** on the

History of the United Kingdom

United Kingdom portal

- v
- t
- e[2]

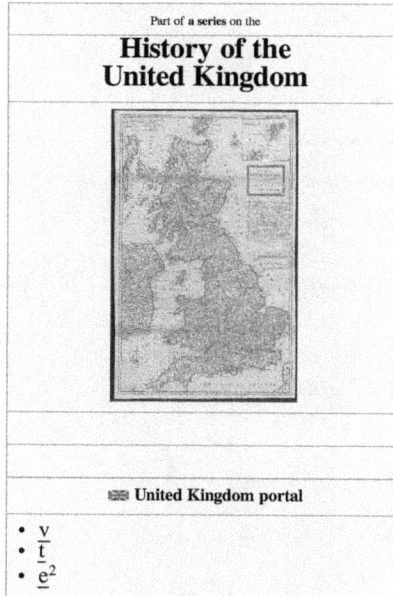

Brexit (/ˈbrɛksɪt, <wbr />ˈbrɛgzɪt/) is the impending withdrawal of the United Kingdom (UK) from the European Union (EU). In a referendum on 23 June 2016, a majority of British voters supported leaving the EU. On 29 March 2017, the UK government invoked Article 50 of the Treaty on European Union. The United Kingdom is due to leave the EU on 29 March 2019 at

11 p.m. UTC (midnight Central European Time), when the period for negotiating a withdrawal agreement will end unless an extension is agreed.

Prime Minister Theresa May announced the government's intention not to seek permanent membership of the European single market or the EU customs union after leaving the EU and promised to repeal the European Communities Act of 1972 and incorporate existing European Union law into UK domestic law. A new government department, the Department for Exiting the European Union, was created in July 2016.

Negotiations with the EU officially started in June 2017, aiming to complete the withdrawal agreement by October 2018. In June 2018, the UK and the EU published a joint progress report outlining agreement on issues including customs, VAT and Euratom.

The UK joined the European Communities (EC) in 1973, with membership confirmed by a referendum in 1975. In the 1970s and 1980s, withdrawal from the EC was advocated mainly by Labour Party members and trade union figures. From the 1990s, the main advocates of withdrawal were the newly founded UK Independence Party (UKIP) and an increasing number of Eurosceptic Conservative Party members. Prime Minister David Cameron held the referendum in fulfilment of a 2015 manifesto pledge. Cameron, who had campaigned for "Remain", resigned after the referendum result and was succeeded by Theresa May, who called a snap general election less than a year later, in which she lost her overall majority. Her minority government is supported in key votes by the Democratic Unionist Party.

Six weeks after the referendum, the Bank of England introduced quantitative easing and lower interest rates, thus allowing both depreciation of sterling and a rise in inflation that outpaced wage growth for most of 2017. The drop in the value of sterling has been claimed to have been caused in part by hedge-fund managers betting on Brexit against polls predicting a narrow victory for the "Remain" camp.[3]

There is a broad consensus in existing economic modeling that Brexit is likely to reduce the UK's real per capita income in the medium term and long term. There is also agreement among economists that the Brexit referendum itself damaged the economy in the subsequent two years. Studies on effects that have materialised since the referendum show annual losses of £404 for the average UK household, and losses between 1.3% and 2.1% of UK GDP. Brexit is likely to reduce immigration from European Economic Area (EEA) countries to the UK, and poses challenges for UK higher education and academic research. As of August 2018[4], the size of the "divorce bill", the UK's inheritance of existing EU trade agreements, and relations with Ireland and other EU member states remain uncertain. The precise impact on the UK depends on whether the process will be a "hard" or a "soft" Brexit.

Terminology

In the wake of the referendum, many new pieces of Brexit-related jargon have entered popular use.

Brexit

Brexit (like its early variant, *Brixit*) is a portmanteau of "British" and "exit". In popular usage, it was derived by analogy from Grexit, referring to a hypothetical withdrawal of Greece from the eurozone (and possibly also the EU).[5] However, the term *Brexit* may have first been used in reference to a possible UK withdrawal from the EU by Peter Wilding, in a Euractiv blog post on 15 May 2012; this is given as the first attestation in the *Oxford English Dictionary*).

Hard and soft Brexit

The terms "hard Brexit" and "soft Brexit" are often used unofficially in terms of the process, but commonly by news media, and are understood to describe the prospective relationship between the UK and the EU after withdrawal, ranging from *hard*, which could involve the UK trading with the EU under the World Trade Organization's Bali Package, but with no obligation to accept free movement of people, to *soft*, which might involve retaining membership of the EU single market for goods and services and at least some free movement of people, according to European Economic Area rules.

Divorce bill

It is expected that the UK will make a contribution toward financial commitments that were approved while the UK was still a member of the EU but are still outstanding. In the first phase of negotiations the total amount was referred to as the *single financial settlement*, or just *the settlement*. Especially in the media, this has been called an *exit bill* or *divorce bill*, while the EU talk of *settling the accounts*. Brexit Secretary Dominic Raab has said the UK will not pay its financial settlement to the EU in a no-deal scenario.

Chequers plan

The short name given by the media to *"The future relationship between the United Kingdom and the European Union"*, the government's white paper drawn up at Chequers and published on 12 July 2018 which sets out the sort of relationship the UK wants with the EU after Brexit.

Brexiteer

Those supporting Brexit are sometimes referred to as "Brexiteers".

Remainer

Those in favour of the UK remaining in the EU are sometimes referred to as "Remainers". The derogatory term "Remoaner" (a portmanteau of "remainer" and "moaner") is sometimes used by pro-Brexit media outlets.

Background

The "Inner Six" European countries signed the Treaty of Paris in 1951, establishing the European Coal and Steel Community (ECSC). The 1955 Messina Conference deemed that the ECSC was a success, and resolved to extend the concept further, thereby leading to the 1957 Treaties of Rome establishing the European Economic Community (EEC) and the European Atomic Energy Community (Euratom). In 1967 these became known as the European Communities (EC). The UK attempted to join in 1963 and 1967, but these applications were vetoed by the President of France, Charles de Gaulle. After de Gaulle relinquished the French presidency the UK successfully applied for membership and the Conservative prime minister Edward Heath signed the Treaty of Accession in 1972, Parliament passed the European Communities Act later in the year and the UK became a member of the EC on 1 January 1973 with Denmark and Ireland.

The opposition Labour Party contested the October 1974 general election with a commitment to renegotiate Britain's terms of membership of the EC and then hold a referendum on whether to remain in the EC on the new terms.[6] After Labour won the election, the United Kingdom held its first national referendum on whether the UK should remain in the European Communities in 1975. Despite significant division within the ruling Labour Party all major political parties and the mainstream press supported continuing membership of the EC. On 5 June 1975, 67.2% of the electorate and all but two[7] UK counties and regions voted to stay in; support for the UK to leave the EC in 1975 appears unrelated to the support for Leave in the 2016 referendum.

The Labour Party campaigned in the 1983 general election on a commitment to withdraw from the EC without a referendum, although after a heavy defeat Labour changed its policy. In 1985, the Thatcher government ratified the Single European Act—the first major revision to the Treaty of Rome—without a referendum.

In October 1990, under pressure from senior ministers and despite Margaret Thatcher's deep reservations, the United Kingdom joined the European Exchange Rate Mechanism (ERM), with the pound sterling pegged to the deutschmark. Thatcher resigned as Prime Minister the following month, amid Conservative Party divisions arising partly from her increasingly Eurosceptic views. The United Kingdom and Italy were forced to withdraw from the ERM in September 1992, after the pound sterling and the lira came under pressure ("Black Wednesday").

Under the Maastricht Treaty, the European Communities became the European Union on 1 November 1993, reflecting the evolution of the organisation from an economic union into a political union.

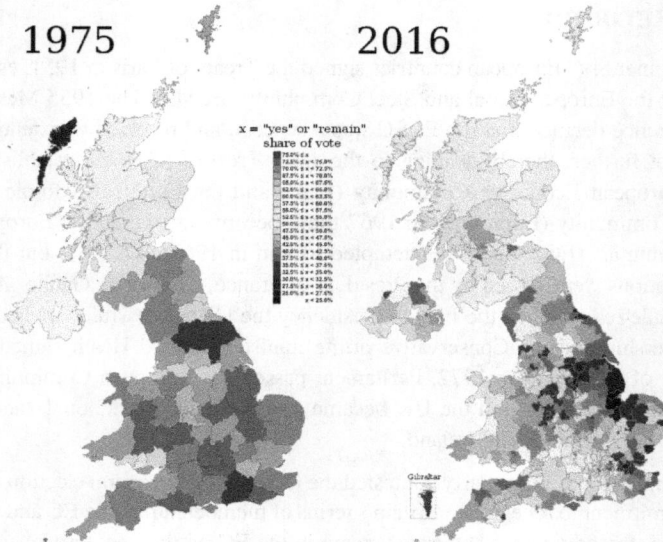

Figure 1: *Comparison of results of 1975 and 2016 referendums*

Referendum Party and UKIP

In 1994, Sir James Goldsmith formed the Referendum Party to contest the 1997 general election on a platform of providing a referendum on the nature of the United Kingdom's relationship with the EU. It fielded candidates in 547 constituencies at that election, and won 810,860 votes or 2.6% of the total votes cast, although it failed to win a single parliamentary seat due to its vote being spread across the country. The Referendum Party disbanded after Goldsmith's death in 1997.

The UK Independence Party (UKIP), a Eurosceptic political party, was also formed in 1993. It achieved third place in the UK during the 2004 European elections, second place in the 2009 European elections and first place in the 2014 European elections, with 27.5% of the total vote. This was the first time since the 1910 general election that any party other than the Labour or Conservative parties had taken the largest share of the vote in a nationwide election. UKIP's electoral success in the 2014 European election has been documented as the strongest correlate of the support for the leave campaign in the 2016 referendum.

UKIP won two by-elections (triggered by defecting Conservative MPs) in 2014; in the 2015 general election it took 12.6% of the total vote, and held one of the two seats won in 2014.

Opinion polls 1977–2015

Both pro- and anti-EU views have had majority support at different times since 1977. In the European Communities membership referendum of 1975, two-thirds of British voters favoured continued EC membership.

In a statistical analysis published in April 2016, Professor John Curtice of Strathclyde University defined Euroscepticism as the wish to sever or reduce the powers of the EU, and conversely Europhilia as the desire to preserve or increase the powers of the EU. According to this definition, the British Social Attitudes (BSA) surveys show an increase in euroscepticism from 38% (1993) to 65% (2015). Euroscepticism should, however, not be confused with the wish to leave the EU: the BSA survey for the period July–November 2015 shows that 60% backed the option "continue as an EU member", and only 30% backed the option to "withdraw".

May 2015 United Kingdom General Election

In the Conservative Party manifesto for the United Kingdom general election, 2015 (held on 7 May 2015), the Conservative Party offered "an EU referendum by 2017".[8,9]

Referendum of 2016

Negotiations for EU reform

In 2012, Prime Minister David Cameron initially rejected calls for a referendum on the UK's EU membership, but then suggested the possibility of a future referendum to endorse his proposed renegotiation of Britain's relationship with the EU. According to the BBC, "The prime minister acknowledged the need to ensure the UK's [renegotiated] position within the European Union had 'the full-hearted support of the British people' but they needed to show 'tactical and strategic patience'." Under pressure from many of his MPs and from the rise of UKIP, in January 2013, Cameron announced that a Conservative government would hold an in–out referendum on EU membership before the end of 2017, on a renegotiated package, if elected in 2015.

The Conservative Party won the 2015 general election with a majority. Soon afterwards the European Union Referendum Act 2015 was introduced into Parliament to enable the referendum. Cameron favoured remaining in a reformed European Union, and sought to renegotiate on four key points: protection of the single market for non-eurozone countries, reduction of "red tape", exempting Britain from "ever-closer union", and restricting EU immigration.

Figure 2: *A "Vote Leave" poster in Omagh, Northern Ireland, saying "We send the EU £50 million every day. Let's spend it on our NHS instead."*

In December 2015, opinion polls showed a clear majority in favour of remaining in the EU; they also showed support would drop if Cameron did not negotiate adequate safeguards for non-eurozone member states, and restrictions on benefits for EU citizens.[10]

The outcome of the renegotiations was announced in February 2016. Some limits to in-work benefits for new EU immigrants were agreed, but before they could be applied, a country such as the UK would have to get permission from the European Commission and then from the European Council.

In a speech to the House of Commons on 22 February 2016, Cameron announced a referendum date of 23 June 2016, and commented on the renegotiation settlement. He spoke of an intention to trigger the Article 50 process immediately following a leave vote, and of the "two-year time period to negotiate the arrangements for exit."

Campaign groups

The official campaign group for leaving the EU was Vote Leave after a contest for the designation with Leave.EU.[11]

The official campaign to stay in the EU, chaired by Stuart Rose, was known as Britain Stronger in Europe, or informally as 'Remain'. Other campaigns supporting remaining in the EU included Conservatives In, Labour in for Britain, #INtogether (Liberal Democrats), Greens for a Better Europe, Scientists for EU, Environmentalists For Europe, Universities for Europe and Another Europe is Possible.

Referendum result

The result was announced on the morning of 24 June: 51.9% voted in favour of leaving the European Union, and 48.1% voted in favour of remaining a member of the European Union. Comprehensive results are available from the UK Electoral Commission Referendum Results site. A petition calling for a second referendum attracted more than four million signatures, but was rejected by the government on 9 July.

United Kingdom European Union membership referendum, 2016
National result

Choice	Votes	%
Leave the European Union	**17,410,742**	**51.89%**
Remain a member of the European Union	16,141,241	48.11%
Valid votes	33,551,983	99.92%
Invalid or blank votes	25,359	0.08%
Total votes	33,577,342	100.00%
Registered voters and turnout	46,500,001	72.21%
Voting age population and turnout	51,356,768	65.38%

Source: Electoral Commission

National referendum results (without spoiled ballots)

Leave: 17,410,742 (51.9%)	Remain: 16,141,241 (48.1%)
▲	

<templatestyles src="Multiple_image/styles.css" />

Results by region (left) and by council district (GB) & UK Parliament constituency (NI) (right)

Leave

Remain

Demographic analysis of voters

According to Thomas Sampson, an economist at the London School of Economics, "Older and less-educated voters were more likely to vote 'leave'... A majority of white voters wanted to leave, but only 33 percent of Asian voters and 27 percent of black voters chose leave. There was no gender split in the vote, with 52 percent of both men and women voting to leave. Leaving the European Union received support from across the political spectrum... Voting to leave the European Union was strongly associated with holding socially conservative political beliefs, opposing cosmopolitanism, and thinking life in Britain is getting worse rather than better." Econometric studies show "first, education and, to a lesser extent, age were the strongest demographic predictors of voting behavior... Second, poor economic outcomes at the individual or area level were associated with voting to leave... Third, support for leaving the European Union is strongly associated with self-reported opposition to immigration, but not with exposure to immigration."

Resignations, contests, and appointments

After the result was declared, Cameron announced that he would resign by October. He stood down on 13 July 2016, with Theresa May becoming Prime Minister after a leadership contest. George Osborne was replaced as Chancellor of the Exchequer by Philip Hammond, former Mayor of London Boris Johnson was appointed Secretary of State for Foreign and Commonwealth Affairs, and David Davis became Secretary of State for Exiting the European Union. Labour leader Jeremy Corbyn lost a vote of confidence among his parliamentary party, and an unsuccessful leadership challenge was launched. On 4 July, Nigel Farage announced his resignation as leader of UKIP.

Irregularities

On 11 May 2018, the Electoral Commission found against Leave.EU, which ran a separate campaign to the official pro-Brexit group Vote Leave, following its investigations into alleged irregularities during the referendum campaign. Leave.EU's co-founder Arron Banks has stated that he rejects the outcome of the investigation and will be challenging it in court.

In July 2018, the UK Electoral Commission found Vote Leave to have broken electoral law, spending over its limit.[12] Also, the House of Commons Culture, Media and Sport Select Committee released an interim report on *Disinformation and 'fake news'*, stating that the largest donor in the Brexit campaign, Arron Banks, used money from UK sources, and may have been financed by the Russian government.[13] This has led to litigation to declare the result is void.[14,15]

Procedure for leaving the EU

Withdrawal from the European Union is governed by Article 50 of the Treaty on European Union. Under the Article 50 invocation procedure, a member notifies the European Council, whereupon the EU is required to *negotiate and conclude an agreement with [the leaving] State, setting out the arrangements for its withdrawal, taking account of the framework for its future relationship with the [European] Union.* The negotiation period is limited to two years unless extended, after which the treaties cease to apply.[16] There was a discussion whether parallel negotiation of withdrawal terms and future relationships under Article 50 are appropriate (Chancellor Merkel's initial view) or whether Britain did not have the right to negotiate future trade with the EU27 as this power is arguably reserved to the EU as long as the UK is a member (the view of a European Commission lawyer).

Although the 2015 Referendum Act did not expressly require Article 50 to be invoked, the UK government stated that it would expect a leave vote to be followed by withdrawal.[17] Following the referendum result, Cameron resigned and said that it would be for the incoming Prime Minister to invoke Article 50.

The Supreme Court ruled in the Miller case in January 2017 that the government needed parliamentary approval to trigger Article 50. Subsequently, the House of Commons overwhelmingly voted, on 1 February 2017, for a government bill authorising the prime minister to invoke Article 50, and the bill passed into law as the European Union (Notification of Withdrawal) Act 2017. Theresa May then signed a letter invoking Article 50 on 28 March 2017, which was delivered on 29 March by Tim Barrow, the UK's ambassador to the EU, to European Council President Donald Tusk.

Reversibility

It has been argued that the Article 50 withdrawal process may be halted unilaterally by the British government, with which opinion the author of Article 50 itself, Lord Kerr, has expressed agreement. The European Parliament's Brexit committee has noted that unilateral revocation, regardless of its legality, poses a substantial moral hazard, with EU member states potentially able to abuse it to blackmail the Union.[18]

Date of Brexit

Wikisourcehas original text related to this article:
The Withdrawal Clause

Both parties to the withdrawal negotiation are bound by Article 50 (3), which states explicitly that the EU treaties will cease to apply "from the date of entry into force of the withdrawal agreement or, failing that, two years after" the withdrawal notification unless the EU Council and UK agree to extend the two-year period.

On the EU side, the EU's *Directives for the negotiation of an agreement* notes that "The Agreement should set a withdrawal date which is at the latest 30 March 2019 at 00:00 (Brussels time)," —i.e. Central European Time— "unless the European Council, in agreement with the United Kingdom, unanimously decides to extend this period in accordance with Article 50(3) of the Treaty on European Union."

On the British side, the European Union (Withdrawal) Act 2018, section 20(1) defines "exit day" as "29 March 2019 at 11.00 p.m".

Negotiations

Timing

The British and EU negotiators agreed that initial negotiations, relating espe-cially to residency rights, would commence in June 2017 (immediately after the French presidential and parliamentary elections), and full negotiations, re-lating especially to trading agreements, could commence in October 2017 (im-mediately after the German federal election, 2017). The first day of talks was 19 June.

History

On 28 June 2016, Chancellor of Germany Angela Merkel, and on the following day European Council President Tusk, stated that the UK could remain in the European Single Market (ESM) only if the UK accepted its four freedoms of movement: for goods, capital, services, and labour. In October, Prime Minister Theresa May emphasised that ending the jurisdiction of EU law and free movement from Europe were the UK's priorities, along with British and EU companies having maximum freedom to trade in the UK and the ESM.

In November 2016, May proposed that Britain and the other EU countries mutually guarantee the residency rights of the 3.3 million EU immigrants in

Britain and those of the 1.2 million British citizens living on the Continent, in order to exclude their fates being bargained during Brexit negotiations. Despite initial approval from a majority of EU states, May's proposal was blocked by Tusk and Merkel.

In January 2017, the Prime Minister presented 12 negotiating objectives and confirmed that the UK government would not seek permanent single market membership. The European Parliament's lead negotiator Guy Verhofstadt responded that there could be no "cherry-picking" by the UK in the talks.

The statutory period for negotiation began on 29 March 2017, when the UK formally submitted a letter notifying withdrawal. The letter called for a "deep and special relationship" between the UK and the EU, and warned that failure to reach an agreement would result in EU-UK trade under World Trade Organisation terms, and a weakening of the UK's co-operation in the fight against crime and terrorism. The letter suggested prioritising an early deal on the rights of EU citizens in the UK and vice versa, and stated that the UK would not seek to remain within the ESM. Instead, the UK would seek a free trade agreement with the EU. In response, Merkel insisted that the EU would not discuss future co-operation without first settling the terms of leaving the EU; Verhofstadt referred to the letter as "blackmail" with regard to the point on security and terrorism, and EU Commission president Jean-Claude Juncker said the UK's decision to quit the block was a "choice they will regret one day".

On 29 April 2017, immediately after the first round of French presidential elections, the EU27 heads of state accepted negotiating guidelines prepared by Tusk. The guidelines take the view that Article 50 permits a two-phased negotiation, in which the UK first agrees to a financial commitment and to lifelong benefits for EU citizens in Britain, and then negotiations on a future relationship can begin. In the first phase, the EU27 would demand the UK pay a "divorce bill", initially estimated as amounting to £52bn[19] and then, after additional financial demands from Germany, France, and Poland, to £92bn. A report of the European Union Committee of the House of Lords, published on 4 March 2017, stated that if there is no post-Brexit deal at the end of the negotiating period, the UK could withdraw without payment.[20]

On 22 May 2017, the European Council authorised its negotiators to start the Brexit talks and it adopted its negotiating directives. The first day of talks took place on 19 June, where Davis and Michel Barnier, European Chief Negotiator for Brexit, agreed to prioritise the question of residency rights, while Davis conceded that a discussion of the Northern Irish border would have to await future trade agreements.[21]

On 22 June 2017, Prime Minister May guaranteed that no EU citizen living legally in the UK would be forced to leave, and offered that any EU citizen who lived in the UK for more than five years until an unspecified deadline between March 2017 and March 2019 would enjoy the same rights as a UK citizen, conditional on the EU providing the same offer to British expatriates living in the EU. The Prime Minister detailed her residency proposals on 26 June, but drew no concessions from EU negotiators, who had declined to expedite agreement on expatriates by the end of June 2017, and who are hoping for European courts to continue to have jurisdiction in the UK with regards to EU citizens, according to their negotiation aims published in May 2017.

The second round of negotiations began in mid-July 2017. Progress was made on the Northern Irish border question; UK negotiators requested a detailed breakdown of the "divorce bill" demand; and the EU negotiators criticised the UK's citizenship rights offer. David Davis did not commit to a net payment by the UK to the EU with regards to the requested divorce bill, while Michel Barnier would not compromise on his demand for the European Court of Justice to have continuing jurisdiction over the rights of EU citizens living in the UK after Brexit, rejecting the compromise proposal of a new international body made up of British and EU judges.

On 16 August 2017, the UK government disclosed the first of several papers detailing British ambitions following Brexit, discussing trade and customs arrangements. On 23 August, Theresa May announced that Britain will leave the EU Court of Justice's direct jurisdiction when the Brexit transition period that is planned after March 2019 ends, but that both the British courts and the EU Court of Justice will also keep "half an eye" on each other's rulings afterwards as well. One of the UK government's position papers published in August called for no additional restrictions for goods already on the market in the UK and EU.

The third round of negotiations began on 28 August 2017. There was disagreement over the financial settlement; The *Irish Times* explained that British negotiators referred to the seven-year Multiannual Financial Framework (MFF or Maff) for the period 2014–2020 agreed by member states and the EU parliament as a "planning tool" for the next period rather than a legally-binding financial obligation on member states. The British case is that the MFF sets ceilings on spending under various headings and is later radically revised during the annual budget process when real legal obligations on each state arises. This contrasts with the EU Commission's methodology for calculating the UK Brexit bill which involves dividing the MFF into the shares historically agreed by each member state. On the Irish border question there was a "breakthrough", with the British side guaranteeing free movement of EU citizens within the Common travel area constituting Ireland and the United Kingdom.

On 5 September 2017, Davis said that "concrete progress" had been made over the summer in areas such as protecting the rights of British expats in the EU to access healthcare and over the future of the Irish border, while significant differences over the "divorce bill" remained. On 9 September, the EU Commission published several negotiating papers, including one in which the EU concedes/declares that it is the responsibility of the UK to propose solutions for the post-Brexit Irish border. The paper envisages that a "unique" solution would be permissible here; in other words, any such exceptional Irish solution would not necessarily be a template for post-Brexit relationships with the other EU members.

On 22 September 2017, May announced further details of her Brexit proposal. In addition to offering 20 billion euros over a two-year transition period and continued acceptance of European immigrants, she also offered a "bold new security relationship" with the EU which would be "unprecedented in its depth" and to continue to make "an ongoing contribution" to projects considered greatly to the EU and UK's advantage, such as science and security projects. She also confirmed that the UK would not "stand in the way" of Juncker's proposals for further EU integration. Barnier welcomed May's proposal as "constructive," but that it also "must be translated into negotiating positions to make meaningful progress". Similarly, President of France Emmanuel Macron was adamant that the EU would not begin negotiations on future EU-UK relationships until "the regulation of European citizens, the financial terms of the exit, and the questions of Ireland" were "clarified" by the UK.

The fourth round of talks began on 25 September, with Barnier declaring he had no mandate from the EU27 to discuss a transition deal suggested by Prime Minister May. Davis reiterated that the UK could honour commitments made during its EU membership only in the context of a future "special partnership" deal with the EU.

At the European Council meeting of 19/20 October 2017, the 27 leaders of the EU states were to decide whether or not to start trade negotiations with the UK. However, Davis has conceded that so soon after the German elections on 24 September, a German coalition government may not be in place in time for making this decision in October, delaying any European Council decision until their December meeting.

EU negotiators have stated that an agreement must be reached between Britain and the EU by October 2018 in order to leave time for national parliaments to endorse Brexit.

On 9 October 2017, May announced to the British Parliament that Britain could operate as an "independent trading nation" after Brexit if no trade deal is reached with the EU.

In December 2017, EU leaders announced an agreement to begin the next phase of negotiations, with talks on a transition period after March 2019 to begin in early 2018 and discussions on the future UK-EU relationship, including trade and security, to begin in March.

After elections in March 2018, the Italian president appointed a eurosceptic Italian government on 1 June 2018, a development expected to affect the Brexit outcome.

On 10 June 2018, the Irish Prime Minister Leo Varadkar cleared the path for the June negotiations by postponing the Irish border question until the final Brexit deal in October 2018.

On 19 June 2018, the UK and the EU published a joint statement outlining agreements at the negotiators' level. Michel Barnier praised the "dedication and commitment" of the negotiating teams, and said progress had been made in issues like customs, VAT and the European nuclear agreement, Euratom.

Post-Article 50 British legislation

European Union (Withdrawal) Act 2018

In October 2016, Theresa May promised a "Great Repeal Bill", which would repeal the European Communities Act 1972 and restate in UK law all enactments previously in force under EU law. Subsequently renamed the European Union (Withdrawal) bill, it was introduced to the House of Commons on 13 July 2017.

On 12 September 2017, the bill passed its first vote and second reading by a margin of 326 votes to 290 votes in the House of Commons. The bill was further amended on a series of votes in both Houses of Parliament. After the Act became law on 26 June 2018, the European Council decided on 29 June to renew its call on Member States and Union institutions to step up their work on preparedness at all levels and for all outcomes.[22]

The Withdrawal Act fixes the period ending 21 January 2019 for the government to decide on how to proceed if the negotiations have not reached agreement in principle on both the withdrawal arrangements and the framework for the future relationship between the UK and EU; while, alternatively, making future ratification of the withdrawal agreement as a treaty between the UK and EU depend upon the prior enactment of another act of Parliament for approving the final terms of withdrawal when the current Brexit negotiations are completed. In any event, the act does not alter the two-year period for negotiating allowed by Article 50 that ends at the latest on 29 March 2019 if the UK has not by then ratified a withdrawal agreement.

The Withdrawal Act which became law in June 2018 allows for various outcomes including no negotiated settlement.

Additional government bills

A report published in March 2017 by the Institute for Government commented that, in addition to the European Union (Withdrawal) bill, primary and secondary legislation will be needed to cover the gaps in policy areas such as customs, immigration and agriculture.[23] The report also commented that the role of the devolved legislatures was unclear, and could cause problems, and as many as fifteen new additional Brexit Bills may be required, which would involve strict prioritisation and limiting Parliamentary time for in-depth examination of new legislation.

In 2016 and 2017, the House of Lords published a series of reports on Brexit-related subjects, including:

- Brexit: the options for trade[24]
- Brexit: UK-Irish relations[25]
- Brexit: future UK-EU security and police cooperation[26]
- Brexit: fisheries[27]
- Brexit: environment and climate change[28]
- Brexit: the Crown Dependencies[29]
- Brexit: justice for families, individuals and businesses?[30]
- Brexit: trade in non-financial services[31]

Euratom

The Nuclear Safeguards Bill 2017–19, relating to withdrawal from Euratom, was presented to Parliament in October 2017 and began its Report Stage in January 2018.

Voting on the final outcome

Replying to questions at a parliamentary committee about Parliament's involvement in voting on the outcome of the negotiations with the EU, the Prime Minister said that "delivering on the vote of the British people to leave the European Union" was her priority. The shadow Brexit secretary, Keir Starmer, commented that the government did not want a vote at the beginning of the process, to trigger Article 50, nor a vote at the end.

Developments since the Referendum of 2016

Elections

Opinion polls in the fortnight following the referendum suggested that the immediate reaction in the Netherlands and other European countries was a decline in support for Eurosceptic movements.

A general election was held on 8 June 2017, announced at short notice by the new Prime Minister Theresa May. The Conservative Party, Labour and UKIP made manifesto pledges to implement the referendum, although the Labour manifesto differed in its approach to Brexit negotiations, such as unilaterally offering permanent residence to EU immigrants. The Liberal Democrat Party and the Green Party manifestos proposed a policy of remaining in the EU via a second referendum. The Scottish Nationalist Party manifesto proposed a policy of waiting for the outcome of the Brexit negotiations and then holding a referendum on Scottish independence. Compared to the 2015 general election, the Conservatives gained votes (but nevertheless lost seats and their majority in the House of Commons). Labour gained significantly on votes and seats, retaining its position as the second-largest party. The DUP and Sinn Féin also made gains in votes and seats. Parties losing votes included the SNP, Liberals, Greens, and especially UKIP.

On 26 June 2017, Conservatives and the DUP reached a confidence and supply agreement whereby the DUP would back the Conservatives in key votes in the House of Commons over the course of the parliament. The agreement included additional funding of £1 billion for Northern Ireland, highlighted mutual support for Brexit and national security, expressed commitment to the Good Friday Agreement, and indicated that policies such as the state pension triple lock and winter fuel payments would be maintained.

Economy

Six weeks after the referendum, the Bank of England sought to cushion the potential shock to the economy by lowering interest rates to the record low of 0.25%, and by creating 70 billion pounds of new money, thereby depreciating the pound and encouraging commercial banks to pass on lower borrowing costs.

A year-long "wage squeeze" attributed to the referendum ended in February 2018, with wage growth catching up with inflation. Inflation had gradually risen to 3% before receding again. Since the referendum, absolute employment has continuously risen to previously unrecorded levels, and by early 2018 relative unemployment reached its lowest level (4.2%) recorded since 1975.

During 2017 the UK continued to be the favourite European destination for foreign physical investment (as distinct from company takeovers), creating 50,000 new jobs, ahead of Germany (31,000 jobs) and France. Factors mentioned were sterling devaluation since the referendum, broadband, and American investment.

Immigration

Official figures for June 2017 (published in February 2018) showed that net EU immigration to the UK had slowed to about 100,000 immigrants per year, corresponding to the immigration level of 2014. Meanwhile, immigration from non-EU countries had increased. Taken together, the two inflows into the UK result in an only slightly reduced net immigration of 230,000 newcomers in the year to June 2017. The Head of the Office of National Statistics suggested that Brexit could well be a factor for the slowdown in EU immigration, but cautioned there might be other reasons.

Domestic impact on the United Kingdom

The Department for Exiting the European Union (DExEU) produced reports on the economic impact on 58 industries of Britain leaving the EU. The Labour Party made a freedom of information request for details about the reports, but DExEU said that publishing the information would undermine policy formulation, and that it needed to carry out policymaking in a "safe space". Labour then proposed a motion of a rarely-used type known as a "humble address" in the Commons on 1 November 2017, calling for the papers to be released; the motion was passed unanimously. The leader of the house, Andrea Leadsom, said that there could be some delay while ministers decided how to release the information without prejudicing Brexit negotiations.

Immigration

Long term

Immigration was cited as the second-most important reason for those voting to Leave. KPMG, based on a 2017 survey of 2,000 EU workers in the UK, estimated that about a million EU citizens working in the UK saw their future in Britain as over or hanging in the balance.

A 2017 paper by King's College London economists Giuseppe Forte and Jonathan Portes found that "while future migration flows will be driven by a number of factors, macroeconomic and otherwise, Brexit and the end of free movement will result in a large fall in immigration from EEA countries to the UK." According to a 2016 study by Portes, "The spectrum of options for

UK immigration policy post Brexit remains wide... However, almost any plausible outcome will result in an increase in regulatory burdens on business; a reduction in the flows of both unskilled and skilled workers; and an increase in illegal working. The key question for policymakers will be how to minimise these negative impacts while at the same time addressing domestic political demands for increased control without antagonising our EU partners to the point of prejudicing other key aspects of the negotiations. This will not be an easy task." Will Somerville of the Migration Policy Institute wrote that "Future migration levels are impossible to predict in the absence of policy and economic certainty", but estimated immediately after the referendum that the UK "would continue to receive 500,000 or more immigrants (from EU and non-EU countries taken together) per year, with annual net migration around 200,000".

The decline in EEA immigration is likely to have an adverse impact on the British health sector. According to the *New York Times*, Brexit "seems certain" to make it harder and costlier for the NHS, which already suffers from chronic understaffing, to recruit nurses, midwives and doctors from the rest of Europe.

Immediate effects

Official figures in March 2017 indicated that EU immigration to the UK continued to exceed emigration, but the difference between immigration and emigration ("net migration") had fallen to its lowest for three years. The number of EU nurses registering with the NHS fell from 1,304 in July 2016 to 46 in April 2017.

Economic effects

Immediate effects

Research on the effects that have already materialised in the United Kingdom since the referendum results show that the referendum result pushed up UK inflation by 1.7 percentage points, leading to an annual cost of £404 for the average British household. Another study on the effects that had already materialised found "contrary to public perception, by the third quarter of 2017 the economic costs of the Brexit vote are already 1.3% of GDP. The cumulative costs amount to almost 20 billion pounds and are expected to grow to more than 60 billion pounds by end-2018." An extension of the latter study to June 2018 showed that the losses amounted to 2.1% of GDP and that the fiscal costs were £23 billion (£440 million a week).

According to a *Financial Times* analysis, the Brexit referendum results had by December 2017 reduced national British income by between 0.6% and

1.3%, which amounts to almost £350 million a week. University of California, Berkeley, economist Barry Eichengreen noted in August 2017 that some of the adverse effects of uncertainty brought about by the Brexit referendum were being made apparent, as British consumer confidence was down and spending had declined to its lowest level in four years. In November 2017, it was reported that European banks had reduced their UK-related assets by €350bn in the 12 months after Brexit vote, and that the trend was expected to increase ahead of the March 2019 Brexit deadline.

Long-term economic analyses

There is overwhelming or near-unanimous agreement among economists that leaving the European Union will adversely affect the British economy in the medium- and long-term.[32]</ref> Surveys of economists in 2016 showed overwhelming agreement that Brexit would likely reduce the UK's real per-capita income level. A 2017 survey of the existing academic literature found "the research literature displays a broad consensus that in the long run Brexit will make the United Kingdom poorer because it will create new barriers to trade, foreign direct investment, and immigration. However, there is substantial uncertainty over how large the effect will be, with plausible estimates of the cost ranging between 1 and 10 percent of the UK's income per capita." These estimates differ depending on whether the UK stays in the European Single Market (for instance, by joining the EEA), makes a free trade agreement with the EU, or reverts to the trade rules that govern relations between all World Trade Organization members. In January 2018, the UK government's own Brexit analysis was leaked; it showed that UK economic growth would be stunted by 2%–8% for at least 15 years following secession from the EU, depending on the leave scenario.

Most economists, including the UK Treasury, argue that being in the EU has a strong positive effect on trade and as a result the UK's trade would be worse off if it left the EU. According to a group of University of Cambridge economists, under a "hard Brexit" whereby the UK reverts to WTO rules, one-third of UK exports to the EU would be tariff-free, one-quarter would face high trade barriers and other exports risk tariffs in the range of 1–10%. A 2017 study based on data from 2010 found that "almost all UK regions are systematically more vulnerable to Brexit than regions in any other country. Due to their longstanding trade integration with the UK, Irish regions have levels of Brexit exposure, which are similar to those of the UK regions with the lowest levels of exposure, namely London and northern parts of Scotland. Meanwhile, the other most risk-exposed EU regions are all in southern Germany, with levels of risk which are typically half that of any UK or Irish region, and one third of that displayed by many UK regions. There is also a very noticeable economic geography logic to the levels of exposure with north-western European regions typically being the most exposed to Brexit, while regions in southern and eastern Europe are barely affected at all by Brexit, at least in terms of the trade linkages... Overall, the UK is far more exposed to Brexit risks than the rest of the EU."

After the referendum, the Institute for Fiscal Studies published a report funded by the Economic and Social Research Council which warned that Britain would lose up to £70 billion in reduced economic growth if it did not retain Single Market membership, with new trade deals unable to make up the difference. One of these areas is financial services, which are helped by EU-wide "passporting" for financial products, which an Oliver Wyman report for a pro-EU lobby group estimated indirectly accounted for up to 71,000 jobs and £10 billion of tax annually,Wikipedia:Verifiability and some banks announced plans to relocate some of their operations outside the UK. According to a 2016 article by John Armour, Professor of Law and Finance at Oxford University, "a 'soft' Brexit, whereby the UK leaves the EU but remains in the single market, would be a lower-risk option for the City than other Brexit options, because it would enable financial services firms to continue to rely on regulatory passporting rights."

A 2017 study found, on the basis of "plausible, empirically based estimates of the likely impacts on growth and wages using relationships from the existing empirical literature", that "Brexit-induced reductions in migration are likely to have a significant negative impact on UK GDP *per capita* (and GDP), with marginal positive impacts on wages in the low-skill service sector." It is unclear how changes in trade and foreign investment will interact with immigration, but these changes are likely to be important.

Former Governor of the Bank of England Mervyn King commented that warnings of economic doom regarding leaving the EU were overstated and that the UK should leave the single market and probably the customs union in order to gain more opportunities, which would lead to improved British economic performance.

Short-term economic analyses

Short-term macroeconomic forecasts by the Bank of England and other banks of what would happen immediately after the Brexit referendum proved to be too pessimistic. The assessments assumed that the referendum results would create greater uncertainty on financial markets and in business and reduce consumer confidence more than it did. According to Oxford University economist Simon Wren-Lewis, "short term unconditional macroeconomic forecasts are extremely unreliable" and they are something that academic economists do not do, unlike banks. Wren-Lewis notes that long-term projections of the impact of Brexit, on the other hand, have a strong empirical foundation.

University of California, Berkeley, economist Barry Eichengreen wrote that economists "have had little success at reliably predicting when and why uncertainty arises" and that it is unclear how severe the impact of uncertainty actually is. King's College London economist Jonathan Portes said that "short-term economic forecasting is very unreliable", and compared short-term economic forecasts to weather forecasts and the long-term economic forecasts to climate forecasts: the methodologies used in long-term forecasts are "well-established and robust". Other economists note that central bank forecasts are not intended for pinpoint accuracy. London School of Economics economist Thomas Sampson notes that it is harder to assess the short-term impact that the transition process to Brexit will have, but that long-term assessments of the post-Brexit period are more reliable. According to the *Financial Times*, economists are in agreement that the short-term effects are uncertain.

On 5 January 2017 Andy Haldane, the Chief Economist and the Executive Director of Monetary Analysis and Statistics at the Bank of England, said that the BoE's own forecast predicting an immediate economic downturn due to the referendum result was inaccurate and noted strong market performance immediately after the referendum, although some have pointed to prices rising faster than wages.[33] Haldane said that the field of economics was "to some degree in crisis" because of its failure to predict the financial crisis of 2007–2008, and added that the Brexit economic forecast was only inaccurate in its near-term assessment, and that over time, the Bank still expected that Brexit would harm economic growth. Imperial College London economist David Miles responded to Haldane, saying that there was no crisis in economics, and that economists did not purport to be able to forecast with full certainty or predict the precise timing of events. Miles said that it was widely acknowledged among economists that short-term forecasts, such as the BoE's, are unreliable.

Loss of agencies

Brexit requires relocating the offices and staff of the European Medicines Agency and European Banking Authority, currently based in London. The agencies together employ more than 1,000 people and will respectively relocate to Amsterdam and Paris. The EU is also considering restricting the clearing of euro-denominated trades to eurozone jurisdictions, which would end London's dominance in this sector.

Higher education and academic research

According to a 2016 study by Ken Mayhew, Emeritus Professor of Education and Economic Performance at Oxford University, Brexit poses the following threats to higher education: "loss of research funding from EU sources; loss of students from other EU countries; the impact on the ability of the sector to hire academic staff from EU countries; and the impact on the ability of UK students to study abroad."

The UK received more from the EU for research than it contributed[34] with universities getting just over 10% of their research income from the EU.[35] All funding for net beneficiaries from the EU, including universities, was guaranteed by the government in August 2016. Before the funding announcement, a newspaper investigation reported that some research projects were reluctant to include British researchers due to uncertainties over funding. Currently the UK is part of the European Research Area and the UK is likely to wish to remain an associated member.[36]

Scotland

As suggested by the Scottish Government before the referendum, the First Minister of Scotland announced that officials were planning an independence referendum due to the result of Scotland voting to remain in the European Union when England and Wales voted to leave. In March 2017, the SNP leader and First Minister Nicola Sturgeon requested a second Scottish independence referendum in 2018 or 2019 (before Britain's formal exit from the EU). The UK Prime Minister immediately rejected the requested timing, but not the referendum itself. The referendum was approved by the Scottish Parliament on 28 March 2017. Sturgeon called for a "phased return" of an independent Scotland back to the EU.

After the referendum, First Minister Sturgeon suggested that Scotland might refuse consent for legislation required to leave the EU, though some lawyers argue that Scotland cannot block Brexit.

On 21 March 2018, the Scottish Parliament passed the Scottish Continuity Bill. This was passed due to stalling negotiations between the Scottish Government and the British Government on where powers within devolved policy areas should lie after exit day from the European Union. This Act allows for all devolved policy areas to remain within the remit of the Scottish Parliament and reduces the executive power upon exit day that the UK Withdrawal Bill provides for Ministers of the Crown. The Bill gained Royal Assent on 28 April 2018.

Impact of Brexit on bilateral UK relations

International agreements

The *Financial Times* said that there were approximately 759 international agreements, spanning 168 non-EU countries, that the UK would no longer be a party to upon leaving the EU. This figure does not include World Trade Organisation or United Nations opt-in accords, and excludes "narrow agreements", which may also have to be renegotiated.

Aviation may be heavily affected. The EU has rules allowing its airlines to fly anywhere in the union also domestic, which will not ally to the UK anymore. The British airline EasyJet decided to relocate its headquarter. The EU also has treaties with many countries regulating the right to fly over, take off and land there. Unless permission or new treaties with the UK are made, aviation to and from the UK may stop.

Options for continuing relationship with the EU

The UK's post-Brexit relationship with the remaining EU members could take several forms. A research paper presented to the UK Parliament in July 2013 proposed a number of alternatives to membership which would continue to allow access to the EU internal market. These include remaining in the European Economic Area, negotiating deep bilateral agreements on the Swiss model, or exit from the EU without EEA membership or a trade agreement under the WTO Option. There may be an interim deal between the time the UK leaves the EU and when the final relationship comes in force.

Border with Republic of Ireland

There is concern about whether the border between the Republic of Ireland and Northern Ireland becomes a "hard border" with customs and passport checks on the border, and whether this could affect the Good Friday Agreement that was seen as instrumental in bringing peace to Northern Ireland.[37]

Until March 2019, both the UK and the Republic of Ireland will be members of the EU, and therefore both are in the Customs Union and the Single Market. There is freedom of movement for all EU nationals within the Common Travel Area and there are no customs or fixed immigration controls at the border. Since the 1998 Good Friday Agreement, the border has been essentially invisible. Following Brexit, the border between Northern Ireland and the Republic of Ireland will become a land border between the EU and a non-EU state which may entail checks on goods at the border, depending on the co-operation and alignment of regulations between the two sides. It is therefore

Figure 3: *The UK/Republic of Ireland border crosses this road at Killeen (near Newry), marked only by a speed limit in km/h. (Northern Ireland uses mph.)*

possible that the border will return to being a "hard" one, with fewer, controlled, crossing posts and a customs infrastructure. Both the EU and the UK have agreed this should be avoided.

Creating a border control system between Ireland and Northern Ireland could jeopardise the Good Friday Agreement.[38,39] In order to forestall this the European Union proposed a "backstop agreement" within the Withdrawal Agreement that would put Northern Ireland under a range of EU rules in order to forestall the need for border checks. This has been opposed by the British government.

Border with France

The President of the Regional Council of Hauts-de-France, Xavier Bertrand, stated in February 2016 that "If Britain leaves Europe, right away the border will leave Calais and go to Dover. We will not continue to guard the border for Britain if it's no longer in the European Union," indicating that the juxtaposed controls would end with a leave vote. French Finance Minister Emmanuel Macron also suggested the agreement would be "threatened" by a leave vote. These claims have been disputed, as the Le Touquet 2003 treaty enabling juxtaposed controls was not an EU treaty, and would not be legally void upon leaving.

Figure 4: *Cars crossing into Gibraltar clearing customs formalities.*
Gibraltar is outside the customs union, VAT area and Schengen Zone.

After the Brexit vote, Xavier Bertrand asked François Hollande to renegotiate the Touquet agreement, which can be terminated by either party with two years' notice. Hollande rejected the suggestion, and said: "Calling into question the Touquet deal on the pretext that Britain has voted for Brexit and will have to start negotiations to leave the Union doesn't make sense." Bernard Cazeneuve, the French Interior Minister, confirmed there would be "no changes to the accord". He said: "The border at Calais is closed and will remain so."

Gibraltar and Spain

Gibraltar is outside the European Union's common customs area and common commercial policy and so has a customs border with Spain. Nevertheless, the territory remains within the European Union until Brexit is complete.

During the campaign leading up to the referendum the Chief Minister of Gibraltar warned that Brexit posed a threat to Gibraltar's safety. Gibraltar overwhelmingly voted to remain in the EU. After the result Spain's Foreign Minister renewed calls for joint Spanish–British control of the peninsula. These calls were strongly rebuffed by Gibraltar's Chief Minister and questions were raised over the future of free-flowing traffic at the Gibraltar–Spain border. The UK government states it will only negotiate on the sovereignty of Gibraltar with the consent of its people.[40]

In February 2018, Sir Joe Bossano, Gibraltar's Minister for Enterprise, Training, Employment and Health and Safety (and former Chief Minister) expressed frustration at the EU's attitude, suggesting that Spain was being offered a veto, adding "It's enough to convert me from a supporter of the European Union into a Brexiteer".[41]

In April 2018, Spanish Foreign Minister Alfonso Dastis announced that Spain hopes to sign off on a bilateral agreement with Britain over Gibraltar before October so as not to hinder a Brexit transition deal. Talks between London and Madrid had progressed well. While reiterating the Spanish long-term aim of "recovering" Gibraltar, he said that Spain would not hold Gibraltar as a "hostage" to the EU negotiations.

Relations with CANZUK countries

Brexit has also created a resurgence in academic and political advocacy for negotiating trade and migration agreements with the "CANZUK" countries – those of Canada, Australia, New Zealand and the United Kingdom. This has been echoed by multiple politicians in the four countries, including Liberal Senator, James Paterson in Australia,[42] Shadow Foreign Affairs Minister, Erin O'Toole in Canada and Secretary of State for Foreign and Commonwealth Affairs, Boris Johnson in the United Kingdom. Organisations such as CANZUK International have also championed the movement,[43] stating that relationships between the four countries will flourish after Brexit.[44] However, numerous academics have criticised this alternative for EU membership as "post-imperial nostalgia".

Consequences of withdrawal for the EU

Structure and budget

Shortly after the referendum, the German parliament published an analysis on the consequences of a Brexit on the EU and specifically on the economic and political situation of Germany. According to this, Britain is, after the United States and France, the third-most important export market for German products. In total Germany exports goods and services to Britain worth about €120 billion annually, which is about 8% of German exports, with Germany achieving a trade surplus with Britain worth €36.3 billion (2014). Should there be a "hard Brexit", exports would be subject to WTO customs and tariffs. The trade weighted average tariff is 2.4%, but the tariff on automobiles, for instance, is 9.7%, so trade in automobiles would be particularly affected; this would also affect German automobile manufacturers with production plants in the United Kingdom. In total, 750,000 jobs in Germany depend upon export to Britain, while on the British side about three million jobs depend on export to the EU. The study emphasises however that the predictions on the economic effects of a Brexit are subject to significant uncertainty.

According to the Lisbon Treaty (2009), Council of the EU decisions made by qualified majority voting can only be blocked if at least four members of the Council form a blocking minority. This rule was originally developed to prevent the three most populous members (Germany, France, Britain) from dominating the Council of the EU. However, after a Brexit of the economically liberal British, the Germans and like-minded northern European countries (the Irish, Dutch, Scandinavians and Baltic states) would lose an ally and therefore also their blocking minority. Without this blocking minority, other EU states could overrule Germany and its allies in questions of EU budget discipline or the recruitment of German banks to guarantee deposits in troubled southern European banks.

With Brexit, the EU would lose its second-largest economy, the country with the third-largest population and "the financial capital of the world", as the German newspaper Münchner Merkur put it. Furthermore, the EU would lose its second-largest net contributor to the EU budget (2015: Germany €14.3 billion, United Kingdom €11.5 billion, France €5.5 billion).

Thus, the departure of Britain would result in an additional financial burden for the remaining net contributors, unless the budget is reduced accordingly: Germany, for example, would have to pay an additional €4.5 billion for 2019 and again for 2020; in addition, the UK would no longer be a shareholder in the European Investment Bank, in which only EU members can participate. Britain's share amounts to 16%, €39.2 billion (2013), which Britain would withdraw unless there is an EU treaty change.

Council of the European Union

The departure of the UK is expected to have a major effect on the EU. In many policy votes Britain had allied with the relatively more economically liberal Germany who together with other northern EU allies had a blocking minority of 35% in the Council of the European Union. The exit of the UK from the European Union means that this blocking minority can no longer be assembled leading to speculation that it could enable the other EU countries to enforce specific proposals such as relaxing EU budget discipline or providing EU-wide deposit guarantees within the banking union.[45]

European Parliament

UK MEPs are expected to retain full rights to participate in the European Parliament up to the Article 50 deadline. However, there have been discussions about excluding UK MEPs from key committee positions.

The EU will need to decide on the revised apportionment of seats in the European Parliament in time for the next European Parliament election, expected to be held in June 2019, when the United Kingdom's 73 MEPs will have vacated their seats. In April 2017, a group of European lawmakers discussed what should be done about the vacated seats. One plan, supported by Gianni Pittella and Emmanuel Macron, is to replace the 73 seats with a pan-European constituency list; other options which were considered include dropping the British seats without replacement, and reassigning some or all of the existing seats from other countries to reduce inequality of representation.

Legal system

The UK's exit from the European Union will leave Ireland and Cyprus as the only two remaining common law jurisdictions in the EU. Paul Gallagher, a former Attorney General of Ireland, has suggested this will isolate those countries and deprive them of a powerful partner that shared a common interest in ensuring that EU legislation was not drafted or interpreted in a way that would be contrary to the principles of the common law. Lucinda Creighton, a former Irish government minister for legal affairs, has said that Ireland relies on the "bureaucratic capacity of the UK" to understand, influence and implement EU legislation.

Fishing

The combined EU fishing fleets land about 6 million tonnes of fish per year, of which about 3 million tonnes are from UK waters. The UK's share of the overall EU fishing catch is only 750,000 tonnes (830,000 tons). This proportion is determined by the London Fisheries Convention of 1964 and by the EU's Common Fisheries Policy. The UK government announced in July 2017 that it would end the 1964 convention in 2019. Loss of access to UK waters will particularly affect the Irish fishing industry which obtains a third of its catch there. The Common Fisheries Policy gives access for any member country to the waters of any other member country. The policy is generally considered a disadvantage to fish-rich countries and is a major reason why Norway and Iceland are not members. The European Economic Area treaty gives access to the inner market but does not include fishing.

World Trade Organization

Questions have arisen over how existing international arrangements with the EU under World Trade Organization (WTO) terms should evolve. Some countries – such as Australia and the United States – wish to challenge the basis for division (i.e., division between the UK and the continuing EU) of the trade schedules previously agreed between them and the EU, because it reduces their flexibility.

As of 2018[4], the WTO does not have any protocols covering trade in services.

Public opinion and comment

Public comment up to February 2017 UK white paper

Various EU leaders said that they would not start any negotiation before the UK formally invokes Article 50. Jean-Claude Juncker ordered all members of the EU Commission not to engage in any kind of contact with UK parties regarding Brexit. In October 2016, he stated that he was agitated that the British had not developed a sense of community with Europeans during 40 years of membership; Juncker denied that Brexit was a warning for the EU, envisaged developing an EU defence policy without the British after Brexit, and rejected a suggestion that the EU should negotiate in such a way that Britain would be able to hold a second referendum. On 5 November 2016, Juncker reacted to reports of some European businesses seeking to make agreements with the UK government, and warned: "I am telling them [companies] that they should not interfere in the debate, as they will find that I will block their path." Juncker stated in February 2017 that the UK would be expected to pay outstanding commitments to EU projects and pensions as part of the withdrawal process, suggesting such bills would be "very hefty."

German foreign secretary Frank-Walter Steinmeier met Britain's foreign secretary Boris Johnson on 4 November 2016; Johnson stressed the importance of British-German relationships, whereas Steinmeier responded that the German view was that the UK should have voted to stay in the EU and that the German priority now was to preserve the remaining union of 27 members. There could be no negotiations before the UK formally gives notice. A long delay before beginning negotiations would be detrimental. Britain could not keep the advantages of the single market but at the same time cancel the "less pleasant rules".

Newly appointed prime minister Theresa May made clear that negotiations with the EU required a "UK-wide approach". On 15 July 2016, she said: "I have already said that I won't be triggering article 50 until I think that we have a UK approach and objectives for negotiations – I think it is important that we establish that before we trigger article 50."

According to *The Daily Telegraph*, the Department for Exiting the European Union spent over £250,000 on legal advice from top Government lawyers in two months, and had plans to recruit more people. Nick Clegg said the figures showed the Civil Service was unprepared for the very complex negotiations ahead.

In the wake of the United Kingdom's vote to leave the European Union, the Department for International Trade (DIT) for striking and extending trade agreements between the UK and non-EU states was created by Prime Minister Theresa May, shortly after she took office on 13 July 2016. It employs about 200 trade negotiators[46] and is overseen by the Secretary of State for International Trade, currently Liam Fox.

On 17 January 2017, Prime Minister Theresa May, announced a series of 12 negotiating objectives in a speech at Lancaster House. These consist of an end to European Court of Justice jurisdiction, withdrawal from the single market with a "comprehensive free-trade agreement" replacing this, a new customs agreement excluding the common external tariff and the EU's common commercial policy, an end to free movement of people, co-operation in crime and terrorism, collaboration in areas of science and technology, engagement with devolved administrations, maintaining the Common Travel Area with Ireland, and preserving existing workers' rights. She also confirmed, "that the Government will put the final deal that is agreed between the UK and the EU to a [meaningful] vote in both Houses of Parliament, before it comes into force."

The Government has stated its intention to "secure the specific interests of Scotland, Wales and Northern Ireland, as well as those of all parts of England". Through the Joint Ministerial Committee on EU Negotiations (JMC(EN)), the Government intends to involve the views of the Scottish Parliament, the Welsh Assembly and the Northern Ireland Assembly in the process of negotiating the UK's exit from the EU. For instance, at the January 2017 meeting of the JMC(EN), the Scottish Government's proposal to remain in the European Economic Area was considered.

Public comment pre- and post-Article 50 notification

EU negotiator Guy Verhofstadt, the European parliament's chief negotiator, said that: "All British citizens today have also EU citizenship. That means a number of things: the possibility to participate in the European elections, the freedom of travel without problem inside the union. We need to have an arrangement in which this arrangement can continue for those citizens who on an individual basis are requesting it." The suggestion being an "associate citizenship".

An EU meeting to discuss Brexit was called for 29 April 2017, Donald Tusk stating that the "priority would be giving "clarity" to EU residents, business and member states about the talks ahead". Barnier called for talks to be completed by October 2018 to give time for any agreement to be ratified before the UK leaves in March 2019.

Sinn Féin called for a referendum to create a united Ireland, following the Northern Ireland majority decision (56% to 44%) to vote no to Brexit and 2 March election to the Northern Ireland Assembly wherein Sinn Féin increased its number of seats.

In early May, Jean-Claude Juncker said that the UK leaving the EU was a "tragedy" and that it is partly the responsibility of the EU. "The EU, in many respects has done too much, especially the Commission", including "too much regulation and too many interferences in the lives of our fellow citizens". The European Commission has, following the "Better regulation" initiative, in place since before Brexit, reduced the number of legislative proposals from 130 to 23 per year.

Post-referendum opinion polling

Right / Wrong

Following the EU referendum, there have been several opinion polls on the question of whether **the UK was "right" or "wrong" to vote to leave the EU**. The results of these polls are shown in the table below.

Date(s) conducted	Right	Wrong	Unde-cided	Lead	Sam-ple	Conducted by	Polling type	Notes
4-5 Sep 2018	43%	**46%**	11%	3%	1,628	YouGov[47]	Online	
3-4 Sep 2018	42%	**48%**	11%	6%	1,883	YouGov[48]	Online	
28-29 Aug 2018	42%	**47%**	11%	5%	1,664	YouGov[49]	Online	
20-21 Aug 2018	41%	**47%**	12%	6%	1,697	YouGov[50]	Online	
13-14 Aug 2018	43%	**45%**	12%	2%	1,660	YouGov[51]	Online	
8-9 Aug 2018	42%	**45%**	13%	3%	1,675	YouGov[52]	Online	
22-23 Jul 2018	42%	**46%**	12%	4%	1,650	YouGov[53]	Online	

16-17 Jul 2018	42%	**47%**	12%	5%	1,657	YouGov[54]	Online	
10-11 Jul 2018	41%	**46%**	12%	5%	1,732	YouGov[55]	Online	
8-9 Jul 2018	Brexit Secretary David Davis and Foreign Secretary Boris Johnson resign.							
8-9 Jul 2018	42%	**46%**	12%	4%	1,669	YouGov[56]	Online	
6 Jul 2018	*The UK Cabinet agrees the Chequers Statement, setting out a proposal on the future UK-EU relationship.*							
3-4 Jul 2018	41%	**46%**	13%	5%	1,641	YouGov[57]	Online	
25-26 Jun 2018	43%	**46%**	11%	3%	1,645	YouGov[58]	Online	
19-20 Jun 2018	44%	**45%**	11%	1%	1,663	YouGov[59]	Online	
18-19 Jun 2018	43%	**44%**	13%	1%	1,606	YouGov[60]	Online	
11-12 Jun 2018	43%	**46%**	12%	3%	1,638	YouGov[61]	Online	
4-5 Jun 2018	**44%**	**44%**	13%	0%	1,619	YouGov[62]	Online	
28-29 May 2018	40%	**47%**	13%	7%	1,670	YouGov[63]	Online	
20-21 May 2018	43%	**44%**	13%	1%	1,660	YouGov[64]	Online	
13-14 May 2018	44%	**45%**	12%	1%	1,634	YouGov[65]	Online	
8-9 May 2018	43%	**45%**	12%	2%	1,648	YouGov[66]	Online	
30 Apr-1 May 2018	42%	**47%**	11%	5%	1,585	YouGov[67]	Online	
24-25 Apr 2018	42%	**45%**	13%	3%	1,668	YouGov[68]	Online	
16-17 Apr 2018	42%	**45%**	13%	3%	1,631	YouGov[69]	Online	
9-10 Apr 2018	42%	**46%**	12%	4%	1,639	YouGov[70]	Online	
26-27 Mar 2018	42%	**45%**	13%	3%	1,659	YouGov[71]	Online	
5-6 Mar 2018	43%	**45%**	12%	2%	1,641	YouGov[72]	Online	
2 Mar 2018	*Theresa May makes Mansion House speech, outlining the UK Government's policy on the future UK-EU relationship.*							
26-27 Feb 2018	44%	**45%**	11%	1%	1,622	YouGov[73]	Online	

Date					Sample	Pollster	Method	
19-20 Feb 2018	42%	**45%**	12%	3%	1,650	YouGov[74]	Online	
12-13 Feb 2018	42%	**46%**	12%	4%	1,639	YouGov[75]	Online	
5-6 Feb 2018	43%	**44%**	13%	1%	2,000	YouGov[76]	Online	
28-29 Jan 2018	40%	**46%**	14%	6%	1,669	YouGov[77]	Online	
16-17 Jan 2018	**45%**	44%	12%	1%	1,672	YouGov[78]	Online	
7-8 Jan 2018	42%	**46%**	12%	4%	1,663	YouGov[79]	Online	
19-20 Dec 2017	42%	**45%**	12%	3%	1,610	YouGov[80]	Online	
15 Dec 2017	*The European Council decides to proceed to the second phase of the Brexit negotiations.*							
10-11 Dec 2017	44%	**45%**	11%	1%	1,680	YouGov[81]	Online	
4-5 Dec 2017	42%	**45%**	13%	3%	1,638	YouGov[82]	Online	
7-8 Nov 2017	42%	**46%**	12%	4%	2,012	YouGov[83]	Online	
23-24 Oct 2017	43%	**45%**	12%	2%	1,637	YouGov[84]	Online	
18-19 Oct 2017	42%	**45%**	14%	3%	1,648	YouGov[85]	Online	
10-11 Oct 2017	42%	**47%**	11%	5%	1,680	YouGov[86]	Online	
22-24 Sep 2017	44%	**45%**	11%	1%	1,716	YouGov[87]	Online	
22 Sep 2017	*Theresa May makes Florence speech, in an attempt to 'unblock' the Brexit negotiations.*							
30-31 Aug 2017	**44%**	**44%**	12%	0%	1,658	YouGov[88]	Online	
21-22 Aug 2017	43%	**45%**	11%	2%	1,664	YouGov[89]	Online	
31 Jul-1 Aug 2017	**45%**	**45%**	10%	0%	1,665	YouGov[90]	Online	
18-19 Jul 2017	**43%**	**43%**	14%	0%	1,593	YouGov[91]	Online	
10-11 Jul 2017	**45%**	43%	12%	2%	1,700	YouGov[92]	Online	
21-22 Jun 2017	44%	**45%**	11%	1%	1,670	YouGov[93]	Online	
19 Jun 2017	*Brexit negotiations begin.*							

12-13 Jun 2017	44%	**45%**	11%	1%	1,651	YouGov[94]	Online	
8 Jun 2017	*United Kingdom general election, 2017*							
5-7 Jun 2017	**45%**	**45%**	10%	0%	2,130	YouGov[95]	Online	
30-31 May 2017	44%	**45%**	11%	1%	1,875	YouGov[96]	Online	
24-25 May 2017	**46%**	43%	11%	3%	2,052	YouGov[97]	Online	
16-17 May 2017	**46%**	43%	11%	3%	1,861	YouGov[98]	Online	
3-14 May 2017	**45%**	41%	14%	4%	1,952	GfK[99]	Online	
9-10 May 2017	44%	**45%**	11%	1%	1,651	YouGov[100]	Online	
2-3 May 2017	**46%**	43%	11%	3%	2,066	YouGov[101]	Online	
25-26 Apr 2017	43%	**45%**	12%	2%	1,590	YouGov[102]	Online	
20-21 Apr 2017	**44%**	**44%**	12%	0%	1,590	YouGov[103]	Online	
18-19 Apr 2017	**46%**	43%	11%	3%	1,727	YouGov[104]	Online	
12-13 Apr 2017	**45%**	43%	12%	2%	2,069	YouGov[105]	Online	
5-6 Apr 2017	**46%**	42%	11%	4%	1,651	YouGov[106]	Online	
29 Mar 2017	*The United Kingdom invokes Article 50.*							
26-27 Mar 2017	**44%**	43%	13%	1%	1,957	YouGov[107]	Online	
20-21 Mar 2017	**44%**	**44%**	12%	0%	1,627	YouGov[108]	Online	
1-15 Mar 2017	**46%**	41%	13%	5%	1,938	GfK[109]	Online	
13-14 Mar 2017	**44%**	42%	15%	2%	1,631	YouGov[110]	Online	
10-14 Mar 2017	**49%**	41%	10%	8%	2,003	Opinium[111]	Online	
27-28 Feb 2017	**45%**	44%	11%	1%	1,666	YouGov[112]	Online	
21-22 Feb 2017	**45%**	**45%**	10%	0%	2,060	YouGov[113]	Online	
12-13 Feb 2017	**46%**	42%	12%	4%	2,052	YouGov[114]	Online	

Date					Sample	Pollster	Method	
30-31 Jan 2017	45%	42%	12%	3%	1,705	YouGov[115]	Online	
17-18 Jan 2017	46%	42%	12%	4%	1,654	YouGov[116]	Online	
17 Jan 2017		*Theresa May makes Lancaster House speech, setting out the UK Government's negotiating priorities.*						
9-12 Jan 2017	52%	39%	9%	13%	2,005	Opinium[117]	Online	
9-10 Jan 2017	46%	42%	12%	4%	1,660	YouGov[118]	Online	
3-4 Jan 2017	45%	44%	11%	1%	1,740	YouGov[119]	Online	
18-19 Dec 2016	44%	44%	12%	0%	1,595	YouGov[120]	Online	
4-5 Dec 2016	44%	42%	14%	2%	1,667	YouGov[121]	Online	
28-29 Nov 2016	44%	45%	11%	1%	1,624	YouGov[122]	Online	
14-15 Nov 2016	46%	43%	11%	3%	1,717	YouGov[123]	Online	
19-20 Oct 2016	45%	44%	11%	1%	1,608	YouGov[124]	Online	
11-12 Oct 2016	45%	44%	11%	1%	1,669	YouGov[125]	Online	
2 Oct 2016	*Theresa May makes Conservative Party Conference speech, announcing her intention to invoke Article 50 by 31 March 2017.*							
13-14 Sep 2016	46%	44%	10%	2%	1,732	YouGov[126]	Online	
30-31 Aug 2016	47%	44%	9%	3%	1,687	YouGov[127]	Online	
22-23 Aug 2016	45%	43%	12%	2%	1,660	YouGov[128]	Online	
16-17 Aug 2016	46%	43%	11%	3%	1,677	YouGov[129]	Online	
8-9 Aug 2016	45%	44%	12%	1%	1,692	YouGov[130]	Online	
1-2 Aug 2016	46%	42%	12%	4%	1,722	YouGov[129]	Online	
13 Jul 2016	*Theresa May becomes Prime Minister of the United Kingdom.*							

- v
- t
- e[131]

Second referendum: Remain / Leave

There have also been opinion polls on how people would vote in **a second referendum on the same question**. The results of these polls are shown in the table below.

Date(s) con-ducted	Re-main	Leave	Nei-ther	Lead	Sam-ple	Conducted by	Polling type	Notes
6-11 Sep 2018	**63%**	18%	19%	45%	1,645	YouGov[132]	Online	18-24 age group
	69%	13%	18%	56%	480			Respon-dents of voting age only since 2016's refer-endum
7 Sep 2018	**47%**	46%	8%	1%	854	Survation[133]	Online	Likely voters
	46%	44%	10%	2%	975			Possible voters
30 Aug-5 Sep 2018	**55%**	37%	8%	18%	620	YouGov[134]	Online	GMB members
30 Aug-5 Sep 2018	**68%**	27%	6%	41%	1,081	YouGov[135]	Online	UNISON members
30 Aug-5 Sep 2018	**61%**	35%	4%	26%	1,058	YouGov[136]	Online	Unite the Union members
31 Jul-04 Sep 2018	**46%**	41%	13%	5%	25,641	YouGov[137]	Online	
31 Jul-3 Sep 2018	**58%**	30%	11%	28%	3,051	YouGov[138]	Online	London only
31 Aug-1 Sep 2018	**47%**	**47%**	6%	0%	1,017	Survation[139]	Online	Likely voters
14-20 Aug 2018	**46%**	41%	13%	5%	10,299	YouGov[140]	Online	

31 Jul-20 Aug 2018	46%	40%	13%	6%	18,772	YouGov[141]	Online	
31 Jul-20 Aug 2018	42%	42%	16%	0%	807	YouGov[142]	Online	North East England only
31 Jul-19 Aug 2018	44%	42%	14%	2%	939	YouGov[143]	Online	Wales only
8-14 Aug 2018	58%	30%	12%	28%	1,977	YouGov[144]	Online	Scotland only
9-13 Aug 2018	40%	35%	25%	5%	1,119	Kantar[145]	Online	
6-10 Aug 2018	50%	43%	7%	7%	1,481	BMG Research[146]	Online	
31 Jul-7 Aug 2018	46%	40%	14%	6%	10,121	YouGov[147]	Online	
31 Jul-7 Aug 2018	46%	43%	11%	3%	930	YouGov[148]	Online	South West England only
25-26 Jul 2018	45%	42%	13%	3%	1,631	YouGov[149]	Online	
23-24 Jul 2018	47%	41%	12%	6%	1,627	YouGov[150]	Online	
19-20 Jul 2018	44%	40%	16%	4%	1,668	YouGov[151]	Online	
12-14 Jul 2018	45%	45%	11%	0%	1,484	Deltapoll[152]	Online	
8-9 Jul 2018	*Brexit Secretary David Davis and Foreign Secretary Boris Johnson resign.*							
5-9 Jul 2018	40%	32%	28%	8%	1,086	Kantar[153]	Online	
7 Jul 2018	49%	45%	5%	4%	1,007	Survation[154]	Online	
6 Jul 2018	*The UK Cabinet agrees the Chequers Statement, setting out a proposal on the future UK-EU relationship.*							

28 Jun-2 Jul 2018	44%	39%	17%	5%	1,031	YouGov[155]	Online	Wales only
26-27 Jun 2018	44%	44%	12%	0%	1,626	YouGov[156]	Online	
19-20 Jun 2018	50%	44%	6%	6%	1,022	Survation[157]	Online	
10-11 Jun 2018	45%	40%	15%	5%	1,654	YouGov[158]	Online	
31 May-4 Jun 2018	48%	47%	5%	1%	2,012	Survation[159]	Online	
9-16 May 2018	47%	42%	11%	5%	2,006	Deltapoll[160]	Online	
8-10 May 2018	47%	47%	6%	0%	1,585	Survation[161]	Online	
25-30 Apr 2018	45%	42%	13%	3%	1,637	YouGov[162]	Online	
14 Apr 2018	47%	46%	7%	1%	2,060	Survation[163]	Online	
6-8 Apr 2018	45%	44%	11%	1%	2,012	ICM[164]	Online	
5-6 Apr 2018	44%	41%	15%	3%	1,636	YouGov[165]	Online	
13-16 Mar 2018	49%	42%	9%	7%	1,815	BMG Research[166]	Online	
12-15 Mar 2018	45%	44%	12%	1%	1,015	YouGov[167]	Online	Wales only
7-8 Mar 2018	44%	49%	7%	5%	2,092	ORB[168]	Online	
2 Mar 2018	43%	46%	12%	3%	1,096	ComRes[169]	Online	
2 Mar 2018								
27-28 Feb 2018	44%	41%	14%	3%	1,646	YouGov[170]	Online	
14-16 Feb 2018	46%	42%	13%	4%	1,482	Sky Data[171]	Online	

2 Mar 2018: *Theresa May makes Mansion House speech, outlining the UK Government's policy on the future UK-EU relationship.*

Date					Sample	Pollster	Method	Notes
26-29 Jan 2018	**49%**	46%	6%	3%	1,059	Survation[172]	Online	
18-22 Jan 2018	**46%**	42%	12%	4%	1,633	YouGov[173]	Online	
16-19 Jan 2018	**49%**	41%	10%	8%	1,096	Sky Data[174]	Online	
10-19 Jan 2018	**45%**	43%	12%	2%	5,075	ICM[175]	Online	
11 Jan 2018	**51%**	43%	6%	8%	1,049	ComRes[176]	Online	
15 Dec 2017					*The European Council decides to proceed to the second phase of the Brexit negotiations.*			
8-10 Dec 2017	**46%**	43%	11%	3%	2,006	ICM[177]	Online	
5-8 Dec 2017	**51%**	41%	8%	10%	1,509	BMG Research[178]	Online	
30 Nov-1 Dec 2017	**49%**	46%	6%	3%	1,003	Survation[179]	Online	
21-24 Nov 2017	**45%**	40%	15%	5%	1,016	YouGov[180]	Online	Wales only
16-17 Nov 2017	**43%**	**43%**	14%	0%	1,672	YouGov[181]	Online	
14-17 Nov 2017	**45%**	**45%**	10%	0%	1,509	BMG Research[178]	Online	
18-24 Oct 2017	**44%**	40%	16%	4%	1,648	YouGov[182]	Online	
19-20 Oct 2017	**46%**	45%	9%	1%	1,005	Opinium[183]	Online	
17-20 Oct 2017	**47%**	44%	8%	3%	1,506	BMG Research[178]	Online	
4-5 Oct 2017	**49%**	45%	6%	4%	2,047	Survation[184]	Online	
23 Sep 2017	46%	**47%**	6%	1%	1,174	Survation[185]	Online	
22 Sep 2017					*Theresa May makes Florence speech, in an attempt to 'unblock' the Brexit negotiations.*			

19-22 Sep 2017	45%	44%	12%	1%	2,004	Opinium[186]	Online	
15-20 Sep 2017	47%	47%	5%	0%	1,614	Survation[187]	Online	
12-15 Sep 2017	47%	43%	10%	4%	1,447	BMG Research[188]	Online	
12-15 Sep 2017	45%	45%	10%	0%	2,009	Opinium[189]	Online	
4-7 Sep 2017	46%	42%	12%	4%	1,011	YouGov[190]	Online	Wales only
15-18 Aug 2017	47%	44%	9%	3%	2,006	Opinium[191]	Online	
8-11 Aug 2017	46%	45%	9%	1%	1,512	BMG Research[192]	Online	
23-24 Jul 2017	46%	43%	11%	3%	1,609	YouGov[193]	Online	
14-15 Jul 2017	47%	48%	5%	1%	1,024	Survation[194]	Online	
11-14 Jul 2017	46%	45%	9%	1%	1,518	BMG Research[192]	Online	
28-30 Jun 2017	52%	44%	5%	8%	1,017	Survation[195]	Telephone	
23-30 Jun 2017	46%	42%	13%	4%	1,661	YouGov[196]	Online	
16-21 Jun 2017	46%	50%	4%	4%	5,481	Panelbase[197]	Online	
19 Jun 2017	*Brexit negotiations begin.*							
16-17 Jun 2017	50%	48%	3%	2%	1,005	Survation[198]	Telephone	Likely voters
10 Jun 2017	48%	46%	6%	2%	1,036	Survation[199]	Online	
8 Jun 2017	*United Kingdom general election, 2017*							
2-7 Jun 2017	46%	51%	3%	5%	3,018	Panelbase[200]	Online	
2-5 Jun 2017	47%	44%	9%	3%	1,503	BMG Research[192]	Online	

Date					Sample	Pollster	Method	Notes
26 May-1 Jun 2017	47%	**49%**	4%	2%	1,224	Panelbase[201]	Online	
29-31 May 2017	42%	**45%**	13%	3%	1,014	YouGov[202]	Online	Wales only
25-30 May 2017	35%	**38%**	27%	3%	1,199	Kantar TNS[203]	Online	
19-22 May 2017	**45%**	**45%**	10%	0%	1,499	BMG Research[192]	Online	
18-21 May 2017	**45%**	43%	13%	2%	1,025	YouGov[204]	Online	Wales only
12-15 May 2017	47%	**50%**	3%	3%	1,026	Panelbase[205]	Online	
5-9 May 2017	47%	**49%**	4%	2%	1,027	Panelbase[206]	Online	
5-7 May 2017	43%	**44%**	13%	1%	1,018	YouGov[207]	Online	Wales only
28 Apr-2 May 2017	48%	**49%**	3%	1%	1,034	Panelbase[208]	Online	Likely voters
21-24 Apr 2017	**45%**	**45%**	10%	0%	1,552	BMG Research[192]	Online	
20-24 Apr 2017	46%	**50%**	4%	4%	1,026	Panelbase[209]	Online	Likely voters
19-21 Apr 2017	**43%**	**43%**	14%	0%	1,029	YouGov[210]	Online	Wales only
28-31 Mar 2017	**46%**	**46%**	8%	0%	1,576	BMG Research[192]	Online	
23-30 Mar 2017	**44%**	43%	14%	1%	1,643	YouGov[211]	Online	
29 Mar 2017	*The United Kingdom invokes Article 50.*							
21-24 Feb 2017	45%	**46%**	9%	1%	1,543	BMG Research[192]	Online	
19-24 Jan 2017	43%	**44%**	13%	1%	1,643	YouGov[212]	Online	

Date					Sample	Pollster	Method	
17 Jan 2017	*Theresa May makes Lancaster House speech, setting out the UK Government's negotiating priorities.*							
6-9 Jan 2017	44%	**45%**	11%	1%	1,520	BMG Research[192]	Online	
14-21 Dec 2016	**44%**	43%	13%	1%	1,569	YouGov[213]	Online	
6-9 Dec 2016	43%	**46%**	11%	3%	1,532	BMG Research[192]	Online	
25-27 Nov 2016	46%	**47%**	6%	1%	2,035	ComRes[214]	Online	
22-25 Nov 2016	**43%**	**43%**	14%	0%	1,523	BMG Research[192]	Online	
20-25 Oct 2016	**44%**	43%	13%	1%	1,631	YouGov[215]	Online	
19-24 Oct 2016	**45%**	43%	12%	2%	1,546	BMG Research[216]	Online	
10-12 Oct 2016	**44%**	**44%**	12%	0%	1,002	Survation[217]	Online	
2 Oct 2016	*Theresa May makes Conservative Party Conference speech, announcing her intention to invoke Article 50 by 31 March 2017.*							
16-20 Sep 2016	42%	**46%**	11%	4%	1,601	YouGov[218]	Online	
31 Aug-9 Sep 2016	43%	**45%**	13%	2%	1,711	YouGov[219]	Online	
20-27 Jul 2016	43%	**44%**	13%	1%	1,673	YouGov[220]	Online	
13 Jul 2016	*Theresa May becomes Prime Minister of the United Kingdom.*							
3-4 Jul 2016	**45%**	**45%**	10%	0%	1,820	YouGov[221]	Online	
29-30 Jun 2016	**45%**	37%	19%	8%	1,017	BMG Research[222]	Online	
28-30 Jun 2016	**48%**	42%	9%	6%	2,006	Opinium[223]Wikipedia:Link rot	Online	
23 Jun 2016	*United Kingdom European Union membership referendum, 2016*							

- $\dfrac{v}{t}$
- $\dfrac{v}{t}$
- $\underline{e}^{224}$

Three-option referendum

On 6 July 2018, the UK Cabinet agreed a statement at Chequers that set out a proposal for the future relationship between the United Kingdom and the European Union, following which two members of the Cabinet resigned. On 16 July 2018 the former Education Secretary Justine Greening noted the lack of a political consensus behind the Chequers proposal and said that, due to a 'stalemate' in the House of Commons, the issue of Brexit should be referred back to the electorate. She proposed a referendum with three options: to leave the EU on such terms as might be agreed between the UK Government and the EU 27; to leave the EU without agreed terms; or to remain in the EU. Voters would be asked to mark a first and second preference using the supplementary vote system. If there were no majority for any particular option among first-preference votes, the third-placed option would be eliminated and second preferences would be used to determine the winner from the two remaining options.

The following table shows opinion polls that have been conducted on how people would vote in such a **three-option referendum**. The table shows the poll results for a first round in which all three options would be available, and for a second round in which only the top two options in the first round would be available.

Date(s) conducted	Round	Re-main	Deal	No Deal	None	Lead	Sample	Con-ducted by	Polling type	Notes
6-11 Sep 2018	I	**58%**	10%	9%	23%	48%	1,645	YouGov[132]	Online	18-24 age group
	II	**82%**	18%			64%				
31 Jul-7 Aug 2018	I	**40%**	11%	27%	22%	13%	10,121	YouGov[225]	Online	
	II	**56%**		44%		12%				
20-23 Jul 2018	I	**48%**	13%	27%	11%	21%	1,466	Sky Data[226]	Online	
	II	**59%**		41%		18%				
19-20 Jul 2018	I	**41%**	9%	31%	19%	10%	1,668	YouGov[227]	Online	
	II	**54%**		46%		8%				

16-17 Jul 2018	I	42%	15%	28%	15%	14%	1,657	YouGov[228]	Online	
	II	55%		45%		10%				

8-9 Jul 2018	*Brexit Secretary David Davis and Foreign Secretary Boris Johnson resign.*
6 Jul 2018	*The UK Cabinet agrees the Chequers Statement, setting out a proposal on the future UK-EU relationship.*
23 Jun 2016	*United Kingdom European Union membership referendum, 2016*

- v
- t
- e[229]

Support for a second referendum

There have been opinion polls to gauge **support for a second referendum** on whether to accept or reject the final Brexit deal.

Date(s) conducted	Support	Oppose	Neither	Lead	Sample	Conducted by	Polling type	Notes
6-11 Sep 2018	52%	22%	25%	30%	1,645	YouGov[132]	Online	18-24 age group
4-5 Sep 2018	40%	41%	18%	1%	1,628	YouGov[230]	Online	
30 Aug-5 Sep 2018	56%	33%	10%	23%	620	YouGov[231]	Online	GMB members
30 Aug-5 Sep 2018	66%	22%	11%	44%	1,081	YouGov[232]	Online	UNISON members
30 Aug-5 Sep 2018	59%	33%	8%	26%	1,058	YouGov[233]	Online	Unite the Union members
31 Jul-4 Sep 2018	45%	35%	21%	10%	25,641	YouGov[234]	Online	
31 Jul-3 Sep 2018	52%	30%	19%	22%	3,051	YouGov[235]	Online	London only
31 Aug-1 Sep 2018	40%	43%	17%	3%	1,600	YouGov[236]	Online	
31 Jul-20 Aug 2018	45%	33%	22%	12%	18,772	YouGov[141]	Online	
31 Jul-19 Aug 2018	44%	36%	21%	8%	939	YouGov[237]	Online	Wales only
25-26 Jul 2018	42%	40%	18%	2%	1,631	YouGov[149]	Online	

Date								
24 Jul 2018	*The Independent launches its campaign for a second referendum.*							
16-17 Jul 2018	40%	**42%**	18%	2%	1,657	YouGov[238]	Online	
	36%	**47%**	17%	11%				Three-option referendum
10-11 Jul 2018	37%	**41%**	23%	4%	1,732	YouGov[239]	Online	
8-9 Jul 2018	*Brexit Secretary David Davis and Foreign Secretary Boris Johnson resign.*							
5-8 Jul 2018	14%	**82%**	4%	68%	966	YouGov[240]	Online	Conservative Party members
6 Jul 2018	*The UK Cabinet agrees the Chequers Statement, setting out a proposal on the future UK-EU relationship.*							
28 Jun-2 Jul 2018	40%	**45%**	15%	5%	1,031	YouGov[155]	Online	Wales only
27-30 Jun 2018	**57%**	34%	9%	23%	902	YouGov[241]	Online	Unite the Union members
13-14 May 2018	38%	**46%**	16%	8%	1,634	YouGov[242]	Online	
12 May 2018	*The National Union of Students calls for a referendum on the final deal.*							
1-4 May 2018	**53%**	31%	16%	22%	2,005	Opinium[243]		
15 Apr 2018	*People's Vote campaign launched.*							
10-12 Apr 2018	**52%**	31%	17%	21%	2,008	Opinium[244]	Online	
9-10 Apr 2018	38%	**45%**	17%	7%	1,639	YouGov[245]	Online	
26-27 Mar 2018	36%	**42%**	22%	6%	1,659	YouGov[246]	Online	
12-15 Mar 2018	39%	**49%**	12%	10%	1,015	YouGov[167]	Online	Wales only
5-6 Mar 2018	36%	**43%**	20%	7%	1,641	YouGov[247]	Online	
2 Mar 2018	*Theresa May makes Mansion House speech, outlining the UK Government's policy on the future UK-EU relationship.*							
10-19 Jan 2018	**47%**	34%	19%	13%	5,075	ICM[248]	Online	
9-10 Jan 2018	36%	**43%**	21%	7%	1,714	YouGov[249]	Online	
15 Dec 2017	*The European Council decides to proceed to the second phase of the Brexit negotiations.*							

10-11 Dec 2017	33%	**42%**	24%	9%	1,680	YouGov[250]	Online	
30 Nov-1 Dec 2017	**50%**	34%	16%	16%	1,003	Survation[251]	Online	
21-24 Nov 2017	**44%**	43%	13%	1%	1,016	YouGov[180]	Online	Wales only
23-24 Oct 2017	32%	**46%**	22%	14%	1,637	YouGov[252]	Online	
22-24 Sep 2017	34%	**46%**	21%	12%	1,716	YouGov[253]	Online	
22 Sep 2017	*Theresa May makes Florence speech, in an attempt to 'unblock' the Brexit negotiations.*							
12-13 Sep 2017	34%	**47%**	19%	13%	1,660	YouGov[254]	Online	
4-7 Sep 2017	40%	**48%**	12%	8%	1,011	YouGov[255]	Online	Wales only
14-15 Jul 2017	**46%**	39%	15%	7%	1,024	Survation[256]	Online	
7-11 Jul 2017	41%	**48%**	12%	7%	2,005	Opinium[257]		
28-30 Jun 2017	46%	**48%**	6%	2%	1,017	Survation[258]	Telephone	
16-20 Jun 2017	38%	**51%**	11%	13%	2,005	Opinium[257]		
19 Jun 2017	*Brexit negotiations begin.*							
16-17 Jun 2017	**48%**	43%	9%	5%	1,005	Survation[259]	Telephone	
16-17 Jun 2017	38%	**57%**	4%	19%	1,005	Survation[260]	Telephone	
8 Jun 2017	*United Kingdom general election, 2017*							
29-31 May 2017	33%	**56%**	11%	23%	1,025	YouGov[202]	Online	Wales only
18-21 May 2017	37%	**52%**	11%	15%	1,025	YouGov[204]	Online	Wales only
5-7 May 2017	37%	**53%**	10%	16%	1,018	YouGov[207]	Online	Wales only
28 Apr-2 May 2017	36%	**53%**	11%	17%	2,003	Opinium[257]		
27-28 Apr 2017	31%	**49%**	20%	18%	1,612	YouGov[261]	Online	

Date								
20-21 Apr 2017	31%	**48%**	21%	17%	1,590	YouGov[262]	Online	
19-21 Apr 2017	35%	**53%**	12%	18%	1,029	YouGov[210]	Online	Wales only
29 Mar 2017	*The United Kingdom invokes Article 50.*							
17-21 Mar 2017	38%	**52%**	10%	14%	2,003	Opinium[257]		
17 Jan 2017	*Theresa May makes Lancaster House speech, setting out the UK Government's negotiating priorities.*							
13-16 Dec 2016	33%	**52%**	15%	19%	2,000	Opinium[257]		
2 Oct 2016	*Theresa May makes Conservative Party Conference speech, announcing her intention to invoke Article 50 by 31 March 2017.*							
13 Jul 2016	*Theresa May becomes Prime Minister of the United Kingdom.*							
29-30 Jun 2016	32%	**60%**	7%	28%	1,017	BMG Research[263]	Online	
23 Jun 2016	*United Kingdom European Union membership referendum, 2016*							

- v
- t
- e[224]

In July 2017, LSE/Opinium research indicated that 60% of Britons wanted to retain EU citizenship after Brexit.[264]

US position

Rex Tillerson, former United States Secretary of State, considers that the European Union and the United Kingdom should perform a fast Brexit to avoid useless disagreement.

Cultural responses to the referendum vote

Brexit in the visual arts

The response of artists and writers to Brexit has in general been negative, reflecting a reported overwhelming percentage of people involved in Britain's creative industries voting against leaving the European Union.[265]

Responses by visual artists to Brexit include a mural, painted in May 2017, by the secretive graffiti artist Banksy near the ferry port at Dover in southern England. It shows a workman using a chisel to chip off one of the stars on the European Union Flag.[266]

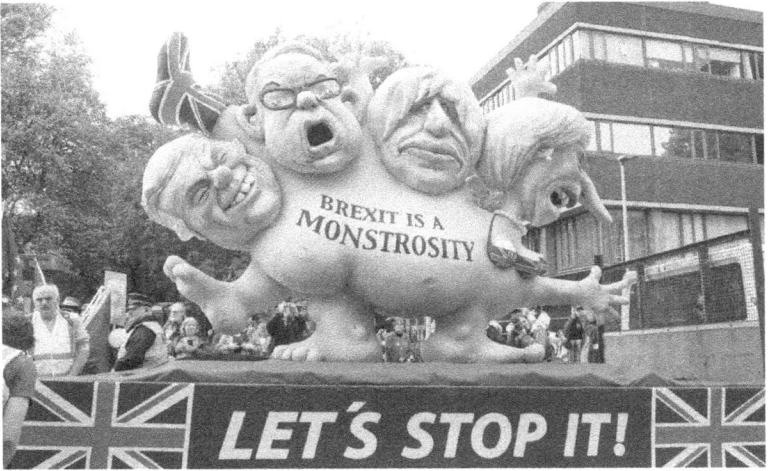

Figure 5: *Anti-Brexit protesters in Manchester*

Figure 6: *Düsseldorf carnival parade in February 2018*

In his 2017 art exhibition at the Serpentine Gallery in London, the artist Grayson Perry showed a series of ceramic, tapestry and other works of art dealing with the divisions in Britain during the Brexit campaign and in its aftermath. This included two large ceramic pots, Perry called his *Brexit Vases*, standing on plinths ten feet apart, on the first of which were scenes involving pro-European British citizens, and on the second scenes involving anti-European British citizens. These were derived from what Perry called his "Brexit tour of Britain."[267]

Brexit in novels

In Daphne Du Maurier's 1972 novel *Rule Britannia* the UK is brought to the brink of bankrupcy after withdrawal from the EEC.[268]

One of the first novels to engage with a post-Brexit Britain was *Rabbitman* by Michael Paraskos (published 9 March 2017). *Rabbitman* is a dark comic fantasy in which the events that lead to the election of a right-wing populist American president, who happens also to be a rabbit, and Britain's vote to leave the European Union, were the result of a series of Faustian pacts with the Devil. As a result, *Rabbitman* is set partly in a post-Brexit Britain in which society has collapsed and people are dependent on European Union food aid.[269]

Mark Billingham's *Love Like Blood* (published 1 June 2017) is a crime thriller in which Brexit sees a rise in xenophobic hate crime.[270] In the novel *The Remains of the Way* (published 6 June 2017), David Boyle imagines Brexit was a conspiracy led by a forgotten government quango, still working away in Whitehall, originally set up by Thomas Cromwell in the sixteenth century during the reign of King Henry VIII, and now dedicated to a Protestant Brexit.[271]

Post-Brexit Britain is also the setting for Amanda Craig's *The Lie of the Land* (published 13 June 2017), a satirical novel set ten years after the vote to leave the European Union, in which an impoverished middle class couple from Islington in north London are forced to move from the heart of the pro-European Union capital, to the heart of the pro-Brexit countryside in Devon.[272]

Brexit is also the baseline for Douglas Board's comic political thriller *Time of Lies* (published 23 June 2017). In this novel, the first post-Brexit general election in 2020 is won by a violent right-wing former football hooligan called Bob Grant. Board charts the response to this of the hitherto pro-European Union metropolitan political elite.[273]

Stanley Johnson's *Kompromat* (scheduled for July 2017) is a political thriller that suggests the vote to leave the European Union was a result of Russian influence on the referendum, although Johnson has insisted his book is not intended to point the finger at Russia's secret services, but is "just meant to be fun."[274]

Brexit in theatre

In June 2017, the National Theatre in London presented a play by Carol Ann Duffy, entitled *My Country; a work in progress*. An allegorical work, the play uses the device of a convention called by the goddess Britannia, who is concerned about the future of the British people.[275] The play differs from some artistic responses in that Duffy and the National Theatre-based the attitudes of the characters in part on the responses of ordinary people in interviews that were conducted by the regional offices of the UK Arts Councils, but excluding responses from London and the south-east of England, where most people voted not to leave the EU. As a result, according to Dominic Cavendish, writing in *The Daily Telegraph*, "the bias is towards the Leave camp".[276]

Brexit in film

In 2016, the television director Martin Durkin wrote and directed an 81 minute long documentary film titled "Brexit: The Movie" which advocated with the withdrawal of the United Kingdom from the European Union. The film was produced by the production company Wag TV with a budget of £300,000. The production costs were sourced primarily through crowdfunding via Kickstarter alongside a £50,000 contribution from the hedge fund Spitfire Capital. In May 2016 the film premiered in Leicester Square, with notable figures such as Nigel Farage and David Davis (who later became Secretary of State for Exiting the European Union) in attendance.

Establishment of pro-European political organisations

Following the Brexit vote, there have been several attempts to set up a new pro-European political party. Examples include 'The Democrats' (a proposal by former *Daily Mail* political editor James Chapman), 'The Radicals' (proposed by Jeremy Cliffe, former Berlin bureau chief of *The Economist*) and the Renew Britain party.

In 2017, newly elected Liberal Democrats leader Vince Cable criticised 'pop up' anti-Brexit parties formed following the 2016 referendum, saying of those groups policies "...it is the kind of ideology-free, technocratic, authoritarian centrism that would be more at home in, say, Singapore." and "Voters beware."

Further reading

- William Outhwaite (ed.), *Brexit: Sociological Responses* (London: Anthem Press, 2017). ISBN 9781783086443
- Hobolt, Sara B. (7 September 2016). "The Brexit vote: a divided nation, a divided continent"[277]. *Journal of European Public Policy*. **23** (9): 1259–1277. doi: 10.1080/13501763.2016.1225785[278]. ISSN 1350-1763[279].
- Peers, Steve (2016). *The Brexit: The Legal Framework for Withdrawal from the EU or Renegotiation of EU Membership*. Oxford, UK: Hart Publishing. ISBN 978-1-84946-874-9. OCLC 917161408[280].
- Ansorg, N. & Haastrup, T.: "Brexit Beyond the UK's Borders: What It Means for Africa", GIGA Focus Afrika No. 03/2016[281]

External links

Wikisourcehas original text related to this article:
The withdrawal clause

Look up *Brexit*in Wiktionary, the free dictionary.

- UK government's Brexit information[282]
- UK government's official negotiation documents[283]
- EU's official negotiation documents[284]
- UK Parliament – Brexit News[285]
- Reading list of post-EU Referendum publications by Parliament and the Devolved Assemblies[286] – House of Commons Library
- Record of Brexit-related business in the devolved legislatures[287] (Northern Ireland, Scotland and Wales) – House of Commons Library
- Gov UK – Department for Exiting the European Union[288]
- BBC: "Brexit: What are the options?" (10 October 2016)[289]
- *The Brexit Papers*, Bar Council, December 2016[290]
- *Plan for Britain: The government's negotiating objectives for exiting the EU*: PM's speech delivered and published on 17 January 2017[291] – transcript of speech as delivered at Lancaster House, London
- *The United Kingdom's exit from and new partnership with the European Union*, February 2017 ("White paper")[292]
- Brexit[293] at Curlie (based on DMOZ)
- Quotes about Brexit[294] on Euronews
- European Council Brexit Guidelines[295]

- *The Principle of Loyalty in EU Law*, 2014, by Marcus Klamert, Legal Officer, European Commission[296]

Relating to court cases

- Judgment[297] of the Supreme Court of the United Kingdom in *R (Miller) v Secretary of State for Exiting the European Union*

Background

History of European Union–United Kingdom relations

Part of a series of articles on the
United Kingdom in the European Union
Accession
• 1973 EC enlargement • 1975 Referendum Act • 1975 EC membership referendum • 1972 EC Act • UK rebate • 2011 EU Act

Membership

- The Euro
- European Movement UK
- Nationality law
- UK Euroscepticism
  - Maastricht Rebels
- Black Wednesday
- **Officials and bodies**
- EU Committee
- European Scrutiny Committee
- Northern Ireland Executive in Brussels
- EU Representative in London
- Young European Movement UK
- UK European Commissioners
- Permanent EU Representatives

Legislation

- 1972 EC Act
- 1986 EC (Amendment) Act
- 1993 EC (Amendment) Act
- 1998 EC (Amendment) Act
- 2002 EC (Amendment) Act
- 2008 EU (Amendment) Act
- 2011 EU Act

European Parliament Elections

- 1979
- 1984
- 1989
- 1994
- 1999
- 2004
- 2009
- 2014

  - 1973 delegation
  - 1st
  - 2nd
  - 3rd
  - 4th
  - 5th
  - 6th
  - 7th
  - 8th

Withdrawal

- 2004–05 EU Bill
- 2013–14 EU (Referendum) Bill
- 2015–16 EU membership renegotiation
- 2015 EU Referendum Act
- 2016 EU (Referendum) Act (Gibraltar)
- **2016 EU membership referendum**
- Issues
- Endorsements
- Opinion polling
- Results
- Causes
- **Campaigns**
- **Organisations advocating and campaigning for a referendum**
- People's Pledge
- Labour for a Referendum
- **Leave**
- **Vote Leave** (official lead group)
  - Business for Britain
  - Conservatives for Britain
  - Students for Britain
- Labour Leave
- Leave.EU
  - Bpoplive
- Grassroots Out
- Get Britain Out
- The Freedom Association
  - Better Off Out
- **Other anti-EU advocacy organisations**
- Bruges Group
- Campaign for an Independent Britain
- **Remain**
- **Britain Stronger in Europe** (official lead group)
- Labour In for Britain
- European Movement UK
- **Other pro-EU advocacy organisations**
- Britain in Europe
- British Influence
- Business for New Europe
- Nucleus
- **Pejorative term for pro-EU advocacy**
- Project Fear
- **Media coverage**
- *Brexit: The Movie*
- *In or Out*
- **Aftermath**
- International reactions
- Terms of Withdrawal from EU (Referendum) Bills
- 2016 Conservative Party election
- 2016 Labour Party election
- 2017 Liberal Democrats Party election
- Proposed second Scottish independence referendum
- Proposed London independence
- *The New European*
- European Union (Withdrawal) Act 2018 (including meaningful vote)
- European Union (Withdrawal Agreement) Bill 2017-19
- Gibraltar
- 2017 General Election
- EU Withdrawal Agreement (Public Vote) Bill 2017-19
- UK's relations with EU after 2019
- **Triggering of Article 50 & Negotiations**
- *R (Miller) v Secretary of State for Exiting the European Union'*
- EU (Notification of Withdrawal) Act 2017
- UK invocation of Article 50
- Brexit negotiations
- Department for Exiting the EU (Brexit Department)
- Department for International Trade
- Post-referendum organisations

Calls for second vote

- European Union Withdrawal Agreement (Public Vote) Bill 2017-19
- **Organisations campaigning**
  for a second vote via People's Vote
- Britain for Europe
- European Movement UK
- For our Future's Sake
- Healthier IN the EU
- Open Britain
- Our Future Our Choice
- Scientists for EU
- **Other organisations campaigning**
  for a second vote
- Best for Britain
- **See also**
- Opposition to Brexit in the United Kingdom

- <u>v</u>
- <u>t</u>
- <u>e</u>[298]

Since the foundation of the European Communities, the United Kingdom has been an important neighbour and is currently a major member, until its withdrawal.

Research shows that the United Kingdom's membership of the European Union has contributed to higher incomes, played an important role in stopping British economic decline during the 1950s and 1960s,Wikipedia:Please clarify and has increased trade and reduced trade costs.

EU roots and British accession (1957–1973)

The UK was not a signatory of the three original treaties that were incorporated into what was then the European Communities, including the most well known of these, the 1957 Treaty of Rome, establishing the European Economic Community (EEC). The UK's applications to join in 1963 and 1967 were vetoed by the President of France, Charles de Gaulle, who said that "a number of aspects of Britain's economy, from working practices to agriculture" had "made Britain incompatible with Europe" and that Britain harboured a "deep-seated hostility" to any pan-European project.

Once de Gaulle had relinquished the French presidency in 1969, the UK made a third and successful application for membership. The question of sovereignty had been discussed at the time in an official Foreign and Commonwealth Office document. It listed among "Areas of policy in which parliamentary freedom to legislate will be affected by entry into the European Communities": Customs duties, Agriculture, Free movement of labour, services and capital, Transport, and Social Security for migrant workers. The document concluded (paragraph

26) that it was advisable to put the considerations of influence and power before those of formal sovereignty.[299]

The Treaty of Accession was signed in January 1972 by the then prime minister Edward Heath, leader of the Conservative Party. Parliament's European Communities Act 1972 was enacted on 17 October, and the UK's instrument of ratification was deposited the next day (18 October), letting the United Kingdom's membership of the EC come into effect on 1 January 1973.

Referendum of 1975

In 1975, the United Kingdom held its first ever national referendum on whether the UK should remain in the European Communities. The opposition Labour Party, led by Harold Wilson, had contested the October 1974 general election with a commitment to renegotiate Britain's terms of membership of the EC and then hold a referendum on whether to remain in the EC on the new terms.[300] All of the major political parties and the mainstream press supported continuing membership of the EC. However, there were significant divides within the ruling Labour Party; a 1975 one-day party conference voted by two to one in favour of withdrawal,[301] and seven of the 23 cabinet ministers were opposed to EC membership, with Harold Wilson suspending the constitutional convention of Cabinet collective responsibility to allow those ministers to publicly campaign against the government.

On 5 June 1975, the electorate were asked to vote yes or no on the question: "Do you think the UK should stay in the European Community (Common Market)?" Every administrative county and region in the UK returned majority "Yes" votes, apart from the Shetland Islands and the Outer Hebrides. With a turnout of just under 65%, the outcome of the vote was 67.2% in favour of staying in, and the United Kingdom remained a member of the EC. Support for the UK to leave the EC in 1975, in the data, appears unrelated to the support for Leave in the 2016 referendum.

From Referendum to Maastricht Treaty (1975–1992)

In 1979, the United Kingdom opted out of the newly formed European Monetary System (EMS), which was the precursor to the creation of the euro currency.

The opposition Labour Party campaigned in the 1983 general election on a commitment to withdraw from the EC without a referendum. It was heavily

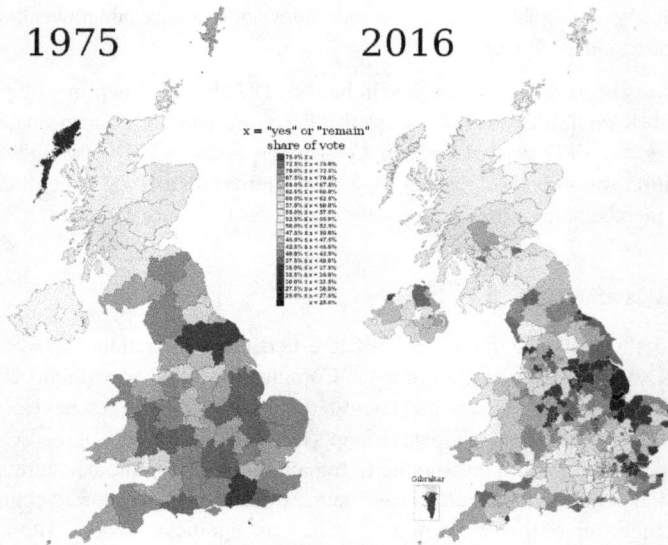

Figure 7: *Comparison of results of 1975 and 2016 referendums*

defeated; the Conservative government of Margaret Thatcher was re-elected. The Labour Party subsequently changed its policy.

In 1985, the United Kingdom ratified the Single European Act—the first major revision to the Treaty of Rome — without a referendum, with the full support of the Thatcher government.Wikipedia:Citation needed

In October 1990 — despite the deep reservations of Margaret Thatcher,Wikipedia:Citation needed who was under pressure from her senior ministersWikipedia:Citation needed — the United Kingdom joined the European Exchange Rate Mechanism (ERM), with the pound sterling pegged to the deutschmark.

Maastricht Treaty and Referendum Party

Thatcher resigned as Prime Minister in November 1990, amid internal divisions within the Conservative Party that arose partly from her increasingly Eurosceptic views. The United Kingdom was forced to withdraw from the ERM in September 1992, after the pound sterling came under pressure from currency speculators (an episode known as Black Wednesday). The resulting cost to UK taxpayers was estimated to be in excess of £3 billion.

As a result of the Maastricht Treaty, the European Communities became the European Union on 1 November 1993. The new name reflected the evolution of the organisation from an economic union into a political union. As a result of the Lisbon Treaty, which entered into force on 1 December 2009, the Maastricht Treaty is now known, in updated form as, the Treaty on European Union (2007) or TEU, and the Treaty of Rome is now known, in updated form, as the Treaty on the Functioning of the European Union (2007) or TFEU.

The Referendum Party was formed in 1994 by Sir James Goldsmith to contest the 1997 general election on a platform of providing a referendum on the UK's membership of the EU. It fielded candidates in 547 constituencies at that election, and won 810,860 votes or 2.6% of the total votes cast. It failed to win a single parliamentary seat because its vote was spread out across the country, and lost its deposit (funded by Goldsmith) in 505 constituencies.

Role of UKIP (1993–2016)

The UK Independence Party (UKIP), a Eurosceptic political party, was also formed, in 1993. It achieved third place in the UK during the 2004 European elections, second place in the 2009 European elections and first place in the 2014 European elections, with 27.5% of the total vote. This was the first time since the 1910 general election that any party other than the Labour or Conservative parties had taken the largest share of the vote in a nationwide election. UKIP's electoral success in the 2014 European election has been documented as the strongest correlate of the support for the leave campaign in the 2016 referendum.

In 2014, UKIP won two by-elections, triggered by defecting Conservative MPs, and in the 2015 general election took 12.6% of the total vote and held one of the two seats won in 2014.

Controversy on the European Court of Human Rights in 2013

The European Convention on Human Rights (ECHR) was drafted in 1950, largely under British leadership,Wikipedia:Citation needed and its court (ECtHR) was established in 1953. EU institutions are bound under article 6 of the Treaty of NiceWikipedia:Citation needed to respect human rights under the Convention, over and above for example the Law of the United Kingdom. The Court was criticised especially within the Conservative Party for ruling in favour of British prisoners obtaining the right to vote. During the referendum the then Home Secretary, Theresa May, had called for the UK to leave the ECHR

Euroscepticism (1993–2016)

In a statistical analysis published in April 2016, Professor John Curtice of Strathclyde University defined Euroscepticism as the wish to sever or reduce the powers of the EU, and conversely Europhilia as the desire to preserve or increase the powers of the EU. According to this definition, the British Social Attitudes (BSA) surveys show an increase in euroscepticism from 38% (1993) to 65% (2015). Euroscepticism should however not be confused with the wish to leave the EU: the BSA survey for the period July–November 2015 shows that 60% backed the option "continue as an EU member", and only 30% backed the option to "withdraw".

Opinion polling

Since 1977, both pro- and anti-European views have had majority support at different times, with some dramatic swings between the two camps. In the United Kingdom European Communities membership referendum of 1975, two-thirds of British voters favoured continued EC membership. The highest-ever rejection of membership was in 1980, the first full year of Prime Minister Margaret Thatcher's term of office, with 65% opposed to and 26% in favour of membership.

After Thatcher had negotiated a rebate of British membership payments in 1984, those favouring the EC maintained a lead in the opinion polls, except during 2000, as Prime Minister Tony Blair aimed for closer EU integration, including adoption of the euro currency, and around 2011, as immigration into the United Kingdom became increasingly noticeable. As late as December 2015 there was, according to ComRes, a clear majority in favour of remaining in the EU, albeit with a warning that voter intentions would be considerably influenced by the outcome of Prime Minister David Cameron's ongoing EU reform negotiations, especially with regards to the two issues of "safeguards for non-Eurozone member states" and "immigration".[302] The following events are relevant.

Brexit (2017–2019)

From 2017 to 2019, UK has engaged in negotiating a Brexit between the European Union and herself. Between UK and EU, this Brexit would consist in a withdrawal agreement and a trade agreement, while at a global level this would/might also split various FTA. The withdrawal agreement is viewed by the EU as a "settlement of accounts" unrelated to the post-exit trade agreement, and viewed by the UK as a 'goodwill payment' to enable a fair post-exit trade agreement. In the event of a no-deal scenario each side will consequently have different views as to the validity of any payment.

Opinion polling for the United Kingdom European Union membership referendum

Part of a series of articles on the

United Kingdom in the European Union

Accession

- 1973 EC enlargement
- 1975 Referendum Act
- 1975 EC membership referendum
- 1972 EC Act
- UK rebate
- 2011 EU Act

Membership

- The Euro
- European Movement UK
- Nationality law
- UK Euroscepticism
  - Maastricht Rebels
- Black Wednesday
- **Officials and bodies**
- EU Committee
- European Scrutiny Committee
- Northern Ireland Executive in Brussels
- EU Representative in London
- Young European Movement UK
- UK European Commissioners
- Permanent EU Representatives

Legislation

- 1972 EC Act
- 1986 EC (Amendment) Act
- 1993 EC (Amendment) Act
- 1998 EC (Amendment) Act
- 2002 EC (Amendment) Act
- 2008 EU (Amendment) Act
- 2011 EU Act

European Parliament Elections

- 1979
- 1984
- 1989
- 1994
- 1999
- 2004
- 2009
- 2014

  - 1973 delegation
  - 1st
  - 2nd
  - 3rd
  - 4th
  - 5th
  - 6th
  - 7th
  - 8th

Withdrawal

- 2004–05 EU Bill
- 2013–14 EU (Referendum) Bill
- 2015–16 EU membership renegotiation
- 2015 EU Referendum Act
- 2016 EU (Referendum) Act (Gibraltar)
- **2016 EU membership referendum**
- Issues
- Endorsements
- Opinion polling
- Results
- Causes
- **Campaigns**
- **Organisations advocating and campaigning for a referendum**
- People's Pledge
- Labour for a Referendum
- **Leave**
- **Vote Leave** (official lead group)
  - Business for Britain
  - Conservatives for Britain
  - Students for Britain
- Labour Leave
- Leave.EU
  - Bpoplive
- Grassroots Out
- Get Britain Out
- The Freedom Association
  - Better Off Out
- **Other anti-EU advocacy organisations**
- Bruges Group
- Campaign for an Independent Britain
- **Remain**
- **Britain Stronger in Europe** (official lead group)
- Labour In for Britain
- European Movement UK
- **Other pro-EU advocacy organisations**
- Britain in Europe
- British Influence
- Business for New Europe
- Nucleus
- **Pejorative term for pro-EU advocacy**
- Project Fear
- **Media coverage**
- *Brexit: The Movie*
- *In or Out*
- **Aftermath**
- International reactions
- Terms of Withdrawal from EU (Referendum) Bills
- 2016 Conservative Party election
- 2016 Labour Party election
- 2017 Liberal Democrats Party election
- Proposed second Scottish independence referendum
- Proposed London independence
- *The New European*
- European Union (Withdrawal) Act 2018 (including meaningful vote)
- European Union (Withdrawal Agreement) Bill 2017-19
- Gibraltar
- 2017 General Election
- EU Withdrawal Agreement (Public Vote) Bill 2017-19
- UK's relations with EU after 2019
- **Triggering of Article 50 & Negotiations**
- *R (Miller) v Secretary of State for Exiting the European Union*'
- EU (Notification of Withdrawal) Act 2017
- UK invocation of Article 50
- Brexit negotiations
- Department for Exiting the EU (Brexit Department)
- Department for International Trade
- Post referendum organisations

Calls for second vote

- European Union Withdrawal Agreement (Public Vote) Bill 2017-19
- **Organisations campaigning
  for a second vote via People's Vote**
- Britain for Europe
- European Movement UK
- For our Future's Sake
- Healthier IN the EU
- Open Britain
- Our Future Our Choice
- Scientists for EU
- **Other organisations campaigning
  for a second vote**
- Best for Britain
- **See also**
- Opposition to Brexit in the United Kingdom

- v
- t
- e[304]

The referendum on EU membership took place on 23 June 2016. **Opinion polling for the United Kingdom European Union membership referendum** was ongoing in the months between the announcement of a referendum and the referendum polling day. Polls on the general principle of Britain's membership of the European Union were carried out for a number of years prior to the referendum. Opinion polls of voters in general tended to show roughly equal proportions in favour of remaining and leaving. Polls of business leaders, scientists, and lawyers showed majorities in favour of remaining. Among non-British citizens in other EU member states, polling suggested that a majority were in favour of the UK remaining in the EU in principle, but that a similarly sized majority believed that if the UK were only able to remain in the EU on renegotiated terms then it should leave.

Analysis

Demographics

Younger voters tended to support remaining in the EU (but are generally less likely to vote) whereas older people tended to support leaving. There was no significant difference in attitudes between the genders. According to two out of three pollsters, managerial, professional and administrative workers were most likely to favour staying in the EU, while semi-skilled and unskilled workers, plus those reliant on benefits, were the largest demographic supporting leave. University graduates are generally more likely to vote remain compared to those with no qualifications. White voters were evenly split, and all ethnic minority groups leant towards backing Remain, but registration is lower and turnout can be up to 25% lower in this demographic. Support for remaining

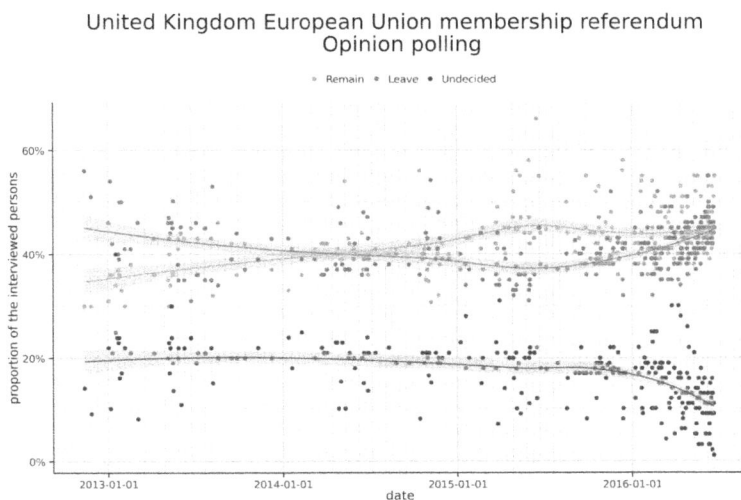

Figure 8: *Opinion polling on the referendum since 2013, showing "remain" in green, "leave" in red, and "undecided" in blue (as of 23 June 2016[303])*

in the EU was known to be significantly higher in Scotland than it is in Great Britain as a whole.

Polling methods

The way voters are polled is known to affect the outcome. Telephone polls have consistently found more support for remaining in the EU than online polls. YouGov, which uses online polling, has criticised telephone polls because they "have too high a percentage of graduates", skewing the results. Ipsos MORI and ComRes, and Peter Kellner, the former president of YouGov, have said telephone polls are more reliable. ICM has said "as good a guess as any is that the right answer lies somewhere in between". A joint study by Populus and Number Cruncher Politics in March 2016 concluded that telephone polls were likely to better reflect the state of public opinion on the issue.

The results of the Referendum, as with the results of the 2015 General Election, show that there is still a problem with the polling methodology. Overall, however, online polls seem to have had a better performance than phone polls. Online surveys, on average, predicted a "leave" win with a 1.2% margin, whereas those with a phone methodology had "remain" win with a 2.6% margin. All in all, 63% of online polls predicted a Leave victory, while 78% of phone polls predicted that Remain would win. Kantar TNS and Opinium,

both pollsters with online methodologies, were the two groups that forecast a
Leave victory just ahead of the vote.

Polls of polls

Several different groups have calculated polls of polls, which collect and average the results of opinion polls across different companies. They have different
methodologies; for example, some give more weight to recent polls than others, some deal with undecided voters differently, and some attempt to adjust
for the consistent gap between telephone and online polling. As a result, the
polls of polls give a spread of results.

Conducted by	Date	Re-main	Leave	Unde-cided	Lead	Notes
What UK Thinks: EU	23 June	52%	48%	N/A	4%	Six most recent polls.
Elections Etc.	23 June	50.6%	49.4%	N/A	1.2%	Twelve most recent polls. Telephone polls are adjusted in favour of Leave and online polls in favour of Remain.
HuffPost Pollster	23 June	45.8%	45.3%	9%	0.5%	
Number Cruncher Politics	22 June	46%	44%	10%	2%	Equal weighting to phone and online polls.
Financial Times	13 June	48%	46%	6%	2%	Five most recent polls.
The Telegraph	21 June	51%	49%	N/A	2%	Six most recent polls.
The Economist	6 June	44%	44%	9%	0%	Excludes polls with fewer than 900 participants.

Standard polling on EU membership

The tables show polling on whether the UK should be in or out of the EU.
Polling generally weights the sample to be nationally representative. Polls were
usually conducted within Great Britain, with Northern Ireland and Gibraltar
normally omitted from the sample. This has historically been the case in British
opinion polling because Northern Ireland has a different set of political parties
from the rest of the UK, reflecting the political divide between unionism and
nationalism or republicanism. Similarly, Gibraltar was not included in standard
polls because it has its own local legislature and does not take part in British
parliamentary elections, although Gibraltar does take part in elections to the
European Parliament and took part in the referendum.

Most of the polls shown here were carried out by members of the British Polling Council (BPC) who fully disclose their findings, methodology and the client who commissioned the poll. As non-members, Qriously, Greenberg Quinlan Rosner Research, Pew Research Center and Lord Ashcroft Polls are not bound by the standards of the BPC, and their polls should be treated with caution.

The percentages who "would not vote" or who refused to answer are not shown below, although some pollsters have excluded these in any case.

2016

Date(s) conducted	Re- main	Leave	Un- de- cided	Lead	Sample	Conducted by	Polling type	Notes
23 June 2016	48.1%	**51.9%**	N/A	3.8%	33,577,342	*Results of the United Kingdom European Union membership referendum, 2016*	*UK-wide referendum*	
23 June	**52%**	48%	N/A	4%	4,772	YouGov[305]	Online	On the day poll
22 June	**55%**	45%	N/A	10%	4,700	Populus[306]	Online	
20–22 June	**51%**	49%	N/A	2%	3,766	YouGov[307]	Online	Includes Northern Ireland (turnout weighted)
20–22 June	**49%**	46%	1%	3%	1,592	Ipsos MORI[308]	Telephone	
20–22 June	44%	**45%**	9%	1%	3,011	Opinium[309]	Online	
17–22 June	**54%**	46%	N/A	8%	1,032	ComRes[310]	Telephone	Those expressing a voting intention (turnout weighted)
	48%	42%	11%	6%				All UK adults (turnout weighted)
16–22 June	41%	**43%**	16%	2%	2,320	TNS[311]	Online	
20 June	**45%**	44%	11%	1%	1,003	Survation/IG Group[312]	Telephone	

Date	Remain	Leave	Undecided	Other	Sample size	Conducted by	Method	Notes
18–19 June	42%	**44%**	13%	2%	1,652	YouGov[313]	Online	
16–19 June	**53%**	46%	2%	7%	800	ORB/-Telegraph[314]	Telephone	Definite voters only
17–18 June	**45%**	42%	13%	3%	1,004	Survation[315]	Telephone	
16–17 June	**44%**	43%	9%	1%	1,694	YouGov[316]	Online	
14–17 June	**44%**	**44%**	12%	N/A	2,006	Opinium[317]	Online	Most fieldwork conducted before the death of Jo Cox.
16 June	All official campaigning suspended until 19 June after the fatal shooting of Jo Cox MP.							
15–16 June	42%	**44%**	9%	2%	1,734	YouGov[318]	Online	
15 June	42%	**45%**	13%	3%	1,104	Survation[319]	Telephone	
10–15 June	37%	**47%**	16%	10%	1,468	BMG Research[320]	Online	
10–15 June	**46%**	43%	11%	3%	1,064	BMG Research[321]	Telephone	
11–14 June	43%	**49%**	3%	6%	1,257	Ipsos MORI[322]	Telephone	
12–13 June	39%	**46%**	15%	7%	1,905	YouGov[323]	Online	
10–13 June	45%	**50%**	5%	5%	1,000	ICM[324]	Telephone	Final ICM polls. Only include those "definite" to vote. Paired telephone/-online polls by otherwise identical methodology
	44%	**49%**	7%	5%	2,001		Online	
9–13 June	**46%**	45%	9%	1%	1,002	ComRes[325]	Telephone	
7–13 June	40%	**47%**	13%	7%	2,497	TNS[326]	Online	
9–12 June	48%	**49%**	3%	1%	800	ORB[327]	Telephone	Measures only those "definite" to vote
16 May–12 June	**53%**	47%	N/A	6%	N/A	NATCEN[328]	Online/-Telephone	Primarily online, those who failed to respond were followed up by phone

Date	Remain	Leave	Undecided	Other	Sample	Pollster	Method	Notes
9–10 June	42%	**43%**	11%	1%	1,671	YouGov[329]	Online	
7–10 June	**44%**	42%	13%	2%	2,009	Opinium[330]	Online	
8–9 June	45%	**55%**	N/A	10%	2,052	ORB[331]	Online	Weighted according to "definite" voters
5–6 June	**43%**	42%	11%	1%	2,001	YouGov[332]	Online	Remainder "won't vote"
3–5 June	43%	**48%**	9%	5%	2,047	ICM[333]	Online	
2–5 June	**48%**	47%	5%	1%	800	ORB[334]	Telephone	Weighted according to "definite" to vote
1–3 June	41%	**45%**	11%	4%	3,405	YouGov[335]	Online	
31 May–3 June	**43%**	41%	16%	2%	2,007	Opinium[336]	Online	Weighted by new methodology
	40%	**43%**	16%	3%				Weighted by previous methodology
30–31 May	**41%**	**41%**	13%	N/A	1,735	YouGov[337]	Online	
27–29 May	42%	**45%**	15%	3%	1,004	ICM[338]	Telephone	Paired telephone/-online polls by otherwise identical methodology
	44%	**47%**	9%	3%	2,052		Online	
25–29 May	**51%**	46%	3%	5%	800	ORB[339]	Telephone	
20–25 May	44%	**45%**	12%	1%	1,638	BMG Research[340]	Online	
24 May	**44%**	38%	18%	6%	1,013	Survation[341]	Telephone	
23–24 May	**41%**	**41%**	13%	N/A	1,756	YouGov[342]	Online	
19–23 May	41%	**43%**	16%	2%	1,213	TNS[343]	Online	
20–22 May	**45%**	**45%**	10%	N/A	2,003	ICM[344]	Online	

18–22 May	55%	42%	3%	13%	800	ORB[345]	Telephone	Poll was said to reflect the private polling conducted for the government
17–19 May	**44%**	40%	14%	4%	2,008	Opinium[346]	Online	
16–17 May	**44%**	40%	12%	4%	1,648	YouGov[347]	Online	
14–17 May	**52%**	41%	7%	11%	1,000	ComRes[348]	Telephone	
14–16 May	**55%**	37%	5%	18%	1,002	Ipsos MORI[349]	Telephone	
13–15 May	**47%**	39%	14%	8%	1,002	ICM[350]	Telephone	Paired telephone/-online polls by otherwise identical methodology
	43%	**47%**	10%	4%	2,048		Online	
11–15 May	**55%**	40%	5%	15%	800	ORB[351]	Telephone	
10–12 May	38%	**41%**	21%	3%	1,222	TNS[352]	Online	
29 Apr–12 May	36%	**39%**	22%	3%	996	YouGov[353]	Telephone	
29 Apr–12 May	38%	**40%**	16%	2%	1,973	YouGov[353]	Online	
6–8 May	44%	**46%**	11%	2%	2,005	ICM[354]	Online	
4–6 May	**42%**	40%	13%	2%	3,378	YouGov[355]	Online	Remainder "won't vote"
29 Apr–3 May	44%	**45%**	11%	1%	2,040	ICM[356]	Online	
27–29 Apr	43%	**46%**	11%	3%	2,029	ICM[357]	Online	
26–29 Apr	**42%**	41%	14%	1%	2,005	Opinium[358]	Online	24% of respondents preferred not to say; the stated percentages are of the other 76%
27–29 Apr	49%	**51%**	N/A	2%	2,000	ORB[359]	Online	

Date					Sample	Pollster	Method	Notes
26–28 Apr	**39%**	36%	26%	3%	1,221	TNS[360]	Online	
25–26 Apr	41%	**42%**	13%	1%	1,650	YouGov[361]	Online	Remainder "won't vote"
25–26 Apr	**45%**	38%	17%	7%	1,003	Survation[362]	Telephone	
22–26 Apr	43%	**45%**	13%	2%	2,001	BMG Research[363]	Online	
22–24 Apr	44%	**46%**	10%	2%	2,001	ICM[364]	Online	
20–24 Apr	**51%**	43%	6%	8%	800	ORB[365]	Telephone	
16–19 Apr	**51%**	40%	9%	9%	1,002	ComRes[366]	Telephone	
16–18 Apr	**49%**	39%	8%	10%	1,026	Ipsos MORI[367]	Telephone	
15–17 Apr	**48%**	41%	11%	7%	1,003	ICM[368]	Telephone	Paired telephone/-online polls by otherwise identical methodology
	43%	**44%**	13%	1%	2,008		Online	
13–17 Apr	**53%**	41%	6%	12%	800	ORB[369]	Telephone	
15 April	*The EU referendum campaign officially begins.*							
12–14 Apr	**38%**	34%	28%	4%	1,198	TNS[370]	Online	
12–14 Apr	**40%**	39%	16%	1%	3,371	YouGov[371]	Online	Remainder "won't vote"
11–12 Apr	**39%**	**39%**	17%	N/A	1,693	YouGov[372]	Online	Remainder "won't vote"
7–11 Apr	**35%**	**35%**	30%	N/A	1,198	TNS[373]	Online	
8–10 Apr	**45%**	38%	17%	7%	1,002	ComRes[374]	Telephone	
8–10 Apr	42%	**45%**	12%	3%	2,030	ICM[375]	Online	
7 April	*HM Government starts sending a pro-Remain pamphlet to 27 million UK households and begins a pro-Remain digital advertising campaign.*							
6–7 Apr	**40%**	38%	16%	2%	1,612	YouGov[376]	Online	Remainder "won't vote"
29 Mar–4 Apr	**39%**	38%	18%	1%	3,754	YouGov[377]	Online	Remainder "won't vote"
1–3 Apr	**44%**	43%	13%	1%	2,007	ICM[378]	Online	

Date	Remain	Leave	Undecided	Other	Sample size	Pollster	Method	Notes
29 Mar–3 Apr	**51%**	44%	5%	7%	800	ORB[379]	Telephone	
29 Mar–1 Apr	39%	**43%**	18%	4%	1,966	Opinium[380]	Online	
24–29 Mar	**35%**	**35%**	30%	N/A	1,193	TNS[381]	Online	
24–29 Mar	41%	**45%**	14%	4%	1,518	BMG Research[363]	Online	Includes Northern Ireland
24–28 Mar	**51%**	49%	N/A	2%	2,002	ORB[382]	Online	
22–24 Mar	**45%**	43%	12%	2%	1,970	ICM[383]	Online	Original poll is no longer available on ICM Unlimted
19–22 Mar	**49%**	41%	10%	8%	1,023	Ipsos MORI[384]	Telephone	
17–22 Mar	**40%**	37%	19%	3%	1,688	YouGov[385]	Online	Remainder "won't vote"
18–20 Mar	**48%**	41%	11%	7%	1,002	ComRes[386]	Telephone	
18–20 Mar	41%	**43%**	17%	2%	2,000	ICM[387]	Online	
17–19 Mar	**46%**	35%	19%	11%	1,006	Survation[388]	Telephone	Includes Northern Ireland
11–14 Mar	47%	**49%**	4%	2%	823	ORB[389]	Telephone	
11–13 Mar	**43%**	41%	16%	2%	2,031	ICM[390]	Online	
4–11 Mar	**45%**	40%	16%	5%	2,282	Greenberg Quinlan Rosner Research[391]	Online	
2–10 Mar	**48%**	45%	7%	3%	4,047	Populus/-Number Cruncher Politics[392]	Online	
4–6 Mar	**49%**	35%	15%	14%	966	Populus/-Number Cruncher Politics[392]	Telephone	
4–6 Mar	40%	**41%**	19%	1%	2,051	ICM[393]	Online	
2–3 Mar	**40%**	37%	18%	3%	1,695	YouGov[394]	Online	

1–2 Mar	**40%**	35%	19%	5%	1,705	YouGov[395]	Online	
29 Feb–1 Mar	**39%**	37%	19%	2%	2,233	YouGov[396]	Online	
26–29 Feb	41%	41%	18%	N/A	2,003	ICM[397]	Online	
26–28 Feb	39%	**45%**	18%	6%	2,071	Populus/-Number Cruncher Politics[392]	Online	
26–28 Feb	**48%**	37%	15%	11%	1,002	Populus/-Number Cruncher Politics[392]	Telephone	
24–25 Feb	48%	**52%**	N/A	4%	2,014	ORB[398]	Online	
21–23 Feb	37%	**38%**	25%	1%	3,482	YouGov[399]	Online	
20 Feb					*David Cameron announces the date of UK's In/-Out EU referendum after an EU summit in Brussels.*			
17–23 Feb	**38%**	36%	25%	2%	1,517	BMG Research[400]	Online	Includes Northern Ireland
19–22 Feb	**42%**	40%	17%	2%	2,021	ICM[401]	Online	
19–22 Feb	**51%**	39%	10%	12%	1,000	ComRes[402]	Telephone	
13–20 Feb	**45%**	32%	23%	13%	938	Survation[403]	Telephone	
18–19 Feb	40%	**41%**	19%	1%	1,033	Opinium[404]	Online	Conducted before the conclusion of the negotiations; exact time frame was not com-municated
13–16 Feb	**54%**	36%	10%	18%	497	Ipsos MORI[405]	Telephone	
11–15 Feb	36%	**39%**	25%	3%	1,079	TNS[406]	Online	
12–14 Feb	**43%**	39%	18%	4%	2,001	ICM[407]	Online	Original poll is no longer available on ICM Unlimted
11–14 Feb	**49%**	41%	10%	8%	1,105	ComRes[408]	Telephone	

Date	Remain	Leave	Undecided	N/A	Sample	Conducted by	Method	Notes
5–7 Feb	41%	**42%**	17%	1%	2,018	ICM[409]	Online	
3–4 Feb	36%	**45%**	19%	9%	1,675	YouGov/The Times[410]	Online	
29–31 Jan	**42%**	39%	19%	3%	2,002	ICM[411]	Online	
27–28 Jan	38%	**42%**	20%	4%	1,735	YouGov[412]	Online	
23–25 Jan	**55%**	36%	9%	19%	513	Ipsos MORI[413]	Telephone	
21–25 Jan	**44%**	42%	14%	2%	1,511	BMG Research[414]	Online	Includes Northern Ireland
22–24 Jan	**54%**	36%	10%	18%	1,006	ComRes[415]	Telephone	
22–24 Jan	**41%**	41%	18%	N/A	2,010	ICM[416]	Online	
20–21 Jan	**52%**	48%	N/A	4%	2,015	ORB[417]	Online	
15–17 Jan	**42%**	40%	17%	2%	2,023	ICM[418]	Online	
15–16 Jan	38%	**40%**	22%	2%	1,017	Survation[419]	Online	Includes Northern Ireland
8–14 Jan	42%	**45%**	12%	3%	2,087	Panelbase[420]	Online	
8–10 Jan	**44%**	38%	18%	6%	2,055	ICM[421]	Online	

2015

Date(s) conducted	Remain	Leave	Undecided	Sample	Conducted by	Notes		
17–18 Dec	41%	**42%**	17%	1,598	YouGov[422]			
12–14 Dec	**58%**	32%	10%	529	Ipsos MORI[423]			
11–13 Dec	**56%**	35%	8%	1,001	ComRes[424]			
11–13 Dec	**42%**	41%	17%	2,053	ICM[425]			
4–6 Dec	**43%**	39%	17%	2,022	ICM[426]			
2–3 Dec	36%	**43%**	21%	1,001	ORB[427]			
30 Nov–3 Dec	40%	**42%**	18%	10,015	Survation[428]	Includes Northern Ireland		
20–24 Nov	**41%**	41%	18%	4,317	YouGov[429]			
19–24 Nov	**40%**	38%	22%	1,699	YouGov[430]			

20–22 Nov	**45%**	38%	17%	2,002	ICM[431]	
17–19 Nov	48%	**52%**	N/A	2,067	ORB[432]	
16–17 Nov	**43%**	40%	18%	1,546	Survation[433]	Includes Northern Ireland
11–17 Nov	**39%**	**39%**	22%	1,528	BMG Research[434]	Includes Northern Ireland
13–15 Nov	**43%**	38%	19%	2,000	ICM[435]	
9–11 Nov	38%	**41%**	21%	2,007	Survation[436]	Includes Northern Ireland
6–8 Nov	**46%**	38%	16%	2,024	ICM[437]	
30 Oct–1 Nov	**44%**	38%	18%	2,060	ICM[438]	
28–29 Oct	39%	**41%**	19%	1,664	YouGov[439]	
22–27 Oct	**40%**	**40%**	20%	1,738	YouGov[440]	
23–25 Oct	**45%**	38%	17%	2,049	ICM[441]	
23–25 Oct	**53%**	47%	N/A	2,015	ORB[442]	
22–23 Oct	**42%**	39%	16%	1,625	YouGov[443]	
19–20 Oct	**42%**	40%	17%	1,690	YouGov[444]	
17–19 Oct	**52%**	36%	12%	498	Ipsos MORI[445]	
14–19 Oct	**42%**	39%	19%	2,372	GQRR[446]	
16–18 Oct	**44%**	38%	18%	2,023	ICM[447]	
7 Oct	**44%**	39%	17%	1,947	ICM[448]	
25–28 Sep	**55%**	36%	8%	1,009	ComRes[449]	
25–27 Sep	**45%**	38%	17%	2,005	ICM[450]	
17–22 Sep	38%	**41%**	21%	2,781	YouGov[451]	
10–17 Sep	38%	**40%**	22%	11,171	YouGov[452]	
11–13 Sep	**43%**	40%	17%	2,006	ICM[453]	
12 Sep	Jeremy Corbyn is **elected** leader of the Labour Party					
3–4 Sep	**40%**	40%	20%	1,004	Survation[454]	
18–19 Aug	**44%**	37%	20%	1,676	YouGov[455]	
13–17 Aug	**50%**	40%	10%	3,402	YouGov[456]	
23–29 Jul	**45%**	37%	19%	1,708	YouGov[457]	
16 Jul	Tim Farron is **elected** leader of the Liberal Democrats					
29 Jun–6 Jul	**45%**	37%	18%	5,008	Survation[458]	Includes Northern Ireland
19–24 Jun	**44%**	38%	18%	1,653	YouGov[459]	
19–21 Jun	**55%**	45%	N/A	2,000	ORB[460]	
14–16 Jun	**66%**	22%	12%	501	Ipsos MORI[461]	

Date				N	Pollster	Notes
8–11 Jun	43%	36%	21%	2,381	YouGov[462]	
1–2 Jun	44%	34%	21%	1,063	YouGov[463]	
27 May–2 Jun	42%	35%	22%	2,956	YouGov[464]	
29–31 May	58%	31%	11%	500	ComRes[465]	
28–31 May	47%	33%	20%	680	ICM[466]	
21–22 May	44%	36%	20%	1,532	YouGov[467]	
8–15 May	47%	40%	13%	3,977	Survation[468]	
7 Apr–13 May	55%	36%	9%	999	Pew Research Center[469]	
8–9 May	45%	36%	19%	1,302	YouGov[470]	
8–9 May	45%	38%	18%	1,027	Survation[471]	
7 May	**United Kingdom general election, 2015**					
3–5 May	56%	34%	10%	1,011	ComRes[472]	
3–4 May	45%	33%	21%	1,664	YouGov[473]	
28–29 Apr	52%	32%	16%	1,823	YouGov[474]	
23–28 Apr	47%	33%	20%	1,834	YouGov[475]	
19–20 Apr	45%	35%	20%	2,078	YouGov[476]	
10–12 Apr	40%	39%	21%	2,036	Populus[477]	
8–9 Apr	45%	41%	15%	1,750	Opinium[478]	
26–30 Mar	35%	34%	31%	1,197	TNS-BMRB[479]	
24–26 Mar	49%	44%	7%	1,007	Panelbase[480]	Includes Northern Ireland
18–25 Mar	41%	38%	21%	2,006	YouGov[481]	
22–23 Mar	46%	36%	18%	1,641	YouGov[482]	
18–23 Mar	42%	34%	23%	8,271	YouGov[483]	
23–24 Feb	45%	37%	18%	1,520	YouGov[484]	
22–23 Feb	45%	35%	20%	1,772	YouGov[485]	
17–20 Feb	41%	44%	15%	1,975	Opinium[486]	
25–26 Jan	43%	37%	20%	1,656	YouGov[487]	
18–19 Jan	43%	38%	18%	1,747	YouGov[488]	
15–19 Jan	38%	34%	28%	1,188	TNS-BMRB[489]	
6–8 Jan	37%	40%	23%	1,201	TNS-BMRB[490]	

2014

Date(s) conducted	Remain	Leave	Undecided	Sample	Conducted by	Notes
14–15 Dec	**40%**	39%	21%	1,648	YouGov[491]	
30 Nov–1 Dec	**42%**	39%	20%	1,763	YouGov[492]	
20–26 Nov	38%	**43%**	19%	1,641	YouGov[493]	
21–23 Nov	32%	**48%**	20%	2,049	ComRes[494]	
20–21 Nov	40%	**41%**	19%	1,970	YouGov[495]	
19–21 Nov	40%	**41%**	19%	2,314	YouGov[496]	
16–17 Nov	**39%**	**39%**	21%	1,589	YouGov[497]	
7 Nov	31%	**54%**	15%	1,020	Survation[498]	
2–3 Nov	38%	**41%**	21%	1,652	YouGov[499]	
31 Oct–2 Nov	35%	**49%**	17%	2,012	Survation[500]	
30–31 Oct	37%	**43%**	20%	1,808	YouGov[501]	
27–28 Oct	35%	**44%**	21%	2,052	YouGov[502]	
23–24 Oct	**41%**	40%	19%	2,069	YouGov[503]	
19–20 Oct	**40%**	39%	21%	1,727	YouGov[504]	
11–14 Oct	**56%**	36%	8%	1,002	Ipsos MORI[505]	
21–22 Sep	**42%**	38%	19%	1,671	YouGov[506]	
18 Sep	Scottish independence referendum, 2014					
25–26 Aug	**41%**	40%	19%	2,021	YouGov[507]	
10–11 Aug	**40%**	38%	22%	1,676	YouGov[508]	
13–14 Jul	**41%**	38%	21%	1,745	YouGov[509]	
29–30 Jun	**40%**	39%	21%	1,729	YouGov[510]	
27–29 Jun	36%	**43%**	21%	2,049	ComRes[511]	
27–28 Jun	39%	**47%**	14%	1,000	Survation[512]	
26–27 Jun	**39%**	37%	24%	1,936	YouGov[513]	
19–20 Jun	**39%**	**39%**	21%	2,016	YouGov[514]	
17–19 Jun	37%	**48%**	15%	1,946	Opinium[515]	
15–16 Jun	**44%**	36%	20%	1,696	YouGov[516]	
30 May–1 Jun	40%	**42%**	18%	2,062	ComRes[517]	
29–30 May	**41%**	39%	20%	2,090	YouGov[518]	
22 May	European Parliament election, 2014					
20–21 May	**42%**	37%	21%	6,124	YouGov[519]	

18–19 May	**43%**	37%	20%	1,740	YouGov[520]		
10–12 May	**54%**	37%	10%	1,003	Ipsos MORI[521]		
28 Apr–6 May	**39%**	38%	23%	1,805	YouGov[522]		
2–3 May	39%	**46%**	15%	1,005	Survation[523]		
24–28 Apr	41%	**49%**	10%	1,199	TNS-BMRB[524]		
24–25 Apr	**40%**	37%	23%	1,835	YouGov[525]		
21–22 Apr	**40%**	38%	23%	2,190	YouGov[526]		
3–4 Apr	**42%**	37%	21%	1,998	YouGov[527]		
27–28 Mar	**42%**	36%	21%	1,916	YouGov[528]		
23–24 Mar	**42%**	36%	22%	1,558	YouGov[529]		
9–10 Mar	**41%**	39%	20%	3,195	YouGov[530]		
9–10 Feb	36%	**39%**	25%	1,685	YouGov[531]		
7–20 Jan	**41%**	**41%**	18%	20,058	Lord Ashcroft Polls[532]		
12–13 Jan	33%	**43%**	24%	1,762	YouGov[533]		

2013

Date(s) conducted	Remain	Leave	Undecided	Sample	Conducted by	Notes
1–9 Dec	37%	**43%**	20%	Unknown	YouGov	
10–11 Nov	**39%**	**39%**	22%	Unknown	YouGov	
13–14 Oct	**42%**	37%	20%	Unknown	YouGov	
23–27 Sep	36%	**44%**	20%	1,922	YouGov[534]	
15–16 Sep	**42%**	39%	20%	Unknown	YouGov	
18–19 Aug	**46%**	34%	20%	Unknown	YouGov	
6–8 Aug	32%	**53%**	15%	1,945	Opinium[535]	
4–5 Aug	**43%**	35%	22%	Unknown	YouGov	

18–24 Jul	35%	**45%**	21%	1,968	YouGov[536]	
22–23 Jul	**45%**	35%	21%	Un-known	YouGov	
7–8 Jul	**43%**	36%	21%	Un-known	YouGov	
4–5 Jul	36%	**46%**	19%	1,022	YouGov[537]	
23–24 Jun	**45%**	31%	24%	Un-known	YouGov	
9–10 Jun	**43%**	35%	22%	Un-known	YouGov	
1–3 Jun	44%	**45%**	11%	1,566	Survation[538]	
28–29 May	**43%**	35%	22%	Un-known	YouGov	
21–28 May	**41%**	38%	20%	1,512	YouGov[539]	
17–18 May	36%	**50%**	14%	1,000	Survation[540]	
16–17 May	36%	**45%**	19%	1,809	YouGov[541]	
15–16 May	24%	**46%**	30%	2,017	ComRes/Sunday Mirror/-Independent[542]Wikipedia:Link rot	Northern Ireland not sampled
15–16 May	30%	**46%**	24%	2,017	ICM/The Telegraph[543]	
12–13 May	34%	**44%**	22%	1,748	YouGov/The Sun[544]	Northern Ireland not sampled
10–12 May	40%	**43%**	17%	1,001	ICM/The Guardian[545]	
9–10 May	30%	**47%**	23%	1,945	YouGov/The Sun[546]	Northern Ireland not sampled
7 May	35%	**46%**	20%	719	YouGov/The Times[547]	Northern Ireland not sampled
7–8 April	36%	**43%**	21%	1,765	YouGov/The Sun[548]	Northern Ireland not sampled
4–27 March	46%	46%	8%	1,012	Pew Research Center[549]	Includes Northern Ireland

17–18 February	38%	41%	21%	1,713	YouGov/The Sun[550]	Northern Ireland not sampled
5 February	30%	41%	22%	1,237	TNS BMRB[551]	
29 Jan – 6 Feb	33%	50%	17%	2,114	Financial Times/Harris[552]	
25 January	36%	50%	16%	1,005	Survation/Mail on Sunday[553]	Northern Ireland not sampled
24–25 January	37%	39%	24%	1,943	YouGov/Sunday Times[554]	Northern Ireland not sampled
23 January	37%	40%	23%	2,000	Populus/The Times[555]	
20–21 January	37%	40%	24%	Un-known	YouGov/The Sun[556]	Northern Ireland not sampled
17–18 January	34%	25%	40%	1,912	YouGov/Sunday Times[557]	Northern Ireland not sampled
10–11 January	36%	42%	21%	1,995	YouGov/Sunday Times[558]	Northern Ireland not sampled
6 January	36%	54%	10%	1,002	Survation/Mail on Sunday[559]	Northern Ireland not sampled
2–3 January	31%	46%	22%	Un-known	YouGov/The Sun[556]	Northern Ireland not sampled

2012

Date(s) conducted	Re-main	Leave	Unde-cided	Sample	Conducted by	Notes
27–28 November	30%	51%	9%	Un-known	YouGov/The Sun[556]	Northern Ireland not sampled
13–15 November	30%	56%	14%	1,957	Opinium/-Observer[560]	Northern Ireland not sampled

2011

Date(s) conducted	Re-main	Leave	Unde-cided	Sample	Conducted by	Notes
15–16 December	41%	**41%**	19%	Un-known	YouGov/The Sun[556]	Northern Ireland not sampled
8–9 December	35%	**44%**	20%	Un-known	YouGov/The Sun[556]	Northern Ireland not sampled
7–8 August	30%	**52%**	19%	Un-known	YouGov/The Sun[556]	Northern Ireland not sampled

2010

Date(s) conducted	Re-main	Leave	Unde-cided	Sample	Conducted by	Notes
8–9 September	33%	**47%**	19%	Un-known	YouGov/The Sun[556]	Northern Ireland not sampled

Sub-national polling

England

Date(s) conducted	Remain	Leave	Undecided	Sample	Held by
23 June 2016	46.6%	**53.4%**	N/A	–	England Results
9–16 September 2015	40%	**43%**	17%	1,712	YouGov[561]

England and Wales

Date(s) conducted	Remain	Leave	Undecided	Sample	Held by
23 June 2016	46.7%	53.3%	N/A	–	Results
26 June – 3 July 2015	42%	43%	15%	956	Panelbase/Sunday Times[562]

London

Date(s) conducted	Remain	Leave	Undecided	Sample	Held by
23 June 2016	59.9%	40.1%	N/A	–	London Results
2–6 June 2016	48%	35%	13%	1,179	YouGov[563]
26 April – 1 May 2016	51%	34%	14%	1,005	Opinium/Evening Standard[564]
4–6 January 2016	39%	34%	27%	1,156	YouGov/LBC[565]
17–19 November 2014	45%	37%	14%	1,124	YouGov/Evening Standard[566]
20–25 June 2013	41%	39%	20%	1,269	YouGov/Evening Standard[567]

Scotland

Date(s) conducted	Remain	Leave	Undecided	Sample	Held by
23 June 2016	62.0%	38.0%	N/A	–	Scotland Results
6–12 Jun 2016	58%	33%	8%	1,000	Ipsos Mori/STV[568]
4–22 May 2016	53%	24%	23%	1,008	TNS[569]
6–10 May 2016	54%	32%	14%	1,000	ICM/The Scotsman[570]
1–2 May 2016	58%	19%	19%	1,024	Survation/Daily Record[571]
23–28 April 2016	57%	33%	11%	1,074	Panelbase/Sunday Times[572]
18–25 April 2016	66%	29%	5%	1,015	Ipsos MORI/STV[573]
1–24 April 2016	48%	21%	31%	1,012	TNS[574]
15–20 April 2016	54%	28%	17%	1,005	Survation/Daily Record[575]

Date	For	Against	Undecided	Sample	Pollster/Client
11–15 April 2016	55%	35%	9%	1,013	BMG Research/Herald[576]
6–15 April 2016	55%	33%	12%	1,021	Panelbase/Sunday Times[577]
2–22 March 2016	51%	19%	29%	1,051	TNS[578]
10–17 March 2016	53%	29%	17%	1,051	Survation/Daily Record[579]
7–9 March 2016	48%	31%	21%	1,070	YouGov[580]
11–16 February 2016	52%	27%	21%	951	Survation[581]
1–7 February 2016	62%	26%	12%	1,000	Ipsos MORI[582]
1–4 February 2016	55%	28%	18%	1,022	YouGov/The Times[583]
6–25 January 2016	44%	21%	29%	1,016	TNS[584]
8–14 January 2016	54%	30%	16%	1,053	Panelbase/Sunday Times[420]
8–12 January 2016	52%	27%	21%	1,029	Survation/Daily Record[585]
9–16 November 2015	65%	22%	13%	1,029	Ipsos MORI[586]
9–13 October 2015	51%	31%	17%	1,026	YouGov/Times[587]
9–30 September 2015	47%	18%	29%	1,037	TNS[588]
22–27 September 2015	55%	30%	15%	1,004	YouGov[589]
7–10 September 2015	51%	29%	20%	975	Survation/Scottish Daily Mail[590]
26 June – 3 July 2015	55%	29%	16%	1,002	Panelbase/Sunday Times[562]
3–7 July 2015	51%	26%	23%	1,045	Survation/Scottish Daily Mail[591]
13–30 May 2015	49%	19%	26%	1,031	TNS BMRB[591]
19–21 May 2015	54%	25%	21%	1,001	YouGov/Sunday Post[592]
29 January – 2 February 2015	52%	29%	17%	1,001	YouGov/The Times[593]
9–14 January 2015	42%	37%	21%	1,007	Panelbase/Wings Over Scotland[594]
6–13 November 2014	47%	35%	18%	1,001	Survation/Daily Record[595]
30 October – 5 November 2014	41%	38%	19%	1,000	Panelbase/Wings Over Scotland[596]
4–9 February 2013	54%	33%	13%	1,003	Ipsos MORI/The Times[597]

Wales

Date(s) conducted	Remain	Leave	Undecided	Sample	Held by
23 June 2016	47.5%	52.5%	N/A	–	Wales Results
30 May – 2 June 2016	41%	41%	18%	1,017	YouGov[598]
7–11 April 2016	38%	39%	16%	1,011	YouGov[599]
9–11 February 2016	37%	45%	18%	1,024	YouGov[600]
21–24 September 2015	42%	38%	21%	1,010	YouGov[601]
4–6 May 2015	47%	33%	16%	1,202	YouGov/ITV Wales[602]
24–27 March 2015	44%	38%	14%	1,189	YouGov/ITV Wales[603]
5–9 March 2015	43%	36%	17%	1,279	YouGov/ITV Wales[604]
19–26 February 2015	63%	33%	4%	1,000	ICM/BBC[605]
19–21 January 2015	44%	36%	16%	1,036	YouGov/ITV Wales[606]
2–5 December 2014	42%	39%	15%	1,131	YouGov/ITV Wales[607]
8–11 September 2014	43%	37%	15%	1,025	YouGov/ITV Wales[608]
26 June – 1 July 2014	41%	36%	18%	1,035	YouGov/ITV Wales[609]
21–24 February 2014	54%	40%	6%	1,000	ICM/BBC[610]
14–25 June 2013	29%	37%	35%	1,015	Beaufort Research[611]

Northern Ireland

Date(s) conducted	Remain	Leave	Undecided	Sample	Held by	Notes
23 June 2016	55.8%	44.2%	N/A	–	Northern Ireland Results	
Late June 2016	37%	26%	NA	Over 1,000	Belfast Telegraph / IPSOS MORI	
20 June 2016	57%	43%	Exc. DKs	2,090	The NI Sun/-LucidTalk	
17–19 May 2016	57%	35%	9%	1,090	LucidTalk	
May 2016	44%	20%	35%	1,005	Ipsos MORI	Question phrased differently.
19–21 October 2015	56.5%	28.3%	15.2%	2,517	LucidTalk	
2–16 October 2015	55%	13%	32%	1,012	BBC/RTÉ	

Gibraltar

Date(s) conducted	Remain	Leave	Undecided	Sample	Held by
23 June 2016	**95.9%**	4.1%	N/A	–	Gibraltar Results
13–15 May 2016	**94%**	2%	4%	596	Gibraltar Chronicle[612]
11–15 April 2016	**88%**	8%	3%	596	Gibraltar Chronicle[613]

Renegotiated terms

The UK government renegotiated certain terms of the UK's membership of the European Union before the referendum was held. Prior to the renegotiation in February 2016, some opinion polls asked the referendum question on the assumption that the UK government would say that it was satisfied with the outcome of the renegotiation.

Date(s) conducted	Re-main	Leave	Unde-cided	Sam-ple	Held by	Notes
1–2 June 2015	**55%**	24%	18%	1,063	YouGov/Prospect	Northern Ireland not sampled
8–9 May 2015	**58%**	24%	16%	1,302	YouGov/-Sunday Times	Northern Ireland not sampled
3–4 May 2015	**56%**	20%	20%	1,664	YouGov/The Sun	Northern Ireland not sampled
19–20 April 2015	**57%**	22%	17%	2,078	YouGov/The Sun	Northern Ireland not sampled
22–23 March 2015	**57%**	22%	18%	1,641	YouGov/The Sun	Northern Ireland not sampled
22–23 February 2015	**57%**	21%	17%	1,772	YouGov/The Sun	Northern Ireland not sampled
25–26 January 2015	**54%**	25%	16%	1,656	YouGov/The Sun	Northern Ireland not sampled
18–19 January 2015	**57%**	21%	19%	1,747	YouGov/British Influence	Northern Ireland not sampled
14–15 Dec 2014	**55%**	24%	16%	1,648	YouGov/The Sun	
30 Nov – 1 December 2014	**55%**	25%	17%	1,763	YouGov/The Sun	
17–19 November 2014	**58%**	25%	13%	1,124	YouGov / The Evening Standard	

Date				Sample	Polling organisation/client	
16–17 November 2014	58%	24%	14%	1,589	YouGov / The Sun	
4–7 November 2014	40%	43%	17%	1,707	Opinium/The Observer	
2–3 November 2014	52%	27%	15%	1,652	YouGov / The Sun	
19–20 October 2014	55%	24%	17%	1,727	YouGov / The Sun	
21–22 September 2014	54%	25%	16%	1,671	YouGov / The Sun	
25–26 August 2014	54%	26%	16%	2,021	YouGov / The Sun	
10–11 August 2014	54%	23%	18%	1,676	YouGov / The Sun	
13–14 July 2014	52%	25%	19%	1,745	YouGov / The Sun	
29–30 June 2014	54%	23%	17%	1,729	YouGov / The Sun	
15–16 June 2014	57%	22%	16%	1,696	YouGov / The Sun	
18–19 May 2014	53%	24%	18%	1,740	YouGov	Northern Ireland not sampled
24–25 April 2014	50%	26%	18%	1,835	YouGov/- Sunday Times	Northern Ireland not sampled
21–22 April 2014	52%	26%	18%	2,190	YouGov/The Sun	Northern Ireland not sampled
23–24 March 2014	54%	25%	17%	2,190	YouGov/The Sun	Northern Ireland not sampled
9–10 March 2014	52%	27%	16%	3,195	YouGov/The Sun	Northern Ireland not sampled
9–10 February 2014	47%	27%	18%	1,685	YouGov/The Sun	Northern Ireland not sampled
12–13 January 2014	48%	29%	18%	1,762	YouGov/The Sun	Northern Ireland not sampled
12–13 May 2013	45%	33%	19%	1,748	YouGov/The Sun	Northern Ireland not sampled
9–10 May 2013	45%	32%	20%	1,945	YouGov/- Sunday Times	Northern Ireland not sampled
7–8 April 2013	46%	31%	17%	1,765	YouGov/The Sun	Northern Ireland not sampled
17–18 February 2013	52%	28%	14%	1,713	YouGov/The Sun	Northern Ireland not sampled

Polling within professional groups

Business leaders

The British Chambers of Commerce surveyed 2,200 business leaders in January and February 2016. Of these, 60% supported remaining in the EU and 30% supported exit. In a further poll published in May, these numbers had changed to 54% and 37% respectively.

The Confederation of British Industry reported a survey of 773 of its members, carried out by ComRes. With numbers adjusted to reflect CBI membership, the poll indicated that 80% of CBI members saw a "remain" outcome as the best outcome for their business, with 5% seeing "leave" as the best outcome.

In a poll of 350 board directors of UK businesses, published in June 2015, 82% agreed with the statement that "the UK's membership of the EU is good for British businesses", while 12% disagreed. In a follow-up poll reported in March 2016, 63% agreed that "British businesses are better off inside the European Union than out of it" while 20% disagreed. To the statement, "An EU exit risks stifling British business growth," 59% agreed and 30% disagreed. To the statement, "Our membership of the EU gives British businesses invaluable access to European markets," 71% agreed and 16% disagreed. Thirty-five per cent agreed that "An EU exit would leave British businesses facing a skills shortage" while 50% disagreed.

The manufacturers' organisation EEF used the market research organisation GfK to conduct a survey in late 2015 of 500 senior decision-makers in manufacturing organisations. Of these, 63% wanted the UK to stay in the EU, and 5% wanted it to leave. Three percent said there was no advantage to their businesses for the UK to be in the EU, against 50% who said it was important and a further 20% who said it was critical for their business.

Two surveys by consultants Deloitte asked 120 Chief Financial Officers of large UK companies "whether it is in the interests of UK businesses for the UK to remain a member of the EU." In the first survey, in the final quarter of 2015, 62% agreed while 6% disagreed. A further 28% said they would withhold their judgement until the renegotiation in February 2016. The second survey, in early 2016, had 75% saying it was in the interest of UK businesses to remain, with 8% saying it was not.

In April 2016, the International Chamber of Commerce published a survey of 226 businesses from 27 different countries. Of these international businesses, 46% said they would reduce investment in the UK if it left the EU, while 1% said Brexit would increase their investment in the UK. As to whether the UK should leave the EU, 8% thought it should, while 86% wanted the UK to remain.

In May 2016, law firm King & Wood Mallesons published a survey of 300 businesses, equally split between France, Spain, Italy, and Germany. Asked about the prospect of the UK leaving the EU, 68% said it would adversely affect their businesses and 62% said they would be less likely to do business in the UK. When asked to name ways in which their businesses could benefit from Brexit, a majority of respondents in France, Italy, and Spain said that their countries could benefit as companies move jobs out of the UK.

Scientists

In March 2016, *Nature* reported a survey of 907 active science researchers based in the UK. Of these, 78% said exit from the EU would be "somewhat harmful" or "very harmful" for UK science, with 9% saying it would be "somewhat beneficial" or "very beneficial". Asked, "Should the UK exit the EU or remain?" 83% chose "remain" and 12% "exit". The journal also surveyed a further 954 scientists based in the EU but outside the UK. Of these, 47% said the UK's exit would be "harmful" or "very harmful" for science in the EU, with 11.5% choosing "beneficial" or "very beneficial".

Lawyers

Legal Week surveyed almost 350 partners in legal firms. Of these, 77% said that a UK exit from the EU would have a "negative" or "very negative" effect on the City's position in global financial markets, with 6.2% predicting a "positive" effect. Asked about the effect on their own firms, 59% of the partners predicted a "quite adverse" or "very adverse" effect, while 13% said the effect would be "quite positive" or "very positive".

Economists

The *Financial Times* surveyed 105 economists about how an exit from the EU would affect their views of the UK's prospects, publishing the results in January 2016. In the medium term, 76 respondents (72%) said the UK's prospects would be worse, 8 (7.6%) said they would be better, and 18 (17%) predicted no difference.

Ipsos MORI surveyed members of the Royal Economic Society and the Society of Business Economists for *The Observer*, with 639 responses. Over the next five years, 88% said that Brexit would have a negative effect on GDP, 7% said it would have no impact, and 3% said there would it would have a positive impact, while 82% said it would have a negative effect on household incomes, 9% said it would have no impact, and 7% said it would have a positive effect. Over ten to twenty years, 72% said it would have a negative effect on GDP, 11% said it would have no impact and 11% said it would have a positive effect,

while 73% said it would have a negative effect on household income, 13% said
it would have no impact, and 10% said it would have a positive effect.

Other opinion polling

In a poll released in December 2015, Lord Ashcroft asked 20,000 people in
the UK to place themselves on a scale of 0–100 of how likely they were vote
to remain or leave. A total of 47% placed themselves in the "leave" end of the
scale, 38% in the "remain" end and 14% were completely undecided.

On British withdrawal

*   ▮ France – A poll conducted by French daily newspaper *Le Parisien*
    in January 2013 found that 52% of French voters were in favour of the
    UK withdrawing from the EU. Of the 1,136 people polled, in conjunction
    with French research agency BVA in January 2013, 48% said they would
    rather the UK remained inside the EU.
*   ▮ Germany – A study carried out by Internationale Politik in January
    2013 found 64% of Germans favoured Britain remaining inside the EU –
    with 36% saying they favoured an exit. The biggest support for retaining
    the union with the UK was with the younger generation with 69% of 18-
    to 25-year-olds saying they wanted the UK to stay. Amongst the Ger-
    man political parties, the supporters of the Green Party remained most
    favourable at 85%.

Ashcroft polling

In early 2016, Lord Ashcroft polled individuals in each of the other European
Union member states to gauge opinion on whether they thought the United
Kingdom should leave the EU, whether they thought the UK should remain a
member or whether they believed it did not matter. All member states said that
they wanted the UK to remain a member, except Cyprus, the Czech Republic
and Slovenia, with Lithuania being most in favour, at 78% voting for the UK
to remain in the EU.

Country	Remain	Does Not Matter	Leave
▮ Austria	**41%**	41%	19%
▮ Belgium	**49%**	38%	13%
▮ Bulgaria	**67%**	27%	7%
▬ Croatia	**49%**	41%	10%

Cyprus	35%	**45%**	19%
Czech Republic	40%	**47%**	13%
Denmark	**56%**	31%	13%
Estonia	**65%**	28%	8%
Finland	**50%**	39%	11%
France	**50%**	32%	18%
Germany	**59%**	30%	11%
Greece	**50%**	35%	15%
Hungary	**64%**	30%	7%
Ireland	**72%**	18%	10%
Italy	**67%**	24%	9%
Latvia	**58%**	33%	9%
Lithuania	**78%**	16%	6%
Luxembourg	**55%**	21%	24%
Malta	**76%**	18%	6%
Netherlands	**49%**	42%	10%
Poland	**67%**	27%	6%
Portugal	**74%**	20%	7%
Romania	**70%**	26%	4%
Slovakia	**61%**	32%	7%
Slovenia	43%	**49%**	8%
Spain	**70%**	24%	6%
Sweden	**56%**	33%	12%
EU27	**60%**	30%	10%

Additionally, Ashcroft asked the same group of people whether they would be happy for Britain to remain in the European Union to renegotiated terms or whether they thought the UK should leave if they do not like their current terms of membership. Newer countries to the European Union, countries which have joined the Union since 2004, were the biggest supporters: 52% supported the renegotiated position, compared to just 40% of respondents from EU members who joined before 2004.

Country	Remain	Leave
Austria	24%	76%
Belgium	34%	66%
Bulgaria	52%	48%
Croatia	36%	64%
Cyprus	33%	67%
Czech Republic	42%	58%
Denmark	51%	49%
Estonia	44%	56%
Finland	30%	70%
France	36%	64%
Germany	35%	65%
Greece	39%	61%
Hungary	61%	39%
Ireland	54%	46%
Italy	50%	50%
Latvia	49%	51%
Lithuania	64%	36%
Luxembourg	26%	74%
Malta	69%	31%
Netherlands	37%	63%
Poland	52%	48%
Portugal	61%	39%
Romania	59%	41%
Slovakia	47%	53%
Slovenia	29%	71%
Spain	43%	57%
Sweden	37%	63%
EU27	43%	57%

ICM polling

An ICM online poll of 1,000 adults in each of nine European countries in November 2015 found an average of 53% in favour of the UK's remaining in the EU.

Country	Remain	Leave
Denmark	46%	24%
Finland	49%	19%
France	51%	22%
Germany	55%	19%
Italy	63%	20%
Norway	34%	27%
Portugal	74%	8%
Spain	69%	11%
Sweden	43%	26%

On the possible withdrawal of other countries

- Denmark – A poll commissioned in January 2013 following David Cameron's EU referendum speech found that 52% of Danes would still want their country to stay within the EU even if the UK voted to withdraw. However, 47% said they would like the Danish Government to attempt to renegotiate improved terms of their membership.
- Ireland – A Red C poll, commissioned by European Movement Ireland in January 2013, found most Irish people would opt for Ireland to remain inside the EU – 66% – even if the UK decided to leave. Just 29% of those asked said that Ireland should leave if the UK does.

Post–referendum polling

Right / Wrong

Following the EU referendum, there have been several opinion polls on the question of whether the UK was 'right' or 'wrong' to vote to leave the EU. The results of these polls are shown in the table below.

Date(s) conducted	Right	Wrong	Unde-cided	Lead	Sam-ple	Conducted by	Polling type	Notes
4-5 Sep 2018	43%	46%	11%	3%	1,628	YouGov[614]	Online	
3-4 Sep 2018	42%	48%	11%	6%	1,883	YouGov[615]	Online	

28-29 Aug 2018	42%	**47%**	11%	5%	1,664	YouGov[616]	Online	
20-21 Aug 2018	41%	**47%**	12%	6%	1,697	YouGov[617]	Online	
13-14 Aug 2018	43%	**45%**	12%	2%	1,660	YouGov[618]	Online	
8-9 Aug 2018	42%	**45%**	13%	3%	1,675	YouGov[619]	Online	
22-23 Jul 2018	42%	**46%**	12%	4%	1,650	YouGov[620]	Online	
16-17 Jul 2018	42%	**47%**	12%	5%	1,657	YouGov[621]	Online	
10-11 Jul 2018	41%	**46%**	12%	5%	1,732	YouGov[622]	Online	
8-9 Jul 2018	*Brexit Secretary David Davis and Foreign Secretary Boris Johnson resign.*							
8-9 Jul 2018	42%	**46%**	12%	4%	1,669	YouGov[623]	Online	
6 Jul 2018	*The UK Cabinet agrees the Chequers Statement, setting out a proposal on the future UK-EU relationship.*							
3-4 Jul 2018	41%	**46%**	13%	5%	1,641	YouGov[624]	Online	
25-26 Jun 2018	43%	**46%**	11%	3%	1,645	YouGov[625]	Online	
19-20 Jun 2018	44%	**45%**	11%	1%	1,663	YouGov[626]	Online	
18-19 Jun 2018	43%	**44%**	13%	1%	1,606	YouGov[627]	Online	
11-12 Jun 2018	43%	**46%**	12%	3%	1,638	YouGov[628]	Online	
4-5 Jun 2018	**44%**	**44%**	13%	0%	1,619	YouGov[629]	Online	
28-29 May 2018	40%	**47%**	13%	7%	1,670	YouGov[630]	Online	
20-21 May 2018	43%	**44%**	13%	1%	1,660	YouGov[631]	Online	
13-14 May 2018	44%	**45%**	12%	1%	1,634	YouGov[632]	Online	
8-9 May 2018	43%	**45%**	12%	2%	1,648	YouGov[633]	Online	
30 Apr-1 May 2018	42%	**47%**	11%	5%	1,585	YouGov[634]	Online	
24-25 Apr 2018	42%	**45%**	13%	3%	1,668	YouGov[635]	Online	
16-17 Apr 2018	42%	**45%**	13%	3%	1,631	YouGov[636]	Online	

9-10 Apr 2018	42%	**46%**	12%	4%	1,639	YouGov[637]	Online	
26-27 Mar 2018	42%	**45%**	13%	3%	1,659	YouGov[638]	Online	
5-6 Mar 2018	43%	**45%**	12%	2%	1,641	YouGov[639]	Online	
2 Mar 2018	*Theresa May makes Mansion House speech, outlining the UK Government's policy on the future UK-EU relationship.*							
26-27 Feb 2018	44%	**45%**	11%	1%	1,622	YouGov[640]	Online	
19-20 Feb 2018	42%	**45%**	12%	3%	1,650	YouGov[641]	Online	
12-13 Feb 2018	42%	**46%**	12%	4%	1,639	YouGov[642]	Online	
5-6 Feb 2018	43%	**44%**	13%	1%	2,000	YouGov[643]	Online	
28-29 Jan 2018	40%	**46%**	14%	6%	1,669	YouGov[644]	Online	
16-17 Jan 2018	**45%**	44%	12%	1%	1,672	YouGov[645]	Online	
7-8 Jan 2018	42%	**46%**	12%	4%	1,663	YouGov[646]	Online	
19-20 Dec 2017	42%	**45%**	12%	3%	1,610	YouGov[647]	Online	
15 Dec 2017	*The European Council decides to proceed to the second phase of the Brexit negotiations.*							
10-11 Dec 2017	44%	**45%**	11%	1%	1,680	YouGov[648]	Online	
4-5 Dec 2017	42%	**45%**	13%	3%	1,638	YouGov[649]	Online	
7-8 Nov 2017	42%	**46%**	12%	4%	2,012	YouGov[650]	Online	
23-24 Oct 2017	43%	**45%**	12%	2%	1,637	YouGov[651]	Online	
18-19 Oct 2017	42%	**45%**	14%	3%	1,648	YouGov[652]	Online	
10-11 Oct 2017	42%	**47%**	11%	5%	1,680	YouGov[653]	Online	
22-24 Sep 2017	44%	**45%**	11%	1%	1,716	YouGov[654]	Online	
22 Sep 2017	*Theresa May makes Florence speech, in an attempt to 'unblock' the Brexit negotiations.*							
30-31 Aug 2017	**44%**	**44%**	12%	0%	1,658	YouGov[655]	Online	
21-22 Aug 2017	43%	**45%**	11%	2%	1,664	YouGov[656]	Online	

31 Jul-1 Aug 2017	45%	45%	10%	0%	1,665	YouGov[657]	Online	
18-19 Jul 2017	43%	43%	14%	0%	1,593	YouGov[658]	Online	
10-11 Jul 2017	45%	43%	12%	2%	1,700	YouGov[659]	Online	
21-22 Jun 2017	44%	45%	11%	1%	1,670	YouGov[660]	Online	
19 Jun 2017	*Brexit negotiations begin.*							
12-13 Jun 2017	44%	45%	11%	1%	1,651	YouGov[661]	Online	
8 Jun 2017	*United Kingdom general election, 2017*							
5-7 Jun 2017	45%	45%	10%	0%	2,130	YouGov[662]	Online	
30-31 May 2017	44%	45%	11%	1%	1,875	YouGov[663]	Online	
24-25 May 2017	46%	43%	11%	3%	2,052	YouGov[664]	Online	
16-17 May 2017	46%	43%	11%	3%	1,861	YouGov[665]	Online	
3-14 May 2017	45%	41%	14%	4%	1,952	GfK[666]	Online	
9-10 May 2017	44%	45%	11%	1%	1,651	YouGov[667]	Online	
2-3 May 2017	46%	43%	11%	3%	2,066	YouGov[668]	Online	
25-26 Apr 2017	43%	45%	12%	2%	1,590	YouGov[669]	Online	
20-21 Apr 2017	44%	44%	12%	0%	1,590	YouGov[670]	Online	
18-19 Apr 2017	46%	43%	11%	3%	1,727	YouGov[671]	Online	
12-13 Apr 2017	45%	43%	12%	2%	2,069	YouGov[672]	Online	
5-6 Apr 2017	46%	42%	11%	4%	1,651	YouGov[673]	Online	
29 Mar 2017	*The United Kingdom invokes Article 50.*							
26-27 Mar 2017	44%	43%	13%	1%	1,957	YouGov[674]	Online	
20-21 Mar 2017	44%	44%	12%	0%	1,627	YouGov[675]	Online	
1-15 Mar 2017	46%	41%	13%	5%	1,938	GfK[676]	Online	

Date	Leave	Remain	Undecided	Lead	Sample	Polling org	Type	
13-14 Mar 2017	**44%**	42%	15%	2%	1,631	YouGov[677]	Online	
10-14 Mar 2017	**49%**	41%	10%	8%	2,003	Opinium[678]	Online	
27-28 Feb 2017	**45%**	44%	11%	1%	1,666	YouGov[679]	Online	
21-22 Feb 2017	**45%**	**45%**	10%	0%	2,060	YouGov[680]	Online	
12-13 Feb 2017	**46%**	42%	12%	4%	2,052	YouGov[681]	Online	
30-31 Jan 2017	**45%**	42%	12%	3%	1,705	YouGov[682]	Online	
17-18 Jan 2017	**46%**	42%	12%	4%	1,654	YouGov[683]	Online	
17 Jan 2017	*Theresa May makes Lancaster House speech, setting out the UK Government's negotiating priorities.*							
9-12 Jan 2017	**52%**	39%	9%	13%	2,005	Opinium[684]	Online	
9-10 Jan 2017	**46%**	42%	12%	4%	1,660	YouGov[685]	Online	
3-4 Jan 2017	**45%**	44%	11%	1%	1,740	YouGov[686]	Online	
18-19 Dec 2016	**44%**	**44%**	12%	0%	1,595	YouGov[687]	Online	
4-5 Dec 2016	**44%**	42%	14%	2%	1,667	YouGov[688]	Online	
28-29 Nov 2016	44%	**45%**	11%	1%	1,624	YouGov[689]	Online	
14-15 Nov 2016	**46%**	43%	11%	3%	1,717	YouGov[690]	Online	
19-20 Oct 2016	**45%**	44%	11%	1%	1,608	YouGov[691]	Online	
11-12 Oct 2016	**45%**	44%	11%	1%	1,669	YouGov[692]	Online	
2 Oct 2016	*Theresa May makes Conservative Party Conference speech, announcing her intention to invoke Article 50 by 31 March 2017.*							
13-14 Sep 2016	**46%**	44%	10%	2%	1,732	YouGov[693]	Online	
30-31 Aug 2016	**47%**	44%	9%	3%	1,687	YouGov[694]	Online	
22-23 Aug 2016	**45%**	43%	12%	2%	1,660	YouGov[695]	Online	
16-17 Aug 2016	**46%**	43%	11%	3%	1,677	YouGov[696]	Online	
8-9 Aug 2016	**45%**	44%	12%	1%	1,692	YouGov[697]	Online	

1-2 Aug 2016	**46%**	42%	12%	4%	1,722	YouGov[696]	Online	
13 Jul 2016	*Theresa May becomes Prime Minister of the United Kingdom.*							

- v
- t
- e[698]

Remain / Leave

There have also been polls to gauge support for remaining in or leaving the EU. The following polls, unless the notes state otherwise, asked how respondents would vote in a second referendum.

Date(s) conducted	Re-main	Leave	Nei-ther	Lead	Sam-ple	Conducted by	Polling type	Notes
6-11 Sep 2018	**63%**	18%	19%	45%	1,645	YouGov[699]	Online	18-24 age group
	69%	13%	18%	56%	480			Respondents of voting age only since 2016's referendum
7 Sep 2018	**47%**	46%	8%	1%	854	Survation[700]	Online	Likely voters
	46%	44%	10%	2%	975			Possible voters
30 Aug-5 Sep 2018	**55%**	37%	8%	18%	620	YouGov[701]	Online	GMB members
30 Aug-5 Sep 2018	**68%**	27%	6%	41%	1,081	YouGov[702]	Online	UNISON members
30 Aug-5 Sep 2018	**61%**	35%	4%	26%	1,058	YouGov[703]	Online	Unite the Union members
31 Jul-04 Sep 2018	**46%**	41%	13%	5%	25,641	YouGov[704]	Online	
31 Jul-3 Sep 2018	**58%**	30%	11%	28%	3,051	YouGov[705]	Online	London only

Date					Sample	Pollster	Mode	Notes
31 Aug-1 Sep 2018	47%	47%	6%	0%	1,017	Survation[706]	Online	Likely voters
14-20 Aug 2018	46%	41%	13%	5%	10,299	YouGov[707]	Online	
31 Jul-20 Aug 2018	46%	40%	13%	6%	18,772	YouGov[708]	Online	
31 Jul-20 Aug 2018	42%	42%	16%	0%	807	YouGov[709]	Online	North East England only
31 Jul-19 Aug 2018	44%	42%	14%	2%	939	YouGov[710]	Online	Wales only
8-14 Aug 2018	58%	30%	12%	28%	1,977	YouGov[711]	Online	Scotland only
9-13 Aug 2018	40%	35%	25%	5%	1,119	Kantar[712]	Online	
6-10 Aug 2018	50%	43%	7%	7%	1,481	BMG Research[713]	Online	
31 Jul-7 Aug 2018	46%	40%	14%	6%	10,121	YouGov[714]	Online	
31 Jul-7 Aug 2018	46%	43%	11%	3%	930	YouGov[715]	Online	South West England only
25-26 Jul 2018	45%	42%	13%	3%	1,631	YouGov[716]	Online	
23-24 Jul 2018	47%	41%	12%	6%	1,627	YouGov[717]	Online	
19-20 Jul 2018	44%	40%	16%	4%	1,668	YouGov[718]	Online	
12-14 Jul 2018	45%	45%	11%	0%	1,484	Deltapoll[719]	Online	
8-9 Jul 2018	*Brexit Secretary David Davis and Foreign Secretary Boris Johnson resign.*							
5-9 Jul 2018	40%	32%	28%	8%	1,086	Kantar[720]	Online	

Date	Remain	Leave	Und.	Diff.	Sample	Pollster	Mode	Notes
7 Jul 2018	**49%**	45%	5%	4%	1,007	Survation[721]	Online	
6 Jul 2018						*The UK Cabinet agrees the Chequers Statement, setting out a proposal on the future UK-EU relationship.*		
28 Jun-2 Jul 2018	**44%**	39%	17%	5%	1,031	YouGov[722]	Online	Wales only
26-27 Jun 2018	**44%**	**44%**	12%	0%	1,626	YouGov[723]	Online	
19-20 Jun 2018	**50%**	44%	6%	6%	1,022	Survation[724]	Online	
10-11 Jun 2018	**45%**	40%	15%	5%	1,654	YouGov[725]	Online	
31 May-4 Jun 2018	**48%**	47%	5%	1%	2,012	Survation[726]	Online	
9-16 May 2018	**47%**	42%	11%	5%	2,006	Deltapoll[727]	Online	
8-10 May 2018	**47%**	**47%**	6%	0%	1,585	Survation[728]	Online	
25-30 Apr 2018	**45%**	42%	13%	3%	1,637	YouGov[729]	Online	
14 Apr 2018	**47%**	46%	7%	1%	2,060	Survation[730]	Online	
6-8 Apr 2018	**45%**	44%	11%	1%	2,012	ICM[731]	Online	
5-6 Apr 2018	**44%**	41%	15%	3%	1,636	YouGov[732]	Online	
13-16 Mar 2018	**49%**	42%	9%	7%	1,815	BMG Research[733]	Online	
12-15 Mar 2018	**45%**	44%	12%	1%	1,015	YouGov[734]	Online	Wales only
7-8 Mar 2018	44%	**49%**	7%	5%	2,092	ORB[735]	Online	
2 Mar 2018	43%	**46%**	12%	3%	1,096	ComRes[736]	Online	
2 Mar 2018						*Theresa May makes Mansion House speech, outlining the UK Government's policy on the future UK-EU relationship.*		

27-28 Feb 2018	44%	41%	14%	3%	1,646	YouGov[737]	Online	
14-16 Feb 2018	46%	42%	13%	4%	1,482	Sky Data[738]	Online	
26-29 Jan 2018	49%	46%	6%	3%	1,059	Survation[739]	Online	
18-22 Jan 2018	46%	42%	12%	4%	1,633	YouGov[740]	Online	
16-19 Jan 2018	49%	41%	10%	8%	1,096	Sky Data[741]	Online	
10-19 Jan 2018	45%	43%	12%	2%	5,075	ICM[742]	Online	
11 Jan 2018	51%	43%	6%	8%	1,049	ComRes[743]	Online	
15 Dec 2017								
8-10 Dec 2017	46%	43%	11%	3%	2,006	ICM[744]	Online	
5-8 Dec 2017	51%	41%	8%	10%	1,509	BMG Research[745]	Online	
30 Nov-1 Dec 2017	49%	46%	6%	3%	1,003	Survation[746]	Online	
21-24 Nov 2017	45%	40%	15%	5%	1,016	YouGov[747]	Online	Wales only
16-17 Nov 2017	43%	43%	14%	0%	1,672	YouGov[748]	Online	
14-17 Nov 2017	45%	45%	10%	0%	1,509	BMG Research[745]	Online	
18-24 Oct 2017	44%	40%	16%	4%	1,648	YouGov[749]	Online	
19-20 Oct 2017	46%	45%	9%	1%	1,005	Opinium[750]	Online	
17-20 Oct 2017	47%	44%	8%	3%	1,506	BMG Research[745]	Online	
4-5 Oct 2017	49%	45%	6%	4%	2,047	Survation[751]	Online	

15 Dec 2017 — *The European Council decides to proceed to the second phase of the Brexit negotiations.*

23 Sep 2017	46%	**47%**	6%	1%	1,174	Survation[752]	Online	
22 Sep 2017	*Theresa May makes Florence speech, in an attempt to 'unblock' the Brexit negotiations.*						
19-22 Sep 2017	**45%**	44%	12%	1%	2,004	Opinium[753]	Online	
15-20 Sep 2017	**47%**	**47%**	5%	0%	1,614	Survation[754]	Online	
12-15 Sep 2017	**47%**	43%	10%	4%	1,447	BMG Research[755]	Online	
12-15 Sep 2017	**45%**	**45%**	10%	0%	2,009	Opinium[756]	Online	
4-7 Sep 2017	**46%**	42%	12%	4%	1,011	YouGov[757]	Online	Wales only
15-18 Aug 2017	**47%**	44%	9%	3%	2,006	Opinium[758]	Online	
8-11 Aug 2017	**46%**	45%	9%	1%	1,512	BMG Research[759]	Online	
23-24 Jul 2017	**46%**	43%	11%	3%	1,609	YouGov[760]	Online	
14-15 Jul 2017	47%	**48%**	5%	1%	1,024	Survation[761]	Online	
11-14 Jul 2017	**46%**	45%	9%	1%	1,518	BMG Research[759]	Online	
28-30 Jun 2017	**52%**	44%	5%	8%	1,017	Survation[762]	Telephone	
23-30 Jun 2017	**46%**	42%	13%	4%	1,661	YouGov[763]	Online	
16-21 Jun 2017	46%	**50%**	4%	4%	5,481	Panelbase[764]	Online	
19 Jun 2017	*Brexit negotiations begin.*						
16-17 Jun 2017	**50%**	48%	3%	2%	1,005	Survation[765]	Telephone	Likely voters
10 Jun 2017	**48%**	46%	6%	2%	1,036	Survation[766]	Online	

8 Jun 2017	United Kingdom general election, 2017							
2-7 Jun 2017	46%	**51%**	3%	5%	3,018	Panelbase[767]	Online	
2-5 Jun 2017	**47%**	44%	9%	3%	1,503	BMG Research[759]	Online	
26 May-1 Jun 2017	47%	**49%**	4%	2%	1,224	Panelbase[768]	Online	
29-31 May 2017	42%	**45%**	13%	3%	1,014	YouGov[769]	Online	Wales only
25-30 May 2017	35%	**38%**	27%	3%	1,199	Kantar TNS[770]	Online	
19-22 May 2017	**45%**	**45%**	10%	0%	1,499	BMG Research[759]	Online	
18-21 May 2017	**45%**	43%	13%	2%	1,025	YouGov[771]	Online	Wales only
12-15 May 2017	47%	**50%**	3%	3%	1,026	Panelbase[772]	Online	
5-9 May 2017	47%	**49%**	4%	2%	1,027	Panelbase[773]	Online	
5-7 May 2017	43%	**44%**	13%	1%	1,018	YouGov[774]	Online	Wales only
28 Apr-2 May 2017	48%	**49%**	3%	1%	1,034	Panelbase[775]	Online	Likely voters
21-24 Apr 2017	**45%**	**45%**	10%	0%	1,552	BMG Research[759]	Online	
20-24 Apr 2017	46%	**50%**	4%	4%	1,026	Panelbase[776]	Online	Likely voters
19-21 Apr 2017	**43%**	**43%**	14%	0%	1,029	YouGov[777]	Online	Wales only
28-31 Mar 2017	**46%**	**46%**	8%	0%	1,576	BMG Research[759]	Online	
23-30 Mar 2017	**44%**	43%	14%	1%	1,643	YouGov[778]	Online	
29 Mar 2017	The United Kingdom invokes Article 50.							

21-24 Feb 2017	45%	**46%**	9%	1%	1,543	BMG Research[759]	Online	
19-24 Jan 2017	43%	**44%**	13%	1%	1,643	YouGov[779]	Online	
17 Jan 2017		*Theresa May makes Lancaster House speech, setting out the UK Government's negotiating priorities.*						
6-9 Jan 2017	44%	**45%**	11%	1%	1,520	BMG Research[759]	Online	
14-21 Dec 2016	**44%**	43%	13%	1%	1,569	YouGov[780]	Online	
6-9 Dec 2016	43%	**46%**	11%	3%	1,532	BMG Research[759]	Online	
25-27 Nov 2016	46%	**47%**	6%	1%	2,035	ComRes[781]	Online	
22-25 Nov 2016	**43%**	**43%**	14%	0%	1,523	BMG Research[759]	Online	
20-25 Oct 2016	**44%**	43%	13%	1%	1,631	YouGov[782]	Online	
19-24 Oct 2016	**45%**	43%	12%	2%	1,546	BMG Research[783]	Online	
10-12 Oct 2016	**44%**	**44%**	12%	0%	1,002	Survation[784]	Online	
2 Oct 2016	*Theresa May makes Conservative Party Conference speech, announcing her intention to invoke Article 50 by 31 March 2017.*							
16-20 Sep 2016	42%	**46%**	11%	4%	1,601	YouGov[785]	Online	
31 Aug-9 Sep 2016	43%	**45%**	13%	2%	1,711	YouGov[786]	Online	
20-27 Jul 2016	43%	**44%**	13%	1%	1,673	YouGov[787]	Online	
13 Jul 2016	*Theresa May becomes Prime Minister of the United Kingdom.*							
3-4 Jul 2016	**45%**	**45%**	10%	0%	1,820	YouGov[788]	Online	
29-30 Jun 2016	**45%**	37%	19%	8%	1,017	BMG Research[789]	Online	

28-30 Jun 2016	**48%**	42%	9%	6%	2,006	Opinium[790]Wikipedia:Link rot	Online	
23 Jun 2016	*United Kingdom European Union membership referendum, 2016*							

- v
- t
- e[791]

Three-option referendum

The following table shows opinion polls that have been conducted on how people would vote in a three-option referendum. The table shows the poll results for a first round in which all three options would be available, and for a second round in which only the top two options in the first round would be available.

Date(s) conducted	Round	Re-main	Deal	No Deal	None	Lead	Sample	Conducted by	Polling type	Notes
6-11 Sep 2018	I	**58%**	10%	9%	23%	48%	1,645	YouGov[699]	Online	18-24 age group
	II	**82%**	18%			64%				
31 Jul-7 Aug 2018	I	**40%**	11%	27%	22%	13%	10,121	YouGov[792]	Online	
	II	**56%**		44%		12%				
20-23 Jul 2018	I	**48%**	13%	27%	11%	21%	1,466	Sky Data[793]	Online	
	II	**59%**		41%		18%				
19-20 Jul 2018	I	**41%**	9%	31%	19%	10%	1,668	YouGov[794]	Online	
	II	**54%**		46%		8%				
16-17 Jul 2018	I	**42%**	15%	28%	15%	14%	1,657	YouGov[795]	Online	
	II	**55%**		45%		10%				
8-9 Jul 2018	*Brexit Secretary David Davis and Foreign Secretary Boris Johnson resign.*									
6 Jul 2018	*The UK Cabinet agrees the Chequers Statement, setting out a proposal on the future UK-EU relationship.*									
23 Jun 2016	*United Kingdom European Union membership referendum, 2016*									

- $\frac{v}{}$
- $\frac{t}{}$
- $\frac{e}{}$[796]

On Britain rejoining the EU

Number Cruncher Politics asked people to imagine the UK had now left the EU and how, in that situation, they would answer "Should the UK join the EU, or not?"

Date(s) conducted	Join	Not Join	Unde-cided	Lead	Sam-ple	Conducted by	Polling type
27 Mar-5 Apr 2018	31%	**47%**	22%	16%	1,037	Number Cruncher Politics[797]	Online

Support for a second referendum

There have been opinion polls to gauge support for a second referendum on whether to accept or reject the final Brexit deal.

Date(s) conducted	Sup-port	Op-pose	Nei-ther	Lead	Sample	Conducted by	Polling type	Notes
6-11 Sep 2018	**52%**	22%	25%	30%	1,645	YouGov[699]	Online	18-24 age group
4-5 Sep 2018	40%	**41%**	18%	1%	1,628	YouGov[798]	Online	
30 Aug-5 Sep 2018	**56%**	33%	10%	23%	620	YouGov[799]	Online	GMB members
30 Aug-5 Sep 2018	**66%**	22%	11%	44%	1,081	YouGov[800]	Online	UNISON members
30 Aug-5 Sep 2018	**59%**	33%	8%	26%	1,058	YouGov[801]	Online	Unite the Union members
31 Jul-4 Sep 2018	**45%**	35%	21%	10%	25,641	YouGov[802]	Online	
31 Jul-3 Sep 2018	**52%**	30%	19%	22%	3,051	YouGov[803]	Online	London only
31 Aug-1 Sep 2018	40%	**43%**	17%	3%	1,600	YouGov[804]	Online	
31 Jul-20 Aug 2018	**45%**	33%	22%	12%	18,772	YouGov[708]	Online	

31 Jul-19 Aug 2018	**44%**	36%	21%	8%	939	YouGov[805]	Online	Wales only
25-26 Jul 2018	**42%**	40%	18%	2%	1,631	YouGov[716]	Online	
24 Jul 2018	*The Independent launches its campaign for a second referendum.*							
16-17 Jul 2018	40%	**42%**	18%	2%	1,657	YouGov[806]	Online	
	36%	**47%**	17%	11%				Three-option referendum
10-11 Jul 2018	37%	**41%**	23%	4%	1,732	YouGov[807]	Online	
8-9 Jul 2018	*Brexit Secretary David Davis and Foreign Secretary Boris Johnson resign.*							
5-8 Jul 2018	14%	**82%**	4%	68%	966	YouGov[808]	Online	Conserva-tive Party members
6 Jul 2018	*The UK Cabinet agrees the Chequers Statement, setting out a proposal on the future UK-EU relationship.*							
28 Jun-2 Jul 2018	40%	**45%**	15%	5%	1,031	YouGov[722]	Online	Wales only
27-30 Jun 2018	**57%**	34%	9%	23%	902	YouGov[809]	Online	Unite the Union members
13-14 May 2018	38%	**46%**	16%	8%	1,634	YouGov[810]	Online	
12 May 2018	*The National Union of Students calls for a referendum on the final deal.*							
1-4 May 2018	**53%**	31%	16%	22%	2,005	Opinium[811]		
15 Apr 2018	*People's Vote campaign launched.*							
10-12 Apr 2018	**52%**	31%	17%	21%	2,008	Opinium[812]	Online	
9-10 Apr 2018	38%	**45%**	17%	7%	1,639	YouGov[813]	Online	
26-27 Mar 2018	36%	**42%**	22%	6%	1,659	YouGov[814]	Online	
12-15 Mar 2018	39%	**49%**	12%	10%	1,015	YouGov[734]	Online	Wales only
5-6 Mar 2018	36%	**43%**	20%	7%	1,641	YouGov[815]	Online	
2 Mar 2018	*Theresa May makes Mansion House speech, outlining the UK Government's policy on the future UK-EU relationship.*							
10-19 Jan 2018	**47%**	34%	19%	13%	5,075	ICM[816]	Online	

9-10 Jan 2018	36%	**43%**	21%	7%	1,714	YouGov[817]	Online	
15 Dec 2017	*The European Council decides to proceed to the second phase of the Brexit negotiations.*							
10-11 Dec 2017	33%	**42%**	24%	9%	1,680	YouGov[818]	Online	
30 Nov-1 Dec 2017	**50%**	34%	16%	16%	1,003	Survation[819]	Online	
21-24 Nov 2017	**44%**	43%	13%	1%	1,016	YouGov[747]	Online	Wales only
23-24 Oct 2017	32%	**46%**	22%	14%	1,637	YouGov[820]	Online	
22-24 Sep 2017	34%	**46%**	21%	12%	1,716	YouGov[821]	Online	
22 Sep 2017	*Theresa May makes Florence speech, in an attempt to 'unblock' the Brexit negotiations.*							
12-13 Sep 2017	34%	**47%**	19%	13%	1,660	YouGov[822]	Online	
4-7 Sep 2017	40%	**48%**	12%	8%	1,011	YouGov[823]	Online	Wales only
14-15 Jul 2017	**46%**	39%	15%	7%	1,024	Survation[824]	Online	
7-11 Jul 2017	41%	**48%**	12%	7%	2,005	Opinium[825]		
28-30 Jun 2017	46%	**48%**	6%	2%	1,017	Survation[826]	Telephone	
16-20 Jun 2017	38%	**51%**	11%	13%	2,005	Opinium[825]		
19 Jun 2017	*Brexit negotiations begin.*							
16-17 Jun 2017	**48%**	43%	9%	5%	1,005	Survation[827]	Telephone	
16-17 Jun 2017	38%	**57%**	4%	19%	1,005	Survation[828]	Telephone	
8 Jun 2017	*United Kingdom general election, 2017*							
29-31 May 2017	33%	**56%**	11%	23%	1,025	YouGov[769]	Online	Wales only
18-21 May 2017	37%	**52%**	11%	15%	1,025	YouGov[771]	Online	Wales only
5-7 May 2017	37%	**53%**	10%	16%	1,018	YouGov[774]	Online	Wales only

Date								
28 Apr-2 May 2017	36%	**53%**	11%	17%	2,003	Opinium[825]		
27-28 Apr 2017	31%	**49%**	20%	18%	1,612	YouGov[829]	Online	
20-21 Apr 2017	31%	**48%**	21%	17%	1,590	YouGov[830]	Online	
19-21 Apr 2017	35%	**53%**	12%	18%	1,029	YouGov[777]	Online	Wales only
29 Mar 2017	*The United Kingdom invokes Article 50.*							
17-21 Mar 2017	38%	**52%**	10%	14%	2,003	Opinium[825]		
17 Jan 2017	*Theresa May makes Lancaster House speech, setting out the UK Government's negotiating priorities.*							
13-16 Dec 2016	33%	**52%**	15%	19%	2,000	Opinium[825]		
2 Oct 2016	*Theresa May makes Conservative Party Conference speech, announcing her intention to invoke Article 50 by 31 March 2017.*							
13 Jul 2016	*Theresa May becomes Prime Minister of the United Kingdom.*							
29-30 Jun 2016	32%	**60%**	7%	28%	1,017	BMG Research[831]	Online	
23 Jun 2016	*United Kingdom European Union membership referendum, 2016*							

- v
- t
- e[791]

External links

- Brexit poll tracker[832] – *Financial Times*
- EU referendum poll tracker[833] – BBC News
- EU referendum poll tracker and odds[834] – *The Telegraph*
- EU referendum poll of polls[835] – What UK Thinks: EU

Referendum of 2016

United Kingdom renegotiation of European Union membership, 2015–16

UK renegotiation of EU membership 2015-16

Map of the United Kingdom within the European Union

Signed	19 February 2016
Condition	"Remain" vote in the United Kingdom European Union membership referendum and subsequent approval by European Parliament.
Signatories	David Cameron (Prime Minister of the United Kingdom) Donald Tusk (President of the European Council)
Parties	United Kingdom European Union

Part of a series of articles on theUnited Kingdom
in the
European Union

Accession

- 1973 EC enlargement
- 1975 Referendum Act
- 1975 EC membership referendum
- 1972 EC Act
- UK rebate
- 2011 EU Act

Membership

- The Euro
- European Movement UK
- Nationality law
- UK Euroscepticism
  - Maastricht Rebels
- Black Wednesday
- **Officials and bodies**
- EU Committee
- European Scrutiny Committee
- Northern Ireland Executive in Brussels
- EU Representative in London
- Young European Movement UK
- UK European Commissioners
- Permanent EU Representatives

Legislation

- 1972 EC Act
- 1986 EC (Amendment) Act
- 1993 EC (Amendment) Act
- 1998 EC (Amendment) Act
- 2002 EC (Amendment) Act

- 2008 EU (Amendment) Act
- 2011 EU Act

European Parliament Elections

- 1979
- 1984
- 1989
- 1994
- 1999
- 2004
- 2009
- 2014

  - 1973 delegation
  - 1st
  - 2nd
  - 3rd
  - 4th
  - 5th
  - 6th
  - 7th
  - 8th

Withdrawal

- 2004–05 EU Bill
- 2013–14 EU (Referendum) Bill
- 2015–16 EU membership renegotiation
- 2015 EU Referendum Act
- 2016 EU (Referendum) Act (Gibraltar)

- **2016 EU membership referendum**

- Issues
- Endorsements
- Opinion polling
- Results
- Causes

- **Campaigns**

- **Organisations advocating and campaigning for a referendum**

- People's Pledge
- Labour for a Referendum

- **Leave**

- **Vote Leave** (official lead group)
  - Business for Britain
  - Conservatives for Britain
  - Students for Britain
- Labour Leave
- Leave.EU
  - Bpoplive
- Grassroots Out
- Get Britain Out
- The Freedom Association
  - Better Off Out

- **Other anti-EU advocacy organisations**

- Bruges Group
- Campaign for an Independent Britain

- **Remain**

- **Britain Stronger in Europe** (official lead group)
- Labour In for Britain
- European Movement UK

- **Other pro-EU advocacy organisations**

- Britain in Europe
- British Influence
- Business for New Europe
- Nucleus

- **Pejorative term for pro-EU advocacy**

- Project Fear

- **Media coverage**

- *Brexit: The Movie*
- *In or Out*

- **Aftermath**

- International reactions
- Terms of Withdrawal from EU (Referendum) Bills
- 2016 Conservative Party election
- 2016 Labour Party election
- 2017 Liberal Democrats Party election
- Proposed second Scottish independence referendum
- Proposed London independence
- *The New European*
- European Union (Withdrawal) Act 2018 (including meaningful vote)

- European Union (Withdrawal Agreement) Bill 2017-19
- Gibraltar
- 2017 General Election
- EU Withdrawal Agreement (Public Vote) Bill 2017-19
- UK's relations with EU after 2019

- **Triggering of Article 50 & Negotiations**

- *R (Miller) v Secretary of State for Exiting the European Union*'
- EU (Notification of Withdrawal) Act 2017
- UK invocation of Article 50
- Brexit negotiations
- Department for Exiting the EU (Brexit Department)
- Department for International Trade

- **Post-referendum organisations**

- Change Britain
- More United
- Open Britain

Calls for second vote

- European Union Withdrawal Agreement (Public Vote) Bill 2017-19

- **Organisations campaigning
  for a second vote via People's Vote**

- Britain for Europe
- European Movement UK
- For our Future's Sake
- Healthier IN the EU
- Open Britain
- Our Future Our Choice
- Scientists for EU

- **Other organisations campaigning
  for a second vote**

- Best for Britain

- **See also**

- Opposition to Brexit in the United Kingdom

- <u>v</u>
- <u>t</u>
- <u>e</u>[836]

The **United Kingdom renegotiation of European Union membership** was a package of changes to the United Kingdom's terms of membership to the European Union (EU) and changes to EU rules which was first proposed by the then Prime Minister of the United Kingdom David Cameron in January 2013, with negotiations only beginning following the outcome of the UK General Election in the summer of 2015. The package was agreed by the President of the European Council Donald Tusk, and approved by EU leaders of all 27 other countries at the European Council session in Brussels on 18–19 February 2016 between the United Kingdom and the rest of the European Union. The changes were intended to take effect following a vote for "Remain" in the UK's in-out referendum, at which point suitable legislation would be presented by the European Commission. Due to the Leave result of the referendum, the changes were never implemented.

The renegotiated terms were in addition to the United Kingdom's existing opt-outs in the European Union and the UK rebate. The changes were legally binding insomuch as the intentions and statements made by the EU leaders were enshrined in an international treaty. The implementation of some of the changes would have required legislation by the European Parliament or treaty change within the EU and so the details may have altered, although it would be hard for the European Commission or the European Parliament to directly defy national governments.

After the deal had been approved, Cameron described it as giving the United Kingdom "special status within the European Union" and immediately declared that both he and the UK Government would campaign for a "Remain" vote in the referendum within a "reformed European Union". The following day, after a special meeting of the cabinet, Cameron announced that the in-out referendum would be held on 23 June 2016 under the provisions of the European Union Referendum Act 2015 which had already been agreed by the UK Parliament.

On 23 June 2016 the United Kingdom, on a national turnout of 72%, voted by 51.9% to 48.1% to leave the European Union and indirectly reject the terms of the new agreement. The result received a variety of different reactions internationally.

Emergency brake

The emergency brake mechanism would allow member countries to limit access to in-work benefits for new EU immigrants. This would have needed the agreement of the European Parliament and the UK would need the agreement a majority of other governments through approval in the Foreign Affairs Council (of Member States).

Under current rules, other EU citizens can ultimately claim most of the same benefits as a UK national. Some of the benefits are subject to a test on "Right to Reside" for which EU citizens will almost certainly qualify. Most benefits also require Habitual Residence which means that for the most EU Citizens they will have to wait three months before claiming Jobseeker's Allowance, Child benefit or Child tax credit.

Under the emergency brake (which needs first to be established in EU law), the European Council (of national Heads of Government) could authorise a country that is experiencing migrant flows of "exceptional magnitude" to restrict benefits for new migrants for four years (with migrants starting with no entitlement then gradually gaining rights to benefits). These restrictions could be kept in place for up to seven years but could be used only once. (In this case "established in EU law" means the EU Commission proposing draft legislation for approval by the European Parliament). Subsequently, member states [but specifically the UK] could request and apply it to migrants reasonably quickly, with the Commission already expressing that they believe the UK would be justified in doing so.

The "Red Card"

The "red card" would have allowed a member of the Council of the European Union with the support of 15 other members to return a law to the European Parliament for further changes. This is not a veto as EU lawmakers could still go ahead if they judge that they have addressed the concerns raised by the "red card", which is named after the penalty card used in football.

Cameron backed the "red card" as a means to support the EU's principle of subsidiarity, which he believes is not fully realised. In this way the "red card" is intended for groups of EU leaders to block or reform EU laws where they think it is their job, rather than that of the EU, to make laws on a particular subject. The "red card" will join the existing "yellow card" (which has been triggered twice) and the "orange card" (which has never been used). The use of the "red card" will require backing of 55% of governments at the Council, which is slightly less than is required to approve laws – which is 55% of all countries and votes representing 65% of the EU's population.

Deporting EU immigrants

Free movement of people is an important tenet of the European Union and enshrined in primary law in treaties. The EU deal subtly changes the free movement rules to make it easier for countries to deport EU immigrants. This is achieved by "beefing up" the exceptions to the general rule that EU citizens can live and work where they choose in the EU.

National governments have a carefully restricted ability to restrict the free movement of people about the EU. Once a citizen lives in another EU country the threshold of reason for the local government to remove them becomes progressively higher. The changes planned in the EU-deal are subtle changes of wording to permit governments to take in to account where migrants' behaviour is "likely" to represent a threat, rather than that it "does", and allows government to take in to more account a person's past behaviour rather than just their present.

Until they are implemented and tested in European Law through the EU's European Court of Justice and, possibly, in the (non-EU) European Court of Human Rights, it will be hard to quantify the impact of these changes. The consensus from the EU leadership is that they will give nations more power to deport criminals and prevent their return but not necessarily restrict movement for other reasons.

Child benefit

The deal makes no changes to the principle that child benefit should be paid to citizens no matter where their children reside. However following the deal governments will be able to adjust the payment they make to reflect the standard of living in the country the child lives and the amount of child benefit that would normally be paid in that country.

Although many people have questioned the idea of paying child benefit for children living in other countries, it is a logical consequence of the EU's principal of non-discrimination – as migrants are more likely to have children in another country and would therefore be discriminated against by restricting those benefits. Once the changes to law were passed to reflect this agreed change it would be up to the Court of Justice to clarify if it is legal or there are any unintended consequences if it was subsequently challenged.

"Ever closer union"

In the EU deal there was a statement specifically exempting the UK from "ever closer union". The precise phrasing of the aspiration, which was in the preamble of the EU's founding treaty and every treaty since is "ever closer union of the peoples [of Europe]". The phrase has symbolic political status but it has little or no legal effect in any of the treaties and thus UK's exemption from it is equally symbolic. The deal is explicit in saying that the presence of the "ever closer union" phrase in the treaties does not of itself grant the EU any specific competences or powers.

The UK and the Eurozone

The EU deal attempts to reassure non-Eurozone countries including the UK, that decisions will not be made favouring Eurozone members over them. There will now be a system for non-Eurozone members to object to laws being passed that might harm them but it will not give them a legal opt-out. However EU law already bans discrimination so this is merely an additional protection.

Along with Denmark the UK has an opt-out to the 1992 Maastricht Treaty which means they are not obliged to join the Euro.

Prior to this EU deal there was concern that Eurozone members may discuss matters of the EU and single market separate to the wider membership and therefore come up with a deal they could impose on non-Eurozone countries. In the Council, Eurozone members would have sufficient majority to pass laws if they wished, although those laws would need to be proposed and drafter by the Commission first and also approved by the European Parliament.

In addition to specifically banning such discrimination it also contains a statement of intent that any measures for "economic and monetary union" will be voluntary for non-Eurozone countries, and that those countries will not stand in the way of such measures for those in the Eurozone. For example, non-Eurozone countries will not be required to contribute to bailouts for Eurozone countries.

Limiting residence rights for family members

The European Parliament intends to bring forward legislation to change EU law to limit the ability of a non-EU national to gain the right to live and work anywhere in the EU (including the UK) by becoming the spouse of an EU citizen. There has been some back-and-forth on the matter in the European Court of Justice with existing laws being inconclusive. This change to the law, if approved, should clarify the matter. The changes to the law could still be challenged in both the EU Court of JusticeWikipedia:Citation needed and the Court of Human Rights (which is not an EU institution).

This change in law is not intended to deal with deliberate abuses of the immigration policy (sham marriages) for which existing tools exist.

Legal status and enforcement

The EU deal would have been international law, as it was made by European heads of government acting outside the structure of the EU. The UK intended to register it as such. This would have meant that statements and intentions made within it cannot be challenged by the Court of Justice. However, certain aspects of it would need treaty change within the EU and certain elementsWikipedia:Citing sources would need legislation to become part of EU law. The Commission had already indicatedWikipedia:Manual of Style/Dates and numbers#Chronological items its intention to bring the legislative requirements to the EU Council and Parliament for passage. Cameron stated that he had lodged the documents with the United Nations. UK Independence Party leader and MEP Nigel Farage criticised the deal for not being made legally binding prior to the referendum and stated that in regard to lodging a deal with the EU with the UN, Farage stated "you may as well lodge an old pair of socks".[837]

Outcome

On 27 June 2016, David Cameron said in his statement to the House of Commons on the result of the referendum to "Leave the European Union": "The deal we negotiated at the European Council in February will now be discarded and a new negotiation to leave the EU will begin under a new Prime Minister."

Summary	Approval requirements			Implementation and enforcement	
Renegotiated area	EU Commission	EU Council	EU parliament	Conditions for implementation	Type of law
"Ever closer union"				Remain vote and Treaty	International law
"Red card"				Remain vote	International law
Protection for non-eurozone countries		Yes		Remain vote and rules changed	EU law
Child benefit	Yes	Yes	Yes	Legislation	EU law
Bringing family to the EU	Yes	Yes	Yes	Legislation	EU law
Free movement	Yes	Yes	Yes	Legislation	EU law
"Emergency brake"	Yes	Yes	Yes	Legislation	EU law

United Kingdom European Union membership referendum, 2016

United Kingdom European Union membership referendum	
Should the United Kingdom remain a member of the European Union or leave the European Union?	

Location	United Kingdom Gibraltar
Date	23 June 2016

	Votes	%
Leave	**17,410,742**	**51.89%**
Remain	16,141,241	48.11%
Valid votes	33,551,983	99.92%
Invalid or blank votes	25,359	0.08%
Total votes	**33,577,342**	**100.00%**
Registered voters/turnout	46,500,001	72.21%

Results by voting areas

Leave   Remain

On the map, the darker shades for a colour indicate a larger margin.

**National and regional referendums held within
the United Kingdom and its constituent countries**

Northern Ireland Border Poll	1973
UK EC Membership Referendum	1975
Scottish Devolution Referendum	1979
Welsh Devolution Referendum	1979
Scottish Devolution Referendum	1997
Welsh Devolution Referendum	1997
Greater London Authority Referendum	1998
NI Good Friday Agreement Referendum	1998
NE England Devolution Referendum	2004
Welsh Devolution Referendum	2011
UK AV Referendum	2011
Scottish Independence Referendum	2014
UK EU Membership Referendum	2016

- $\underline{v}$
- $\underline{t}$
- $\underline{e}$[838]

Constitutional documents and events (present & historical) relevant to the status of the United Kingdom and legislative unions of its constituent countries

Treaty of Union	1706
Acts of Union	1707
Wales and Berwick Act	1746
Irish Constitution	1782
Acts of Union	1800
Parliament Act	1911
Government of Ireland Act	1920
Anglo-Irish Treaty	1921

Royal and Parliamentary Titles Act	1927
Statute of Westminster	1931
United Nations Act	1946
Parliament Act	1949
EC Treaty of Accession	1972
NI (Temporary Provisions) Act	1972
European Communities Act	1972
Local Government Act	1972
Local Government (Scotland) Act	1973
NI Border Poll	1973
NI Constitution Act	1973
Referendum Act	1975
EC Membership Referendum	1975
Scotland Act	1978
Wales Act	1978
Scottish Devolution Referendum	1979
Welsh Devolution Referendum	1979
Local Government (Wales) Act	1994
Local Government etc. (Scotland) Act	1994
Referendums (Scotland & Wales) Act	1997
Scottish Devolution Referendum	1997
Welsh Devolution Referendum	1997
Good Friday Agreement	1998
Northern Ireland Act	1998
Government of Wales Act	1998
Human Rights Act	1998
Scotland Act	1998
Government of Wales Act	2006
Northern Ireland Act	2009
Welsh Devolution Referendum	2011
European Union Act	2011
Fixed-term Parliaments Act	2011
Scotland Act	2012
Edinburgh Agreement	2012
Scottish Independence Referendum	2014
Wales Act	2014
European Union Referendum Act	2015

EU Membership Referendum	2016
Scotland Act	2016
Wales Act	2017
EU (Notification of Withdrawal) Act	2017
Invocation of Article 50	2017
European Union (Withdrawal) Act	2018

- $\underline{v}$
- $\underline{t}$
- $\underline{e}^{839}$

Part of a series of articles on theUnited Kingdom
in the
European Union

Accession

- 1973 EC enlargement
- 1975 Referendum Act
- 1975 EC membership referendum
- 1972 EC Act
- UK rebate
- 2011 EU Act

Membership

- The Euro
- European Movement UK
- Nationality law
- UK Euroscepticism
  - Maastricht Rebels
- Black Wednesday

- **Officials and bodies**

- EU Committee
- European Scrutiny Committee
- Northern Ireland Executive in Brussels
- EU Representative in London
- Young European Movement UK

- UK European Commissioners
- Permanent EU Representatives

Legislation

- 1972 EC Act
- 1986 EC (Amendment) Act
- 1993 EC (Amendment) Act
- 1998 EC (Amendment) Act
- 2002 EC (Amendment) Act
- 2008 EU (Amendment) Act
- 2011 EU Act

European Parliament Elections

- 1979
- 1984
- 1989
- 1994
- 1999
- 2004
- 2009
- 2014

  - 1973 delegation
  - 1st
  - 2nd
  - 3rd
  - 4th
  - 5th
  - 6th
  - 7th
  - 8th

Withdrawal

- 2004–05 EU Bill
- 2013–14 EU (Referendum) Bill
- 2015–16 EU membership renegotiation
- 2015 EU Referendum Act
- 2016 EU (Referendum) Act (Gibraltar)

- **2016 EU membership referendum**

- Issues
- Endorsements
- Opinion polling
- Results

- Causes
- **Campaigns**
- **Organisations advocating and campaigning for a referendum**
- People's Pledge
- Labour for a Referendum
- **Leave**
- **Vote Leave** (official lead group)
  - Business for Britain
  - Conservatives for Britain
  - Students for Britain
- Labour Leave
- Leave.EU
  - Bpoplive
- Grassroots Out
- Get Britain Out
- The Freedom Association
  - Better Off Out
- **Other anti-EU advocacy organisations**
- Bruges Group
- Campaign for an Independent Britain
- **Remain**
- **Britain Stronger in Europe** (official lead group)
- Labour In for Britain
- European Movement UK
- **Other pro-EU advocacy organisations**
- Britain in Europe
- British Influence
- Business for New Europe
- Nucleus
- **Pejorative term for pro-EU advocacy**
- Project Fear
- **Media coverage**
- *Brexit: The Movie*
- *In or Out*
- **Aftermath**

- International reactions
- Terms of Withdrawal from EU (Referendum) Bills
- 2016 Conservative Party election
- 2016 Labour Party election
- 2017 Liberal Democrats Party election
- Proposed second Scottish independence referendum
- Proposed London independence
- *The New European*
- European Union (Withdrawal) Act 2018 (including meaningful vote)
- European Union (Withdrawal Agreement) Bill 2017-19
- Gibraltar
- 2017 General Election
- EU Withdrawal Agreement (Public Vote) Bill 2017-19
- UK's relations with EU after 2019

- **Triggering of Article 50 & Negotiations**

- *R (Miller) v Secretary of State for Exiting the European Union*'
- EU (Notification of Withdrawal) Act 2017
- UK invocation of Article 50
- Brexit negotiations
- Department for Exiting the EU (Brexit Department)
- Department for International Trade

- **Post-referendum organisations**

- Change Britain
- More United
- Open Britain

Calls for second vote

- European Union Withdrawal Agreement (Public Vote) Bill 2017-19

- **Organisations campaigning
  for a second vote via People's Vote**

- Britain for Europe
- European Movement UK
- For our Future's Sake
- Healthier IN the EU
- Open Britain
- Our Future Our Choice
- Scientists for EU

- **Other organisations campaigning
  for a second vote**

- Best for Britain
- **See also**
- Opposition to Brexit in the United Kingdom
- $\underline{v}$
- $\underline{t}$
- $\underline{e}^{840}$

The **United Kingdom European Union membership referendum**, also known as the **EU referendum** and the **Brexit referendum**, took place on 23 June 2016 in the United Kingdom (UK) and Gibraltar to gauge support for the country either remaining a member of, or leaving, the European Union (EU) under the provisions of the European Union Referendum Act 2015 and also the Political Parties, Elections and Referendums Act 2000. The referendum resulted in a simple majority of 51.9% (of people who voted) being in favour of leaving the EU. Although legally the referendum was non-binding, the government of that time had promised to implement the result, and it initiated the official EU withdrawal process on 29 March 2017, which put the UK on course to leave the EU by 30 March 2019, after a period of Brexit negotiations.

Membership of the EU and its predecessors has long been a topic of debate in the United Kingdom. The country joined what were then the three European Communities, principally the European Economic Community (EEC, or "Common Market"), in 1973. A previous referendum on continued membership of the then European Communities (Common Market) was held in 1975, and it was approved by 67.2% of "Yes" voters compared to 32.8% of "No" voters.

In May 2015, in accordance with a Conservative Party manifesto commitment following their victory at the 2015 UK general election, the legal basis for a referendum on EU membership was established by the UK Parliament through the European Union Referendum Act 2015. Britain Stronger in Europe was the official group campaigning for the UK to remain in the EU, and was endorsed by the Prime Minister David Cameron and Chancellor George Osborne. Vote Leave was the official group campaigning for the UK to leave the EU, and was fronted by the Conservative MP Boris Johnson, Secretary of State for Justice Michael Gove and Labour MP Gisela Stuart. Other campaign groups, political parties, businesses, trade unions, newspapers and prominent individuals were also involved, and each side had supporters from across the political spectrum.

Immediately after the result, financial markets reacted negatively, and Cameron announced that he would resign as Prime Minister and Leader of the Conservative Party, having campaigned unsuccessfully for a "Remain" vote. It was the first time that a national referendum result had gone against the preferred option of the UK Government. Cameron was succeeded by Home

Secretary Theresa May on 13 July 2016. The opposition Labour Party also faced a leadership challenge as a result of the EU referendum. In response to the result, the devolved Scottish Government announced that it would plan for a possible second referendum on Scottish independence from the United Kingdom. Several campaign groups and parties (supporting both leave and remain) have been fined by the Electoral Commission for campaign finance irregularities. The fine imposed on Leave.EU was constrained by the cap on the commission's fines and the matter has been referred to police. They were also fined by the Information Commissioner's Office, an investigation is ongoing into their relationship with Cambridge Analytica, and their funder – Arron Banks – has been accused of being linked to alleged Russian interference in the referendum.

Background

The European Communities were formed in the 1950s—the European Coal and Steel Community (ECSC) in 1952, and the European Atomic Energy Community (EAEC or Euratom) and European Economic Community (EEC) in 1957. The EEC, the more ambitious of the three, came to be known as the "Common Market". The UK first applied to join them in 1961, but this was vetoed by France. A later application was successful, and the UK joined in 1973; two years later, the first ever national referendum on continuing membership resulted in 67.2% approval. Political integration gained greater focus when the Maastricht Treaty established the European Union (EU) in 1993, which incorporated (and after the Treaty of Lisbon, succeeded) the European Communities.

Growing pressure for a referendum

Prior to the 2010 general election, the then Leader of the Conservative Party David Cameron had given a "cast iron" promise of a referendum on the Lisbon Treaty, which he backtracked on after all EU countries had ratified the treaty before the election.

Whilst attending the May 2012 NATO summit meeting, UK Prime Minister David Cameron, Foreign Secretary William Hague and Ed Llewellyn discussed the idea of using a European Union referendum as a concession to energise the Eurosceptic wing of the Conservative Party. Cameron promised in January 2013 that, should the Conservatives win a parliamentary majority at the 2015 general election, the British government would negotiate more favourable arrangements for continuing British membership of the EU, before holding a referendum on whether the UK should remain in or leave the EU. The Conservative Party published a draft EU Referendum Bill in May 2013, and outlined

Figure 9: *During the 2015 general election campaign, David Cameron promised to renegotiate the terms of the UK's EU membership and later hold a referendum on the subject if a Conservative majority government was elected.*

its plans for renegotiation followed by an in-out vote (i.e. a referendum giving options only of leaving and of remaining in under the current terms, or under new terms if these had become available), were the party to be re-elected in 2015. The draft Bill stated that the referendum had to be held no later than 31 December 2017.

The draft legislation was taken forward as a Private Member's Bill by Conservative MP James Wharton which was known as the European Union (Referendum) Bill 2013. The bill's First Reading in the House of Commons took place on 19 June 2013. Cameron was said by a spokesperson to be "very pleased" and would ensure the Bill was given "the full support of the Conservative Party".

Regarding the ability of the bill to bind the UK Government in the 2015–20 Parliament (which indirectly, as a result of the referendum itself, proved to last only two years) to holding such a referendum, a parliamentary research paper noted that:

> *The Bill simply provides for a referendum on continued EU membership by the end of December 2017 and does not otherwise specify the timing, other than requiring the Secretary of State to bring forward orders by the end of*

2016. [...] If no party obtained a majority at the [next general election due in 2015], there might be some uncertainty about the passage of the orders in the next Parliament.[841]

The bill received its Second Reading on 5 July 2013, passing by 304 votes to none after almost all Labour MPs and all Liberal Democrat MPs abstained, cleared the Commons in November 2013, and was then introduced to the House of Lords in December 2013, where members voted to block the bill.

Conservative MP Bob Neill then introduced an Alternative Referendum Bill to the Commons. After a debate on 17 October 2014, it passed to the Public Bills Committee, but because the Commons failed to pass a money resolution, the bill was unable to progress further before the dissolution of parliament on 27 March 2015.

At the European Parliament election in 2014, the UK Independence Party (UKIP) secured more votes and more seats than any other party, the first time a party other than the Conservatives or Labour had topped a nationwide poll in 108 years, leaving the Conservatives in third place.

Under Ed Miliband's leadership between 2010 and 2015, the Labour Party ruled out an in-out referendum unless and until a further transfer of powers from the UK to the EU were to be proposed. In their manifesto for the 2015 general election, the Liberal Democrats pledged to hold an in-out referendum only in the event of there being a change in the EU treaties. The UK Independence Party (UKIP), the British National Party (BNP), the Green Party,[842] the Democratic Unionist Party[843] and the Respect Party[844] all supported the principle of a referendum.

When the Conservative Party won a majority of seats in the House of Commons at the 2015 general election, Cameron reiterated his party's manifesto commitment to hold an in-out referendum on UK membership of the EU by the end of 2017, but only after "negotiating a new settlement for Britain in the EU".

Renegotiation before the referendum

In early 2014, David Cameron outlined the changes he aimed to bring about in the EU and in the UK's relationship with it. These were: additional immigration controls, especially for citizens of new EU member states; tougher immigration rules for present EU citizens; new powers for national parliaments collectively to veto proposed EU laws; new free-trade agreements and a reduction in bureaucracy for businesses; a lessening of the influence of the European Court of Human Rights on British police and courts; more power for individual member states, and less for the central EU; and abandonment of the EU notion of "ever closer union". He intended to bring these about during a series of negotiations with other EU leaders and then, if re-elected, to announce a referendum.

In November that year Cameron gave an update on the negotiations, and further details of his aims. The key demands made of the EU were: on economic governance, to recognise officially that Eurozone laws would not necessarily apply to non-Eurozone EU members and the latter would not have to bail out troubled Eurozone economies; on competitiveness, to expand the single market and to set a target for the reduction of bureaucracy for businesses; on sovereignty, for the UK to be legally exempted from "ever closer union" and for national parliaments to be able collectively to veto proposed EU laws; and, on immigration, for EU citizens going to the UK for work to be unable to claim social housing or in-work benefits until they had worked there for four years, and for them to be unable to send child benefit payments overseas.

The outcome of the renegotiations was announced in February 2016. The renegotiated terms were in addition to the United Kingdom's existing opt-outs in the European Union and the UK rebate. There was to be no fundamental change to the EU–UK relationship.Wikipedia:Citation needed Some limits to in-work benefits for EU immigrants were agreed, but these would apply on a sliding scale for four years and would be for new immigrants only; before they could be applied, a country would have to get permission from the European Council. Child benefit payments could still be made overseas, but these would be linked to the cost of living in the other country. On sovereignty, the UK was reassured that it would not be required to participate in "ever closer union"; these reassurances were "in line with existing EU law". Cameron's demand to allow national parliaments to veto proposed EU laws was modified to allow national parliaments collectively to object to proposed EU laws, in which case the European Council would reconsider the proposal before itself deciding what to do. On economic governance, anti-discrimination regulations for non-Eurozone members would be reinforced, but they would be unable to veto any legislation. The final two areas covered were proposals to "exclude from the scope of free movement rights, third country nationals who had no prior lawful residence in a Member State before marrying a Union citizen" and to make it easier for member states to deport EU nationals for public policy or public security reasons. The extent to which the various parts of the agreement would be legally binding is complex; no part of the agreement itself changed EU law, but some parts could be enforceable in international law.

The EU had reportedly offered David Cameron a so-called "emergency brake", which would have allowed the UK to withhold social benefits to new immigrants for the first four years after they arrived; this brake could have been applied for a period of seven years. That offer was still on the table at the time of the Brexit referendum, but expired when the vote determined that the

UK would leave the EU. Cameron claimed that "he could have avoided Brexit had European leaders let him control migration", according to the *Financial Times*. However, Angela Merkel said that the offer had not been made by the EU. Merkel stated in the German Parliament: "If you wish to have free access to the single market then you have to accept the fundamental European rights as well as obligations that come from it. This is as true for Great Britain as for anybody else."

Legislation

The planned referendum was included in the Queen's Speech on 27 May 2015. It was suggested at the time that Cameron was planning to hold the referendum in October 2016, but the European Union Referendum Act 2015, which authorised it, went before the House of Commons the following day, just three weeks after the election. On the bill's second reading on 9 June, members of the House of Commons voted by 544 to 53 in favour, endorsing the principle of holding a referendum, with only the Scottish National Party voting against. In contrast to the Labour Party's position prior to the 2015 general election under Miliband, acting Labour leader Harriet Harman committed her party to supporting plans for an EU referendum by 2017.

To enable the referendum to take place, the European Union Referendum Act[845] was passed by the Parliament of the United Kingdom. It extended to include and take legislative effect in Gibraltar, and received royal assent on 17 December 2015. The Act was, in turn, confirmed, enacted and implemented in Gibraltar by the European Union (Referendum) Act 2016 (Gibraltar),[846] which was passed by the Gibraltar Parliament and entered into law upon receiving the assent of the Governor of Gibraltar on 28 January 2016.

The European Union Referendum Act required a referendum to be held on the question of the UK's continued membership of the European Union (EU) before the end of 2017. It did not contain any requirement for the UK Government to implement the results of the referendum. Instead, it was designed to gauge the electorate's opinion on EU membership. The referendums held in Scotland, Wales and Northern Ireland in 1997 and 1998 are examples of this type, where opinion was tested before legislation was introduced. The UK does not have constitutional provisions which would require the results of a referendum to be implemented, unlike, for example, the Republic of Ireland, where the circumstances in which a binding referendum should be held are set out in its constitution. In contrast, the legislation that provided for the referendum held on AV in May 2011 would have implemented the new system of voting without further legislation, provided that the boundary changes also provided for in the Parliamentary Voting System and Constituency Act 2011 were also implemented. In the event, there was a substantial majority against any change. The 1975 referendum was held after the re-negotiated terms of the UK's EC membership had been agreed by all EC Member States, and the terms set out in a command paper and agreed by both Houses.[847] Following the 2016 referendum, the High Court confirmed that the result was not legally binding, owing to the constitutional principles of parliamentary sovereignty and representative democracy, and the legislation authorising the referendum did not contain clear words to the contrary.[848]

Administration

Date

Prior to being officially announced, it was widely speculated that a June date for the referendum was a serious possibility. The First Ministers of Northern Ireland, Scotland, and Wales co-signed a letter to Cameron asking him not to hold the referendum in June, as devolved elections were scheduled to take place the previous month. These elections had been postponed for a year to avoid a clash with the 2015 general election, after Westminster had implemented the Fixed-term Parliament Act. Cameron refused this request, saying people were able to make up their own minds in multiple elections spaced a short time from each other.

In February 2016, Cameron announced that the UK Government would formally recommend to the British people that the UK should remain a member of a reformed European Union and that the referendum would be held on 23 June, marking the official launch of the campaign. He also announced that Parliament would enact secondary legislation on 22 February relating to the European Union Referendum Act 2015. With the official launch, ministers of the UK Government were then free to campaign on either side of the argument in a rare exception to Cabinet collective responsibility.

Eligibility to vote

The right to vote in the referendum in the United Kingdom is defined by the legislation as limited to residents of the United Kingdom who were either also Commonwealth citizens under the British Nationality Act 1948 (which include British citizens and other British nationals), or those who were also citizens of the Republic of Ireland, or both. Members of the House of Lords, who could not vote in general elections, were able to vote in the referendum.

Residents of the United Kingdom who were citizens of other EU countries were not allowed to vote unless they were citizens (or were also citizens) of the Republic of Ireland, of Malta, or of the Republic of Cyprus.

The Representation of the People Acts 1983 *(1983 c. 2)* and 1985 *(1985 c. 50)*, as amended, also permit certain British citizens (but not other British nationals), who had once lived in the United Kingdom, but had since and in the meantime lived outside of the United Kingdom, but for a period of no more than 15 years, to vote.

Voting on the day of the referendum was from 0700 to 2200 BST (WEST) (0700 to 2200 CEST in Gibraltar) in some 41,000 polling stations manned by over 100,000 staff. Each polling station was specified to have no more than 2,500 registered voters.Wikipedia:Citation needed Under the provisions of the Representation of the People Act 2000, postal ballots were also permitted in the referendum and were sent out to eligible voters some three weeks ahead of the vote (2 June 2016).

The minimum age for voters in the referendum was set to 18 years, in line with the Representation of the People Act, as amended. A House of Lords amendment proposing to lower the minimum age to 16 years was rejected.

The deadline to register to vote was initially midnight on 7 June 2016; however, this was extended by 48 hours owing to technical problems with the official registration website on 7 June, caused by unusually high web traffic. Some supporters of the Leave campaign, including the Conservative MP Sir Gerald Howarth, criticised the government's decision to extend the deadline, alleging it gave Remain an advantage because many late registrants were young people who were considered to be more likely to vote for Remain. According to provisional figures from the Electoral Commission, almost 46.5 million people were eligible to vote.

Registration problems

Nottingham City Council emailed a Vote Leave supporter to say that the council was unable to check whether the nationality that people stated on their voting registration form was true, and hence that they simply had to assume that the information that was submitted was, indeed, correct.

Kingston-upon-Thames Council and the Electoral Commission stated that Jakub Pawlowski, a Polish voter in Kingston-upon-Thames declared himself as being British on his registration form, and hence, received a referendum polling card in the post, although he is not a UK citizen and did not have the right to receive such a polling card. The voter stated that he specified that he was a Polish citizen when registering on the electoral roll, but still had received the card in the post. The matter had been referred to the police.

3,462 EU nationals were wrongly sent postal voting cards, due to an IT issue experienced by Xpress, an electoral software supplier to a number of councils. Xpress was initially unable to confirm the exact number of those affected. The

Referendum on the United Kingdom's membership of the European Union
Vote only once by putting a cross **✗** in the box next to your choice
Should the United Kingdom remain a member of the European Union or leave the European Union?
Remain a member of the European Union   ☐
Leave the European Union   ☐

Figure 10: *Sample referendum ballot paper*

matter was resolved by the issuance of a software patch which rendered the wrongly recorded electors ineligible to vote on 23 June.

Crown Dependencies

Residents of the Crown Dependencies (which are not part of the United Kingdom), namely the Isle of Man and the Bailiwicks of Jersey and Guernsey, even if they were British citizens, were excluded from the referendum unless they were also previous residents of the United Kingdom (that is: England and Wales, Scotland and Northern Ireland).

Some residents of the Isle of Man protested that they, as full British citizens under the British Nationality Act 1981 and living within the British Islands, should also have been given the opportunity to vote in the referendum, as the Isle and the Bailiwicks, although not included as if they were part of the United Kingdom for the purpose of European Union (and European Economic Area (EEA)) membership (as is the case with Gibraltar), would also have been significantly affected by the outcome and impact of the referendum.

Referendum question

Research by the Electoral Commission confirmed that its recommended question "was clear and straightforward for voters, and was the most neutral wording from the range of options ... considered and tested", citing responses to its consultation by a diverse range of consultees. The proposed question was accepted by the government in September 2015, shortly before the bill's third reading. The question that appeared on ballot papers in the referendum under the Act was: <templatestyles src="Template:Quote/styles.css"/>

> ***Should the United Kingdom remain a member of the European Union or leave the European Union?***

with the responses to the question to be (to be marked with a single (X)): <templatestyles src="Template:Quote/styles.css"/>

> ***Remain a member of the European Union***
>
> ***Leave the European Union***

and in Welsh: <templatestyles src="Template:Quote/styles.css"/>

> ***A ddylai'r Deyrnas Unedig aros yn aelod o'r Undeb Ewropeaidd neu adael yr Undeb Ewropeaidd?***

with the responses (to be marked with a single (X)): <templatestyles src="Template:Quote/styles.css"/>

> ***Aros yn aelod o'r Undeb Ewropeaidd***
>
> ***Gadael yr Undeb Ewropeaidd***

Campaign

As of October 2015[849], there was a cross-party, formal group campaigning for Britain to remain a member of the EU, called Britain Stronger in Europe, while there were two groups promoting British withdrawal from the EU which sought to be the official Leave campaign: Leave.EU (supported by most of UKIP, including Nigel Farage), and Vote Leave (supported by Conservative Party Eurosceptics). The Electoral Commission announced on 13 April 2016 that Vote Leave was the official leave campaign. This gave it the right to spend up to £7,000,000, a free mailshot, TV broadcasts and £600,000 in public funds. Leave.EU also had an umbrella group offshoot, the cross-party Grassroots Out. The UK Government's official position was to support the "Remain" option. Nevertheless, Cameron announced that Conservative Ministers and MPs were free to campaign in favour of remaining in the EU or leaving it, according to their conscience. This decision came after mounting pressure for a free vote for ministers. In an exception to the usual rule of cabinet collective responsibility, Cameron allowed cabinet ministers to campaign publicly for EU withdrawal. A Government-backed campaign was launched in April. On 16 June, all official

Figure 11: *Britain Stronger in Europe campaigners, London, June 2016*

Figure 12: *Referendum posters for both the Leave and Remain campaigns in Pimlico, London*

national campaigning was suspended until 19 June after the murder of MP Jo Cox.

HM Government distributed a leaflet to every household in England in the week commencing on 11 April, and in Scotland, Wales and Northern Ireland on 5 May (after devolved elections). It gave details on why the government's position was that the UK should remain in the EU. The rationale was that internal polls showed that 85% of the UK population wanted more information from the Government. It was criticised by those wanting to leave as being an unfair advantage, inaccurate and a waste of money costing £9,300,000 for the campaign.

In the week beginning on 16 May, the Electoral Commission sent a voting guide regarding the referendum to every household within the UK and Gibraltar to raise awareness of the upcoming referendum. The eight-page guide contained details on how to vote, as well as a sample of the actual ballot paper, and a whole page each was given to the campaign groups Britain Stronger in Europe and Vote Leave to present their case.

Those who favoured withdrawal from the European Union – commonly referred to as *Brexit* – argued that the EU has a democratic deficit and that being a member undermined national sovereignty, while those who favoured membership argued that in a world with many supranational organisations any loss of sovereignty was compensated by the benefits of EU membership.Wikipedia:Citation needed Those who wanted to leave the EU argued that it would allow the UK to better control immigration, thus reducing pressure on public services, housing and jobs; save billions of pounds in EU membership fees; allow the UK to make its own trade deals; and free the UK from EU regulations and bureaucracy that they saw as needless and costly.Wikipedia:Citation needed Those who wanted to remain argued that leaving the EU would risk the UK's prosperity; diminish its influence over world affairs; jeopardise national security by reducing access to common European criminal databases and result in trade barriers between the UK and the EU.Wikipedia:Citation needed In particular, they argued that it would lead to job losses, delays in investment into the UK and risks to business.

Responses to the referendum campaign

Party policies

The table lists political parties with representation either in the House of Commons or in the House of Lords, or in the European Parliament, or in the Scottish Parliament, Northern Ireland Assembly or the Welsh Assembly, or in the Gibraltar Parliament.

Great Britain

Position	Political parties	Ref
Remain	Green Party of England and Wales	
	Labour Party	
	Liberal Democrats	
	Plaid Cymru – The Party of Wales	
	Scottish Green Party	
	Scottish National Party (SNP)	
Leave		
	UK Independence Party (UKIP)	
Neutral	Conservative Party	

Northern Ireland

Position	Political parties	Ref
Remain	Alliance Party of Northern Ireland	
	Green Party in Northern Ireland	
	Sinn Féin	
	Social Democratic and Labour Party (SDLP)	
	Ulster Unionist Party (UUP)	
Leave		
	Democratic Unionist Party (DUP)	
	People Before Profit Alliance (PBP)	
	Traditional Unionist Voice (TUV)	

Gibraltar

Position	Political parties	Ref
Remain	Gibraltar Social Democrats	
	Gibraltar Socialist Labour Party	
	Liberal Party of Gibraltar	

Minor parties

Among minor parties, the Socialist Labour Party, the Communist Party, Britain First, the British National Party (BNP), Éirígí, Respect Party, Trade Unionist and Socialist Coalition (TUSC), the Social Democratic Party, Liberal Party, and Independence from Europe supported leaving the EU. The Scottish Socialist Party (SSP) supported remaining in the EU. The Women's Equality Party had no official position on the issue.

Cabinet ministers

The Cabinet of the United Kingdom is a body responsible for making decisions on policy and organising governmental departments; it is chaired by the Prime Minister and contains most of the government's ministerial heads. Following the announcement of the referendum in February, 23 of the 30 Cabinet ministers (including attendees) supported the UK staying in the EU. Iain Duncan Smith, in favour of leaving, resigned on 19 March and was replaced by Stephen Crabb who was in favour of remaining. Crabb was already a cabinet member, as the Secretary of State for Wales, and his replacement, Alun Cairns, was in favour of remaining, bringing the total number of pro-remain Cabinet members to 25.

Business

Various UK multinationals have stated that they would not like the UK to leave the EU because of the uncertainty it would cause, such as Shell, BT and Vodafone, with some assessing the pros and cons of Britain exiting. The banking sector was one of the most vocal advocating to stay in the EU, with the British Bankers' Association saying: "Businesses don't like that kind of uncertainty". RBS warned of potential damage to the economy. Furthermore, HSBC and foreign-based banks JP Morgan and Deutsche Bank claim a Brexit might result in the banks' changing domicile. According to Goldman Sachs and the City of London's policy chief, all such factors could impact on the City of London's present status as a European and global market leader in financial services. In February 2016, leaders of 36 of the FTSE 100 companies, including Shell,

BAE Systems, BT and Rio Tinto, officially supported staying in the EU. Moreover, 60% of the Institute of Directors and the EEF memberships supported staying.

Many UK-based businesses, including Sainsbury's, remained steadfastly neutral, concerned that taking sides in the divisive issue could lead to a backlash from customers.

Richard Branson stated that he was "very fearful" of the consequences of a UK exit from the EU. Alan Sugar expressed similar concern.

James Dyson, founder of the Dyson company, argued in June 2016 that the introduction of tariffs would be less damaging for British exporters than the appreciation of the pound against the Euro, arguing that, because Britain ran a 100 billion pound trade deficit with the EU, tariffs could represent a significant revenue source for the Treasury.[850] Pointing out that languages, plugs and laws differ between EU member states, Dyson said that the 28-country bloc was not a single market, and argued the fastest growing markets were outside the EU. Engineering company Rolls-Royce wrote to employees to say that it did not want the UK to leave the EU.

Surveys of large UK businesses showed a strong majority favoured the UK remaining in the EU. Small and medium-sized UK businesses were more evenly split. Polls of foreign businesses found that around half would be less likely to do business in the UK, while 1% would increase their investment in the UK. Two large car manufacturers, Ford and BMW, warned in 2013 against Brexit, suggesting it would be "devastating" for the economy. Conversely, in 2015, some other manufacturing executives told Reuters that they would not shut their plants if the UK left the EU, although future investment might be put at risk. The CEO of Vauxhall stated that a Brexit would not materially affect its business. Foreign-based Toyota CEO Akio Toyoda confirmed that, whether or not Britain left the EU, Toyota would carry on manufacturing cars in Britain as they had done before.

Exchange rates and stock markets

In the week following conclusion of the UK's renegotiation (and especially after Boris Johnson announced that he would support the UK leaving), the pound fell to a seven-year low against the dollar and economists at HSBC warned that it could drop even more.[851] At the same time, Daragh Maher, head of HSBC, suggested that if Sterling dropped in value so would the Euro. European banking analysts also cited Brexit concerns as the reason for the Euro's decline. Immediately after a poll in June 2016 showed that the Leave campaign was 10 points ahead, the pound dropped by a further one per cent. In the same month, it was announced that the value of goods exported from the UK in April had shown a month-on-month increase of 11.2%, "the biggest rise since records started in 1998".

Uncertainty over the referendum result, together with several other factors—US interest rates rising, low commodity prices, low Eurozone growth and concerns over emerging markets such as China—contributed to a high level of stock market volatility in January and February 2016. During this period, the FTSE 100 rose or fell by more than 1.5% on 16 days. On 14 June, polls showing that a Brexit was more likely led to the FTSE 100 falling by 2%, losing £98 billion in value. After further polls suggested a move back towards Remain, the pound and the FTSE recovered.

On the day of the referendum, sterling hit a 2016 high of $1.5018 and the FTSE 100 also climbed to a 2016 high, as a new poll suggested a win for the Remain campaign. Initial results suggested a vote for 'Remain' and the value of the pound held its value. However, when the result for Sunderland was announced, it indicated an unexpected swing to 'Leave'. Subsequent results appeared to confirm this swing and sterling fell in value to $1.3777, its lowest level since 1985. However, the following Monday when the markets opened, sterling fell to a new low of $1.32.

When the London Stock Exchange opened on the morning of 24 June, the FTSE 100 fell from 6338.10 to 5806.13 in the first ten minutes of trading. It recovered to 6091.27 after a further 90 minutes, before further recovering to 6162.97 by the end of the day's trading. When the markets reopened the following Monday, the FTSE 100 showed a steady decline losing over 2% by mid-afternoon. Upon opening later on the Friday after the referendum, the US Dow Jones Industrial Average dropped nearly 450 points or about 2½% in less than half an hour. The Associated Press called the sudden worldwide stock market decline a stock market crash. Investors in worldwide stock markets lost more than the equivalent of US$2 trillion on 24 June 2016, making it the worst single-day loss in history, in absolute terms. The market losses amounted to US$3 trillion by 27 June. The value of the pound sterling against the US dollar fell to a 31-year low. The UK's and the EU's sovereign debt credit rating was also lowered by Standard & Poor's.

By mid-afternoon on 27 June 2016, sterling was at a 31-year low, having fallen 11% in two trading days, and the FTSE 100 had surrendered £85 billion; however, by 29 June it had recovered all its losses since the markets closed on polling day and the value of the pound had begun to rise.

European responses

Czech prime minister Bohuslav Sobotka suggested in February 2016 that the Czech Republic would start discussions on leaving the EU if the UK voted for an EU exit.[852]

Marine Le Pen, the leader of the French *Front national*, described the possibility of a Brexit as "like the fall of the Berlin Wall" and commented that "Brexit would be marvellous – extraordinary – for all European peoples who long for freedom". A poll in France in April 2016 showed that 59% of the French people were in favour of Britain remaining in the EU.

Polish President Andrzej Duda lent his support for the UK remaining within the EU. Moldovan Prime Minister Pavel Filip asked all citizens of Moldova living in the UK to speak to their British friends and convince them to vote for the UK to remain in the EU.

Spanish foreign minister José García-Margallo said Spain would demand control of Gibraltar the "very next day" after a British withdrawal from the EU. Margallo also threatened to close the border with Gibraltar if Britain left the EU.

The Dutch politician Geert Wilders, leader of the Party for Freedom, said that the Netherlands should follow Britain's example: "Like in the 1940s, once again Britain could help liberate Europe from another totalitarian monster, this time called 'Brussels'. Again, we could be saved by the British."[853]

Swedish foreign minister Margot Wallström said on 11 June 2016 that if Britain left the EU, other countries would have referendums on whether to leave the EU, and that if Britain stayed in the EU, other countries would negotiate, ask and demand to have special treatment.[854]

Non-European responses

International Monetary Fund

Christine Lagarde, the managing director of the International Monetary Fund, warned in February 2016 that the uncertainty over the outcome of the referendum would be bad "in and of itself" for the British economy. In response, Leave campaigner Priti Patel said a previous warning from the IMF regarding the coalition government's deficit plan for the UK was proven incorrect and that the IMF "were wrong then and are wrong now".

United States

In October 2015, United States Trade Representative Michael Froman declared that the United States was not keen on pursuing a separate free-trade agreement (FTA) with Britain if it were to leave the EU, thus, according to *The Guardian*, undermining a key economic argument of proponents of those who say Britain would prosper on its own and be able to secure bilateral FTAs with trading partners. Also in October 2015, the United States Ambassador to the United Kingdom Matthew Barzun said that UK participation in NATO and the EU made each group "better and stronger" and that, while the decision to remain or leave is a choice for the British people, it was in the US interest that it remain. In April 2016, eight former US Secretaries of the Treasury, who had served both Democratic and Republican presidents, urged Britain to remain in the EU.[855]

In July 2015, President Barack Obama confirmed the long-standing US preference for the UK to remain in the EU. Obama said: "Having the UK in the EU gives us much greater confidence about the strength of the transatlantic union, and is part of the cornerstone of the institutions built after World War II that has made the world safer and more prosperous. We want to make sure that the United Kingdom continues to have that influence." Obama's intervention was criticised by Republican Senator Ted Cruz as "a slap in the face of British self-determination as the president, typically, elevated an international organisation over the rights of a sovereign people", and stated that "Britain will be at the front of the line for a free trade deal with America", were a Brexit to occur. Two years later, one of Obama's former aides recounted that the public intervention was made following a request by Cameron.

Prior to the vote, Republican presidential candidate Donald Trump anticipated that Britain would leave based on its concerns over migration, while Democratic presidential candidate Hillary Clinton hoped that Britain would remain in the EU to strengthen transatlantic co-operation.

Other states

In October 2015, Chinese President Xi Jinping declared his support for Britain remaining in the EU, saying "China hopes to see a prosperous Europe and a united EU, and hopes Britain, as an important member of the EU, can play an even more positive and constructive role in promoting the deepening development of China-EU ties". Chinese diplomats have stated "off the record" that the People's Republic sees the EU as a counterbalance to American economic power, and that an EU without Britain would mean a stronger United States.

In February 2016, the finance ministers from the G20 major economies warned that leaving the EU would lead to "a shock" in the global economy.

In May 2016, the Australian Prime Minister Malcolm Turnbull said that Australia would prefer the UK to remain in the EU, but that it was a matter for the British people, and "whatever judgment they make, the relations between Britain and Australia will be very, very close".

Indonesian president Joko Widodo stated during a European trip that he was not in favour of Brexit.

Sri Lankan Prime Minister Ranil Wickremesinghe issued a statement of reasons why he was "very concerned" at the possibility of Brexit.

Russian President Vladimir Putin said: "I want to say it is none of our business, it is the business of the people of the UK." Maria Zakharova, the official Russian foreign ministry spokesperson, said: "Russia has nothing to do with Brexit. We are not involved in this process in any way. We don't have any interest in it."

Economists

In November 2015, the Governor of the Bank of England Mark Carney said that the Bank of England would do what was necessary to help the UK economy if the British people voted to leave the EU.[856] In March 2016, Carney told MPs that an EU exit was the "biggest domestic risk" to the UK economy, but that remaining a member also carried risks, related to the European Monetary Union, of which the UK is not a member.[857] In May 2016, Carney said that a "technical recession" was one of the possible risks of the UK leaving the EU. However, Iain Duncan Smith said Carney's comment should be taken with "a pinch of salt", saying "all forecasts in the end are wrong".

In December 2015, the Bank of England published a report about the impact of immigration on wages. The report concluded that immigration put downward pressure on workers' wages, particularly low-skilled workers: a 10 percent point rise in the proportion of migrants working in low-skilled services drove down the average wages of low-skilled workers by about 2 percent.[858] The 10 percentage point rise cited in the paper is larger than the entire rise observed since the 2004–06 period in the semi/unskilled services sector, which is about 7 percentage points.

In March 2016, Nobel prize-winning economist Joseph Stiglitz argued that he might reconsider his support for the UK remaining in the EU if the proposed Transatlantic Trade and Investment Partnership (TTIP) were to be agreed to.[859] Stiglitz warned that under the investor-state dispute settlement provision in current drafts of the TTIP, governments risked being sued for loss of profits resulting from new regulations, including health and safety regulations to limit the use of asbestos or tobacco.

The German economist Clemens Fuest wrote that there was a liberal, free-trade bloc in the EU comprising the UK, the Netherlands, the Czech Republic, Sweden, Denmark, Ireland, Slovakia, Finland, Estonia, Latvia and Lithuania, controlling 32% of the votes in the European Council and standing in opposition to the *dirigiste*, protectionist policies favoured by France and its allies. Germany with its 'social market' economy stands midway between the French *dirigiste* economic model and the British free-market economic model. From the German viewpoint, the existence of the liberal bloc allows Germany to play off free-market Britain against *dirigiste* France, and that if Britain were to leave, the liberal bloc would be severely weakened, thereby allowing the French to take the EU into a much more *dirigiste* direction that would be unattractive from the standpoint of Berlin.

A study by Oxford Economics for the Law Society of England and Wales has suggested that Brexit would have a particularly large negative impact on the UK financial services industry and the law firms that support it, which could cost the law sector as much as £1.7bn per annum by 2030. The Law Society's own report into the possible effects of Brexit notes that leaving the EU would be likely to reduce the role played by the UK as a centre for resolving disputes between foreign firms, whilst a potential loss of "passporting" rights would require financial services firms to transfer departments responsible for regulatory oversight overseas.

World Pensions Forum director M. Nicolas Firzi has argued that the Brexit debate should be viewed within the broader context of economic analysis of EU law and regulation in relation to English common law, arguing: "Every year, the British Parliament is forced to pass tens of new statutes reflecting the latest EU directives coming from Brussels – a highly undemocratic process known as 'transposition'... Slowly but surely, these new laws dictated by EU commissars are conquering English common law, imposing upon UK businesses and citizens an ever-growing collection of fastidious regulations in every field".

Institute for Fiscal Studies

In May 2016, the Institute for Fiscal Studies said that an EU exit could mean two more years of austerity cuts as the government would have to make up for an estimated loss of £20 billion to £40 billion of tax revenue. The head of the IFS, Paul Johnson said that the UK "could perfectly reasonably decide that we are willing to pay a bit of a price for leaving the EU and regaining some sovereignty and control over immigration and so on. That there would be some price though, I think is now almost beyond doubt."

Lawyers

A poll of lawyers conducted by a legal recruiter in late May 2016 suggested 57% of lawyers wanted to remain in the EU.

During a Treasury Committee shortly following the vote, economic experts generally agreed that the leave vote would be detrimental to the UK economy.

Michael Dougan, Professor of European law and Jean Monnet Chair in EU Law at the University of Liverpool and a constitutional lawyer, described the Leave campaign as "one of the most dishonest political campaigns this country [the UK] has ever seen", for using arguments based on constitutional law that he said were readily demonstrable as false.

NHS officials

Simon Stevens, head of NHS England, warned in May 2016 that a recession following a Brexit would be "very dangerous" for the National Health Service, saying that "when the British economy sneezes, the NHS catches a cold." Three-quarters of a sample of NHS leaders agreed that leaving the EU would have a negative effect on the NHS as a whole. In particular, eight out of 10 respondents felt that leaving the EU would have a negative impact on trusts' ability to recruit health and social care staff. In April 2016, a group of nearly 200 health professionals and researchers warned that the NHS would be in jeopardy if Britain left the European Union. The leave campaign reacted by saying more money would be available to be spent on the NHS if the UK left the EU.

British charities

Guidelines by the Charity Commission for England and Wales that forbid political activity for registered charities have kept them silent on the EU poll. According to Simon Wessely, head of psychological medicine at the Institute of Psychiatry, King's College London – neither a special revision of the guidelines from 7 March 2016, nor Cameron's encouragement have made health organisations, most of which support the remain campaign, willing to speak out.

Fishing industry

A June 2016 survey of British fishermen found that 92% intended to vote to leave the EU. The EU's Common Fisheries Policy was mentioned as a central reason for their near-unanimity. More than three-quarters believed that they would be able to land more fish, and 93% stated that leaving the EU would benefit the fishing industry. More than half of fish caught in British waters are caught by non-UK vessels due to the EU's Common Fisheries Policy.

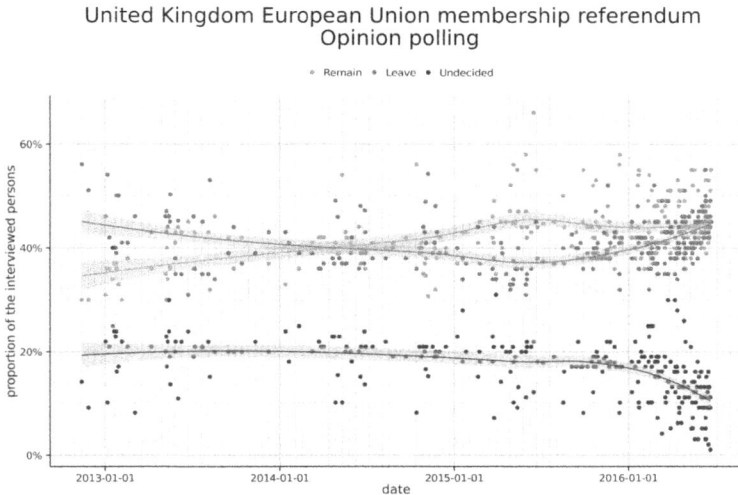

Figure 13: *Opinion polling on the referendum*

Historians

In May 2016, more than 300 historians wrote in a joint letter to *The Guardian* that Britain could play a bigger role in the world as part of the EU. They said: "As historians of Britain and of Europe, we believe that Britain has had in the past, and will have in the future, an irreplaceable role to play in Europe."

Exit plan competition

Following David Cameron's announcement of an EU referendum, British think tank the Institute of Economic Affairs (IEA) announced in July 2013 a competition to find the best plan for a UK exit from the European Union, declaring that a departure is a "real possibility" after the 2015 general election. Iain Mansfield, a Cambridge graduate and UKTI diplomat, submitted the winning thesis: *A Blueprint for Britain: Openness not Isolation*. Mansfield's submission focused on addressing both trade and regulatory issues with member states as well as other global trading partners.

Opinion polling

Opinion polls from 2010 onwards suggested the British public were relatively evenly divided on the question, with opposition to EU membership peaking in November 2012 at 56% compared with 30% who prefer to remain in, while in

June 2015 those in favour of Britain remaining in the EU reached 43% versus those opposed 36%. The largest ever poll (of 20,000 people, in March 2014) showed the public evenly split on the issue, with 41% in favour of withdrawal, 41% in favour of membership, and 18% undecided. However, when asked how they would vote if Britain renegotiated the terms of its membership of the EU, and the UK Government stated that British interests had been satisfactorily protected, more than 50% indicated that they would vote for Britain to stay in.

Analysis of polling suggested that young voters tended to support remaining in the EU, whereas those older tend to support leaving, but there was no gender split in attitudes. In February 2016 YouGov also found that euroscepticism correlated with people of lower income and that "higher social grades are more clearly in favour of remaining in the EU", but noted that euroscepticism also had strongholds in "the more wealthy, Tory shires". Scotland, Wales and many English urban areas with large student populations were more pro-EU. Big business was broadly behind remaining in the EU, though the situation among smaller companies was less clear cut. In polls of economists, lawyers, and scientists, clear majorities saw the UK's membership of the EU as beneficial. Ladbrokes offered 6/1 odds on the day of the referendum against voters choosing to leave the EU. The American company TickerTags accurately predicted the results using Twitter data.

On the day YouGov Poll

Remain	Leave	Undecided	Lead	Sample	Conducted by
52%	48%	N/A	4%	4,772	YouGov[860]

Shortly after the polls closed at 10pm on 23 June, the British polling company YouGov released a poll conducted among almost 5,000 people on the day; it suggested a narrow lead for "Remain", which polled 52% with Leave polling 48%. It was later criticised for overestimating the margin of the "Remain" vote, when it became clear a few hours later that the UK had voted 51.9% to 48.1% in favour of leaving the European Union.

Issues

The number of jobs lost or gained by a withdrawal was a dominant issue; the BBC's outline of issues warned that a precise figure was difficult to find. The Leave campaign argued that a reduction in red tape associated with EU regulations would create more jobs and that small to medium-sized companies who trade domestically would be the biggest beneficiaries. Those arguing to remain

Figure 14: *Boris Johnson MP played a key role in the Vote Leave campaign*

in the EU, claimed that millions of jobs would be lost. The EU's importance as a trading partner and the outcome of its trade status if it left was a disputed issue. Whilst those wanting to stay cited that most of the UK's trade was made with the EU, those arguing to leave say that its trade was not as important as it used to be. Scenarios of the economic outlook for the country if it left the EU were generally negative. The United Kingdom also paid more into the EU budget than it received.

Citizens of EU countries, including the United Kingdom, have the right to travel, live and work within other EU countries, as free movement is one of the four founding principles of the EU. Campaigners for remaining said that EU immigration had positive impacts on the UK's economy, citing that the country's growth forecasts were partly based upon continued high levels of net immigration. The Office for Budget Responsibility also claimed that taxes from immigrants boost public funding. A recent academic paper suggests that migration from Eastern Europe put pressure on wage growth at the lower end of the wage distribution, while at the same time increasing pressures on public services and housing. The Leave campaign believed reduced immigration would ease pressure in public services such as schools and hospitals, as well as giving British workers more jobs and higher wages. According to official Office for National Statistics data, net migration in 2015 was 333,000, which was the second highest level on record, far above David Cameron's target of tens of thousands.[861,862] Net migration from the EU was 184,000. The figures also showed that 77,000 EU migrants who came to Britain were looking for work.

After the announcement had been made as to the outcome of the referendum, Rowena Mason, political correspondent for *The Guardian* offered the following assessment: "Polling suggests discontent with the scale of migration to the UK has been the biggest factor pushing Britons to vote out, with the contest turning into a referendum on whether people are happy to accept free movement in return for free trade." A columnist for *The Times*, Philip Collins, went a step further in his analysis: "This was a referendum about immigration disguised as a referendum about the European Union."

The Conservative MEP (Member of the European Parliament) representing South East England, Daniel Hannan, predicted on the BBC program *Newsnight* that the level of immigration would remain high after Brexit. "Frankly, if people watching think that they have voted and there is now going to be zero immigration from the EU, they are going to be disappointed. ... you will look in vain for anything that the Leave campaign said at any point that ever suggested there would ever be any kind of border closure or drawing up of the drawbridge."

The EU had offered David Cameron a so-called "emergency brake" which would have allowed the UK to withhold social benefits to new immigrants for the first four years after they arrived; this brake could have been applied for a period of seven years." That offer was still on the table at the time of the Brexit referendum but expired when the vote determined that the UK would leave the EU.

The possibility that the UK's smaller constituent countries could vote to remain within the EU but find themselves withdrawn from the EU led to discussion about the risk to the unity of the United Kingdom. Scotland's First Minister, Nicola Sturgeon, made it clear that she believed that a second independence referendum would "almost certainly" be demanded by Scots if the UK voted to leave the EU but Scotland did not. The First Minister of Wales, Carwyn Jones, said: "If Wales votes to remain in [the EU] but the UK votes to leave, there will be a... constitutional crisis. The UK cannot possibly continue in its present form if England votes to leave and everyone else votes to stay".

There was concern that the Transatlantic Trade and Investment Partnership (TTIP), a proposed trade agreement between the United States and the EU, would be a threat to the public services of EU member states.[863,864,865,866] Jeremy Corbyn, on the Remain side, said that he pledged to veto TTIP in Government.[867] John Mills, on the Leave side, said that the UK could not veto

TTIP because trade pacts were decided by Qualified Majority Voting in the European Council.[868]

There was debate over the extent to which the European Union membership aided security and defence in comparison to the UK's membership of NATO and the United Nations. Security concerns over the union's free movement policy were raised too, because people with EU passports were unlikely to receive detailed checks at border control.

Debates, Q&A sessions and interviews

A debate was held by *The Guardian* on 15 March 2016, featuring the leader of UKIP Nigel Farage, Conservative MP Andrea Leadsom, the leader of Labour's "yes" campaign Alan Johnson and former leader of the Liberal Democrats Nick Clegg.

Earlier in the campaign, on 11 January, a debate took place between Nigel Farage and Carwyn Jones, who was at the time the First Minister of Wales and leader of the Welsh Labour Party. Reluctance to have Conservative Party members argue against one another has seen some debates split, with Leave and Remain candidates interviewed separately.

The Spectator held a debate hosted by Andrew Neil on 26 April, which featured Nick Clegg, Liz Kendall and Chuka Umunna arguing for a remain vote, and Nigel Farage, Daniel Hannan and Kate Hoey arguing for a leave vote. The *Daily Express* held a debate on 3 June, featuring Nigel Farage, Labour MP Kate Hoey and Conservative MP Jacob Rees-Mogg debating Labour MPs Siobhain McDonagh and Chuka Umunna and businessman Richard Reed, co-founder of Innocent drinks. *Essex TV* produced a documentary named 'Is Essex IN or OUT' released on 20 June, featuring Boris Johnson, local public figures and various members of the public from Essex. Andrew Neil presented four interviews ahead of the referendum. The interviewees were Hilary Benn, George Osborne, Nigel Farage and Iain Duncan Smith on 6, 8, 10 and 17 May, respectively.

The scheduled debates and question sessions included a number of question and answer sessions with various campaigners. and a debate on ITV held on 9 June that included Angela Eagle, Amber Rudd and Nicola Sturgeon, Boris Johnson, Andrea Leadsom, and Gisela Stuart.

EU Referendum: The Great Debate was held at Wembley Arena on 21 June and hosted by David Dimbleby, Mishal Husain and Emily Maitlis in front of an audience of 6,000. The audience was split evenly between both sides. Sadiq Khan, Ruth Davidson and Frances O'Grady appeared for Remain. Leave was represented by the same trio as the ITV debate on 9 June (Johnson, Leadsom

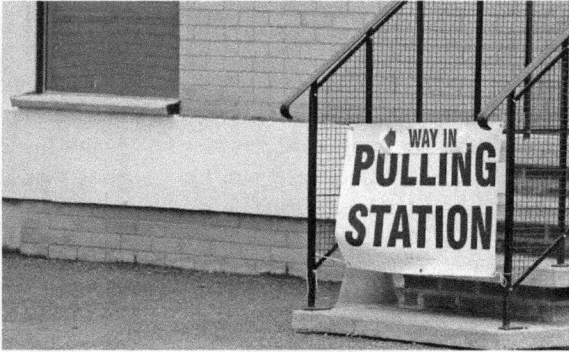

Figure 15: *Sign outside a polling station in England on the morning of the referendum*

and Stuart). *Europe: The Final Debate with Jeremy Paxman* was held the following day on Channel 4.

Voting, voting areas and counts

Voting took place from 0700 BST (WEST) until 2200 BST (Same hours CEST in Gibraltar) in 41,000 polling stations across 382 voting areas, with each polling station limited to a maximum of 2,500 voters.[869] The referendum was held across all four countries of the United Kingdom, as well as in Gibraltar, as a single majority vote. The 382 voting areas were grouped into twelve regional counts and there was separate declarations for each of the regional counts.

In England, as happened in the 2011 AV referendum, the 326 districts were used as the local voting areas and the returns of these then fed into nine English regional counts. In Scotland the local voting areas were the 32 local councils which then fed their results into the Scottish national count, and in Wales the 22 local councils were their local voting areas before the results were then fed into the Welsh national count. Northern Ireland, as was the case in the AV referendum, was a single voting and national count area although local totals by Westminster parliamentary constituency areas were announced.

Gibraltar was a single voting area, but as Gibraltar was to be treated and included as if it were a part of South West England, its results was included together with the South West England regional count.

The following table shows the breakdown of the voting areas and regional counts that were used for the referendum.

Country	Counts and voting areas
United Kingdom (together with **Gibraltar**, treated as if it were a [full] part of the United Kingdom)	Referendum declaration; 12 regional counts; 382 voting areas (381, 1 in Gibraltar)

Constituent countries	Counts and voting areas
England (together with **Gibraltar**, treated as if it were a part of South West England)	9 regional counts; 327 voting areas (326, 1 in Gibraltar)
Northern Ireland	National count and single voting area; 18 local totals
Scotland	National count; 32 voting areas
Wales	National count; 22 voting areas

Disturbances

On 16 June 2016, one pro-EU Labour MP, Jo Cox, was shot and killed in Birstall, West Yorkshire the week before the referendum by a man calling himself "death to traitors, freedom for Britain", and a man who intervened was injured. The two rival official campaigns suspended their activities as a mark of respect to Cox. David Cameron cancelled a planned rally in Gibraltar supporting British EU membership. Campaigning resumed on 19 June. Polling officials in the Yorkshire and Humber region also halted counting of the referendum ballots on the evening of 23 June to observe a minute of silence. The Conservative Party, Liberal Democrats, UK Independence Party and the Green Party all announced that they would not contest the ensuing by-election in Cox's constituency as a mark of respect;

On polling day itself two polling stations in Kingston upon Thames were flooded by rain and had to be relocated. In advance of polling day, concern had been expressed that the courtesy pencils provided in polling booths could allow votes to be later altered. Although this was widely dismissed as a conspiracy theory, some Leave campaigners advocated that voters should instead use pens to mark their ballot papers. On polling day in Winchester an emergency call was made to police about "threatening behaviour" outside the polling station. After questioning a woman who had been offering to lend her pen to voters, the police decided that no offence was being committed.

Figure 16:
*Of the 382 voting areas a total of 263 returned majority votes in
favour of "Leave" whilst 119 returned majority votes in favour of
"Remain" in the referendum including all 32 areas in Scotland.*
Leave
Remain

Result

The final result was announced on Friday 24 June 2016 at 07:20 BST by then-
Electoral Commission Chairwoman Jenny Watson at Manchester Town Hall
after all 382 voting areas and the twelve UK regions had declared their totals.
With a national turnout of 72% across the United Kingdom and Gibraltar the
target to secure the majority win for the winning side was 16,788,672 votes.
The decision by the electorate was to "Leave the European Union" which won
by a majority of 1,269,501 votes (3.8%) over those who had voted in favour
of "Remain a member of the European Union".Wikipedia:Verifiability The
national turnout of 72% was the highest ever for a UK-wide referendum and
the highest for any national vote since the 1992 general election.

Choice	Votes	%
Leave the European Union	**17,410,742**	**51.89**
Remain a member of the European Union	16,141,241	48.11
Valid votes	33,551,983	99.92
Invalid or blank votes	25,359	0.08
Total votes	**33,577,342**	**100.00**
Registered voters and turnout	46,500,001	72.21
Source: Electoral Commission[870]		

National referendum results (without spoiled ballots)

Leave: 17,410,742 (51.9%)	Remain: 16,141,241 (48.1%)
▲	

Regional count results

Region	Elec-torate	Voter turnout, of eligible	Votes		Proportion of votes	
			Remain	Leave	Remain	Leave
East Midlands	3,384,299	74.2%	1,033,036	**1,475,479**	41.18%	**58.82%**
East of England	4,398,796	75.7%	1,448,616	**1,880,367**	43.52%	**56.48%**
Greater London	5,424,768	69.7%	**2,263,519**	1,513,232	**59.93%**	40.07%
North East England	1,934,341	69.3%	562,595	**778,103**	41.96%	**58.04%**
North West England	5,241,568	70.0%	1,699,020	**1,966,925**	46.35%	**53.65%**
Northern Ireland	1,260,955	62.7%	**440,707**	349,442	**55.78%**	44.22%
Scotland	3,987,112	67.2%	**1,661,191**	1,018,322	**62.00%**	38.00%
South East England	6,465,404	76.8%	2,391,718	**2,567,965**	48.22%	**51.78%**
South West England (including Gibraltar)	4,138,134	76.7%	1,503,019	**1,669,711**	47.37%	**52.63%**
Wales	2,270,272	71.7%	772,347	**854,572**	47.47%	**52.53%**
West Midlands	4,116,572	72.0%	1,207,175	**1,755,687**	40.74%	**59.26%**
Yorkshire and the Humber	3,877,780	70.7%	1,158,298	**1,580,937**	42.29%	**57.71%**

Results by constituent countries

Country	Electorate	Voter turnout, of eligible	Votes		Proportion of votes	
			Remain	Leave	Remain	Leave
England (including Gibraltar)	39,005,781	73.0%	13,266,996	**15,188,406**	46.62%	**53.38%**
Northern Ireland	1,260,955	62.7%	**440,707**	349,442	**55.78%**	44.22%
Scotland	3,987,112	67.2%	**1,661,191**	1,018,322	**62.00%**	38.00%
Wales	2,270,272	71.7%	772,347	**854,572**	47.47%	**52.53%**

Voting demographics and trends

Voting figures from local referendum counts and ward-level data (using local demographic information collected in the 2011 census) suggested that Leave votes were strongly correlated with lower education and higher age. The data were obtained from approximately one in nine wards in England and Wales, with no information coming from Northern Ireland and very little coming from Scotland. A YouGov survey reported similar findings; these are summarised in the figures below.

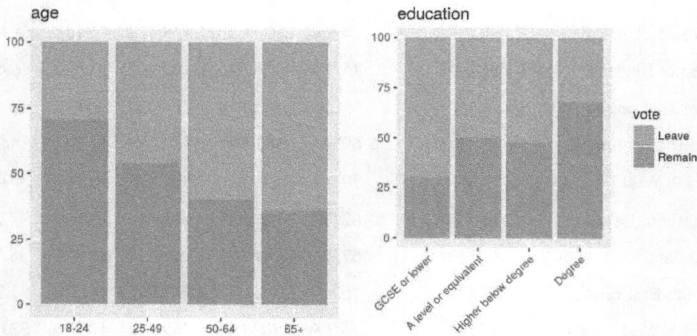

Figure 17: *EU referendum vote by age and education, based on a YouGov survey. UNIQ-ref-1-f025349a66ac0d2b-QINU*

Reactions to the result

Immediate reaction to the vote

Youth protests and non-inclusion of underage citizens

The referendum was criticised for not granting people younger than 18 years of age a vote. Unlike in the 2014 Scottish independence referendum, the vote was not extended to 16- and 17-year-old citizens. Critics argued that these people would live with the consequences of the referendum for longer than those who were able to vote. Some supporters for the inclusion of these young citizens considered this exclusion a violation of democratic principles and a major shortcoming of the referendum.

Increase of applications for passports of other EU countries

The foreign ministry of Ireland stated on 24 June 2016 that the number of applications from the UK for Irish passports had increased significantly. Enquiries about passports also increased: the Irish Embassy in London reported 4,000 a day immediately after the vote to leave, in comparison with the normal 200 a day. Other EU nations also had increases in requests for passports from British citizens, including France and Belgium.

Abuse and hate crimes

More than a hundred racist abuse and hate crimes were reported in the immediate aftermath of the referendum, with many citing the plan to leave the European Union. On 24 June 2016, a Polish school in Cambridgeshire was vandalised with a sign reading "Leave the EU. No more Polish vermin". Following the referendum result, similar signs were distributed outside homes and schools in Huntingdon, with some left on the cars of Polish residents collecting their children from school. On 26 June, the London office of the Polish Social and Cultural Association was vandalised with racist graffiti. Both incidents were investigated by the police. In Wales, a Muslim woman was told to leave after the referendum, even though she had been born and raised in the United Kingdom. Other instances of racism occurred as perceived foreigners were targeted in supermarkets, on buses and on street corners, and told to leave the country immediately. All such incidents were widely condemned by politicians and religious leaders.

By September 2016, it was reported, according to the LGBT anti-violence charity Galop, that attacks on LGBT people in the United Kingdom had risen by 147% in the three months after the referendum.

The killing of a Polish national Arkadiusz Jozwik in Harlow, Essex in August 2016 was widely speculated to be linked to the Leave result. A BBC Newsnight report by John Sweeney showed an interview with someone who knew the victim who then claimed that Leading Brexit campaigner Nigel Farage had "blood on his hands". It was mentioned in the European Parliament by the EU Commissioner Jean-Claude Juncker who said: "We Europeans can never accept Polish workers being harassed, beaten up or even murdered on the streets of Harlow." A teenager was subsequently convicted of manslaughter and sentenced to three and a half years in a young offender institution but the trial did not conclude that the altercation resulting in Jozwik's death was a hate crime. Nigel Farage criticised the "sensationalist" reporting of the issue and complained to the BBC about broadcasting the "blood on his hands" remark.

Petition for a new referendum

Within hours of the result's announcement, a petition, calling for a second referendum to be held in the event that a result was secured with less than 60% of the vote and on a turnout of less than 75%, attracted tens of thousands of new signatures. The petition had actually been initiated by someone favouring an exit from the EU, one William Oliver Healey of the English Democrats on 24 May 2016, when the Remain faction had been leading in the polls, and had received 22 signatures prior to the referendum result being declared. On 26 June, Healey made it clear on his Facebook page that the petition had actually been started to favour an exit from the EU and that he was a strong supporter of the Vote Leave and Grassroots Out campaigns. Healey also claimed that the petition had been "hijacked by the remain campaign". English Democrats chairman Robin Tilbrook suggested those who had signed the petition were experiencing "sour grapes" about the result of the referendum. It attracted more than four million signatures, meaning it was considered for debate in Parliament; this debate took place on 5 September 2016.

On 27 June 2016, David Cameron's spokesperson stated that holding another vote on Britain's membership to the European Union was "not remotely on the cards." Home Secretary Theresa May made the following comment when announcing her candidacy to replace Cameron as Conservative leader (and hence as Prime Minister) on 30 June: "The campaign was fought ... and the public gave their verdict. There must be no attempts to remain inside the EU ... and no second referendum. ... Brexit means Brexit." The petition was rejected by the government on 9 July. Its response said that the referendum vote "must be respected" and that the government "must now prepare for the process to exit the EU".

Sadiq Khan fears there can be only no deal or a bad deal (which Khan maintains will be worse) because there is insufficient time to negotiate anything better.

Figure 18: *Prime Minister David Cameron announces his resignation following the outcome of the referendum.*

Khan stated, "They are both incredibly risky and I don't believe Theresa May has the mandate to gamble so flagrantly with the British economy and people's livelihood." Khan blames what he sees as the government's poor performance for there being no good alternative to a second referendum. "This means a public vote on any Brexit deal obtained by the government, or a vote on a 'no-deal' Brexit if one is not secured, alongside the option of staying in the EU. People didn't vote to leave the EU to make themselves poorer, to watch their businesses suffer, to have NHS wards understaffed, to see the police preparing for civil unrest or for our national security to be put at risk if our cooperation with the EU in the fight against terrorism is weakened."[871]

Political

Conservative Party

On 24 June, the Conservative Party leader and Prime Minister David Cameron announced that he would resign by October because the Leave campaign had been successful in the referendum. The leadership election was scheduled for 9 September. The new leader would be in place before the autumn conference set to begin on 2 October. Unexpectedly, Boris Johnson, who had been a leading figure for Vote Leave, declined to be nominated shortly before the deadline

Figure 19: *Theresa May succeeded David Cameron as Prime Minister following the vote.*

for nominations. On 13 July, almost three weeks after the vote, Theresa May succeeded Cameron as Prime Minister.

Labour Party

The Labour Party leader Jeremy Corbyn faced growing criticism from his party, which had supported remaining within the EU, for poor campaigning. On 26 June 2016, Corbyn sacked Hilary Benn (the shadow foreign secretary) for apparently leading a coup against him. This led to a string of Labour MPs quickly resigning their roles in the party. A no confidence motion was held on 28 June; Corbyn lost the motion with more than 80% (172) of MPs voting against him. Corbyn responded with a statement that the motion had no "constitutional legitimacy" and that he intended to continue as the elected leader. The vote did not require the party to call a leadership election but after Angela Eagle and Owen Smith launched leadership challenges to Corbyn, the Labour Party (UK) leadership election, 2016 was triggered. Corbyn won the contest, with a larger share of the vote than in 2015.

UK Independence Party

On 4 July 2016 Nigel Farage stood down as the leader of UKIP, stating that his "political ambition has been achieved" following the result of the referendum. Following the resignation of the elected party leader Diane James, Farage became an interim leader on 5 October 2016.

Scottish independence

Scottish First Minister Nicola Sturgeon said on 24 June 2016 that it was "clear that the people of Scotland see their future as part of the European Union" and that Scotland had "spoken decisively" with a "strong, unequivocal" vote to remain in the European Union. On the same day, the Scottish Government announced that officials would plan for a "highly likely" second referendum on independence from the United Kingdom and start preparing legislation to that effect. Former First Minister Alex Salmond said that the vote was a "significant and material change" in Scotland's position within the United Kingdom, and that he was certain his party would implement its manifesto on holding a second referendum. Sturgeon said she will communicate to all EU member states that "Scotland has voted to stay in the EU and I intend to discuss all options for doing so."

New political movement

In reaction to the lack of a unified pro-EU voice following the referendum, the Liberal Democrats and others discussed the launch of a new centre-left political movement. This was officially launched on 24 July 2016 as More United.

Economy

On the morning of 24 June, the pound sterling fell to its lowest level against the US dollar since 1985. The drop over the day was 8% – the biggest one-day fall in the pound since the introduction of floating exchange rates following the collapse of the Bretton Woods system in 1971.

The FTSE 100 initially fell 8%, then recovered to be 3% down by the close of trading on 24 June. The FTSE 100 index fully recovered by 29 June and subsequently rose above its pre-referendum levels.

The referendum result also had an immediate impact on some other countries. The South African rand experienced its largest single-day decline since 2008, dropping over 8% against the United States dollar. Other countries affected included Canada, whose stock exchange fell 1.70%, Nigeria and Kenya.

On 28 June 2016, former governor of Bank of England Mervyn King said that current governor Mark Carney would help to guide Britain through the next few months, adding that the BOE would undoubtedly lower the temperature of the post-referendum uncertainty, and that British citizens should keep calm, wait and see.

On 5 January 2017, Andy Haldane, chief economist and the executive director of monetary analysis and statistics at the Bank of England, admitted that the bank's forecasts (predicting an economic downturn should the referendum favour Brexit) had proved inaccurate given the subsequent strong market performance. He stated that the bank's models "were rather narrow and fragile [and] ill-equipped to making sense of behaviours that were deeply irrational" and said that his "profession is to some degree in crisis" due to this and the unforeseen 2007–2008 crisis.

Electoral Reform Society

In August 2016 the Electoral Reform Society published a highly critical report on the referendum and called for a review of how future events are run. Contrasting it very unfavourably with the 'well-informed grassroots' campaign for Scottish independence, Katie Ghose described it as "dire" with "glaring democratic deficiencies" which left voters bewildered. Ghose noted a generally negative response to establishment figures with 29% of voters saying David Cameron made them more likely to vote leave whilst only 14% said he made them want to vote remain. Looking ahead, the society called for an official organisation to highlight misleading claims and for Office of Communications (Ofcom) to define the role that broadcasters were expected to play.

Television coverage

The BBC, ITV and Sky News all provided live coverage of the counts and the reaction to the result. ITV's coverage was presented by Tom Bradby, Robert Peston and Allegra Stratton. The BBC simulcast their domestic coverage on the BBC World News Channel, BBC One and the BBC News Channel which was presented by David Dimbleby, Laura Kuenssberg and John Curtice.

The BBC called the referendum result for Leave with its projected forecast at 04:40 BST on 24 June. David Dimbleby announced it with the words:

"   **"**

Well, at twenty minutes to five, we can now say the decision taken in 1975 by this country to join the Common Market has been reversed by this referendum to leave the EU. We are absolutely clear now that there is no way that the Remain side can win. It looks as if the gap is going to be something like 52 to 48, so a four-point lead for leaving the EU, and that is the result of this referendum, which has been preceded by weeks and months of argument and dispute and all the rest of it. The British people have spoken and the answer is: we're out!

The remark about 1975 was incorrect: the UK had joined the Common Market in 1973 and the 1975 referendum was on whether to remain in it.

Television coverage			
Timeslot	**Programme**	**Presenters**	**Broad-caster**
22:00 – 06:00	EU Referendum Live	Tom Bradby, Robert Peston & Allegra Stratton	ITV
06:00 – 09:30	Good Morning Britain	Susanna Reid, Piers Morgan & Charlotte Hawkins	
09:30 – 14:00	ITV News	Alastair Stewart	
18:00 – 19:00	ITV News	Mark Austin, Robert Peston & Mary Nightingale	
22:00 – 22:45	ITV News	Tom Bradby, Robert Peston & Allegra Stratton	
21:55 – 09:00	EU Referendum – The Result	David Dimbleby, Laura Kuenssberg & John Curtice	BBC
09:00 – 13:00	EU Referendum – The Reaction	Sophie Raworth, Victoria Derbyshire & Norman Smith	
13:00 – 13:45	BBC News at One	Sophie Raworth	
13:45 – 14:00	Regional news		

Investigations into campaigns

On 9 May 2016, Leave.EU was fined £50,000 by the UK Information Commissioner's Office 'for failing to follow the rules about sending marketing messages': they sent people text messages without having first gained their permission to do so.[872,873]

On 4 March 2017, the Information Commissioner's Office also reported that it was 'conducting a wide assessment of the data-protection risks arising from the use of data analytics, including for political purposes' in relation to the Brexit campaign. It was specified that among the organisations to be investigated was Cambridge Analytica and its relationship with the Leave.EU campaign.[874,875]

Possible Russian interference

In the run-up to the Brexit referendum, Prime Minister David Cameron suggested that Russia "might be happy" with a positive Brexit vote, while the Remain campaign accused the Kremlin of secretly backing a "Leave" vote in the referendum.[876] Steve Rosenberg, the Moscow correspondent for BBC News, suggested on 26 June 2016 that the Russian government stood to gain from Brexit in several ways: (1) enabling Russian state media "to contrast post-referendum upheaval and uncertainty abroad with a picture of 'stability' back home and images of a 'strong' President Putin at the helm" in a way that bolstered the ruling United Russia party; (2) to place the value of the British pound under pressure and thereby exact retaliation for sanctions against Russia imposed after its occupation of Crimea; (3) to "make the European Union more friendly towards Russia" in the absence of British membership; and (4) to force the resignation of Cameron, who had been critical of Russian actions. After the referendum result Putin said that Brexit brought "positives and negatives".

In December 2016, MP Ben Bradshaw speculated in parliament that Russia may have interfered in the referendum.[877] In February 2017, he called on the GCHQ intelligence service to reveal the information it had on Russian interference.[878] In April 2017, the House of Commons Public Administration and Constitutional Affairs Select Committee (PACAC) issued a report suggesting that there were technical indications that a June 2016 crash of the voter-registration website was caused by a distributed denial-of-service attack using botnets.[879] The Cabinet Office, in response, stated that it did not believe that "malign intervention" had caused the crash, and instead attributed the crash "to a spike in users just before the registration deadline."

In October 2017, MP Damian Collins, chairman of the House of Commons Digital, Culture, Media and Sport Committee, sent a letter to Facebook CEO Mark Zuckerberg requesting documents relating to possible Russian government manipulation of Facebook during the Brexit referendum and the general election the following year.

In October 2017, a study by researchers at City, University of London was published in the journal *Social Science Computer Review*. The article identified 13,493 Twitter accounts that posted a total of about 65,000 messages in the last four weeks of the Brexit referendum campaign, the vast majority campaigning for a "Leave" vote; they were deleted shortly after the referendum.[880,881] A further 26,538 Twitter accounts suddenly changed their username. The research findings "raised questions about the possibility that a coordinated 'bot army' was deployed, and also about the possibility that Twitter itself may have detected and removed them without disclosing the manipulation."

In November 2017, the Electoral Commission told *The Times* that it had launched an inquiry to "examine the growing role of social media in election campaigns amid concerns from the intelligence and security agencies that Russia is trying to destabilise the democratic process in Britain."[882] The Commission was in contact with Facebook and Twitter as part of the inquiry.

After denying it for over a year, Facebook admitted in November 2017 that it was targeted by Russian trolls in the run-up to the Brexit referendum. According to Facebook, Russian-based operatives spent 97 cents to place three

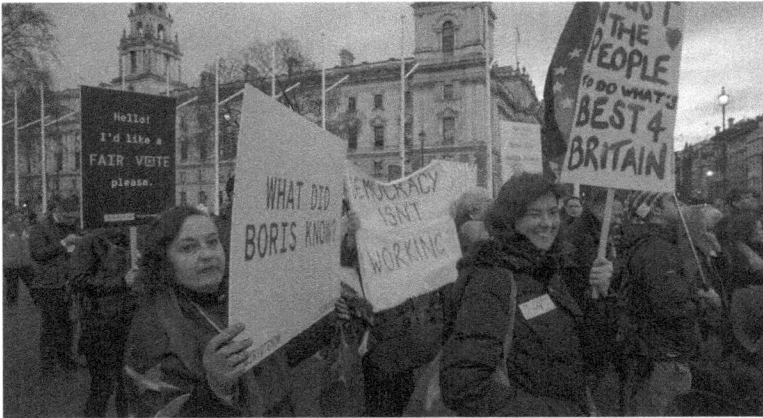

Figure 20: *A protest following the Cambridge Analytica allegations, 29 March 2018*

adverts on the social network in the run-up to the referendum, which were viewed 200 times.

On 10 June 2018, *The Guardian* reported that investigators from *The Observer* had seen evidence that Leave.EU funder Arron Banks had met Russian officials "multiple times" from 2015 to 2017 and had discussed "a multibillion dollar opportunity to buy Russian goldmines".

Campaign spending

In February 2017, the Electoral Commission announced that it was investigating the spending of Stronger In and Vote Leave, along with smaller parties, as they had not submitted all the necessary invoices, receipts, or details to back up their accounts.[883] In April 2017, the Commission specified that 'there were reasonable grounds to suspect that potential offences under the law may have occurred' in relation to Leave.EU.[884]

In May 2017, *The Irish Times* reported that £425,622 donated by the Constitutional Research Council to the Democratic Unionist Party for spending during the referendum may have originated in Saudi Arabia.[885]

In November 2017, the Electoral Commission said that it was investigating allegations that Arron Banks, an insurance businessman and the largest single financial supporter of Brexit, violated campaign spending laws.[886] The Commission's investigation focuses on both Banks and Better for the Country Limited, a company of which Banks is a director and majority shareholder.[887] The company donated £2.4 million to groups supporting British withdrawal from the EU. The investigation began after the Commission found "initial grounds to suspect breaches of electoral law."[888] The Commission specifically seeks to determine "whether or not Mr Banks was the true source of loans reported by a referendum campaigner in his name" and "whether or not Better for the Country Limited was the true source of donations made to referendum campaigners in its name, or if it was acting as an agent."

In December 2017, the Electoral Commission announced several fines related to breaches of campaign finance rules during the referendum campaign.[889] The Liberal Democrats were fined £18,000; The Immigrants Political Party was fined £2,500; the Traditional Unionist Voice had to pay £1,850; and Open Britain (formerly Britain Stronger in Europe) paid £1,250 in fines. The maximum possible fine was £20,000.

DW reported in March 2018 that Canadian whistleblower Christopher Wylie "told UK lawmakers during a committee hearing...that a firm linked to Cambridge Analytica helped the official Vote Leave campaign [the official pro-Brexit group headed by Boris Johnson and Michael Gove] circumvent campaign financing laws during the Brexit referendum."[890]

In May 2018, the Electoral Commission reported that Leave.EU had unlawfully overspent at least £77,380 – 10% more than the statutory spending limit. Additionally, its investigations found that Leave.EU inaccurately reported three loans it had received, including "a lack of transparency and incorrect reporting around who provided the loans, the dates the loans were entered into, the repayment date and the interest rate." Finally, Leave.EU had also failed to provide the required invoices for "97 payments of over £200, totalling £80,224." The Electoral Commission's director of political finance and regulation and legal counsel said that the "level of fine we have imposed has been constrained by the cap on the commission's fines". The Electoral Commission has referred the matter to the police – to date, the only such incidence in its investigations into the 2016 EU referendum.Wikipedia:Verifiability

In the same month, the Electoral Commission issued minor fines to one EU referendum permitted participant and two unions.[891]

Further reading

- George, Stephen (January 2000). "Britain: anatomy of a Eurosceptic state"[892]. *Journal of European Integration*. Taylor and Francis. **22** (1): 15–33. doi: 10.1080/07036330008429077[893].

- Usherwood, Simon (March 2007). "Proximate factors in the mobilization of anti-EU groups in France and the UK: the European Union as first-order politics"[894]. *Journal of European Integration*. Taylor and Francis. **29** (1): 3–21. doi: 10.1080/07036330601144177[895].
- Emerson, Michael (April 2016). "The Economics of a Brexit"[896]. *Intereconomics*. Springer Science+Business Media. **51** (2): 46–47. doi: 10.1007/s10272-016-0574-2[897].
- LSE Library (March 2017), " Collection of campaigning leaflets from the referendum[898]"

External links

- Examples of leaflets used during the referendum campaign[898]
- European Union[899] at Curlie (based on DMOZ)
- Electoral Commission guide to the EU Referendum[900]
- BBC News – EU Referendum[901]
- BBC Radio 4 *Why Did People Vote to Leave*[902]
- BBC Radio 4 *How We Voted Brexit*[903]

Campaigning in the United Kingdom European Union membership referendum, 2016

Part of a series of articles on the
United Kingdom in the European Union

Accession
• 1973 EC enlargement • 1975 Referendum Act • 1975 EC membership referendum • 1972 EC Act • UK rebate • 2011 EU Act

Membership

- The Euro
- European Movement UK
- Nationality law
- UK Euroscepticism
  - Maastricht Rebels
- Black Wednesday
- **Officials and bodies**
- EU Committee
- European Scrutiny Committee
- Northern Ireland Executive in Brussels
- EU Representative in London
- Young European Movement UK
- UK European Commissioners
- Permanent EU Representatives

Legislation

- 1972 EC Act
- 1986 EC (Amendment) Act
- 1993 EC (Amendment) Act
- 1998 EC (Amendment) Act
- 2002 EC (Amendment) Act
- 2008 EU (Amendment) Act
- 2011 EU Act

European Parliament Elections

- 1979
- 1984
- 1989
- 1994
- 1999
- 2004
- 2009
- 2014

- 1973 delegation
- 1st
- 2nd
- 3rd
- 4th
- 5th
- 6th
- 7th
- 8th

Withdrawal

- 2004–05 EU Bill
- 2013–14 EU (Referendum) Bill
- 2015–16 EU membership renegotiation
- 2015 EU Referendum Act
- 2016 EU (Referendum) Act (Gibraltar)
- **2016 EU membership referendum**
- Issues
- Endorsements
- Opinion polling
- Results
- Causes
- **Campaigns**
- **Organisations advocating and campaigning for a referendum**
- People's Pledge
- Labour for a Referendum
- **Leave**
- **Vote Leave** (official lead group)
  - Business for Britain
  - Conservatives for Britain
  - Students for Britain
- Labour Leave
- Leave.EU
  - Bpoplive
- Grassroots Out
- Get Britain Out
- The Freedom Association
  - Better Off Out
- **Other anti-EU advocacy organisations**
- Bruges Group
- Campaign for an Independent Britain
- **Remain**
- **Britain Stronger in Europe** (official lead group)
- Labour In for Britain
- European Movement UK
- **Other pro-EU advocacy organisations**
- Britain in Europe
- British Influence
- Business for New Europe
- Nucleus
- **Pejorative term for pro-EU advocacy**
- Project Fear
- **Media coverage**
- *Brexit: The Movie*
- *In or Out*
- **Aftermath**
- International reactions
- Terms of Withdrawal from EU (Referendum) Bills
- 2016 Conservative Party election
- 2016 Labour Party election
- 2017 Liberal Democrats Party election
- Proposed second Scottish independence referendum
- Proposed London independence
- *The New European*
- European Union (Withdrawal) Act 2018 (including meaningful vote)
- European Union (Withdrawal Agreement) Bill 2017-19
- Gibraltar
- 2017 General Election
- EU Withdrawal Agreement (Public Vote) Bill 2017-19
- UK's relations with EU after 2019
- **Triggering of Article 50 & Negotiations**
- *R (Miller) v Secretary of State for Exiting the European Union*'
- EU (Notification of Withdrawal) Act 2017
- UK invocation of Article 50
- Brexit negotiations
- Department for Exiting the EU (Brexit Department)
- Department for International Trade
- Post-referendum organisations

Calls for second vote

- European Union Withdrawal Agreement (Public Vote) Bill 2017-19
- **Organisations campaigning for a second vote via People's Vote**
- Britain for Europe
- European Movement UK
- For our Future's Sake
- Healthier IN the EU
- Open Britain
- Our Future Our Choice
- Scientists for EU
- **Other organisations campaigning for a second vote**
- Best for Britain
- **See also**
- Opposition to Brexit in the United Kingdom

- v
- t
- e[904]

Campaigning in the United Kingdom European Union membership referendum began unofficially on 20 February 2016 when Prime Minister David Cameron formally announced under the terms of the European Union Referendum Act 2015 that a referendum would be held on the issue of the United Kingdom's membership of the European Union. The official campaign period for the 2016 referendum ran from 15 April 2016 until the day of the poll on 23 June 2016.

Position of political parties

Position	Political parties (Great Britain) (England and Wales, and Scotland)	Ref
Remain	Green Party of England and Wales	
	Labour Party	
	Liberal Democrats	
	Plaid Cymru – The Party of Wales	
	Scottish Green Party	
	Scottish National Party (SNP)	
Leave		
	UK Independence Party (UKIP)	
Neutral	Conservative Party	

Figure 21: *Britain Stronger in Europe campaigners, London, June 2016.*

Figure 22: *Referendum posters for both the
Leave and Remain votes in Pimlico, London.*

Position	Political parties (Northern Ireland)	Ref
Remain	Alliance Party of Northern Ireland	
	Green Party in Northern Ireland	
	Sinn Féin	
	Social Democratic and Labour Party (SDLP)	
	Ulster Unionist Party (UUP)	
Leave		
	Democratic Unionist Party (DUP)	
	People Before Profit Alliance (PBP)	
	Traditional Unionist Voice (TUV)	

Position	Political parties (Gibraltar)	Ref
Remain	Gibraltar Social Democrats	
	Gibraltar Socialist Labour Party	
	Liberal Party of Gibraltar	

Designation of official campaign groups

At the close of applications on 31 March only Britain Stronger in Europe had applied to the Electoral Commission for the official "remain" designation. Three competing applications were submitted for the official "leave" designation. The Electoral Commission announced the designated campaign groups for the leave and remain sides on 13 April 2016, two days before the official ten-week campaign period began.[905]

- Designated official leading Remain campaigning group: Britain Stronger in Europe
- Designated official leading Leave campaigning group: Vote Leave[906]

Remain groups

The Remain Campaign was led by Britain Stronger in Europe, a cross-party lobbying group that was declared as the official "Remain" campaign for the referendum by the Electoral Commission. However there were a number of other groups that were involved in leading more specialist campaigns.

Figure 23: *A "Vote Leave" poster in Omagh saying "We send the EU £50 million every day. Let's spend it on our NHS instead."*

Leave groups

Examples of leaflets used by the remain groups can be found on the LSE Library's collection of referendum leaflets[907].

Vote Leave

Vote Leave was the lead organisation campaigning for a leave vote in the referendum. On 13 April 2016, Vote Leave was designated by the Electoral Commission as the official campaign in favour of leaving the European Union for the United Kingdom European Union membership referendum. Vote Leave was created in October 2015 and was a cross-party campaign, including members of Parliament from Conservatives, Labour, and UKIP.

Paul Marshall, a hedge fund manager gave £100,000 to Vote Leave.[908]

Leave.EU

Leave.EU campaigned for a Leave vote, and tried to become the lead campaigner. Founded in July 2015 as The Know, the campaign was relaunched in September 2015 with its present name to reflect altered wording in the referendum question. The campaign, along with rival organisation Vote Leave, aimed to be formally designated as the lead campaign for the Leave vote by the Electoral Commission. On 13 April 2016, Vote Leave was designated by the Electoral Commission as the official campaign.

Grassroots Out

Grassroots Out was formed in January 2016 as a result of infighting between Vote Leave and Leave.EUWikipedia:Citation needed and officially launched on 23 January 2016 in Kettering. Despite its name, it was started by politicians from a mixture of political parties including Peter Bone, Tom Pursglove, Liam Fox of the Conservatives, Kate Hoey of Labour, Nigel Farage of UKIP, Sammy Wilson of the DUP and George Galloway of Respect.

Labour Leave

Labour Leave campaigned within the Labour Party (UK) against the United Kingdom's continued membership of the European Union and led by Labour MP's Kate Hoey, Graham Stringer, Kelvin Hopkins, and Roger Godsiff.

Left Leave

Left Leave was a left-wing group campaigning for the United Kingdom's withdrawal from the European Union. It was made up of a coalition of left-wing political parties and organisations, such as the Communist Party of Great Britain, the Respect Party and the National Union of Rail, Maritime and Transport Workers. The Left Leave campaign was chaired by Robert Griffiths, the General Secretary of the Communist Party of Great Britain.

Trade Union and Socialist Coalition

The Trade Union and Socialist Coalition also applied to be the official "leave" campaign. It purports to represent anti-austerity campaigners who wish to leave the EU rather than other leave groups who represent "pro-business" views.

Green Leaves

Within the Green Party (which supports Remain): An organisation of Green Party members who are campaigning to leave the EU. Baroness Jenny Jones the Leader of the Green Party in the House of Lords, was a supporter.

Liberal Leave

Within the Liberal Democrats (which supports Remain): A campaign group of Liberal Democrat activists who want to leave the EU, includes councillors and former MP for Hereford, Paul Keetch. Also supported by the Liberal Party.

Campaign anthems

Both the Remain and Leave campaigns have released *songs* to promote their messages. Gruff Rhys for the Remain team entitles his song *I love EU*. For the Leave campaign, UKIP Parliamentary Candidate Mandy Boylett[909] created a parody of the Three Lions anthem. David Baddiel, who penned the original *Three Lions*, described this version as "brilliantly naff". Guido Fawkes used Mandy Boylett's song as the backing track to his end of referendum summary, *Guido's referendum best bits*.

On 13 June 2016 Mandy Boylett launched a follow up Brexit song, penning new words to Pink's *Get this party started*. The new song was immediately reported across the British Press including the Daily Express, City AM

Individual endorsements

A number of politicians, public figures, newspapers and magazines, businesses and other organisations endorsed an official position during the Referendum campaign. These are listed in the article above.

Campaigning in Gibraltar

Unlike all other British overseas territories, Gibraltar is part of the UK's EU membership and consequently the territory will participate in the referendum. As of March 2016, all major parties within the Gibraltarian parliament support a "remain" vote.Wikipedia:Citation needed

Official investigations into campaigns

On 9 May 2016, Leave.EU was fined £50,000 by the UK Information Commissioner's Office 'for failing to follow the rules about sending marketing messages': they sent people text messages without having first gained their permission to do so.[910],[911]

On 4 March 2017, the Information Commissioner's Office also reported that it was 'conducting a wide assessment of the data-protection risks arising from the use of data analytics, including for political purposes' in relation to the Brexit campaign. It was specified that among the organisations to be investigated was Cambridge Analytica and its relationship with the Leave.EU campaign. The findings were expected to be published sometime in 2017.[912,913]

On 21 April 2017, the Electoral Commission announced that it was investigating 'whether one or more donations – including of services – accepted by Leave.EU was impermissible; and whether Leave.EU's spending return was complete', because 'there were reasonable grounds to suspect that potential offences under the law may have occurred'.[914]

Results of the United Kingdom European Union membership referendum, 2016

United Kingdom European Union membership referendum		
Should the United Kingdom remain a member of the European Union or leave the European Union?		
Location	United Kingdom Gibraltar	
Date	23 June 2016	
	Votes	**%**
Leave	**17,410,742**	**51.89%**
Remain	16,141,241	48.11%
Valid votes	33,551,983	99.92%
Invalid or blank votes	25,359	0.08%
Total votes	**33,577,342**	**100.00%**
Registered voters/turnout	46,500,001	72.21%

Results by voting areas

Gibraltar

Leave   Remain

On the map, the darker shades for a colour indicate a larger margin.

Part of a series of articles on theUnited Kingdom
in the
European Union

Accession

- 1973 EC enlargement
- 1975 Referendum Act
- 1975 EC membership referendum
- 1972 EC Act
- UK rebate
- 2011 EU Act

Membership

- The Euro
- European Movement UK
- Nationality law
- UK Euroscepticism
  - Maastricht Rebels
- Black Wednesday

- **Officials and bodies**

- EU Committee
- European Scrutiny Committee
- Northern Ireland Executive in Brussels
- EU Representative in London
- Young European Movement UK
- UK European Commissioners
- Permanent EU Representatives

Legislation

- 1972 EC Act
- 1986 EC (Amendment) Act
- 1993 EC (Amendment) Act
- 1998 EC (Amendment) Act

- 2002 EC (Amendment) Act
- 2008 EU (Amendment) Act
- 2011 EU Act

European Parliament Elections

- 1979
- 1984
- 1989
- 1994
- 1999
- 2004
- 2009
- 2014

  - 1973 delegation
  - 1st
  - 2nd
  - 3rd
  - 4th
  - 5th
  - 6th
  - 7th
  - 8th

Withdrawal

- 2004–05 EU Bill
- 2013–14 EU (Referendum) Bill
- 2015–16 EU membership renegotiation
- 2015 EU Referendum Act
- 2016 EU (Referendum) Act (Gibraltar)

- **2016 EU membership referendum**

- Issues
- Endorsements
- Opinion polling
- Results
- Causes

- **Campaigns**

- **Organisations advocating and campaigning
  for a referendum**

- People's Pledge
- Labour for a Referendum

- **Leave**
- **Vote Leave** (official lead group)
  - Business for Britain
  - Conservatives for Britain
  - Students for Britain
- Labour Leave
- Leave.EU
  - Bpoplive
- Grassroots Out
- Get Britain Out
- The Freedom Association
  - Better Off Out

- **Other anti-EU advocacy organisations**
- Bruges Group
- Campaign for an Independent Britain

- **Remain**
- **Britain Stronger in Europe** (official lead group)
- Labour In for Britain
- European Movement UK

- **Other pro-EU advocacy organisations**
- Britain in Europe
- British Influence
- Business for New Europe
- Nucleus

- **Pejorative term for pro-EU advocacy**
- Project Fear

- **Media coverage**
- *Brexit: The Movie*
- *In or Out*

- **Aftermath**
- International reactions
- Terms of Withdrawal from EU (Referendum) Bills
- 2016 Conservative Party election
- 2016 Labour Party election
- 2017 Liberal Democrats Party election
- Proposed second Scottish independence referendum
- Proposed London independence

- *The New European*
- European Union (Withdrawal) Act 2018 (including meaningful vote)
- European Union (Withdrawal Agreement) Bill 2017-19
- Gibraltar
- 2017 General Election
- EU Withdrawal Agreement (Public Vote) Bill 2017-19
- UK's relations with EU after 2019

- **Triggering of Article 50 & Negotiations**

- *R (Miller) v Secretary of State for Exiting the European Union*'
- EU (Notification of Withdrawal) Act 2017
- UK invocation of Article 50
- Brexit negotiations
- Department for Exiting the EU (Brexit Department)
- Department for International Trade

- **Post-referendum organisations**

- Change Britain
- More United
- Open Britain

Calls for second vote

- European Union Withdrawal Agreement (Public Vote) Bill 2017-19

- **Organisations campaigning
  for a second vote via People's Vote**

- Britain for Europe
- European Movement UK
- For our Future's Sake
- Healthier IN the EU
- Open Britain
- Our Future Our Choice
- Scientists for EU

- **Other organisations campaigning
  for a second vote**

- Best for Britain

- **See also**

- Opposition to Brexit in the United Kingdom

- <u>v</u>
- <u>t</u>
- <u>e</u>[915]

The **United Kingdom European Union membership referendum**, also known as the **EU referendum**, took place in the United Kingdom and Gibraltar on 23 June 2016. Membership of the European Union has been a topic of debate in the United Kingdom since the country joined the European Communities (the Common Market), as it was known then, in 1973. The referendum was conducted very differently to the European Communities membership referendum in 1975 with a more localised and regionalised counting procedure and was also overseen by the Electoral Commission, a public body which did not exist at the time of the first vote. This article lists, by voting area, all the results of the referendum, each ordered into national and regional sections.

Under the provisions of the European Union Referendum Act 2015 there were a total of 382 voting areas across twelve regions using the same boundaries as used in European Parliamentary elections since 1999 under the provisions of the European Parliamentary Elections Act 2002 with votes counted at local authority level: in England the 326 local government districts were used as the voting areas; these consist of all unitary authorities, all metropolitan boroughs, all shire districts, the London boroughs, the City of London and the Isles of Scilly.[916] The nine regions of England were then also used to count the votes at the regional level with Gibraltar being regarded as part of South West England. Northern Ireland was a single voting area, as well as being a regional count, although local totals by Westminster parliamentary constituency area were announced. In Scotland the 32 Scottish council areas were used as voting areas and a single national count. In Wales the 22 Welsh council areas were used as the voting areas and a single national count.

Counting began as soon as the polls closed on 23 June from 2200 BST onwards making it the first UK-wide referendum to be counted overnight and took nine hours and twenty minutes to complete. The result of the referendum was forecast by the BBC just before 04:40 BST (around 6 hours 40 minutes after polls closed), with around 308 results declared at the time. The first result announced was Gibraltar, and the last was Cornwall.

On 23 June 2016 the recorded result was that UK voters favoured leaving the European Union, by 51.9% for Leave, and 48.1% for Remain with 263 (68.85%) voting areas voting to "Leave the European Union" to 119 (31.15%) voting areas who voted to "Remain a member of the European Union". In July 2018, three reports were issued by the Electoral Commission,[917] the Information Commissioner's Office,[918] and the House of Commons Digital, Culture, Media and Sport Committee finding criminal offences of overspending by Vote Leave, data offences, and foreign interference by Russia.[919] In August 2018, this led to legal challenges to declare the referendum void for violating common law and UK constitutional law.[920]

Figure 24:
Of the 382 voting areas in the United Kingdom a total of 263 re-
turned majority votes in favour of "Leave the European Union"
whilst 119 returned majority votes in favour of "Remain a member
of the European Union" including all 32 voting areas in Scotland.
Leave
Remain

United Kingdom

The final result of the referendum for the United Kingdom and Gibraltar was declared at Manchester Town Hall at 0720 BST on Friday 24 June 2016 after all the 382 voting areas and the twelve UK regions had declared their results by the then "chief counting officer" (CCO) for the referendum, Jenny Watson. In a UK-wide referendum, the position of "chief counting officer" (CCO) is held by the chair of the Electoral Commission. The following figures are as reported by the Electoral Commission.[921]

With a national turnout of 72% the target to secure the majority win for the winning side was 16,788,672 votes. The decision by the electorate was to "Leave the European Union" which won by a majority of 1,269,501 votes (3.78%) over those who had voted in favour of "Remain a member of the European Union" with England and Wales voting to "Leave" whilst Scotland and Northern Ireland voted to "Remain".Wikipedia:Verifiability

United Kingdom European Union membership referendum, 2016

Choice	Votes	%
Leave the European Union	**17,410,742**	**51.89**
Remain a member of the European Union	16,141,241	48.11
Valid votes	33,551,983	99.92
Invalid or blank votes	25,359	0.08
Total votes	**33,577,342**	**100.00**
Registered voters and turnout	46,500,001	72.21
Voting age population and turnout	51,356,768	65.38
Source: Electoral Commission[922]		

National referendum results (without spoiled ballots)

Leave: *17,410,742(51.9%)*	Remain: *16,141,241 (48.1%)*
▲	

Results by United Kingdom regions

Region	Elec-torate	Voter turnout, of eligible	Votes		Proportion of votes	
			Remain	Leave	Remain	Leave
East Midlands	3,384,299	74.2%	1,033,036	**1,475,479**	41.18%	**58.82%**
East of England	4,398,796	75.7%	1,448,616	**1,880,367**	43.52%	**56.48%**
Greater London	5,424,768	69.7%	**2,263,519**	1,513,232	**59.93%**	40.07%
North East England	1,934,341	69.3%	562,595	**778,103**	41.96%	**58.04%**
North West England	5,241,568	70.0%	1,699,020	**1,966,925**	46.35%	**53.65%**
Northern Ireland	1,260,955	62.7%	**440,707**	349,442	**55.78%**	44.22%
Scotland	3,987,112	67.2%	**1,661,191**	1,018,322	**62.00%**	38.00%
South East England	6,465,404	76.8%	2,391,718	**2,567,965**	48.22%	**51.78%**
South West England (including Gibraltar)	4,138,134	76.7%	1,503,019	**1,669,711**	47.37%	**52.63%**
Wales	2,270,272	71.7%	772,347	**854,572**	47.47%	**52.53%**
West Midlands	4,116,572	72.0%	1,207,175	**1,755,687**	40.74%	**59.26%**
Yorkshire and the Humber	3,877,780	70.7%	1,158,298	**1,580,937**	42.29%	**57.71%**

Results by United Kingdom constituent states

Country	Electorate	Voter turnout, of eligible	Votes		Proportion of votes	
			Remain	Leave	Remain	Leave
England (including Gibraltar)	39,005,781	73.0%	13,266,996	**15,188,406**	46.62%	**53.38%**
Northern Ireland	1,260,955	62.7%	**440,707**	349,442	**55.78%**	44.22%
Scotland	3,987,112	67.2%	**1,661,191**	1,018,322	**62.00%**	38.00%
Wales	2,270,272	71.7%	772,347	**854,572**	47.47%	**52.53%**

Returns from United Kingdom major cities

Out of over 33.5 million valid votes cast across the United Kingdom, over 8.8 million, or just over one quarter, were cast in thirty major cities that each gathered 100,000 votes or more.

In those 30 cities, votes to Remain outnumbered those to Leave by over 900,000 (4,872,810 to 3,955,595 or 55.2% to 44.8%), while in the other voting areas, the votes to Leave outnumbered those to Remain by nearly 2.2 million (13,455,147 to 11,268,431, or 54.4% to 45.6%).

City	Voting region (& Remain %) [b]	Total votes	Turn-out	Votes			Percent of votes [b]	
				Remain	Leave	Margin [c]	Re-main	Leave
Greater London	London (59.9%)	3,776,751	69.7%	**2,263,519**	1,513,232	+750,287	**59.9%**	40.1%
Birmingham	W. Midlands (40.7%)	450,702	63.7%	223,451	**227,251**	–3,800	49.6%	**50.4%**
Leeds	Yorks/-Humber (42.3%)	387,337	71.3%	**194,863**	192,474	+2,389	**50.3%**	49.7%
Sheffield	Yorks/-Humber (42.3%)	266,753	67.3%	130,735	**136,018**	–5,283	49.0%	**51.0%**
Glasgow	Scotland (62.0%)	252,809	56.2%	**168,335**	84,474	+83,861	**66.6%**	33.4%

Edinburgh	**Scot-land** (62.0%)	252,294	*72.9%*	**187,796**	64,498	+123,298	**74.4%**	25.6%
Bradford	Yorks/-Humber (42.3%)	228,488	*66.7%*	104,575	**123,913**	–19,338	45.8%	**54.2%**
Bristol	South West (41.2%)	228,445	*73.1%*	**141,027**	87,418	+53,609	**61.7%**	38.3%
Liverpool	North West (46.3%)	203,554	*64.0%*	**118,453**	85,101	+33,352	**58.2%**	41.8%
Manch-ester	North West (46.3%)	201,814	*59.7%*	**121,823**	79,991	+41,832	**60.4%**	39.6%
Wakefield	Yorks/-Humber (42.3%)	175,042	*71.1%*	58,877	**116,165**	–57,288	33.6%	**66.4%**
Cardiff	**Wales** (47.5%)	169,604	*69.6%*	**101,788**	67,816	+33,972	**60.0%**	40.0%
greater **Belfast**[923]	**N. Ireland** (55.8%)	158,365	—	**94,915**	63,450	+31,465	**59.9%**	40.1%
Coventry	W. Mid-lands (40.7%)	153,064	*69.2%*	67,967	**85,097**	–17,130	44.4%	**55.6%**
Brighton & Hove	South East (48.2%)	146,675	*74.0%*	**100,648**	46,027	+54,621	**68.6%**	31.4%
Leicester	E. Mid-lands (41.2%)	138,972	*65.0%*	**70,980**	67,992	+2,988	**51.1%**	48.9%
Sunder-land	North East (42.0%)	134,324	*64.8%*	51,930	**82,394**	–30,464	38.7%	**61.3%**
Plymouth	South West (41.2%)	133,455	*71.4%*	53,458	**79,997**	–26,539	40.1%	**59.9%**
Newcastle *upon* **Tyne**	North East (42.0%)	129,003	*67.6%*	**65,405**	63,598	+1,807	**50.7%**	49.3%
Notting-ham	E. Mid-lands (41.2%)	120,661	*61.8%*	59,318	**61,343**	–2,025	49.2%	**50.8%**
Derby	E. Mid-lands (41.2%)	120,655	*70.5%*	51,612	**69,043**	–17,431	42.8%	**57.2%**

Swansea	Wales (47.5%)	120,243	69.5%	58,307	**61,936**	−3,629	48.5%	**51.5%**
Wolver-hampton	W. Mid-lands (40.7%)	117,936	67.5%	44,138	**73,798**	−29,660	37.4%	**62.6%**
Stoke-on-Trent	W. Mid-lands (40.7%)	117,590	65.7%	36,027	**81,563**	−45,536	30.6%	**69.4%**
Kingston *upon* Hull	Yorks/-Humber (42.3%)	113,355	62.9%	36,709	**76,646**	−39,937	32.4%	**67.6%**
Salford	North West (46.3%)	109,815	63.2%	47,430	**62,385**	−14,955	43.2%	**56.8%**
York	Yorks/-Humber (42.3%)	109,600	70.6%	**63,617**	45,983	+17,634	**58.0%**	42.0%
Southamp-ton	South East (48.2%)	107,665	68.1%	49,738	**57,927**	−8,189	46.2%	**53.8%**
Aberdeen	**Scot-land** (62.0%)	104,714	67.9%	**63,985**	40,729	+23,256	**61.1%**	38.9%
Portsmouth	South East (48.2%)	98,720	70.3%	41,384	**57,336**	−15,952	41.9%	**58.1%**
Total of 30 cities	U.K. (48.1%)	**8,828,405**	—	**4,872,810**	3,955,595	+917,215	**55.2%**	44.8%
Other voting areas	U.K. (48.1%)	**24,723,578**	—	11,268,431	**13,455,147**	−2,186,716	45.6%	**54.4%**
United Kingdom	U.K.	**33,551,983**	72.2%	16,141,241	**17,410,742**	−1,269,501	48.1%	**51.9%**

Notes:
[a] Vote totals for Belfast are based on the returns from the four parliamentary constituencies in Belfast.
  These include areas in districts outside the City of Belfast.
[b] Lighter shades indicate a prevailing Remain or Leave vote of 52.0% or less; darker shades one of 58.0% or more.
[c] Margins are (arbitrarily) positive (+) when they indicate the excess of Remain votes over Leave,
  and negative (−) when they indicate the excess of Leave votes over Remain.

England

The English local districts were used as the voting areas for the referendum in England; these consist of all unitary authorities, all metropolitan boroughs, all shire districts, the London boroughs, the City of London and the Isles of Scilly.

Unlike the other constituent countries of the United Kingdom there was no centralised national count of the votes in England as counting was done within the nine separate regions. It should also be noted that figures from Gibraltar are also included.

United Kingdom European Union membership referendum, 2016 England (including Gibraltar)		
Choice	**Votes**	**%**
Leave the European Union	**15,188,406**	**53.38%**
Remain a member of the European Union	13,266,996	46.62%
Valid votes	28,455,482	99.92%
Invalid or blank votes	22,184	0.08%
Total votes	28,477,666	100.00%
Registered voters and turnout	39,005,781	73.01%

England referendum results (without spoiled ballots):

Leave: *15,188,406* (**53.4%**)	Remain: *13,266,996* (46.6%)
▲	

England was broken down into 9 regional count areas using the same regional constituency boundaries as used in European Parliamentary elections.

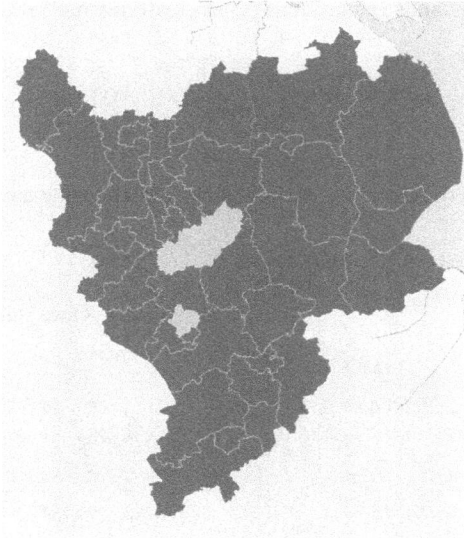

Figure 25:
Voting areas of the East Midlands region
Leave
Remain

East Midlands

United Kingdom European Union membership referendum, 2016 East Midlands		
Choice	Votes	%
Leave the European Union	**1,475,479**	**58.82%**
Remain a member of the European Union	1,033,036	41.18%
Vaild votes	2,508,515	99.92%
Invalid or blank votes	1,891	0.08%
Total votes	2,510,496	100.00%
Registered voters and turnout	3,384,299	74.18%
Source: Electoral Commission[922]		

East Midlands referendum results (without spoiled ballots):

Leave: *1,475,479* **(58.9%)**	Remain: *1,033,036* (41.1%)
▲	

The East Midlands region was broken down into 40 voting areas.

District	Voter turnout, of eligible	Votes		Proportion of votes	
		Remain	Leave	Remain	Leave
Amber Valley	76.3%	29,319	**44,501**	39.7%	**60.3%**
Ashfield	72.8%	20,179	**46,720**	30.2%	**69.8%**
Bassetlaw	74.8%	20,575	**43,392**	32.2%	**67.8%**
Blaby	76.5%	22,888	**33,583**	40.5%	**59.5%**
Bolsover	72.3%	12,242	**29,730**	29.2%	**70.8%**
Boston	77.2%	7,430	**22,974**	24.4%	**75.6%**
Broxtowe	78.3%	29,672	**35,754**	45.4%	**54.6%**
Charnwood	70.4%	43,500	**50,672**	46.2%	**53.8%**
Chesterfield	71.9%	22,946	**34,478**	40.0%	**60.0%**
Corby	74.1%	11,470	**20,611**	35.8%	**64.2%**
Daventry	80.9%	20,443	**28,938**	41.4%	**58.6%**
Derby	70.5%	51,612	**69,043**	42.8%	**57.2%**
Derbyshire Dales	81.9%	22,633	**24,095**	48.4%	**51.6%**
East Lindsey	74.9%	23,515	**56,613**	29.3%	**70.7%**
East Northamptonshire	76.9%	21,680	**30,894**	41.2%	**58.8%**
Erewash	76.0%	25,791	**40,739**	38.8%	**61.2%**
Gedling	76.5%	30,035	**37,542**	44.4%	**55.6%**
High Peak	75.6%	27,116	**27,717**	49.5%	**50.5%**
Harborough	81.4%	27,028	**27,850**	49.3%	**50.7%**
Hinckley & Bosworth	76.7%	25,969	**39,501**	39.7%	**60.3%**
Kettering	76.4%	21,030	**32,877**	39.0%	**61.0%**
Leicester	65.0%	**70,980**	67,992	**51.1%**	48.9%
Lincoln	69.3%	18,902	**24,992**	43.1%	**56.9%**
Mansfield	72.6%	16,417	**39,927**	29.1%	**70.9%**
Melton	81.3%	12,695	**17,610**	41.9%	**58.1%**

Newark and Sherwood	76.8%	26,571	**40,516**	39.6%	**60.4%**
North East Derbyshire	75.2%	22,075	**37,235**	37.2%	**62.8%**
Northampton	72.6%	43,805	**61,454**	41.6%	**58.4%**
North Kesteven	78.4%	25,570	**42,183**	37.7%	**62.3%**
North West Leicester-shire	77.9%	22,642	**34,969**	39.3%	**60.7%**
Nottingham	61.8%	59,318	**61,343**	49.2%	**50.8%**
Oadby and Wigston	73.7%	14,292	**17,173**	45.4%	**54.6%**
Rushcliffe	81.5%	**40,522**	29,888	**57.6%**	42.4%
Rutland	78.1%	11,353	**11,613**	49.4%	**50.6%**
South Derbyshire	76.8%	22,479	**34,216**	39.6%	**60.4%**
South Holland	75.3%	13,074	**36,423**	26.4%	**73.6%**
South Kesteven	78.2%	33,047	**49,424**	40.1%	**59.9%**
South Northamptonshire	79.4%	25,853	**30,771**	45.7%	**54.3%**
Wellingborough	75.4%	15,462	**25,679**	37.6%	**62.4%**
West Lindsey	74.5%	20,906	**33,847**	38.2%	**61.8%**

East of England

United Kingdom European Union membership referendum, 2016 East of England		
Choice	**Votes**	**%**
Leave the European Union	**1,880,367**	**56.48%**
Remain a member of the European Union	1,448,616	43.52%
Vaild votes	3,328,983	99.93%
Invalid or blank votes	2,329	0.07%
Total votes	3,331,312	100.00%
Registered voters and turnout	4,398,796	75.73%
Source: Electoral Commission[922]		

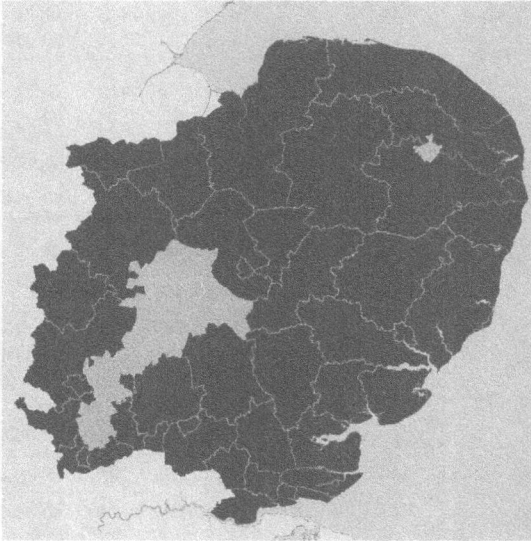

Figure 26:
Voting areas of the East of England region
Leave
Remain

East of England referendum results (without spoiled ballots):

Leave: 1,880,367 (56.5%)	Remain: 1,448,616 (43.5%)
▲	

The East of England region was broken down into 47 voting areas.

District	Voter turnout, of eligible	Votes		Proportion of votes	
		Remain	Leave	Remain	Leave
Babergh	78.2%	25,309	**29,933**	45.8%	**54.2%**
Basildon	73.8%	30,748	**67,251**	31.4%	**68.6%**
Bedford	72.1%	41,497	**44,569**	48.2%	**51.8%**
Braintree	76.6%	33,523	**52,713**	38.9%	**61.1%**
Breckland	74.3%	26,313	**47,235**	35.8%	**64.2%**
Brentwood	79.5%	19,077	**27,627**	40.8%	**59.2%**
Broadland	78.3%	35,469	**42,268**	45.6%	**54.4%**
Broxbourne	73.7%	17,166	**33,706**	33.7%	**66.3%**
Cambridge	72.2%	**42,682**	15,117	**73.8%**	26.2%
Castle Point	75.3%	14,154	**37,691**	27.3%	**72.7%**
Central Bedfordshire	77.8%	69,670	**89,134**	43.9%	**56.1%**
Chelmsford	77.6%	47,545	**53,249**	47.2%	**52.8%**
Colchester	75.1%	44,414	**51,305**	46.4%	**53.6%**
Dacorum	79.1%	42,542	**43,702**	49.3%	**50.7%**
East Cambridgeshire	77.0%	23,599	**24,487**	49.1%	**50.9%**
East Hertfordshire	80.3%	42,372	**42,994**	49.6%	**50.4%**
Epping Forest	76.8%	28,676	**48,176**	37.3%	**62.7%**
Fenland	73.7%	15,055	**37,571**	28.6%	**71.4%**
Forest Heath	72.5%	9,791	**18,160**	35.0%	**65.0%**
Great Yarmouth	69.0%	14,284	**35,844**	28.5%	**71.5%**
Harlow	73.5%	13,867	**29,602**	31.9%	**68.1%**
Hertsmere	76.6%	27,593	**28,532**	49.2%	**50.8%**
Huntingdonshire	77.8%	45,729	**54,198**	45.8%	**54.2%**
Ipswich	72.5%	27,698	**38,655**	41.7%	**58.3%**
King's Lynn and West Norfolk	74.7%	28,587	**56,493**	33.6%	**66.4%**
Luton	66.2%	36,708	**47,773**	43.5%	**56.5%**
Maldon	79.1%	14,529	**24,302**	37.4%	**62.6%**
Mid Suffolk	78.1%	27,391	**33,794**	44.8%	**55.2%**
North Hertfordshire	78.2%	**42,234**	35,438	**54.4%**	45.6%
North Norfolk	76.8%	26,214	**37,576**	41.1%	**58.9%**

Norwich	69.1%	**37,326**	29,040	**56.2%**	43.8%
Peterborough	72.3%	34,176	**53,216**	39.1%	**60.9%**
Rochford	78.8%	17,510	**34,937**	33.4%	**66.6%**
South Cambridgeshire	81.2%	**56,128**	37,061	**60.2%**	39.8%
Southend-on-Sea	72.8%	39,348	**54,522**	41.9%	**58.1%**
South Norfolk	78.5%	38,817	**41,541**	48.3%	**51.7%**
St Albans	82.4%	**54,208**	32,237	**62.7%**	37.3%
St. Edmundsbury	76.7%	26,986	**35,224**	43.4%	**56.6%**
Stevenage	73.7%	18,659	**27,126**	40.8%	**59.2%**
Suffolk Coastal	80.6%	37,218	**41,966**	47.0%	**53.0%**
Tendring	74.4%	25,210	**57,447**	30.5%	**69.5%**
Three Rivers	78.4%	25,751	**27,097**	48.7%	**51.3%**
Thurrock	72.7%	22,151	**57,765**	27.7%	**72.3%**
Uttlesford	80.2%	25,619	**26,324**	49.3%	**50.7%**
Watford	71.6%	23,167	**23,419**	49.7%	**50.3%**
Waveney	72.6%	24,356	**41,290**	37.1%	**62.9%**
Welwyn Hatfield	75.0%	27,550	**31,060**	47.0%	**53.0%**

Greater London

United Kingdom European Union membership referendum, 2016 Greater London		
Choice	**Votes**	**%**
Remain a member of the European Union	**2,263,519**	**59.93%**
Leave the European Union	1,513,232	40.07%
Vaild votes	3,776,751	99.88%
Invalid or blank votes	4,453	0.12%
Total votes	3,781,204	100.00%
Registered voters and turnout	5,424,768	69.70%
Source: Electoral Commission[922]		

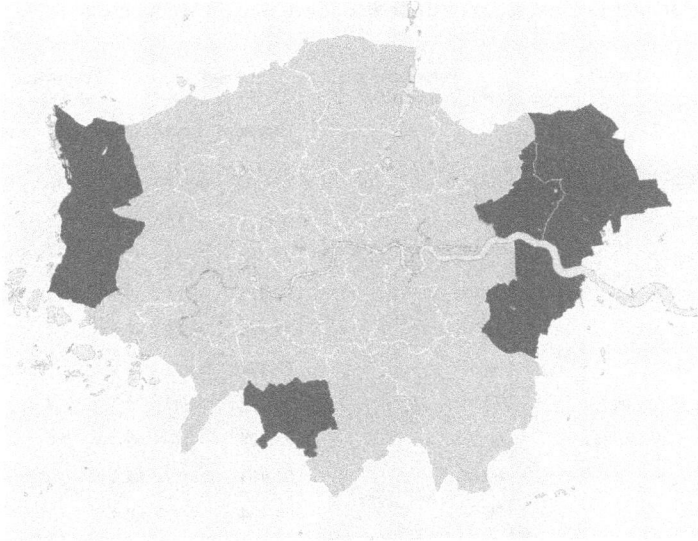

Figure 27:
Voting areas of the London region
Leave
Remain

Greater London referendum results (without spoiled ballots):

Leave: 1,513,232 (40%)	Remain: 2,263,519 (60%)
▲	

The Greater London region was broken down into 33 voting areas.

District	Voter turnout, of eligible	Votes		Proportion of votes	
		Remain	Leave	Remain	Leave
Barking and Dagenham	63.8%	27,750	**46,130**	37.6%	**62.4%**
Barnet	72.1%	**100,210**	60,823	**62.2%**	37.8%
Bexley	75.2%	47,603	**80,886**	37.0%	**63.0%**
Brent	65.0%	**72,523**	48,881	**59.7%**	40.3%
Bromley	78.8%	**92,398**	90,034	**50.6%**	49.4%
Camden	65.4%	**71,295**	23,838	**74.9%**	25.1%
City of London	73.5%	**3,312**	1,087	**75.3%**	24.7%
City of Westminster	64.9%	**53,928**	24,268	**69.0%**	31.0%
Croydon	69.8%	**92,913**	78,221	**54.3%**	45.7%
Ealing	70.0%	**90,024**	59,017	**60.4%**	39.6%
Enfield	69.0%	**76,425**	60,481	**55.8%**	44.2%
Greenwich	69.5%	**65,248**	52,117	**55.6%**	44.4%
Hackney	65.1%	**83,398**	22,868	**78.5%**	21.5%
Haringey	70.5%	**79,991**	25,855	**75.6%**	24.4%
Harrow	72.2%	**64,042**	53,183	**54.6%**	45.4%
Hammersmith and Fulham	69.9%	**56,188**	24,054	**70.0%**	30.0%
Havering	76.0%	42,201	**96,885**	30.3%	**69.7%**
Hillingdon	68.9%	58,040	**74,982**	43.6%	**56.4%**
Hounslow	69.7%	**58,755**	56,321	**51.1%**	48.9%
Islington	70.3%	**76,420**	25,180	**75.2%**	24.8%
Kensington and Chelsea	65.9%	**37,601**	17,138	**68.7%**	31.3%
Kingston upon Thames	78.3%	**52,533**	32,737	**61.6%**	38.4%
Lambeth	67.3%	**111,584**	30,340	**78.6%**	21.4%
Lewisham	63.0%	**86,955**	37,518	**69.9%**	30.1%
Merton	73.4%	**63,003**	37,097	**62.9%**	37.1%
Newham	59.2%	**55,328**	49,371	**52.8%**	47.2%
Redbridge	67.5%	**69,213**	59,020	**54.0%**	46.0%
Richmond upon Thames	82.0%	**75,396**	33,410	**69.3%**	30.7%
Southwark	66.1%	**94,293**	35,209	**72.8%**	27.2%
Sutton	76.0%	49,319	**57,241**	46.3%	**53.7%**

Tower Hamlets	64.5%	**73,011**	35,224	**67.5%**	32.5%
Waltham Forest	66.6%	**64,156**	44,395	**59.1%**	40.9%
Wandsworth	71.9%	**118,463**	39,421	**75.0%**	25.0%

North East England

United Kingdom European Union membership referendum, 2016 North East England		
Choice	Votes	%
Leave the European Union	**778,103**	**58.04%**
Remain a member of the European Union	562,595	41.96%
Vaild votes	1,340,698	99.95%
Invalid or blank votes	689	0.05%
Total votes	1,341,387	100.00%
Registered voters and turnout	1,934,341	69.35%
Source: Electoral Commission[922]		

North East England referendum results (without spoiled ballots):

Leave: 778,103 (58%)	Remain: 562,595 (42%)
▲	

The North East England region was broken down into 12 voting areas.

District	Voter turnout, of eligible	Votes		Proportion of votes	
		Remain	Leave	Remain	Leave
Darlington	71.0%	24,172	**30,994**	43.8%	**56.2%**
Durham	68.7%	113,521	**153,877**	42.5%	**57.5%**
Gateshead	70.6%	44,429	**58,529**	43.2%	**57.8%**
Hartlepool	65.5%	14,029	**32,071**	30.4%	**69.6%**
Middlesbrough	64.9%	21,181	**40,177**	34.5%	**65.5%**
Newcastle upon Tyne	67.6%	**65,405**	63,598	**50.7%**	49.3%

North Tyneside	72.3%		52,873	60,589	46.6%	53.4%
Northumberland	74.3%		82,022	96,699	45.9%	54.1%
Redcar and Cleveland	70.2%		24,586	48,128	33.8%	66.2%
South Tyneside	68.2%		30,014	49,065	38.0%	62.0%
Stockton-on-Tees	71.0%		38,433	61,982	38.3%	61.7%
Sunderland	64.8%		51,930	82,394	38.7%	61.3%

North West England

United Kingdom European Union membership referendum, 2016 North West England		
Choice	Votes	%
Leave the European Union	1,966,925	53.65%
Remain a member of the European Union	1,699,020	46.35%
Valid votes	3,665,945	99.93%
Invalid or blank votes	2,682	0.07%
Total votes	3,668,627	100.00%
Registered voters and turnout	5,241,568	69.99%
Source: Electoral Commission[922]		

North West England referendum results (without spoiled ballots):

Leave: 1,966,925 (53.6%)	Remain: 1,699,020 (46.4%)

▲

The North West England region was broken down into 39 voting areas.

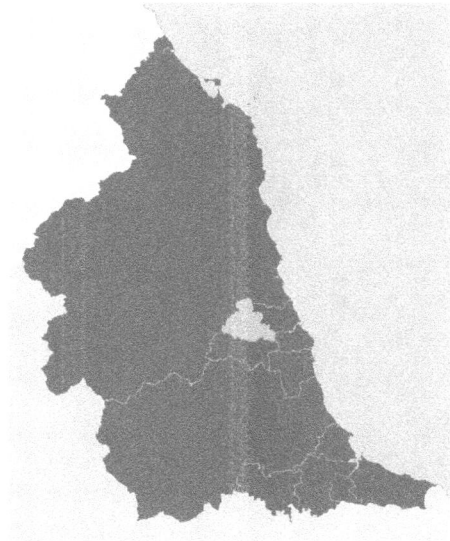

Figure 28:
Voting areas of the North East England region
Leave
Remain

District	Voter turnout, of eligible	Votes		Proportion of votes	
		Remain	Leave	Remain	Leave
Allerdale	72.9%	22,429	**31,809**	41.4%	**58.6%**
Barrow-in-Furness	67.8%	14,207	**21,867**	39.4%	**60.6%**
Blackburn with Darwen	65.2%	28,522	**36,799**	43.7%	**56.3%**
Blackpool	65.4%	21,781	**45,146**	32.5%	**67.5%**
Bolton	70.1%	57,589	**80,491**	41.7%	**58.3%**
Burnley	67.2%	14,462	**28,854**	33.4%	**66.6%**
Bury	71.3%	46,354	**54,674**	45.9%	**54.1%**
Carlisle	74.5%	23,788	**35,895**	39.9%	**60.1%**
Cheshire East	77.3%	107,962	**113,163**	48.8%	**51.2%**
Cheshire West and Chester	74.5%	95,455	**98,082**	49.3%	**50.7%**
Chorley	75.5%	27,417	**36,098**	43.2%	**56.8%**
Copeland	70.0%	14,419	**23,528**	38.0%	**62.0%**

Eden	75.7%	14,807	**16,911**	46.7%	**53.3%**
Fylde	75.5%	19,889	**26,317**	43.0%	**57.0%**
Halton	68.2%	27,678	**37,327**	42.6%	**57.4%**
Hyndburn	64.7%	13,569	**26,568**	33.8%	**66.2%**
Knowsley	63.5%	34,345	**36,558**	48.4%	**51.6%**
Lancaster	72.6%	35,732	**37,309**	48.9%	**51.1%**
Liverpool	64.0%	**118,453**	85,101	**58.2%**	41.8%
Manchester	59.7%	**121,823**	79,991	**60.4%**	39.6%
Oldham	67.9%	42,034	**65,369**	39.1%	**60.9%**
Pendle	70.2%	16,704	**28,631**	36.8%	**63.2%**
Preston	68.7%	30,227	**34,518**	46.7%	**53.3%**
Ribble Valley	79.0%	15,892	**20,550**	43.6%	**56.4%**
Rochdale	65.9%	41,217	**62,014**	39.9%	**60.1%**
Rossendale	72.4%	15,012	**23,169**	39.3%	**60.7%**
Salford	63.2%	47,430	**62,385**	43.2%	**56.8%**
Sefton	71.7%	**76,702**	71,176	**51.9%**	48.1%
South Lakeland	79.7%	**34,531**	30,800	**52.9%**	47.1%
South Ribble	75.3%	26,406	**37,318**	41.4%	**58.6%**
St. Helens	68.8%	39,322	**54,357**	42.0%	**58.0%**
Stockport	74.9%	**85,559**	77,930	**52.5%**	47.5%
Tameside	66.0%	43,118	**67,829**	38.9%	**61.1%**
Trafford	75.8%	**72,293**	53,018	**57.7%**	42.3%
Warrington	73.3%	52,657	**62,487**	45.7%	**54.3%**
West Lancashire	74.4%	28,546	**35,323**	44.7%	**55.3%**
Wigan	69.2%	58,942	**104,331**	36.1%	**63.9%**
Wirral	70.9%	**88,931**	83,069	**51.7%**	48.3%
Wyre	74.6%	22,816	**40,163**	36.2%	**63.8%**

Figure 29:
Voting areas of the North West England region
Leave
Remain

South East England

United Kingdom European Union membership referendum, 2016 South East England		
Choice	**Votes**	**%**
Leave the European Union	**2,567,965**	**51.78%**
Remain a member of the European Union	2,391,718	48.22%
Vaild votes	4,959,683	99.93%
Invalid or blank votes	3,427	0.07%
Total votes	4,963,110	100.00%
Registered voters and turnout	6,465,404	76.76%
Source: Electoral Commission[922]		

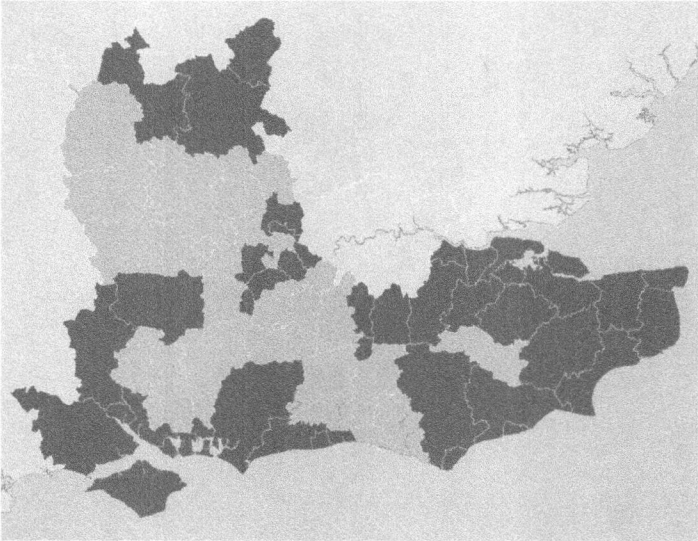

Figure 30:
Voting areas of the South East England region
Leave
Remain

South East England referendum results (without spoiled ballots):

Leave: 2,567,965 (51.8%)	Remain: 2,391,718 (48.2%)
▲	

The South East England region was broken down into 67 voting areas.

District	Voter turnout, of eligible	Votes		Proportion of votes	
		Remain	Leave	Remain	Leave
Adur	76.4%	16,914	**20,315**	45.4%	**54.6%**
Arun	77.8%	34,193	**56,936**	37.5%	**62.5%**
Ashford	77.1%	28,314	**41,472**	40.6%	**59.4%**
Aylesbury Vale	78.4%	52,877	**53,956**	49.5%	**50.5%**
Basingstoke and Deane	78.0%	48,257	**52,071**	48.1%	**51.9%**
Bracknell Forest	76.1%	29,888	**35,002**	46.1%	**53.9%**
Brighton & Hove	74.0%	**100,648**	46,027	**68.6%**	31.4%
Canterbury	75.0%	40,169	**41,879**	49.0%	**51.0%**
Cherwell	75.5%	40,668	**41,168**	49.7%	**50.3%**
Chichester	77.8%	35,011	**36,326**	49.1%	**50.9%**
Chiltern	83.5%	**32,241**	26,363	**55.0%**	45.0%
Crawley	73.2%	22,388	**31,447**	41.6%	**58.4%**
Dartford	75.5%	19,985	**35,870**	35.8%	**64.2%**
Dover	76.5%	24,606	**40,410**	37.8%	**62.2%**
Eastbourne	74.7%	22,845	**30,700**	42.7%	**57.3%**
Eastleigh	78.2%	36,172	**39,902**	47.5%	**52.5%**
East Hampshire	81.6%	**37,346**	36,576	**50.5%**	49.5%
Elmbridge	78.1%	**45,841**	31,162	**59.5%**	40.5%
Epsom and Ewell	80.4%	**23,596**	21,707	**52.1%**	47.9%
Fareham	79.6%	32,210	**39,525**	44.9%	**55.1%**
Gosport	73.5%	16,671	**29,456**	36.1%	**63.9%**
Gravesham	74.9%	18,876	**35,643**	34.6%	**65.4%**
Guildford	76.9%	**44,155**	34,458	**56.2%**	43.8%
Hart	82.6%	**30,282**	27,513	**52.4%**	47.6%
Hastings	71.6%	20,011	**24,339**	45.1%	**54.9%**
Havant	74.1%	26,582	**44,047**	37.6%	**62.4%**
Horsham	81.6%	**43,785**	41,303	**51.5%**	48.5%
Isle of Wight	72.3%	30,207	**49,173**	38.1%	**61.9%**
Lewes	77.8%	**30,974**	28,508	**52.1%**	47.9%
Maidstone	76.0%	36,762	**52,365**	41.2%	**58.8%**
Medway	72.1%	49,889	**88,997**	35.9%	**64.1%**

Mid Sussex	80.7%	**46,471**	41,057	**53.1%**	46.9%
Milton Keynes	73.6%	63,393	**67,063**	48.6%	**51.4%**
Mole Valley	82.1%	**29,088**	25,708	**53.1%**	46.9%
New Forest	79.2%	47,199	**64,541**	42.2%	**57.8%**
Oxford	72.3%	**49,424**	20,913	**70.3%**	29.7%
Portsmouth	70.3%	41,384	**57,336**	41.9%	**58.1%**
Reading	72.5%	**43,385**	31,382	**58.0%**	42.0%
Reigate and Banstead	78.2%	40,181	**40,980**	49.5%	**50.5%**
Rother	79.3%	23,916	**33,753**	41.5%	**58.5%**
Runnymede	76.0%	20,259	**24,035**	45.7%	**54.3%**
Rushmoor	74.1%	20,384	**28,396**	41.8%	**58.2%**
Sevenoaks	80.6%	32,091	**38,258**	45.6%	**54.4%**
Shepway	74.9%	22,884	**37,729**	37.8%	**62.2%**
Slough	62.1%	24,911	**29,631**	45.7%	**54.3%**
Southampton	68.1%	49,738	**57,927**	46.2%	**53.8%**
South Bucks	78.0%	20,077	**20,647**	49.3%	**50.7%**
South Oxfordshire	80.7%	**46,245**	37,865	**55.0%**	45.0%
Spelthorne	77.9%	22,474	**34,135**	39.7%	**60.3%**
Surrey Heath	79.8%	25,638	**26,667**	49.0%	**51.0%**
Swale	74.2%	28,481	**47,388**	37.5%	**62.5%**
Tandridge	80.3%	24,251	**27,169**	47.2%	**52.8%**
Test Valley	79.6%	36,170	**39,091**	48.1%	**51.9%**
Thanet	72.7%	26,065	**46,037**	36.2%	**63.8%**
Tonbridge and Malling	79.6%	32,792	**41,229**	44.3%	**55.7%**
Tunbridge Wells	79.1%	**35,676**	29,320	**54.9%**	45.1%
Vale of White Horse	81.1%	**43,462**	33,192	**56.7%**	43.3%
Waverley	82.3%	**44,341**	31,601	**58.4%**	41.6%
Wealden	80.0%	44,084	**52,808**	45.5%	**54.5%**
West Berkshire	79.9%	**48,300**	44,977	**51.8%**	48.2%
West Oxfordshire	79.7%	**35,236**	30,435	**53.7%**	46.3%
Winchester	81.2%	**42,878**	29,886	**58.9%**	41.4%
Windsor and Maiden-head	79.7%	**44,086**	37,706	**53.9%**	46.1%
Woking	77.4%	**31,007**	24,214	**56.2%**	43.8%
Wokingham	79.2%	**55,272**	42,229	**56.7%**	43.3%

| Worthing | 75.4% | 28,851 | **32,515** | 47.0% | **53.0%** |
| Wycombe | 75.7% | **49,261** | 45,529 | **52.0%** | 48.0% |

South West England (including Gibraltar)

United Kingdom European Union membership referendum, 2016 South West England (including Gibraltar)		
Choice	**Votes**	**%**
Leave the European Union	**1,669,711**	**52.62%**
Remain a member of the European Union	1,503,019	47.37%
Vaild votes	3,172,730	99.93%
Invalid or blank votes	2,179	0.07%
Total votes	3,174,909	100.00%
Registered voters and turnout	4,138,134	73.01%
Source: Electoral Commission[922]		

South West England (including Gibraltar) referendum results (without spoiled ballots):

Leave: *1,669,711* **(52.6%)**	Remain: *1,503,019* (47.4%)
▲	

The South West England region was broken down into 38 voting areas.

District	Voter turnout, of eligible	Votes		Proportion of votes	
		Remain	Leave	Remain	Leave
Bath and North East Somerset	77.1%	**60,878**	44,352	**57.9%**	42.1%
Bournemouth	69.2%	41,473	**50,453**	45.1%	**54.9%**
Bristol	73.1%	**141,027**	87,418	**61.7%**	38.3%
Cheltenham	75.8%	**37,081**	28,932	**56.2%**	43.8%

Christchurch	79.3%	12,782	**18,268**	41.2%	**58.8%**
Cornwall	77.0%	140,540	**182,665**	43.5%	**56.5%**
Cotswold	79.8%	**28,015**	26,806	**51.1%**	48.9%
East Devon	78.9%	40,743	**48,040**	45.9%	**54.1%**
East Dorset	81.3%	24,786	**33,702**	42.4%	**57.6%**
Exeter	73.8%	**35,270**	28,533	**55.3%**	44.7%
Forest of Dean	77.4%	21,392	**30,251**	41.4%	**58.6%**
Gloucester	72.0%	26,801	**37,776**	41.5%	**58.5%**
Isles of Scilly	79.2%	**803**	621	**56.4%**	43.6%
Mendip	76.9%	**33,427**	32,028	**51.1%**	48.9%
Mid Devon	79.3%	22,400	**25,606**	46.7%	**53.3%**
North Dorset	79.7%	18,399	**23,802**	43.6%	**56.4%**
North Devon	76.8%	24,931	**33,100**	43.0%	**57.0%**
North Somerset	77.4%	59,572	**64,976**	47.8%	**52.2%**
Plymouth	71.4%	53,458	**79,997**	40.1%	**59.9%**
Poole	75.3%	35,741	**49,707**	41.8%	**58.2%**
Purbeck	78.9%	11,754	**16,966**	40.9%	**59.1%**
Sedgemoor	76.3%	26,545	**41,869**	38.8%	**61.2%**
South Gloucestershire	76.2%	74,928	**83,405**	47.3%	**52.7%**
South Hams	80.2%	**29,308**	26,142	**52.9%**	47.1%
South Somerset	78.6%	42,527	**56,940**	42.8%	**57.2%**
Stroud	80.0%	**40,446**	33,618	**54.6%**	45.4%
Swindon	75.8%	51,220	**61,745**	45.3%	**54.7%**
Taunton Deane	78.1%	30,944	**34,789**	47.1%	**52.9%**
Teignbridge	79.3%	37,949	**44,363**	46.1%	**53.9%**
Tewkesbury	79.1%	25,084	**28,568**	46.8%	**53.2%**
Torbay	73.6%	27,935	**47,889**	36.8%	**63.2%**
Torridge	78.3%	16,229	**25,200**	39.2%	**60.8%**
West Dorset	79.4%	31,924	**33,267**	49.0%	**51.0%**
West Devon	81.2%	16,658	**18,937**	46.8%	**53.2%**
West Somerset	79.1%	8,566	**13,168**	39.4%	**60.6%**
Wiltshire	78.8%	137,258	**151,637**	47.5%	**52.5%**
Weymouth and Portland	75.8%	14,903	**23,352**	39.0%	**61.0%**

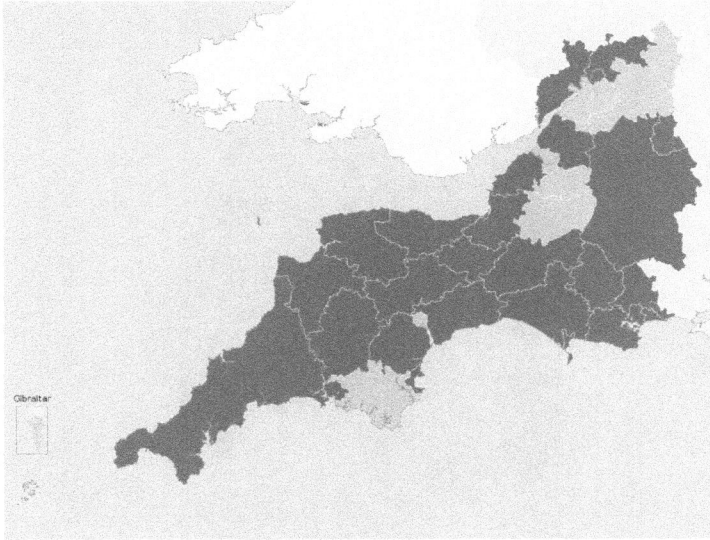

Figure 31:
Voting areas of the South West England region (together with Gibraltar)
Leave
Remain

Gibraltar

For the purposes of this referendum and as has been the case with European Parliamentary elections, the overseas territory of Gibraltar was a single voting area placed in the South West England constituency. It is the first time the territory has taken part in any UK-wide referendum as they did not participate in either the original 1975 EC Referendum or the 2011 AV Referendum as Gibraltar does not send any Members of Parliament to the House of Commons in Westminster.

Overseas Territory	Voter turnout, of eligible	Votes		Proportion of votes	
		Remain	Leave	Remain	Leave
Gibraltar	83.6%	**19,322**	823	**95.9%**	4.1%

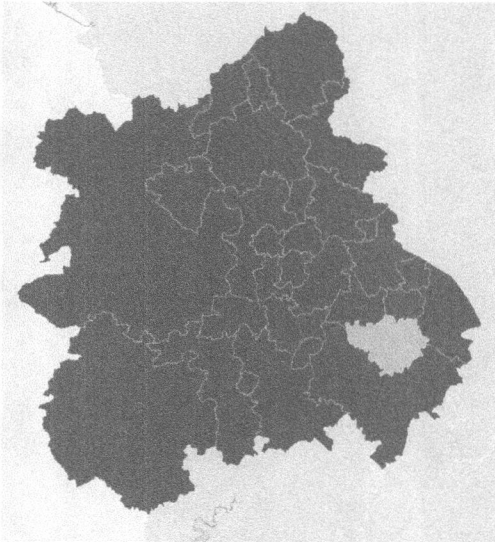

Figure 32:
Voting areas of the West Midlands region
Leave
Remain

West Midlands

United Kingdom European Union membership referendum, 2016 West Midlands		
Choice	**Votes**	**%**
Leave the European Union	**1,755,687**	**59.26%**
Remain a member of the European Union	1,207,175	40.74%
Vaild votes	2,962,862	99.92%
Invalid or blank votes	2,507	0.08%
Total votes	2,965,369	100.00%
Registered voters and turnout	4,116,572	72.03%
Source: Electoral Commission[922]		

West Midlands referendum results (without spoiled ballots):

Leave: *1,775,687* (59.3%)	Remain: *1,207,175* (40.7%)
▲	

The West Midlands region was broken down into 30 voting areas.

District	Voter turnout, of eligible	Votes		Proportion of votes	
		Remain	Leave	Remain	Leave
Birmingham	63.7%	223,451	**227,251**	49.6%	**50.4%**
Bromsgrove	79.3%	26,252	**32,563**	44.6%	**55.4%**
Cannock Chase	71.4%	16,684	**36,894**	31.1%	**68.9%**
Coventry	69.2%	67,967	**85,097**	44.4%	**55.6%**
Dudley	71.7%	56,780	**118,446**	32.4%	**67.6%**
East Staffordshire	74.3%	22,850	**39,266**	36.8%	**63.2%**
Herefordshire	78.3%	44,148	**64,122**	40.8%	**59.2%**
Lichfield	78.7%	26,064	**37,214**	41.2%	**58.8%**
Malvern Hills	80.5%	23,203	**25,294**	47.8%	**52.2%**
Newcastle-under-Lyme	74.3%	25,477	**43,457**	37.0%	**63.0%**
North Warwickshire	76.2%	12,569	**25,385**	33.1%	**66.9%**
Nuneaton and Bed- worth	74.3%	23,736	**46,095**	34.0%	**66.0%**
Redditch	75.2%	17,303	**28,579**	37.7%	**62.3%**
Rugby	79.0%	25,350	**33,199**	43.3%	**56.7%**
Sandwell	66.5%	49,004	**98,250**	33.3%	**66.7%**
Shropshire	77.3%	78,987	**104,166**	43.1%	**56.9%**
Solihull	76.0%	53,466	**68,484**	43.8%	**56.2%**
South Staffordshire	77.8%	23,444	**43,248**	35.2%	**64.8%**
Stafford	77.8%	34,098	**43,386**	44.0%	**56.0%**
Staffordshire Moor- lands	75.3%	21,076	**38,684**	35.3%	**64.7%**
Stoke-on-Trent	65.7%	36,027	**81,563**	30.6%	**69.4%**
Stratford-on-Avon	80.8%	38,341	**40,817**	48.4%	**51.6%**
Tamworth	74.1%	13,705	**28,424**	32.5%	**67.5%**
Telford and Wrekin	72.1%	32,954	**56,649**	36.8%	**63.2%**
Walsall	69.6%	43,572	**92,007**	32.1%	**67.9%**

Warwick	79.2%	**47,976**	33,642	**58.8%**	41.2%
Wolverhampton	67.5%	44,138	**73,798**	37.4%	**62.6%**
Worcester	73.8%	25,125	**29,114**	46.3%	**53.7%**
Wychavon	80.8%	32,188	**44,201**	42.1%	**57.9%**
Wyre Forest	74.0%	21,240	**36,392**	36.9%	**63.1%**

Yorkshire and the Humber

United Kingdom European Union membership referendum, 2016 Yorkshire and the Humber		
Choice	**Votes**	**%**
Leave the European Union	**1,580,937**	**57.71%**
Remain a member of the European Union	1,158,298	42.29%
Vaild votes	2,739,235	99.93%
Invalid or blank votes	1,937	0.07%
Total votes	2,741,172	100.00%
Registered voters and turnout	3,877,780	70.69%
Source: Electoral Commission[922]		

Yorkshire and the Humber referendum results (without spoiled ballots):

Leave: *1,580,937* **(57.7%)**	Remain: *1,158,298 (42.3%)*
▲	

The Yorkshire and the Humber region was broken down into 21 voting areas.

District	Voter turnout, of eligible	Votes		Proportion of votes	
		Remain	Leave	Remain	Leave
Barnsley	69.9%	38,951	**83,958**	31.7%	**68.3%**
Bradford	66.7%	104,575	**123,913**	45.8%	**54.2%**
Calderdale	71.0%	46,950	**58,975**	44.3%	**55.7%**
Craven	81.0%	16,930	**18,961**	47.2%	**52.8%**

Doncaster	69.5%		46,922	104,260	31.0%	69.0%
East Riding of York-shire	74.9%		78,779	120,136	39.6%	60.4%
Hambleton	78.4%		25,480	29,502	46.3%	53.7%
Harrogate	78.8%		48,211	46,374	51.0%	49.0%
Kingston upon Hull	62.9%		36,709	76,646	32.4%	67.6%
Kirklees	70.8%		98,485	118,755	45.3%	54.7%
Leeds	71.3%		194,863	192,474	50.3%	49.7%
North East Lincolnshire	67.9%		23,797	55,185	30.1%	69.9%
North Lincolnshire	71.9%		29,947	58,915	33.7%	66.3%
Richmondshire	75.1%		11,945	15,691	43.2%	56.8%
Rotherham	69.5%		44,115	93,272	32.1%	67.9%
Ryedale	77.2%		14,340	17,710	44.7%	55.3%
Scarborough	73.0%		22,999	37,512	38.0%	62.0%
Selby	79.1%		21,071	30,532	40.8%	59.2%
Sheffield	67.3%		130,735	136,018	49.0%	51.0%
Wakefield	71.1%		58,877	116,165	33.6%	66.4%
York	70.6%		63,617	45,983	58.0%	42.0%

Northern Ireland

Northern Ireland was a single voting area, as well as being a regional count although local totals were announced in each of the Westminister Parliamentary constituency areas within Northern Ireland but did not constitute as voting areas.

United Kingdom European Union membership referendum, 2016 Northern Ireland		
Choice	Votes	%
Remain a member of the European Union	**440,707**	**55.78%**
Leave the European Union	349,442	44.22%
Vaild votes	790,149	99.95%
Invalid or blank votes	374	0.05%
Total votes	790,523	100.00%
Registered voters and turnout	1,260,955	62.69%

Northern Ireland referendum results (without spoiled ballots):

Leave: 349,442 (44.2%)	Remain: 470,707 (55.8%)

▲

Northern Ireland local totals by Parliamentary constituencies.

Constituency	Voter turnout, of eligible	Votes		Proportion of votes	
		Remain	Leave	Remain	Leave
Belfast East	65.8%	20,728	21,918	48.1%	51.4%
Belfast North	57.5%	20,128	19,844	50.4%	49.6%
Belfast South	67.6%	30,960	13,596	69.5%	30.5%
Belfast West	48.9%	23,099	8,092	74.1%	25.9%
East Antrim	65.2%	18,616	22,929	44.8%	55.2%
East Londonderry	59.7%	21,098	19,455	52.0%	48.0%
Fermanagh and South Tyrone	67.8%	28,200	19,958	58.6%	41.4%
Foyle	57.4%	32,064	8,905	78.3%	21.7%
Lagan Valley	66.6%	22,710	25,704	46.9%	53.1%
Mid Ulster	61.6%	25,612	16,799	60.4%	39.6%
Newry and Armagh	63.9%	31,963	18,659	62.9%	36.9%
North Antrim	64.9%	18,782	30,938	37.8%	62.2%
North Down	67.7%	23,131	21,046	52.4%	47.6%
South Antrim	63.1%	21,498	22,055	49.4%	50.6%
South Down	62.2%	32,076	15,625	67.2%	32.8%
Strangford	64.5%	18,727	23,383	44.5%	55.5%
Upper Bann	63.6%	24,550	27,262	47.4%	52.6%
West Tyrone	61.8%	26,765	13,274	66.8%	33.2%

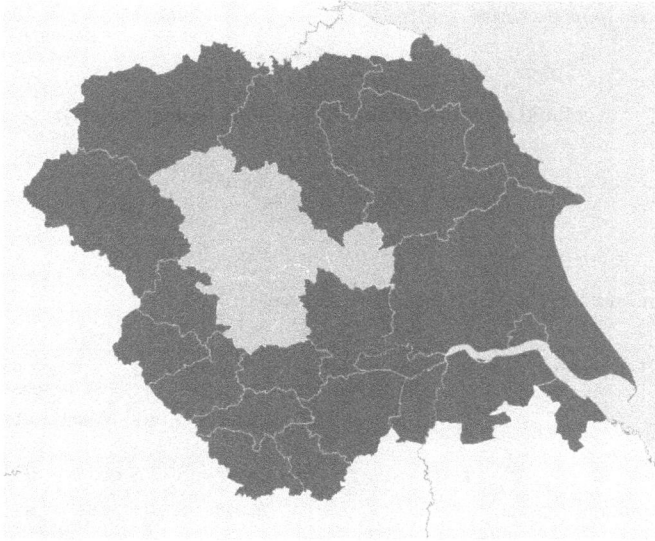

Figure 33:
Voting areas of the Yorkshire and the Humber region
Leave
Remain

Scotland

The Scottish council areas were used as the voting areas for the referendum throughout Scotland.

United Kingdom European Union membership referendum, 2016 Scotland		
Choice	**Votes**	**%**
Remain a member of the European Union	**1,661,191**	**62.00%**
Leave the European Union	1,018,322	38.00%
Vaild votes	2,679,513	99.94%
Invalid or blank votes	1,666	0.06%
Total votes	2,681,179	100.00%

| Registered voters and turnout | 3,987,112 | 67.25% |

Source: Electoral Commission[922]

Scotland referendum results (without spoiled ballots):

| Leave:
1,018,322 (38%) | Remain:
1,661,191 (62%) |

▲

Scotland was broken down into 32 voting areas.

Council area	Voter turnout, of eligible	Votes		Proportion of votes	
		Remain	Leave	Remain	Leave
Aberdeen City	67.9%	63,985	40,729	61.1%	38.9%
Aberdeenshire	70.6%	76,445	62,516	55.0%	45.0%
Angus	68.0%	32,747	26,511	55.3%	44.7%
Argyll and Bute	73.1%	29,494	19,202	60.6%	39.4%
Clackmannanshire	67.2%	14,691	10,736	57.8%	42.2%
Dumfries and Galloway	71.4%	43,864	38,803	53.1%	46.9%
Dundee City	62.9%	39,688	26,697	59.8%	40.2%
East Ayrshire	62.9%	33,891	23,942	58.6%	41.4%
East Dunbartonshire	75.1%	44,534	17,840	71.4%	28.6%
East Lothian	71.7%	36,026	19,738	64.6%	35.4%
East Renfrewshire	76.1%	39,345	13,596	74.3%	25.7%
City of Edinburgh	72.9%	187,796	64,498	74.4%	25.6%
Falkirk	67.5%	44,987	34,271	56.8%	43.2%
Fife	66.7%	106,754	75,466	58.6%	41.4%
Glasgow City	56.2%	168,335	84,474	66.6%	33.4%
Highland	71.6%	70,308	55,349	56.0%	44.0%
Inverclyde	66.0%	24,688	14,010	63.8%	36.2%
Midlothian	68.1%	28,217	17,251	62.1%	37.9%
Moray	67.4%	24,114	23,992	50.1%	49.9%
North Ayrshire	64.6%	38,394	29,110	56.9%	43.1%
North Lanarkshire	60.9%	95,549	59,400	61.7%	38.3%
Perth and Kinross	73.7%	49,641	31,614	61.1%	38.9%
Renfrewshire	69.2%	57,119	31,010	64.8%	35.2%

Scottish Borders	73.4%	37,952	26,962	58.5%	41.5%
Stirling	74.0%	33,112	15,787	67.7%	32.3%
South Lanarkshire	65.3%	102,568	60,024	63.1%	36.9%
South Ayrshire	69.8%	36,265	25,241	59.0%	41.0%
West Dunbartonshire	63.9%	26,794	16,426	62.0%	38.0%
West Lothian	67.6%	51,560	36,948	58.3%	41.7%
Na h-Eileanan Siar (Western Isles)	70.1%	8,232	6,671	55.2%	44.8%
Orkney	68.3%	7,189	4,193	63.2%	36.8%
Shetland	70.3%	6,907	5,315	56.5%	43.5%

Whilst all council counting areas show a majority for Remain one constituency, Banff and Buchan, voted to Leave the European Union at the 2016 European Union membership referendum on an estimated margin of 54% Leave 46% Remain. The Leave vote in the area was concentrated around the north coast of Aberdeenshire between the fishing towns of Banff and Peterhead, where there were 23,707 Leave votes to 14,918 Remain votes (61% Leave 39% Remain).

The areas of Whalsay and South Unst in the Shetland Islands and An Taobh Siar agus Nis in the Na h-Eileanan an Iar (Western Isles) also voted by a majority for Leave, as did the town of Lossiemouth in Moray.

Wales

The Welsh council areas were used as the voting areas for the referendum throughout Wales.

United Kingdom European Union membership referendum, 2016 Wales		
Choice	Votes	%
Leave the European Union **Gadael yr Undeb Ewropeaidd**	**854,572**	**52.53%**
Remain a member of the European Union Aros yn aelod o'r Undeb Ewropeaidd	772,347	47.47%
Vaild votes	1,626,919	99.93%
Invalid or blank votes	1,135	0.07%
Total votes	1,628,054	100.00%

Registered voters and turnout	2,270,272	71.71%
Source: Electoral Commission[922]		

Wales referendum results (without spoiled ballots):

Leave: 854,572 (52.5%)	Remain: 772,347 (47.5%)
▲	

Wales was broken down into 22 voting areas.

Council area	Voter turnout, of eligible	Votes		Proportion of votes	
		Remain	Leave	Remain	Leave
Anglesey	73.8%	18,618	**19,333**	49.1%	**50.9%**
Blaenau Gwent	68.1%	13,215	**21,587**	38.0%	**62.0%**
Bridgend	71.1%	33,723	**40,622**	45.4%	**54.6%**
Caerphilly	70.7%	39,178	**53,295**	42.4%	**57.6%**
Cardiff	69.6%	**101,788**	67,816	**60.0%**	40.0%
Carmarthenshire	74.0%	47,654	**55,381**	46.3%	**53.7%**
Ceredigion	74.4%	**21,711**	18,031	**54.6%**	45.4%
Conwy	71.7%	30,147	**35,357**	46.0%	**54.0%**
Denbighshire	69.1%	23,955	**28,117**	46.0%	**54.0%**
Flintshire	74.8%	37,867	**48,930**	43.6%	**56.4%**
Gwynedd	72.3%	**35,517**	25,665	**58.1%**	41.9%
Merthyr Tydfil	67.4%	12,574	**16,291**	43.6%	**56.4%**
Monmouthshire	77.7%	**28,061**	27,569	**50.4%**	49.6%
Neath Port Talbot	71.5%	32,651	**43,001**	43.2%	**56.8%**
Newport	70.2%	32,413	**41,236**	44.0%	**56.0%**
Pembrokeshire	74.4%	29,367	**39,155**	42.9%	**57.1%**
Powys	77.0%	36,762	**42,707**	46.3%	**53.7%**
Rhondda Cynon Taf	67.4%	53,973	**62,590**	46.3%	**53.7%**
Swansea	69.5%	58,307	**61,936**	48.5%	**51.5%**
Torfaen	69.8%	19,363	**28,781**	40.2%	**59.8%**
Vale of Glamorgan	76.1%	**36,681**	35,628	**50.7%**	49.3%
Wrexham	71.5%	28,822	**41,544**	41.0%	**59.0%**

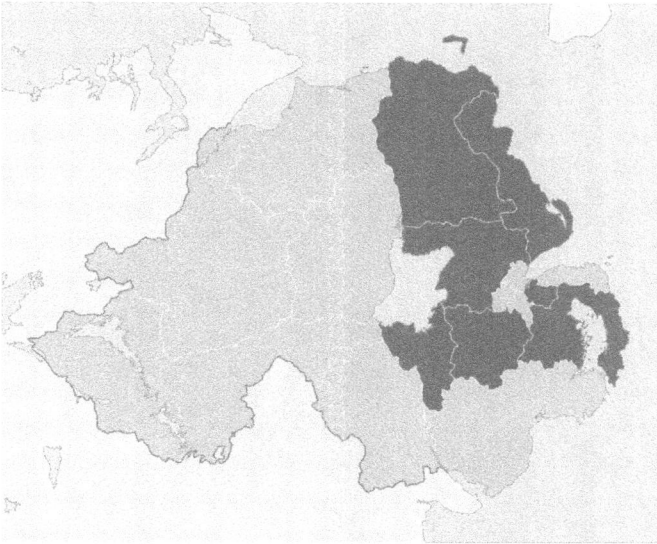

Figure 34:
Northern Ireland
Leave
Remain

Results by constituency

The EU referendum vote was not counted by parliamentary constituencies except for Northern Ireland. However a number of local councils and districts have released the referendum results by electoral ward or constituency. Moreover, several constituency boundaries are coterminous with their local government district. For constituencies elswhere, Dr Chris Hanretty, a Reader in Politics at the University of East Anglia, estimated through a demographic model the 'Leave' and 'Remain' votes in each constituency. Hanretty urges caution in the interpretation of the data as the estimates have a margin of error.

Figure 35:
Voting areas of Scotland
Remain

Constituency results by party

Party	Remain	Leave	Remain %	Leave %
Conservative Party	80	247	26%	74%
Labour Party	84	148	36%	64%
Scottish National Party	55	1	98%	2%
Liberal Democrats	6	2	75%	25%
Democratic Unionist Party	2	6	25%	75%
Sinn Féin	4	0	100%	0%
Plaid Cymru	2	1	67%	33%
Social Democratic and Labour Party	3	0	100%	0%
Independent	1	1	50%	50%
Ulster Unionist Party	1	1	50%	50%
Green Party	1	0	100%	0%
Speaker	1	0	100%	0%
Total	**242**	**406**	**37%**	**63%**

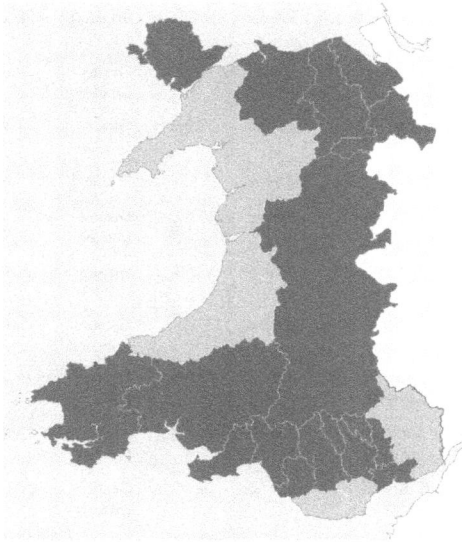

Figure 36:
Voting areas of Wales
Leave
Remain

List of constituency results

Constituency	Member of Parliament	MP position	MP's majority	Region	Proportion of votes		Notes
					Re-main %	Leave %	
Streatham	Chuka Umunna	Remain	27.9%	Greater London	**79.5%**	20.5%	924
Bristol West	Thangam Debbonaire	Remain	8.4%	South West England	**79.3%**	20.7%	
Hackney North and Stoke Newington	Diane Abbott	Remain	48.1%	Greater London	**79.1%**	20.9%	
Glasgow North	Patrick Grady	Remain	25.2%	Scotland	**78.4%**	21.6%	
Islington North	Jeremy Corbyn	Remain	43.0%	Greater London	**78.4%**	21.6%	
Foyle	Mark Durkan	Remain	16.3%	Northern Ireland	**78.3%**	21.7%	

Edinburgh North and Leith	Deidre Brock	Remain	9.6%	Scotland	**78.2%**	21.8%	
Dulwich and West Norwood	Helen Hayes	Remain	31.4%	Greater London	**78.0%**	22.0%	
Hackney South and Shoreditch	Meg Hillier	Remain	50.9%	Greater London	**77.9%**	22.1%	
Edinburgh South	Ian Murray	Remain	5.4%	Scotland	**77.8%**	22.2%	
Vauxhall	Kate Hoey	Leave	26.5%	Greater London	**77.6%**	22.4%	
Battersea	Jane Ellison	Remain	15.6%	Greater London	**77.0%**	23.0%	
Hampstead and Kilburn	Tulip Siddiq	Remain	2.1%	Greater London	**76.6%**	23.4%	
Tottenham	David Lammy	Remain	55.4%	Greater London	**76.2%**	23.8%	
Lewisham Deptford	Vicky Fox-croft	Remain	45.4%	Greater London	**75.4%**	24.6%	
Hornsey and Wood Green	Catherine West	Remain	19.1%	Greater London	**75.0%**	25.0%	
Tooting	Rosena Allin-Khan	Remain	19.9%	Greater London	**74.7%**	25.3%	
East Renfrewshire	Kirsten Os-wald	Remain	6.6%	Scotland	**74.3%**	25.7%	
Belfast West	Paul Maskey	Remain	35.0%	Northern Ireland	**74.1%**	25.9%	
Cambridge	Daniel Zeich-ner	Remain	1.2%	East of England	**73.8%**	26.2%	925
Manchester Withington	Jeff Smith	Remain	29.8%	North West England	**73.7%**	26.3%	
Brighton Pavilion	Caroline Lucas	Remain	14.6%	South East England	**73.4%**	26.6%	
East Dunbartonshire	John Nicolson	Remain	4.0%	Scotland	**73.3%**	26.7%	
Holborn and St Pancras	Keir Starmer	Remain	31.0%	Greater London	**73.3%**	26.7%	
Richmond Park	Zac Gold-smith	Leave	38.9%	Greater London	**73.3%**	27.7%	
Liverpool Riverside	Louise Ell-man	Remain	55.3%	North West England	**73.2%**	26.8%	
Putney	Justine Greening	Remain	23.8%	Greater London	**73.2%**	26.8%	
Bermondsey and Old Southwark	Neil Coyle	Remain	8.7%	Greater London	**73.0%**	27.0%	
Edinburgh East	Tommy Sheppard	Remain	19.3%	Scotland	**72.4%**	27.6%	

Edinburgh South West	Joanna Cherry	Remain	15.8%	Scotland	**72.1%**	27.9%	
Glasgow South	Stewart Mc-Donald	Remain	25.2%	Scotland	**71.8%**	28.2%	
Islington South and Finsbury	Emily Thorn-berry	Remain	28.7%	Greater London	**71.7%**	28.3%	
Cities of London and Westminster	Mark Field	Remain	26.7%	Greater London	**71.4%**	28.6%	
Edinburgh West	Michelle Thomson	Remain	5.9%	Scotland	**71.2%**	28.8%	
Glasgow Central	Alison Thewliss	Remain	19.5%	Scotland	**71.2%**	28.8%	
Ealing Central and Acton	Rupa Huq	Remain	0.5%	Greater London	**70.9%**	29.1%	
Chelsea and Fulham	Greg Hands	Remain	39.8%	Greater London	**70.8%**	29.2%	
Wimbledon	Stephen Hammond	Remain	26.1%	Greater London	**70.6%**	29.4%	
Camberwell and Peckham	Harriet Har-man	Remain	50.1%	Greater London	**69.9%**	30.1%	
Cardiff Central	Jo Stevens	Remain	12.9%	Wales	**69.7%**	30.3%	
Sheffield Central	Paul Blom-field	Remain	39.2%	Yorkshire and the Humber	**69.6%**	30.4%	
Belfast South	Alasdair McDonnell	Remain	2.3%	Northern Ireland	**69.5%**	30.5%	
Bethnal Green and Bow	Rushanara Ali	Remain	45.9%	Greater London	**69.1%**	30.9%	
Finchley and Gold-ers Green	Mike Freer	Remain	11.2%	Greater London	**69.1%**	30.9%	
Hammersmith	Andy Slaugh-ter	Remain	13.6%	Greater London	**69.0%**	31.0%	
Kensington	Victoria Borwick	Leave	21.1%	Greater London	**68.7%**	31.3%	
Glasgow North West	Carol Mon-aghan	Remain	23.6%	Scotland	**68.5%**	31.5%	
Bath	Ben Howlett	Remain	8.1%	South West England	**68.4%**	31.6%	
Aberdeen South	Callum Mc-Caig	Remain	14.9%	Scotland	**67.7%**	32.3%	
Stirling	Steven Pater-son	Remain	23.4%	Scotland	**67.7%**	32.3%	
Oxford East	Andrew David Smith	Remain	30.1%	South East England	**67.7%**	32.3%	
South Down	Margaret Ritchie	Remain	13.8%	Northern Ireland	**67.2%**	32.8%	

Westminster North	Karen Patricia Buck	Remain	5.4%	Greater London	**67.1%**	32.9%	
West Tyrone	Pat Doherty	Remain	26.0%	Northern Ireland	**66.8%**	33.2%	
Walthamstow	Stella Creasy	Remain	23.4%	Greater London	**66.5%**	33.5%	
Birmingham Hall Green	Roger Godsiff	Leave	42.1%	West Midlands	**66.4%**	33.6%	
Twickenham	Tania Mathias	Remain	3.2%	Greater London	**66.4%**	33.6%	
Hove	Peter Kyle	Remain	2.4%	South East England	**66.1%**	33.9%	
Paisley and Renfrewshire South	Mhairi Black	Remain	12.3%	Scotland	**65.9%**	34.1%	
Poplar and Limehouse	Jim Fitzpatrick	Remain	33.1%	Greater London	**65.9%**	34.1%	
Lewisham West and Penge	Jim Dowd	Remain	26.4%	Greater London	**65.6%**	34.4%	
Arfon	Hywel Williams	Remain	13.7%	Wales	**65.1%**	34.9%	
Leeds North West	Greg Mulholland	Remain	6.7%	Yorkshire and the Humber	**64.7%**	35.3%	
East Lothian	George Kerevan	Remain	11.5%	Scotland	**64.6%**	35.4%	
Lanark and Hamilton East	Angela Crawley	Remain	18.3%	Scotland	**64.6%**	35.4%	
Lewisham East	Heidi Alexander	Remain	33.4%	Greater London	**64.6%**	35.4%	
Birmingham Ladywood	Shabana Mahmood	Remain	60.9%	West Midlands	**64.4%**	35.6%	
Greenwich and Woolwich	Matthew Pennycook	Remain	25.6%	Greater London	**64.3%**	35.7%	
Liverpool Wavertree	Luciana Berger	Remain	59.3%	North West England	**64.2%**	35.8%	
Sheffield Hallam	Nick Clegg	Remain	4.2%	Yorkshire and the Humber	**64.1%**	35.9%	
Paisley and Renfrewshire North	Gavin Newlands	Remain	18.0%	Scotland	**64.0%**	36.0%	
Inverclyde	Ronnie Cowan	Remain	24.8%	Scotland	**63.8%**	36.2%	
Manchester Central	Lucy Powell	Remain	47.7%	North West England	**63.4%**	36.6%	
Motherwell and Wishaw	Marion Fellows	Remain	24.6%	Scotland	**63.1%**	36.9%	

Leyton and Wanstead	John Cryer	Leave	27.9%	Greater London	**62.9%**	37.1%
Newry and Armagh	Mickey Brady	Remain	8.4%	Northern Ireland	**62.9%**	37.1%
Leeds North East	Fabian Hamilton	Remain	15.0%	Yorkshire and the Humber	**62.7%**	37.3%
Rutherglen and Hamilton West	Margaret Ferrier	Remain	17.3%	Scotland	**62.7%**	37.3%
St Albans	Anne Main	Leave	23.4%	East of England	**62.6%**	37.4%
Cumbernauld, Kilsyth and Kirkintilloch East	Stuart Mc-Donald	Remain	29.9%	Scotland	**62.1%**	37.9%
East Kilbride, Strathaven and Lesmahagow	Lisa Cameron	Remain	27.3%	Scotland	**62.1%**	37.9%
Enfield Southgate	David Burrowes	Leave	10.4%	Greater London	**62.1%**	37.9%
Manchester Gorton	Gerald Kaufman	Remain	57.3%	North West England	**62.1%**	37.9%
Midlothian	Owen Thompson	Remain	20.4%	Scotland	**62.1%**	37.9%
West Dunbartonshire	Martin Docherty	Remain	27.7%	Scotland	**62.0%**	38.0%
North East Fife	Stephen Gethins	Remain	9.6%	Scotland	**61.9%**	38.1%
Oxford West and Abingdon	Nicola Blackwood	Remain	16.7%	South East England	**61.9%**	38.1%
Dundee East	Stewart Hosie	Remain	39.8%	Scotland	**61.8%**	38.2%
Reading East	Rob Wilson	Remain	12.9%	South East England	**61.8%**	38.2%
Altrincham and Sale West	Graham Brady	Leave	26.3%	North West England	**61.6%**	38.4%
South Cambridgeshire	Heidi Allen	Remain	33.5%	East of England	**61.6%**	38.4%
York Central	Rachael Maskell	Remain	14.1%	Yorkshire and the Humber	**61.5%**	38.5%
West Aberdeenshire and Kincardine	Stuart Donaldson	Remain	12.7%	Scotland	**61.4%**	38.6%
Coatbridge, Chryston and Bellshill	Phil Boswell	Remain	22.7%	Scotland	**61.3%**	38.7%
Cardiff North	Craig Williams	Remain	4.2%	Wales	**60.9%**	39.0%

Ochil and South Perthshire	Tasmina Ahmed-Sheikh	Remain	17.6%	Scotland	**60.8%**	39.2%	
Argyll and Bute	Brendan O'Hara	Remain	16.3%	Scotland	**60.6%**	39.4%	
Kilmarnock and Loudoun	Alan Brown	Remain	25.3%	Scotland	**60.4%**	39.6%	
Mid Ulster	Francie Molloy	Remain	33.3%	Northern Ireland	**60.4%**	39.6%	
Hitchin and Harpenden	Peter Lilley	Leave	36.2%	East of England	**60.3%**	39.7%	
Winchester	Steve Brine	Remain	30.6%	South East England	**60.3%**	39.7%	
Airdrie and Shotts	Neil Gray	Remain	19.8%	Scotland	**60.0%**	40.0%	
Dunfermline and West Fife	Douglas Chapman	Remain	18.5%	Scotland	**60.0%**	40.0%	
Perth and North Perthshire	Pete Wishart	Remain	17.8%	Scotland	**59.9%**	40.1%	
Norwich South	Clive Lewis	Remain	15.8%	East of England	**59.8%**	40.2%	
Orkney and Shetland	Alistair Carmichael	Remain	3.6%	Scotland	**59.7%**	40.3%	
South West Surrey	Jeremy Hunt	Remain	49.8%	South East England	**59.4%**	40.6%	
Glasgow North East	Anne McLaughlin	Remain	24.4%	Scotland	**59.3%**	40.7%	
Chipping Barnet	Theresa Villiers	Leave	14.4%	Greater London	**59.1%**	40.9%	
Croydon North	Steve Reed	Remain	39.9%	Greater London	**59.1%**	40.9%	
Glasgow South West	Chris Stephens	Remain	24.3%	Scotland	**59.1%**	40.9%	
Dundee West	Chris Law	Remain	38.2%	Scotland	**58.9%**	41.1%	
Guildford	Anne Milton	Unknown	41.6%	South East England	**58.9%**	41.1%	
Newcastle upon Tyne East	Nick Brown	Remain	31.9%	North East England	**58.9%**	41.1%	
Warwick and Leamington	Chris White	Remain	13.1%	West Midlands	**58.9%**	41.1%	
Inverness, Nairn, Badenoch and Strathspey	Drew Hendry	Remain	18.8%	Scotland	**58.7%**	41.3%	
Rushcliffe	Kenneth Clarke	Remain	25.1%	East Midlands	**58.7%**	41.3%	

Fermanagh and South Tyrone	Tom Elliott	Leave	1.0%	Northern Ireland	**58.6%**	41.4%	
Kingston and Surbiton	James Berry	Remain	4.8%	Greater London	**58.5%**	41.5%	
Bristol North West	Charlotte Leslie	Leave	9.5%	South West England	**58.4%**	41.6%	
Esher and Walton	Dominic Raab	Leave	50.2%	South East England	**58.4%**	41.6%	
Kirkcaldy and Cowdenbeath	Roger Mullin	Remain	18.9%	Scotland	**58.4%**	41.6%	
Linlithgow and East Falkirk	Martyn Day	Remain	21.0%	Scotland	**58.4%**	41.6%	
Ealing Southall	Virendra Sharma	Remain	43.3%	Greater London	**58.2%**	41.8%	
Falkirk	John McNally	Remain	32.6%	Scotland	**58.1%**	41.9%	
Hendon	Matthew Offord	Leave	7.5%	Greater London	**58.1%**	41.9%	
North Ayrshire and Arran	Patricia Gibson	Remain	25.2%	Scotland	**57.8%**	42.2%	
Central Ayrshire	Philippa Whitford	Remain	26.8%	Scotland	**57.8%**	42.2%	
Wokingham	John Redwood	Leave	43.2%	South East England	**57.6%**	42.4%	
Leicester South	Jon Ashworth	Remain	38.9%	East Midlands	**57.5%**	42.5%	
Swansea West	Geraint Davies	Remain	20.0%	Wales	**57.4%**	42.6%	
Cheadle	Mary Robinson	Remain	12.2%	North West England	**57.3%**	42.7%	926
Cheltenham	Alex Chalk	Remain	12.1%	South West England	**57.3%**	42.7%	
City of Chester	Chris Matheson	Remain	0.2%	North West England	**57.3%**	42.7%	
Ayr, Carrick, and Cumnock	Corri Wilson	Remain	21.6%	Scotland	**57.1%**	42.9%	
Brent Central	Dawn Butler	Remain	41.8%	Greater London	**57.1%**	42.9%	
Nottingham East	Chris Leslie	Remain	33.8%	East Midlands	**57.1%**	42.9%	
Aberdeen North	Kirsty Blackman	Remain	30.5%	Scotland	**57.0%**	43.0%	
Brent North	Barry Gardiner	Remain	20.7%	Greater London	**57.0%**	43.0%	

Henley	John Howell	Remain	45.9%	South East England	**57.0%**	43.0%	
Berwickshire, Roxburgh & Selkirk	Calum Kerr	Remain	0.6%	Scotland	**56.8%**	43.2%	
Brentford and Isleworth	Ruth Cadbury	Remain	0.8%	Greater London	**56.7%**	43.3%	
Ross, Skye and Lochaber	Ian Blackford	Remain	12.3%	Scotland	**56.7%**	43.3%	
Brighton Kemptown	Simon Kirby	Remain	1.5%	South East England	**57.6%**	43.4%	
Harrow West	Gareth Thomas	Remain	4.7%	Greater London	**56.6%**	43.4%	
Glasgow East	Natalie McGarry	Remain	24.5%	Scotland	**56.2%**	43.8%	
Ilford South	Mike Gapes	Remain	38.1%	Greater London	**56.2%**	43.8%	
Livingston	Hannah Bardell	Remain	29.3%	Scotland	**56.2%**	43.8%	
Dumfriesshire, Clydesdale and Tweeddale	David Mundell	Remain	1.5%	Scotland	**56.1%**	43.9%	
Woking	Jonathan Lord	Leave	40.2%	South East England	**56.0%**	44.0%	
City of Durham	Roberta Blackman-Woods	Remain	25.0%	North East England	**55.7%**	44.3%	
Gordon	Alex Salmond	Remain	15.0%	Scotland	**55.5%**	44.5%	
Exeter	Ben Bradshaw	Remain	13.3%	South West England	**55.3%**	44.7%	
Mitcham and Morden	Siobhain McDonagh	Remain	37.5%	Greater London	**55.3%**	44.7%	
Tunbridge Wells	Greg Clark	Remain	44.5%	South East England	**55.3%**	44.7%	
Wirral West	Margaret Greenwood	Remain	1.0%	North West England	**55.3%**	44.7%	
Cardiff West	Kevin Brennan	Remain	15.5%	Wales	**55.2%**	44.8%	
Na h-Eileanan an Iar	Angus MacNeil	Remain	25.7%	Scotland	**55.2%**	44.8%	
Cardiff South and Penarth	Stephen Doughty	Remain	16.0%	Wales	**55.1%**	44.9%	
South East Cambridgeshire	Lucy Frazer	Remain	28.3%	East of England	**55.1%**	44.9%	

York Outer	Julian Sturdy	Leave	24.4%	Yorkshire and the Humber	**55.1%**	44.9%	
Chesham and Amersham	Cheryl Gillan	Leave	45.4%	South East England	**55.0%**	45.0%	
Sefton Central	Bill Esterson	Remain	24.2%	North West England	**54.9%**	45.1%	
Canterbury	Julian Brazier	Leave	18.3%	South East England	**54.7%**	45.3%	
Dumfries and Galloway	Richard Arkless	Remain	11.5%	Scotland	**54.7%**	45.3%	
Hexham	Guy Opperman	Remain	27.8%	North East England	**54.7%**	45.3%	
Ceredigion	Mark Williams	Remain	8.2%	Wales	**54.6%**	45.4%	
Maidenhead	Theresa May	Remain	54.0%	South East England	**54.6%**	45.4%	
Edmonton	Kate Osamor	Remain	37.3%	Greater London	**54.5%**	45.5%	
Southport	John Pugh	Remain	3.0%	North West England	**54.5%**	45.5%	
Croydon South	Chris Philp	Remain	29.7%	Greater London	**54.2%**	45.8%	
Pontypridd	Owen Smith	Remain	23.7%	Wales	**54.2%**	45.8%	
Romsey and Southampton North	Caroline Nokes	Remain	36.6%	South East England	**54.2%**	45.8%	
Tatton	George Osborne	Remain	40.3%	North West England	**54.2%**	45.8%	
North East Hampshire	Ranil Jayawardena	Leave	55.4%	South East England	**54.1%**	45.9%	
Stroud	Neil Carmichael	Remain	8.0%	South West England	**54.1%**	45.9%	
Windsor	Adam Afriyie	Leave	50.0%	South East England	**54.0%**	46.0%	
Ealing North	Stephen Pound	Remain	25.4%	Greater London	**53.7%**	46.3%	
Witney	David Cameron	Remain	14.8%	South East England	**53.7%**	46.3%	
South West Hertfordshire	David Gauke	Remain	40.6%	East of England	**53.7%**	46.3%	
Wantage	Ed Vaizey	Remain	37.3%	South East England	**53.6%**	46.4%	

Glenrothes	Peter Grant	Remain	29.2%	Scotland	**53.6%**	46.4%	
Kenilworth and Southam	Jeremy Wright	Remain	43.0%	West Midlands	**53.5%**	46.5%	
Nottingham South	Lilian Greenwood	Remain	16.0%	East Midlands	**53.5%**	46.5%	
Mid Sussex	Nicholas Soames	Remain	42.2%	South East England	**53.4%**	46.6%	
Wirral South	Alison McGovern	Remain	11.0%	North West England	**53.4%**	46.6%	
Bradford West	Naz Shah	Remain	28.3%	Yorkshire and the Humber	**53.3%**	46.7%	
Bristol East	Kerry McCarthy	Remain	8.6%	South West England	**53.2%**	46.8%	
Stockport	Ann Coffey	Remain	25.4%	North West England	**53.2%**	46.8%	
Lewes	Maria Caulfield	Leave	2.1%	South East England	**53.1%**	46.9%	
Birmingham Selly Oak	Steve McCabe	Remain	18.6%	West Midlands	**53.1%**	46.9%	
East Ham	Stephen Timms	Remain	65.5%	Greater London	**53.1%**	46.9%	
Bristol South	Karin Smyth	Remain	14.0%	South West England	**52.9%**	47.1%	
Truro and Falmouth	Sarah Newton	Remain	27.2%	South West England	**52.9%**	47.1%	
Harrogate and Knaresborough	Andrew Jones	Remain	30.7%	Yorkshire and the Humber	**52.8%**	47.2%	
Birmingham Edgbaston	Gisela Stuart	Leave	6.6%	West Midlands	**52.7%**	47.3%	
West Ham	Lyn Brown	Remain	53.0%	Greater London	**52.7%**	47.3%	
Leeds Central	Hilary Benn	Remain	37.7%	Yorkshire and the Humber	**52.4%**	47.4%	
Westmorland and Lonsdale	Tim Farron	Remain	18.3%	North West England	**52.6%**	47.4%	
Harrow East	Bob Blackman	Leave	9.7%	Greater London	**52.5%**	47.5%	
Newbury	Richard Benyon	Remain	46.0%	South East England	**52.5%**	47.5%	

Mole Valley	Paul Beresford	Remain	46.1%	South East England	**52.5%**	47.5%
North Down	Sylvia Hermon	Remain	25.6%	Northern Ireland	**52.4%**	47.6%
Reigate	Crispin Blunt	Leave	43.5%	South East England	**52.3%**	47.7%
The Cotswolds	Geoffrey Clifton-Brown	Leave	37.9%	South West England	**52.3%**	47.7%
Garston and Halewood	Maria Eagle	Remain	55.4%	North West England	**52.2%**	47.8%
Monmouth	David Davies	Leave	23.1%	Wales	**52.2%**	47.8%
Tynemouth	Alan Campbell	Remain	15.4%	North East England	**52.2%**	47.8%
Epsom and Ewell	Chris Grayling	Leave	42.8%	South East England	**52.1%**	47.9%
Filton and Bradley Stoke	Jack Lopresti	Leave	20.0%	South West England	**52.1%**	47.9%
North Somerset	Liam Fox	Leave	39.2%	South West England	**52.1%**	47.9%
East Londonderry	Gregory Campbell	Leave	22.5%	Northern Ireland	**52.0%**	48.0%
Wycombe	Steve Baker	Leave	28.9%	South East England	**52.0%**	48.0%
Angus	Mike Weir	Remain	25.2%	Scotland	**51.9%**	48.1%
Macclesfield	David Rutley	Remain	29.9%	North West England	**51.9%**	48.1%
Dwyfor Meirionnydd	Liz Saville-Roberts	Remain	18.2%	Wales	**51.7%**	48.3%
Newcastle upon Tyne Central	Chi Onwurah	Remain	36.1%	North East England	**51.7%**	48.3%
Pudsey	Stuart Andrew	Leave	8.8%	Yorkshire and the Humber	**51.7%**	48.3%
Beckenham	Bob Stewart	Leave	37.8%	Greater London	**51.6%**	48.4%
Stretford and Urmston	Kate Green	Remain	25.2%	North West England	**51.6%**	48.4%
Buckingham	John Bercow	Remain	42.7%	South East England	**51.4%**	48.6%
Horsham	Jeremy Quin	Remain	43.3%	South East England	**51.4%**	48.6%

East Hampshire	Damian Hinds	Remain	48.7%	South East England	**51.3%**	48.7%	
Coventry South	Jim Cunning-ham	Remain	7.3%	West Midlands	**51.1%**	48.9%	
Ruislip, Northwood and Pinner	Nick Hurd	Remain	39.5%	Greater London	**51.0%**	49.0%	
Beaconsfield	Dominic Grieve	Remain	49.5%	South East England	**50.8%**	49.2%	
Chingford and Woodford Green	Iain Duncan Smith	Leave	19.1%	Greater London	**50.8%**	49.2%	
Enfield North	Joan Ryan	Remain	2.4%	Greater London	**50.8%**	49.2%	
Hertford and Stort-ford	Mark Prisk	Remain	38.2%	East of England	**50.8%**	49.2%	
Caithness, Suther-land and Easter Ross	Paul Mon-aghan	Remain	11.2%	Scotland	**50.6%**	49.4%	
Belfast North	Nigel Dodds	Leave	13.1%	Northern Ireland	**50.4%**	49.6%	
Bridgend	Madeleine Moon	Remain	4.9%	Wales	**50.4%**	49.6%	
Loughborough	Nicky Mor-gan	Remain	17.7%	East Midlands	**50.4%**	49.6%	
Bromley and Chisle-hurst	Bob Neill	Remain	30.8%	Greater London	**50.2%**	49.8%	
Colne Valley	Jason Mc-Cartney	Leave	9.5%	Yorkshire and the Humber	**50.2%**	49.8%	
Milton Keynes North	Mark Lan-caster	Remain	16.9%	South East England	**50.2%**	49.8%	
Runnymede and Weybridge	Philip Ham-mond	Remain	44.2%	South East England	**50.2%**	49.8%	
Wythenshawe and Sale East	Mike Kane	Remain	24.4%	North West England	**50.2%**	49.8%	
Moray	Angus Robertson	Remain	18.4%	Scotland	**50.1%**	49.9%	
Wallasey	Angela Eagle	Remain	37.7%	North West England	**50.1%**	49.9%	
Gower	Byron Davies	Remain	0.1%	Wales	49.9%	**50.1%**	
Weaver Vale	Graham Evans	Remain	1.7%	North West England	49.9%	**50.1%**	
Liverpool West Derby	Stephen Twigg	Remain	66.7%	North West England	49.8%	**50.2%**	

Croydon Central	Gavin Bar-well	Remain	0.3%	Greater London	49.7%	**50.3%**	
North Wiltshire	James Gray	Leave	41.6%	South West England	49.7%	**50.3%**	
Salisbury	John Glen	Remain	40.3%	South West England	49.7%	**50.3%**	
East Devon	Hugo Swire	Remain	22.4%	South West England	49.6%	**50.4%**	
High Peak	Andrew Bingham	Leave	9.6%	East Midlands	49.5%	**50.5%**	
Banbury	Victoria Prentis	Remain	31.7%	South East England	49.5%	**50.5%**	
Chelmsford	Simon Burns	Remain	35.9%	East of England	49.5%	**50.5%**	
Arundel and South Downs	Nick Herbert	Remain	46.3%	South East England	49.4%	**50.6%**	
Chichester	Andrew Tyrie	Remain	42.7%	South East England	49.4%	**50.6%**	
Southampton Test	Alan White-head	Remain	8.7%	South East England	49.4%	**50.6%**	
South Antrim	Danny Kina-han	Remain	2.6%	Northern Ireland	49.4%	**50.6%**	
Warrington South	David Mowat	Remain	4.6%	North West England	49.4%	**50.6%**	
Hertsmere	Oliver Dow-den	Remain	36.9%	East of England	49.2%	**50.8%**	
Lancaster and Fleet-wood	Cat Smith	Remain	3.0%	North West England	49.1%	**50.9%**	
Saffron Walden	Alan Hasel-hurst	Remain	43.4%	East of England	49.1%	**50.9%**	
Somerton and Frome	David War-burton	Leave	33.6%	South West England	49.1%	**50.9%**	
West Dorset	Oliver Letwin	Remain	28.6%	South West England	49.1%	**50.9%**	
Ynys Môn	Albert Owen	Remain	0.7%	Wales	49.1%	**50.9%**	
Colchester	Will Quince	Leave	11.5%	East of England	49.0%	**51.0%**	
Huddersfield	Barry Sheer-man	Remain	18.1%	Yorkshire and the Humber	49.0%	**51.0%**	

Central Devon	Mel Stride	Remain	39.0%	South West England	48.9%	51.1%
South Norfolk	Richard Bacon	Leave	35.9%	East of England	48.9%	51.1%
Stratford-on-Avon	Nadhim Zahawi	Leave	44.5%	West Midlands	48.9%	51.1%
Watford	Richard Harrington	Remain	17.4%	East of England	48.9%	51.1%
Birmingham Perry Barr	Khalid Mahmood	Remain	35.9%	West Midlands	48.8%	51.2%
Derbyshire Dales	Patrick McLoughlin	Remain	29.7%	East Midlands	48.8%	51.2%
Sutton and Cheam	Paul Scully	Leave	7.9%	Greater London	48.8%	51.2%
Blackley and Broughton	Graham Stringer	Leave	45.5%	North West England	48.7%	51.3%
North East Hertfordshire	Oliver Heald	Remain	36.5%	East of England	48.7%	51.3%
Belfast East	Gavin Robinson	Leave	6.5%	Northern Ireland	48.6%	51.4%
Devizes	Claire Perry	Remain	42.3%	South West England	48.6%	51.4%
Birmingham Hodge Hill	Liam Byrne	Remain	56.9%	West Midlands	48.5%	51.5%
Shipley	Philip Davies	Leave	19.0%	Yorkshire and the Humber	48.5%	51.5%
South Swindon	Robert Buckland	Remain	11.7%	South West England	48.5%	51.5%
Leicester West	Liz Kendall	Remain	20.9%	East Midlands	48.4%	51.6%
Birkenhead	Frank Field	Leave	52.8%	North West England	48.3%	51.7%
Brecon and Radnorshire	Christopher Davies	Leave	12.7%	Wales	48.3%	51.7%
Sutton Coldfield	Andrew Mitchell	Remain	32.3%	West Midlands	48.3%	51.7%
Portsmouth South	Flick Drummond	Remain	12.5%	South East England	48.2%	51.8%
Eltham	Clive Efford	Remain	6.2%	Greater London	48.2%	51.8%

Bedford	Richard Fuller	Leave	2.4%	East of England	48.1%	**51.9%**
Surrey Heath	Michael Gove	Leave	45.6%	South East England	48.1%	**51.9%**
Aylesbury	David Lidington	Remain	31.0%	South East England	47.9%	**52.1%**
North East Somerset	Jacob Rees-Mogg	Leave	24.9%	South West England	47.9%	**52.1%**
Eddisbury	Antoinette Sandbach	Remain	27.4%	North West England	47.8%	**52.2%**
Harborough	Edward Garnier	Remain	37.4%	East Midlands	47.8%	**52.2%**
Hazel Grove	William Wragg	Leave	15.2%	North West England	47.8%	**52.2%**
Mid Bedfordshire	Nadine Dorries	Leave	40.2%	East of England	47.8%	**52.2%**
Chippenham	Michelle Donelan	Remain	18.2%	South West England	47.7%	**52.3%**
Vale of Glamorgan	Alun Cairns	Remain	13.4%	Wales	47.7%	**52.3%**
Broxtowe	Anna Soubry	Remain	8.0%	East Midlands	47.6%	**52.4%**
Knowsley	George Howarth	Remain	68.3%	North West England	47.6%	**52.4%**
Clwyd West	David Jones	Leave	17.7%	Wales	47.5%	**52.5%**
Ilford North	Wes Streeting	Remain	1.2%	Greater London	47.5%	**52.5%**
Mid Derbyshire	Pauline Latham	Remain	26.8%	East Midlands	47.5%	**52.5%**
Tonbridge and Malling	Tom Tugendhat	Remain	44.2%	South East England	47.5%	**52.5%**
Wealden	Nusrat Ghani	Leave	40.3%	South East England	47.5%	**52.5%**
Welwyn Hatfield	Grant Shapps	Remain	24.2%	East of England	47.5%	**52.5%**
West Worcestershire	Harriett Baldwin	Remain	41.7%	West Midlands	47.5%	**52.5%**
Congleton	Fiona Bruce	Leave	32.9%	North West England	47.4%	**52.6%**
Reading West	Alok Sharma	Remain	13.7%	South East England	47.4%	**52.6%**

South Northampton-shire	Andrea Leadsom	Leave	43.4%	East Midlands	47.4%	**52.6%**	
Upper Bann	David Simpson	Leave	4.8%	Northern Ireland	47.4%	**52.6%**	
Meon Valley	George Hollingbery	Remain	46.2%	South East England	47.1%	**52.9%**	
Milton Keynes South	Iain Stewart	Leave	14.7%	South East England	47.1%	**52.9%**	
Taunton Deane	Rebecca Pow	Remain	26.8%	South West England	47.1%	**52.9%**	
Shrewsbury and Atcham	Daniel Kawczynski	Leave	17.7%	West Midlands	47.0%	**53.0%**	
Newport West	Paul Flynn	Remain	8.7%	Wales	47.0%	**53.0%**	
Skipton and Ripon	Julian Smith	Remain	38.1%	Yorkshire and the Humber	47.0%	**53.0%**	
Lagan Valley	Jeffrey Donaldson	Leave	32.7%	Northern Ireland	46.9%	**53.1%**	
Leicester East	Keith Vaz	Remain	38.2%	East Midlands	46.9%	**53.1%**	
Bracknell	Phillip Lee	Remain	38.9%	South East England	46.8%	**53.2%**	
Calder Valley	Craig Whittaker	Remain	8.3%	Yorkshire and the Humber	46.8%	**53.2%**	
Huntingdon	Jonathan Djanogly	Remain	34.7%	East of England	46.8%	**53.2%**	
North East Bedford-shire	Alistair Burt	Remain	43.7%	East of England	46.8%	**53.2%**	
Aberconwy	Guto Bebb	Remain	13.3%	Wales	46.7%	**53.3%**	
Keighley	Kris Hopkins	Remain	6.2%	Yorkshire and the Humber	46.7%	**53.3%**	
Solihull	Julian Knight	Remain	23.6%	West Midlands	46.7%	**53.3%**	
Thornbury and Yate	Luke Hall	Remain	3.1%	South West England	46.7%	**53.3%**	
Wells	James Heappey	Remain	13.3%	South West England	46.6%	**53.4%**	
Bournemouth East	Tobias Ellwood	Remain	32.6%	South West England	46.5%	**53.5%**	

Basingstoke	Maria Miller	Remain	20.8%	South East England	46.4%	**53.6%**
Bury North	David Nuttall	Leave	0.8%	North West England	46.4%	**53.6%**
East Worthing and Shoreham	Tim Loughton	Leave	30.0%	South East England	46.4%	**53.6%**
Salford and Eccles	Rebecca Long-Bailey	Remain	29.0%	North West England	46.4%	**53.6%**
Blackburn	Kate Hollern	Remain	29.0%	North West England	46.3%	**53.7%**
Bury St Edmunds	Jo Churchill	Remain	35.9%	East of England	46.3%	**53.7%**
Carmarthen East and Dinefwr	Jonathan Edwards	Remain	14.2%	Wales	46.3%	**53.7%**
Derby North	Amanda Solloway	Remain	0.1%	East Midlands	46.3%	**53.7%**
Tewkesbury	Laurence Robertson	Leave	39.7%	South West England	46.3%	**53.7%**
Worcester	Robin Walker	Remain	11.4%	West Midlands	46.3%	**53.7%**
Liverpool Walton	Steve Rotheram	Remain	72.3%	North West England	46.2%	**53.8%**
Sevenoaks	Michael Fallon	Remain	39.0%	South East England	46.2%	**53.8%**
Rutland and Melton	Alan Duncan	Remain	39.8%	East Midlands	46.1%	**53.9%**
Slough	Fiona Mac-taggart	Remain	15.2%	South East England	46.1%	**53.9%**
Banff and Buchan	Eilidh White-ford	Remain	31.4%	Scotland	46.0%	**54.0%**
Broadland	Keith Simp-son	Remain	31.7%	East of England	46.0%	**54.0%**
Eastleigh	Mims Davies	Leave	16.5%	South East England	46.0%	**54.0%**
Totnes	Sarah Wollas-ton	Remain	38.8%	South West England	46.0%	**54.0%**
Wyre and Preston North	Ben Wallace	Remain	28.4%	North West England	46.0%	**54.0%**
East Surrey	Sam Gyimah	Remain	40.4%	South East England	45.9%	**54.1%**

South Suffolk	James Cartlidge	Remain	33.8%	East of England	45.9%	**54.1%**	
Neath	Christina Rees	Remain	25.7%	Wales	45.8%	**54.2%**	
St Ives	Derek Thomas	Leave	5.1%	South West England	45.8%	**54.2%**	
Erith and Thamesmead	Teresa Pearce	Remain	22.4%	Greater London	45.7%	**54.3%**	
Central Suffolk and North Ipswich	Dan Poulter	Remain	37.2%	East of England	45.6%	**54.4%**	
Plymouth Sutton and Devonport	Oliver Colvile	Remain	1.1%	South West England	45.6%	**54.4%**	
Bury South	Ivan Lewis	Remain	10.4%	North West England	45.5%	**54.5%**	
North West Hampshire	Kit Malthouse	Leave	43.4%	South East England	45.5%	**54.5%**	
Richmond (Yorks)	Rishi Sunak	Leave	36.2%	Yorkshire and the Humber	45.4%	**54.6%**	
Wolverhampton South West	Rob Marris	Remain	2.0%	West Midlands	45.6%	**54.6%**	
Delyn	David Hanson	Remain	7.8%	Wales	45.3%	**54.7%**	
Bootle	Peter Dowd	Remain	63.6%	North West England	45.2%	**54.8%**	
Leeds West	Rachel Reeves	Remain	27.9%	Yorkshire and the Humber	45.1%	**54.9%**	
North West Durham	Pat Glass	Remain	23.5%	North East England	45.1%	**54.9%**	
West Lancashire	Rosie Cooper	Remain	16.8%	North West England	45.1%	**54.9%**	
Southend West	David Amess	Leave	31.5%	East of England	45.0%	**55.0%**	
Caerphilly	Wayne David	Remain	25.0%	Wales	44.9%	**55.1%**	
Hemel Hempstead	Mike Penning	Leave	29.1%	East of England	44.9%	**55.1%**	
Bradford East	Imran Hussain	Remain	17.1%	Yorkshire and the Humber	44.8%	**55.2%**	
East Antrim	Sammy Wilson	Leave	17.3%	Northern Ireland	44.8%	**55.2%**	

South West Devon	Gary Streeter	Remain	39.9%	South West England	44.8%	**55.2%**	
Carmarthen West and South Pembrokeshire	Simon Hart	Remain	15.0%	Wales	44.7%	**55.3%**	
Penrith and The Border	Rory Stewart	Remain	45.3%	North West England	44.7%	**55.3%**	
Fareham	Suella Fernandes	Leave	40.7%	South East England	44.6%	**55.4%**	
Bromsgrove	Sajid Javid	Remain	31.6%	West Midlands	44.6%	**55.4%**	
Haltemprice and Howden	David Davis	Leave	33.2%	Yorkshire and the Humber	44.6%	**55.4%**	
Llanelli	Nia Griffith	Remain	18.4%	Wales	44.6%	**55.4%**	
Luton South	Gavin Shuker	Remain	13.5%	East of England	44.6%	**55.4%**	
Berwick-upon-Tweed	Anne-Marie Trevelyan	Leave	12.2%	North East England	44.5%	**55.5%**	
Bolton West	Chris Green	Leave	1.6%	North West England	44.5%	**55.5%**	
Strangford	Jim Shannon	Leave	30.0%	Northern Ireland	44.5%	**55.5%**	
Newark	Robert Jenrick	Remain	35.3%	East Midlands	44.3%	**55.7%**	
Preseli Pembrokeshire	Stephen Crabb	Remain	12.3%	Wales	44.3%	**55.7%**	
New Forest West	Desmond Swayne	Leave	43.5%	South East England	44.2%	**55.8%**	
Maidstone and The Weald	Helen Grant	Remain	21.4%	South East England	44.2%	**55.8%**	
Suffolk Coastal	Therese Coffey	Remain	33.9%	East of England	44.2%	**55.8%**	
Feltham and Heston	Seema Malhotra	Remain	23.2%	Greater London	44.1%	**55.9%**	
Montgomeryshire	Glyn Davies	Leave	15.8%	Wales	44.1%	**55.9%**	
Vale of Clwyd	James Davies	Leave	0.7%	Wales	44.1%	**55.9%**	
Gateshead	Ian Mearns	Remain	39.0%	North East England	44.0%	**56.0%**	
Gedling	Vernon Coaker	Remain	6.2%	East Midlands	43.9%	**56.1%**	
Newton Abbot	Anne Marie Morris	Leave	23.4%	South West England	43.9%	**56.1%**	

St Helens South and Whiston	Marie Rimmer	Remain	43.9%	North West England	43.9%	**56.1%**
Wansbeck	Ian Lavery	Remain	28.2%	North East England	43.9%	**56.1%**
Worthing West	Peter Bottomley	Remain	33.2%	South East England	43.9%	**56.1%**
Hastings and Rye	Amber Rudd	Remain	9.4%	South East England	43.8%	**56.2%**
Blaydon	David Anderson	Remain	31.7%	North East England	43.7%	**56.3%**
Carshalton and Wallington	Tom Brake	Remain	3.2%	Greater London	43.7%	**56.3%**
Elmet and Rothwell	Alec Shelbrooke	Remain	14.7%	Yorkshire and the Humber	43.7%	**56.3%**
Uxbridge and South Ruislip	Boris Johnson	Leave	23.9%	Greater London	43.7%	**56.3%**
North Dorset	Simon Hoare	Remain	39.6%	South West England	43.6%	**56.4%**
Thirsk and Malton	Kevin Hollinrake	Remain	37.2%	Yorkshire and the Humber	43.6%	**56.4%**
Chorley	Lindsay Hoyle	Remain	8.8%	North West England	43.5%	**56.5%**
Fylde	Mark Menzies	Remain	30.4%	North West England	43.5%	**56.5%**
Ipswich	Ben Gummer	Remain	7.7%	East of England	43.5%	**56.5%**
Weston-super-Mare	John Penrose	Remain	29.7%	South West England	43.4%	**56.6%**
Barrow and Furness	John Woodcock	Remain	1.8%	North West England	43.3%	**56.7%**
Kingswood	Chris Skidmore	Remain	18.7%	South West England	43.2%	**56.8%**
Preston	Mark Hendrick	Remain	36.1%	North West England	43.2%	**56.8%**
South Ribble	Seema Kennedy	Remain	11.4%	North West England	43.2%	**56.8%**
Cynon Valley	Ann Clwyd	Remain	30.9%	Wales	43.1%	**56.9%**

North West Cambridgeshire	Shailesh Vara	Remain	32.4%	East of England	43.1%	**56.9%**
Poole	Robert Syms	Leave	33.3%	South West England	43.1%	**56.9%**
North Devon	Peter Heaton-Jones	Remain	13.3%	South West England	43.0%	**57.0%**
Torridge and West Devon	Geoffrey Cox	Leave	32.5%	South West England	43.0%	**57.0%**
Newcastle upon Tyne North	Catherine McKinnell	Remain	22.6%	North East England	42.9%	**57.1%**
Stevenage	Stephen McPartland	Leave	10.4%	East of England	42.9%	**57.1%**
Dewsbury	Paula Sherriff	Remain	2.7%	Yorkshire and the Humber	42.8%	**57.2%**
Stafford	Jeremy Lefroy	Remain	18.8%	West Midlands	42.8%	**57.2%**
Lincoln	Karl McCartney	Leave	3.1%	East Midlands	42.7%	**57.3%**
Norwich North	Chloe Smith	Remain	10.2%	East of England	42.7%	**57.3%**
Wrexham	Ian Lucas	Remain	5.6%	Wales	42.7%	**57.3%**
North Swindon	Justin Tomlinson	Leave	22.6%	South West England	42.6%	**57.4%**
Lichfield	Michael Fabricant	Leave	35.3%	West Midlands	42.5%	**57.5%**
Orpington	Jo Johnson	Remain	40.7%	Greater London	42.5%	**57.5%**
Rochdale	Simon Danczuk	Remain	27.4%	North West England	42.5%	**57.5%**
Bexhill and Battle	Huw Merriman	Remain	36.4%	South East England	42.4%	**57.6%**
Eastbourne	Caroline Ansell	Leave	1.4%	South East England	42.4%	**57.6%**
Sheffield Heeley	Louise Haigh	Remain	30.8%	Yorkshire and the Humber	42.4%	**57.6%**
South West Wiltshire	Andrew Murrison	Leave	35.2%	South West England	42.4%	**57.6%**
Tiverton and Honiton	Neil Parish	Remain	37.5%	South West England	42.4%	**57.6%**

Selby and Ainsty	Nigel Adams	Leave	25.7%	Yorkshire and the Humber	42.4%	57.6%	
Alyn and Deeside	Mark Tami	Remain	8.1%	Wales	42.3%	57.7%	
Bolton North East	David Crausby	Remain	10.1%	North West England	42.3%	57.7%	
Ellesmere Port and Neston	Justin Madders	Remain	13.4%	North West England	42.3%	57.7%	
Bournemouth West	Conor Burns	Leave	29.7%	South West England	42.2%	57.8%	
Halton	Derek Twigg	Remain	45.1%	North West England	42.2%	57.8%	
Stockton South	James Wharton	Leave	9.7%	North East England	42.2%	57.8%	
Mid Dorset and North Poole	Michael Tomlinson	Leave	22.6%	South West England	42.1%	57.9%	
Darlington	Jenny Chapman	Remain	7.7%	North East England	42.0%	58.0%	
Forest of Dean	Mark Harper	Remain	22.2%	South West England	42.0%	58.0%	
Meriden	Caroline Spelman	Remain	35.7%	West Midlands	42.0%	58.0%	
Stone	Bill Cash	Leave	34.6%	West Midlands	42.0%	58.0%	
Aldershot	Gerald Howarth	Leave	32.3%	South East England	41.8%	58.2%	
Charnwood	Ed Argar	Remain	32.4%	East Midlands	41.8%	58.2%	
Faversham and Mid Kent	Helen Whately	Remain	36.4%	South East England	41.8%	58.2%	
Luton North	Kelvin Hopkins	Leave	22.3%	East of England	41.8%	58.2%	
North Herefordshire	Bill Wiggin	Leave	41.6%	West Midlands	41.8%	58.2%	
North Norfolk	Norman Lamb	Remain	8.2%	East of England	41.8%	58.2%	
South Leicestershire	Alberto Costa	Remain	31.2%	East Midlands	41.8%	58.2%	
St Helens North	Conor McGinn	Remain	37.4%	North West England	41.8%	58.2%	

The Wrekin	Mark Pritchard	Remain	23.6%	West Midlands	41.8%	**58.2%**	
Rugby	Mark Pawsey	Remain	21.1%	West Midlands	41.7%	**58.3%**	
South East Cornwall	Sheryll Murray	Leave	33.7%	South West England	41.7%	**58.3%**	
Crawley	Henry Smith	Leave	13.4%	South East England	41.6%	**58.4%**	
Merthyr Tydfil and Rhymney	Gerald Jones	Remain	35.2%	Wales	41.6%	**58.4%**	
Ludlow	Philip Dunne	Remain	39.4%	West Midlands	41.5%	**58.5%**	
Rossendale and Darwen	Jake Berry	Remain	11.5%	North West England	41.5%	**58.5%**	
Coventry North West	Geoffrey Robinson	Remain	10.0%	West Midlands	41.4%	**58.6%**	
Ribble Valley	Nigel Evans	Leave	26.0%	North West England	41.4%	**58.6%**	
South West Bedfordshire	Andrew Selous	Remain	34.7%	East of England	41.4%	**58.6%**	
Warrington North	Helen Jones	Remain	19.6%	North West England	41.4%	**58.6%**	
Beverley and Holderness	Graham Stuart	Remain	23.2%	Yorkshire and the Humber	41.3%	**58.7%**	
Daventry	Chris Heaton-Harris	Leave	40.1%	East Midlands	41.3%	**58.7%**	
Halifax	Holly Lynch	Remain	1.0%	Yorkshire and the Humber	41.2%	**58.8%**	
Islwyn	Chris Evans	Remain	29.4%	Wales	45.3%	**58.8%**	
Gloucester	Richard Graham	Remain	13.8%	South West England	41.1%	**58.9%**	
Mid Worcestershire	Nigel Huddleston	Remain	39.3%	West Midlands	41.1%	**58.9%**	
Morecambe and Lunesdale	David Morris	Remain	10.6%	North West England	41.1%	**58.9%**	
Sedgefield	Phil Wilson	Remain	17.7%	North East England	41.1%	**58.9%**	
Crewe and Nantwich	Edward Timpson	Remain	7.3%	North West England	41.0%	**59.0%**	

Coventry North East	Colleen Fletcher	Remain	29.1%	West Midlands	40.8%	**59.2%**	
Yeovil	Marcus Fysh	Leave	9.3%	South West England	40.8%	**59.2%**	
Chesterfield	Toby Perkins	Remain	29.8%	East Midlands	40.7%	**59.3%**	
North Tyneside	Mary Glindon	Remain	36.7%	North East England	40.7%	**59.3%**	
Stalybridge and Hyde	Jonathan Reynolds	Leave	16.3%	North West England	40.7%	**59.3%**	
Hayes and Harlington	John McDonnell	Remain	34.8%	Greater London	40.6%	**59.4%**	
North Shropshire	Owen Paterson	Leave	31.6%	West Midlands	40.6%	**59.4%**	
South Dorset	Richard Drax	Leave	24.7%	South West England	40.6%	**59.4%**	
New Forest East	Julian Lewis	Leave	38.8%	South East England	40.5%	**59.5%**	
North Cornwall	Scott Mann	Leave	13.7%	South West England	40.5%	**59.5%**	
Ashford	Damian Green	Remain	33.6%	South East England	40.5%	**59.5%**	
Northampton South	David Mackintosh	Remain	9.8%	East Midlands	40.4%	**59.6%**	
Morley and Outwood	Andrea Jenkyns	Leave	0.9%	Yorkshire and the Humber	40.3%	**59.7%**	
Ogmore	Chris Elmore	Remain	36.4%	Wales	40.3%	**59.7%**	
Blyth Valley	Ronnie Campbell	Leave	24.0%	North East England	40.2%	**59.8%**	
Christchurch	Christopher Chope	Leave	36.7%	South West England	40.2%	**59.8%**	
Copeland	Jamie Reed	Remain	6.5%	North West England	40.2%	**59.8%**	
Worsley and Eccles South	Barbara Keeley	Remain	14.1%	North West England	40.2%	**59.8%**	
Aberavon	Stephen Kinnock	Remain	33.1%	Wales	40.1%	**59.9%**	
Kingston upon Hull North	Diana Johnson	Remain	36.5%	Yorkshire and the Humber	40.1%	**59.9%**	

Oldham East and Saddleworth	Debbie Abrahams	Remain	13.5%	North West England	40.1%	**59.9%**	
Southampton Itchen	Royston Smith	Leave	5.2%	South East England	40.1%	**59.9%**	
Sunderland Central	Julie Elliott	Remain	26.8%	North East England	40.0%	**60.0%**	
Birmingham Yardley	Jess Phillips	Remain	16.0%	West Midlands	39.9%	**60.1%**	
Corby	Tom Pursglove	Leave	4.3%	East Midlands	39.9%	**60.1%**	
Hereford and South Herefordshire	Jesse Norman	Remain	35.7%	West Midlands	39.9%	**60.1%**	
North Durham	Kevan Jones	Remain	34.0%	North East England	39.9%	**60.1%**	
Clwyd South	Susan Jones	Remain	6.9%	Wales	39.8%	**60.2%**	
Newport East	Jessica Morden	Remain	13.4%	Wales	39.8%	**60.2%**	
Barking	Margaret Hodge	Remain	35.5%	Greater London	39.7%	**60.3%**	
Batley and Spen	Vacant	n/a	81.0%	Yorkshire and the Humber	39.7%	**60.3%**	
South Derbyshire	Heather Wheeler	Leave	22.6%	East Midlands	39.7%	**60.3%**	
Spelthorne	Kwasi Kwarteng	Leave	28.8%	South East England	39.7%	**60.3%**	
Workington	Sue Hayman	Remain	12.2%	North West England	39.7%	**60.3%**	
Carlisle	John Stevenson	Remain	6.5%	North West England	39.6%	**60.4%**	
Rochford and Southend East	James Duddridge	Leave	21.7%	East of England	39.6%	**60.4%**	
Mid Norfolk	George Freeman	Remain	33.1%	East of England	39.5%	**60.5%**	
Bishop Auckland	Helen Goodman	Remain	8.9%	North East England	39.4%	**60.6%**	
Northampton North	Michael Ellis	Remain	8.2%	East Midlands	39.4%	**60.6%**	
Bosworth	David Tredinnick	Remain	20.5%	East Midlands	39.3%	**60.7%**	
North West Leicestershire	Andrew Bridgen	Leave	22.1%	East Midlands	39.3%	**60.7%**	

Brentwood and Ongar	Eric Pickles	Remain	42.0%	East of England	39.2%	**60.8%**
Torfaen	Nick Thomas-Symonds	Remain	21.5%	Wales	39.2%	**60.8%**
Witham	Priti Patel	Leave	41.5%	East of England	39.2%	**60.8%**
Leeds East	Richard Burgon	Remain	32.8%	Yorkshire and the Humber	39.1%	**60.9%**
Denton and Reddish	Andrew Gwynne	Remain	27.2%	North West England	39.0%	**61.0%**
Epping Forest	Eleanor Laing	Un-known	36.4%	East of England	39.0%	**61.0%**
Grantham and Stamford	Nick Boles	Remain	35.3%	East Midlands	39.0%	**61.0%**
Harwich and North Essex	Bernard Jenkin	Leave	31.3%	East of England	39.0%	**61.0%**
Kettering	Philip Hol-lobone	Leave	26.7%	East Midlands	39.0%	**61.0%**
Rhondda	Chris Bryant	Remain	23.6%	Wales	38.8%	**61.2%**
Maldon	John Whittingdale	Leave	45.9%	East of England	38.7%	**61.3%**
Penistone and Stocksbridge	Angela Smith	Remain	14.3%	Yorkshire and the Humber	38.7%	**61.3%**
Scarborough and Whitby	Robert Goodwill	Remain	13.0%	Yorkshire and the Humber	38.7%	**61.3%**
Braintree	James Cleverly	Leave	35.0%	East of England	38.6%	**61.4%**
Redditch	Karen Lumley	Leave	16.0%	West Midlands	38.6%	**61.4%**
Sheffield Brightside and Hillsborough	Gill Furniss	Remain	42.5%	Yorkshire and the Humber	38.6%	**61.4%**
Sleaford and North Hykeham	Caroline Johnson	Leave	40.0%	East Midlands	38.5%	**61.5%**
Derby South	Margaret Beckett	Remain	21.6%	East Midlands	38.4%	**61.6%**
Jarrow	Stephen Hepburn	Remain	36.0%	North East England	38.4%	**61.6%**
Newcastle-under-Lyme	Paul Farrelly	Remain	1.5%	West Midlands	38.4%	**61.6%**
South Thanet	Craig Mackinlay	Leave	5.7%	South East England	38.4%	**61.6%**

Walsall South	Valerie Vaz	Remain	14.4%	West Midlands	38.4%	**61.6%**
Ashton under Lyne	Angela Rayner	Remain	27.6%	North West England	38.2%	**61.8%**
Birmingham North-field	Richard Burden	Remain	5.9%	West Midlands	38.2%	**61.8%**
Folkestone and Hythe	Damian Collins	Remain	25.1%	South East England	38.2%	**61.8%**
Warley	John Spellar	Remain	38.9%	West Midlands	38.2%	**61.8%**
Gosport	Caroline Dinenage	Remain	35.9%	South East England	38.1%	**61.9%**
Washington and Sunderland West	Sharon Hodg-son	Remain	35.3%	North East England	38.1%	**61.9%**
Isle of Wight	Andrew Turner	Leave	19.5%	South East England	38.1%	**61.9%**
Blaenau Gwent	Nick Smith	Remain	40.1%	Wales	38.0%	**62.0%**
Gainsborough	Edward Leigh	Leave	31.4%	East Midlands	38.0%	**62.0%**
Swansea East	Carolyn Harris	Remain	35.8%	Wales	38.0%	**62.0%**
Bridgwater and West Somerset	Ian Liddell-Grainger	Leave	26.8%	South West England	37.9%	**62.1%**
North East Der-byshire	Natascha Engel	Remain	3.9%	East Midlands	37.9%	**62.1%**
Oldham West and Royton	Jim McMa-hon	Remain	34.2%	North West England	37.9%	**62.1%**
Peterborough	Stewart Jack-son	Leave	4.1%	East of England	37.9%	**62.1%**
South Shields	Emma Lewell-Buck	Remain	29.3%	North East England	37.9%	**62.1%**
North Antrim	Ian Paisley, Jr.	Leave	27.6%	Northern Ireland	37.8%	**62.2%**
Havant	Alan Mak	Remain	31.1%	South East England	37.6%	**62.4%**
Heywood and Mid-dleton	Liz McInnes	Remain	10.9%	North West England	37.6%	**62.4%**
St Austell and Newquay	Steve Double	Leave	16.2%	South West England	37.6%	**62.4%**
Wakefield	Mary Creagh	Remain	6.1%	Yorkshire and the Humber	37.4%	**62.6%**

Houghton and Sunderland South	Bridget Phillipson	Remain	33.6%	North East England	37.4%	**62.6%**	
Torbay	Kevin Foster	Remain	6.8%	South West England	37.4%	**62.6%**	
Camborne and Redruth	George Eustice	Leave	15.3%	South West England	37.3%	**62.7%**	
Wigan	Lisa Nandy	Remain	31.4%	North West England	37.3%	**62.7%**	
Wellingborough	Peter Bone	Leave	32.5%	East Midlands	37.1%	**62.9%**	
Birmingham Erdington	Jack Dromey	Remain	14.8%	West Midlands	37.0%	**63.0%**	
Dover	Charlie Elphicke	Remain	12.5%	South East England	36.8%	**63.1%**	
Old Bexley and Sidcup	James Brokenshire	Remain	33.8%	Greater London	36.8%	**63.1%**	
Wyre Forest	Mark Garnier	Remain	26.0%	West Midlands	36.9%	**63.1%**	
Pendle	Andrew Stephenson	Leave	12.3%	North West England	36.8%	**63.2%**	
West Suffolk	Matthew Hancock	Unknown	30.4%	East of England	36.8%	**63.2%**	
Waveney	Peter Aldous	Remain	4.6%	East of England	36.8%	**63.2%**	
East Yorkshire	Greg Knight	Leave	29.9%	Yorkshire and the Humber	36.7%	**63.3%**	
Erewash	Maggie Throup	Remain	7.4%	East Midlands	36.7%	**63.3%**	
Bolton South East	Yasmin Qureshi	Remain	26.8%	North West England	36.6%	**63.4%**	
Leigh	Andy Burnham	Remain	31.2%	North West England	36.6%	**63.4%**	
Bradford South	Judith Cummins	Remain	17.2%	Yorkshire and the Humber	36.5%	**63.5%**	
Gillingham and Rainham	Rehman Chishti	Leave	22.4%	South East England	36.5%	**63.5%**	
Portsmouth North	Penny Mordaunt	Leave	23.2%	South East England	36.4%	**63.6%**	
Stourbridge	Margot James	Remain	14.5%	West Midlands	36.4%	**63.6%**	

Rochester and Strood	Kelly Tolhurst	Remain	13.6%	South East England	36.3%	**63.7%**
Sherwood	Mark Spencer	Remain	9.2%	East Midlands	36.3%	**63.7%**
Nottingham North	Graham Allen	Remain	33.6%	East Midlands	36.2%	**63.8%**
Dartford	Gareth Johnson	Leave	23.6%	South East England	36.0%	**64.0%**
Bognor Regis and Littlehampton	Nick Gibb	Remain	29.6%	South East England	35.8%	**64.2%**
Staffordshire Moorlands	Karen Bradley	Remain	23.9%	West Midlands	35.5%	**64.5%**
Burton	Andrew Griffiths	Remain	22.8%	West Midlands	35.4%	**64.6%**
Chatham and Aylesford	Tracey Crouch	Unknown	26.6%	South East England	35.3%	**64.7%**
Nuneaton	Marcus Jones	Remain	10.7%	West Midlands	35.3%	**64.7%**
North Thanet	Roger Gale	Remain	23.3%	South East England	35.1%	**64.9%**
Bexleyheath and Crayford	David Evennett	Remain	21.3%	Greater London	35.0%	**65.0%**
Makerfield	Yvonne Fovargue	Remain	29.4%	North West England	35.0%	**65.0%**
Middlesbrough South and East Cleveland	Tom Blenkinsop	Remain	5.0%	North East England	35.0%	**65.0%**
Stoke-on-Trent Central	Tristram Hunt	Remain	12.4%	West Midlands	35.0%	**65.0%**
South Staffordshire	Gavin Williamson	Remain	41.1%	West Midlands	34.8%	**65.2%**
Amber Valley	Nigel Mills	Leave	9.2%	East Midlands	34.7%	**65.3%**
Gravesham	Adam Holloway	Leave	16.7%	South East England	34.6%	**65.4%**
Hyndburn	Graham Jones	Remain	10.3%	North West England	34.3%	**65.7%**
Sittingbourne and Sheppey	Gordon Henderson	Leave	24.6%	South East England	34.3%	**65.7%**
Broxbourne	Charles Walker	Leave	36.3%	East of England	34.2%	**65.8%**
Middlesbrough	Andy McDonald	Remain	38.1%	North East England	34.0%	**66.0%**
Tamworth	Christopher Pincher	Leave	24.0%	West Midlands	34.0%	**66.0%**

North West Norfolk	Henry Bellingham	Leave	29.4%	East of England	33.9%	**66.1%**	
Brigg and Goole	Andrew Percy	Leave	25.8%	Yorkshire and the Humber	33.8%	**66.2%**	
South West Norfolk	Elizabeth Truss	Remain	27.7%	East of England	33.8%	**66.2%**	
Doncaster Central	Rosie Winterton	Remain	25.0%	Yorkshire and the Humber	33.7%	**66.3%**	
Halesowen and Rowley Regis	James Morris	Remain	7.0%	West Midlands	33.7%	**66.3%**	
Plymouth Moor View	Johnny Mercer	Remain	2.4%	South West England	33.6%	**66.4%**	
Sheffield South East	Clive Betts	Remain	29.5%	Yorkshire and the Humber	33.6%	**66.4%**	
Easington	Grahame Morris	Remain	42.3%	North East England	33.5%	**66.5%**	
Stockton North	Alex Cunningham	Remain	21.1%	North East England	33.5%	**66.5%**	
Burnley	Julie Cooper	Remain	8.2%	North West England	33.4%	**66.6%**	
Rother Valley	Kevin Barron	Remain	15.5%	Yorkshire and the Humber	33.3%	**66.7%**	
Blackpool North and Cleveleys	Paul Maynard	Leave	8.5%	North West England	33.2%	**66.8%**	
Basildon and Billericay	John Baron	Leave	29.0%	East of England	33.1%	**66.9%**	
Telford	Lucy Allan	Leave	1.8%	West Midlands	33.0%	**67.0%**	
Redcar	Anna Turley	Remain	25.4%	North East England	32.5%	**67.5%**	
West Bromwich East	Tom Watson	Remain	25.3%	West Midlands	32.5%	**67.5%**	
North Warwickshire	Craig Tracey	Leave	6.3%	West Midlands	32.3%	**67.7%**	
Wolverhampton North East	Emma Reynolds	Remain	16.2%	West Midlands	32.3%	**67.7%**	
Aldridge-Brownhills	Wendy Morton	Remain	29.7%	West Midlands	32.2%	**67.8%**	
Blackpool South	Gordon Marsden	Remain	8.0%	North West England	32.2%	**67.8%**	

Kingston upon Hull West and Hessle	Alan Johnson	Remain	29.3%	Yorkshire and the Humber	32.2%	**67.8%**	
Rayleigh and Wickford	Mark Francois	Leave	32.4%	East of England	32.2%	**67.8%**	
Harlow	Robert Halfon	Remain	18.9%	East of England	32.0%	**68.0%**	
Hemsworth	Jon Trickett	Remain	28.5%	Yorkshire and the Humber	31.9%	**68.1%**	
Wolverhampton South East	Pat McFadden	Remain	31.0%	West Midlands	31.8%	**68.2%**	
Barnsley Central	Dan Jarvis	Remain	34.0%	Yorkshire and the Humber	31.7%	**68.3%**	
Bassetlaw	John Mann	Leave	17.9%	East Midlands	31.7%	**68.3%**	
Rotherham	Sarah Champion	Remain	22.3%	Yorkshire and the Humber	31.7%	**68.3%**	
Cleethorpes	Martin Vickers	Leave	17.5%	Yorkshire and the Humber	31.6%	**68.4%**	
Don Valley	Caroline Flint	Remain	20.9%	Yorkshire and the Humber	31.5%	**68.5%**	
Cannock Chase	Amanda Milling	Remain	10.5%	West Midlands	31.1%	**68.9%**	
Wentworth and Dearne	John Healey	Remain	32.0%	Yorkshire and the Humber	31.1%	**68.9%**	
Scunthorpe	Nic Dakin	Remain	8.5%	Yorkshire and the Humber	31.0%	**69.0%**	
West Bromwich West	Adrian Bailey	Remain	22.1%	West Midlands	30.9%	**69.1%**	
Romford	Andrew Rosindell	Leave	28.2%	Greater London	30.8%	**69.2%**	
Normanton, Pontefract and Castleford	Yvette Cooper	Remain	33.6%	Yorkshire and the Humber	30.7%	**69.3%**	
Hornchurch and Upminster	Angela Watkinson	Remain	23.7%	Greater London	30.6%	**69.4%**	
Louth and Horncastle	Victoria Atkins	Remain	29.8%	East Midlands	30.6%	**69.4%**	
North East Cambridgeshire	Stephen Barclay	Leave	32.6%	East of England	30.6%	**69.4%**	
Hartlepool	Iain Wright	Remain	7.7%	North East England	30.4%	**69.6%**	

Dagenham and Rainham	Jon Cruddas	Remain	11.6%	Greater London	30.1%	**69.9%**
Clacton	Douglas Carswell	Leave	7.8%	East of England	30.0%	**70.0%**
Bolsover	Dennis Skinner	Leave	26.8%	East Midlands	29.8%	**70.2%**
Thurrock	Jackie Doyle-Price	Remain	1.1%	East of England	29.8%	**70.2%**
Dudley South	Mike Wood	Leave	11.2%	West Midlands	29.6%	**70.4%**
Ashfield	Gloria De Piero	Remain	18.6%	East Midlands	29.5%	**70.5%**
Barnsley East	Michael Dugher	Remain	31.2%	Yorkshire and the Humber	29.3%	**70.7%**
Stoke-on-Trent South	Robert Flello	Remain	6.5%	West Midlands	29.2%	**70.8%**
Mansfield	Alan Meale	Remain	11.3%	East Midlands	29.1%	**70.9%**
South Holland and the Deepings	John Hayes	Leave	37.7%	East Midlands	28.9%	**71.1%**
Dudley North	Ian Austin	Remain	11.0%	West Midlands	28.6%	**71.4%**
Great Grimsby	Melanie Onn	Remain	13.5%	Yorkshire and the Humber	28.6%	**71.4%**
Great Yarmouth	Brandon Lewis	Remain	13.8%	East of England	28.5%	**71.5%**
Doncaster North	Ed Miliband	Remain	29.8%	Yorkshire and the Humber	28.0%	**72.0%**
Stoke-on-Trent North	Ruth Smeeth	Remain	12.5%	West Midlands	27.9%	**72.1%**
Kingston upon Hull East	Karl Turner	Remain	29.4%	Yorkshire and the Humber	27.4%	**72.6%**
Castle Point	Rebecca Harris	Leave	19.7%	East of England	27.3%	**72.7%**
South Basildon and East Thurrock	Stephen Metcalfe	Leave	16.9%	East of England	27.0%	**73.0%**
Walsall North	David Winnick	Remain	5.2%	West Midlands	25.8%	**74.2%**
Boston and Skegness	Matt Warman	Remain	10.0%	East Midlands	25.1%	**74.9%**

Most Leave areas

The following were the ten voting areas that voted most heavily in favour of leave. All but one of them were in the East Midlands and East of England regions with four voting areas out of the top ten including both the top two located in Lincolnshire.

Rank-ing	Voting Area	Voter turnout, of eligible	Votes		Proportion of votes		Region
			Re-main	Leave	Re-main	Leave	
1	Boston	77.2%	7,430	**22,974**	24.4%	**75.6%**	East Midlands
2	South Holland	75.3%	13,074	**36,423**	26.4%	**73.6%**	East Midlands
3	Castle Point	75.3%	14,154	**37,691**	27.3%	**72.7%**	East of England
4	Thurrock	72.7%	22,151	**57,765**	27.7%	**72.3%**	East of England
5	Great Yarmouth	69.0%	14,284	**35,844**	28.5%	**71.5%**	East of England
6	Fenland	73.7%	15,055	**37,571**	28.6%	**71.4%**	East of England
7	Mansfield	72.6%	16,417	**39,927**	29.1%	**70.9%**	East Midlands
8	Bolsover	72.3%	12,242	**29,730**	29.2%	**70.8%**	East Midlands
9	East Lindsey	74.9%	23,515	**56,613**	29.3%	**70.7%**	East Midlands
10	North East Lincolnshire	67.9%	23,797	**55,185**	30.1%	**69.9%**	Yorkshire and the Humber

Most Remain areas

The following were the ten voting areas that voted most heavily in favour of remain. Of the ten, seven were in the Greater London region.

Rank-ing	Voting Area	Voter turnout, of eligible	Votes		Proportion of votes		Region
			Re-main	Leave	Re-main	Leave	
1	Gibraltar	83.5%	**19,322**	823	**95.9%**	4.1%	South West England
2	Lambeth	67.3%	**111,584**	30,340	**78.6%**	21.4%	Greater London
3	Hackney	65.1%	**83,398**	22,868	**78.5%**	21.5%	Greater London
4	Foyle	57.4%	**32,064**	8,905	**78.3%**	21.7%	Northern Ireland
5	Haringey	70.5%	**79,991**	25,855	**75.6%**	24.4%	Greater London
6	City of London	73.5%	**3,312**	1,087	**75.3%**	24.7%	Greater London
7	Islington	70.3%	**76,420**	25,180	**75.2%**	24.8%	Greater London
8	Wandsworth	71.9%	**118,463**	39,421	**75.0%**	25.0%	Greater London
9	Camden	65.4%	**71,295**	23,838	**74.9%**	25.1%	Greater London
10	City of Edinburgh	72.9%	**187,796**	64,498	**74.4%**	25.6%	Scotland

Most evenly divided areas

The narrowest margin of victory for any of the 382 voting areas in the United Kingdom was in the Scottish council area of Moray which voted by just 122 votes or 0.25% margin in favour of Remain.

In England the narrowest margin of victory for Leave was in Watford which voted by just 252 votes or 0.54% margin in favour of Leave, and in Cherwell which also voted by just 500 votes or 0.61% margin in favour of Leave. The narrowest margin of victory for Remain was in the London Borough of Bromley which voted by just 2,364 votes or a 1.30% margin in favour of Remain.

Narrowest Leave vote

Voting Area	Voter turnout, of eligible	Votes		Proportion of votes		Region	Majority
		Re-main	Leave	Remain	Leave		
Watford	71.6%	23,167	**23,419**	49.7%	**50.3%**	East of England	252

Narrowest Remain vote

Voting Area	Voter turnout, of eligible	Votes		Proportion of votes		Region	Majority
		Re-main	Leave	Remain	Leave		
Moray	67.4%	**24,114**	23,992	**50.1%**	49.9%	Scot-land	122

Turnout by age group

After the referendum, the annual *British Social Attitudes* survey questioned the public on their participation. Interviewing was mainly carried out between July and October 2016 and respondents were subdivided into three age groups (18-34, 35-64 and >65). The survey revealed that turnout was higher in the older age groups, and was 64%, 80% and 89% respectively. The age disparity had also been a feature of previous elections and referenda. However, compared to the previous referendum in 2011, the young voters' turnout in 2016 had increased sharply by 31%, while turnout by the two older age categories had also increased, but only by 26% and 21%.

Irregularities

In July 2018, Vote Leave was found to have broken electoral law, spending over its limit, by the UK Electoral Commission.[927] Connected to this, the Information Commissioner's Office found that data had been unlawfully harvested from UK voters, and issued a notice of intent to fine Facebook £500,000.[928] Also, the House of Commons Culture, Media and Sport Select Committee, released an interim report on 'Disinformation and 'fake news'', stating that Russia had engaged in "unconventional warfare" through Twitter and other social media against the United Kingdom, designed to amplify support for a "leave" vote in Brexit. It also found that it could not be satisfied that the largest donor in the Brexit campaign, Arron Banks, used money from UK sources, and may have been financed by the Russian government.[929] This has led to litigation to declare the result is void.[930] A second campaign group, the Fair Vote Project, which is calling for a public inquiry and supports a second referendum stated: "The issue is too big to have half the country or more than half the country, wonder 'was that actually the result? Is this the future the country wants?' That's first and foremost, let's be certain, everybody play by the rules." Taylor maintains further, "on the basis of fairness, it has to be the same vote posed in the same way".[931]

Aftermath of the United Kingdom European Union membership referendum, 2016

Part of a series of articles on the
United Kingdom in the European Union
Accession
• 1973 EC enlargement • 1975 Referendum Act • 1975 EC membership referendum • 1972 EC Act • UK rebate • 2011 EU Act

Membership

- The Euro
- European Movement UK
- Nationality law
- UK Euroscepticism
  - Maastricht Rebels
- Black Wednesday
- **Officials and bodies**
- EU Committee
- European Scrutiny Committee
- Northern Ireland Executive in Brussels
- EU Representative in London
- Young European Movement UK
- UK European Commissioners
- Permanent EU Representatives

Legislation

- 1972 EC Act
- 1986 EC (Amendment) Act
- 1993 EC (Amendment) Act
- 1998 EC (Amendment) Act
- 2002 EC (Amendment) Act
- 2008 EU (Amendment) Act
- 2011 EU Act

European Parliament Elections

- 1979
- 1984
- 1989
- 1994
- 1999
- 2004
- 2009
- 2014

  - 1973 delegation
  - 1st
  - 2nd
  - 3rd
  - 4th
  - 5th
  - 6th
  - 7th
  - 8th

Withdrawal

- 2004–05 EU Bill
- 2013–14 EU (Referendum) Bill
- 2015–16 EU membership renegotiation
- 2015 EU Referendum Act
- 2016 EU (Referendum) Act (Gibraltar)
- **2016 EU membership referendum**
- Issues
- Endorsements
- Opinion polling
- Results
- Causes
- **Campaigns**
- **Organisations advocating and campaigning for a referendum**
- People's Pledge
- Labour for a Referendum
- **Leave**
- **Vote Leave** (official lead group)
  - Business for Britain
  - Conservatives for Britain
  - Students for Britain
- Labour Leave
- Leave.EU
  - Bpoplive
- Grassroots Out
- Get Britain Out
- The Freedom Association
  - Better Off Out
- **Other anti-EU advocacy organisations**
- Bruges Group
- Campaign for an Independent Britain
- **Remain**
- **Britain Stronger in Europe** (official lead group)
- Labour In for Britain
- European Movement UK
- **Other pro-EU advocacy organisations**
- Britain in Europe
- British Influence
- Business for New Europe
- Nucleus
- **Pejorative term for pro-EU advocacy**
- Project Fear
- **Media coverage**
- *Brexit: The Movie*
- *In or Out*
- **Aftermath**
- International reactions
- Terms of Withdrawal from EU (Referendum) Bills
- 2016 Conservative Party election
- 2016 Labour Party election
- 2017 Liberal Democrats Party election
- Proposed second Scottish independence referendum
- Proposed London independence
- *The New European*
- European Union (Withdrawal) Act 2018 (including meaningful vote)
- European Union (Withdrawal Agreement) Bill 2017-19
- Gibraltar
- 2017 General Election
- EU Withdrawal Agreement (Public Vote) Bill 2017-19
- UK's relations with EU after 2019
- **Triggering of Article 50 & Negotiations**
- *R (Miller) v Secretary of State for Exiting the European Union'*
- EU (Notification of Withdrawal) Act 2017
- UK invocation of Article 50
- Brexit negotiations
- Department for Exiting the EU (Brexit Department)
- Department for International Trade
- **Post-referendum organisations**

Calls for second vote

- European Union Withdrawal Agreement (Public Vote) Bill 2017-19
- **Organisations campaigning for a second vote via People's Vote**
- Britain for Europe
- European Movement UK
- For our Future's Sake
- Healthier IN the EU
- Open Britain
- Our Future Our Choice
- Scientists for EU
- **Other organisations campaigning for a second vote**
- Best for Britain
- **See also**
- Opposition to Brexit in the United Kingdom

- <u>v</u>
- <u>t</u>
- <u>e</u>[932]

After the UK EU membership referendum held on 23 June 2016, in which a majority voted to leave the European Union, the United Kingdom experienced political and economic upsets, with spillover effects across the rest of the European Union and the wider world. Prime Minister David Cameron, who had campaigned for Remain, announced his resignation on 24 June, triggering a Conservative leadership election, won by Home Secretary Theresa May. Following Leader of the Opposition Jeremy Corbyn's loss of a motion of no confidence among the Parliamentary Labour Party, he also faced a leadership challenge, which he won. Nigel Farage stepped down from leadership of the pro-Leave party UKIP in July. After the elected party leader resigned, Farage then became the party's interim leader on 5 October until Paul Nuttall was elected leader on 28 November.

Voting patterns in the referendum varied between areas: Gibraltar, Greater London, many other cities, Scotland and Northern Ireland had majorities for Remain; the remainder of England and Wales and most unionist parts of Northern Ireland showed Leave majorities. This fuelled concern among Scottish and Irish nationalists: the First Minister of Scotland threatened to withhold legislative consent for any withdrawal legislation and has now formally requested permission to hold a second Scottish independence referendum, while the deputy First Minister of Northern Ireland called for a referendum on a united Ireland. The status of Gibraltar and that of London were also questioned.

In late July 2016, the Foreign Affairs Select Committee was told that Cameron had refused to allow the Civil Service to make plans for Brexit, a decision the committee described as "an act of gross negligence".

Economic effects

Economic arguments were a major element of the referendum debate. Remainers, including the UK treasury, argued trade would be worse off outside the EU. Supporters of withdrawal argued that the cessation of net contributions to the EU would allow for some cuts to taxes or increases in government spending.[933]

On the day after the referendum, Bank of England Governor Mark Carney held a press conference to reassure the markets, and two weeks later released £150 billion in lending. Nonetheless, share prices of the five largest British banks fell an average of 21% on the morning after the referendum. All of the Big Three credit rating agencies reacted negatively to the vote in June 2016: Standard & Poor's cut the UK credit rating from AAA to AA, Fitch Group cut from AA+ to AA, and Moody's cut the UK's outlook to "negative".

When the London Stock Exchange opened on Friday 24 June, the FTSE 100 fell from 6338.10 to 5806.13 in the first ten minutes of trading. Near the close of trading on 27 June, the domestically-focused FTSE 250 Index was down approximately 14% compared to the day before the referendum results were published. However, by 1 July the FTSE 100 had risen above pre-referendum levels, to a ten-month high representing the index's largest single-week rise since 2011. On 11 July, it officially entered bull market territory, having risen by more than 20% from its February low. The FTSE 250 moved above its pre-referendum level on 27 July. In the US, the S&P 500, a broader market than the Dow Jones, reached an all-time high on 11 July.

On the morning of 24 June, the pound sterling fell to its lowest level against the US dollar since 1985. The drop over the day was 8% – the biggest one-day fall in the pound since the introduction of floating exchange rates following the collapse of the Bretton Woods system in 1971. The pound remained low, and on 8 July became the worst performing major currency of the year, although the pound's trade-weighted index is only back at levels seen in the period 2008–2013. It was expected that the weaker pound would also benefit aerospace and defence firms, pharmaceutical companies, and professional services companies; the share prices of these companies were boosted after the EU referendum.[934]

After the referendum the Institute for Fiscal Studies published a report funded by the Economic and Social Research Council which warned that Britain would lose up to £70 billion in reduced economic growth if it didn't retain Single Market membership with new trade deals unable to make up the difference. One of these areas is financial services, which are helped by EU-wide "passporting" for financial products, which the Financial Times estimates indirectly accounts for up to 71,000 jobs and 10 billion pounds of tax annually and there are concerns that banks may relocate outside the UK.

On 5 January 2017, Andy Haldane, the Chief Economist and the Executive Director of Monetary Analysis and Statistics at the Bank of England, admitted that forecasts predicting an economic downturn due to the referendum were inaccurate and noted strong market performance after the referendum, although some have pointed to prices rising faster than wages.[935]

Economy and business

On 27 June, Chancellor of the Exchequer George Osborne attempted to reassure financial markets that the UK economy was not in serious trouble. This came after media reports that a survey by the Institute of Directors suggested that two-thirds of businesses believed that the outcome of the referendum would produce negative results as well as falls in the value of sterling and the FTSE 100. Some British businesses had also predicted that investment cuts, hiring freezes and redundancies would be necessary to cope with the results of the referendum. Osborne indicated that Britain was facing the future "from a position of strength" and there was no current need for an emergency Budget. "No-one should doubt our resolve to maintain the fiscal stability we have delivered for this country ... And to companies, large and small, I would say this: the British economy is fundamentally strong, highly competitive and we are open for business."

On 14 July Philip Hammond, Osborne's successor as Chancellor, told BBC News the referendum result had caused uncertainty for businesses, and that it was important to send "signals of reassurance" to encourage investment and spending. He also confirmed there would not be an emergency budget: "We will want to work closely with the governor of the Bank of England and others through the summer to prepare for the Autumn Statement, when we will signal and set out the plans for the economy going forward in what are very different circumstances that we now face, and then those plans will be implemented in the Budget in the spring in the usual way."

On 12 July, the global investment management company BlackRock predicted the UK would experience a recession in late 2016 or early 2017 as a result of the vote to leave the EU, and that economic growth would slow down for at least five years because of a reduction in investment. On 18 July, the UK-based economic forecasting group EY ITEM club suggested the country would experience a "short shallow recession" as the economy suffered "severe confidence effects on spending and business"; it also cut its economic growth forecasts for the UK from 2.6% to 0.4% in 2017, and 2.4% to 1.4% for 2018. The group's chief economic adviser, Peter Soencer, also argued there would be more long-term implications, and that the UK "may have to adjust to a permanent reduction in the size of the economy, compared to the trend that seemed possible prior to the vote". Senior City investor Richard Buxton also argued there would be a "mild recession". On 19 July, the International Monetary Fund (IMF) reduced its 2017 economic growth forecast for the UK from 2.2% to 1.3%, but still expected Britain to be the second fastest growing economy in the G7 during 2016; the IMF also reduced its forecasts for world economic growth by 0.1% to 3.1% in 2016 and 3.4% in 2017, as a result of the referendum, which it said had "thrown a spanner in the works" of global recovery.

On 20 July, a report released by the Bank of England said that although uncertainty had risen "markedly" since the referendum, it was yet to see evidence of a sharp economic decline as a consequence. However, around a third of contacts surveyed for the report expected there to be "some negative impact" over the following year.

In September 2016, following three months of positive economic data after the referendum, commentators suggested that many of the negative statements and predictions promoted from within the "remain" camp had failed to materialise, but by December, analysis began to show that Brexit was having an effect on inflation.

In April 2017 the IMF raised their forecast for the UK economy from 1.5% to 2% for 2017 and from 1.4% to 1.5% for 2018.

Party politics

Conservative

On 24 June, the Conservative Party leader and Prime Minister David Cameron announced that he would resign by October because the Leave campaign had been successful in the referendum. Although most of the Conservative MPs on both sides of the referendum debate had urged him to stay, the UKIP leader, Nigel Farage, called for Cameron to go "immediately". A leadership election was scheduled for 9 September, with the new leader to be in place before the party's autumn conference on 2 October. The two main candidates were predicted to be Boris Johnson, who had been a keen supporter of leaving the EU, and Home Secretary Theresa May, who had campaigned for Remain. The last-minute candidature by Johnson's former ally Michael Gove destabilised the race and forced Johnson to stand down; the final two candidates became May and Andrea Leadsom. Leadsom soon withdrew, leaving May as new party leader and next prime minister. She took office on 13 July.

Figure 37: *Prime Minister David Cameron announces his resignation following the outcome of the referendum*

Labour

The Labour Party leader Jeremy Corbyn faced growing criticism from his parliamentary party MPs, who had supported remaining within the EU, for poor campaigning, and two Labour MPs submitted a vote of no confidence in Corbyn on 24 June. It is claimed that there is evidence that Corbyn deliberately sabotaged Labour's campaign to remain part of the EU, despite remain polling favourably among Labour voters. In the early hours of Sunday 26 June, Corbyn sacked Hilary Benn (the shadow foreign secretary) for apparently leading a coup against him. This led to a string of Labour MPs quickly resigning their roles in the party. By mid-afternoon on 27 June 2016, 23 of the Labour Party's 31 shadow cabinet members had resigned from the shadow cabinet as had seven parliamentary private secretaries. On 27 June 2016, Corbyn filled some of the vacancies and was working to fill the others.

According to a source quoted by the BBC, the party's Deputy Leader Tom Watson told leader Jeremy Corbyn that "it looks like we are moving towards a leadership election." Corbyn stated that he would run again in that event. A no confidence motion was held on 28 June 2016; Corbyn lost the motion with more than 80% (172) of MPs voting against him with a turnout of 95%.

Corbyn responded with a statement that the motion had no "constitutional legitimacy" and that he intended to continue as the elected leader. The vote does not require the party to call a leadership election but, according to *The Guardian*: "the result is likely to lead to a direct challenge to Corbyn as some politicians scramble to collect enough nominations to trigger a formal challenge to his leadership." By 29 June, Corbyn had been encouraged to resign by Labour Party stalwarts such as Dame Tessa Jowell, Ed Miliband and Dame Margaret Beckett. Union leaders rallied behind Corbyn, issuing a joint statement saying that the Labour leader had a "resounding mandate" and a leadership election would be an "unnecessary distraction". Supporting Corbyn, John McDonnell said, "We're not going to be bullied by Labour MPs who refuse to accept democracy in our party."

On 11 July, Angela Eagle announced her campaign for the Labour party leadership after attaining enough support of MPs to trigger a leadership contest, saying that she "can provide the leadership that Corbyn can't". Eagle subsequently dropped out of the race (on 18 July) leaving Owen Smith as the only contender to Jeremy Corbyn.

Smith had supported the campaign for Britain to remain in the European Union, in the referendum on Britain's membership in June 2016. On 13 July 2016, following the vote to leave the EU, three weeks prior, he pledged that he would press for an early general election or offer a further referendum on the final 'Brexit' deal drawn up by the new Prime Minister, were he to be elected Labour leader.

Approximately two weeks later, Smith told the BBC that (in his view) those who had voted with the Leave faction had done so "because they felt a sense of loss in their communities, decline, cuts that have hammered away at vital public services and they haven't felt that any politicians, certainly not the politicians they expect to stand up for them..." His recommendation was to "put in place concrete policies that will bring real improvements to people's lives so I'm talking about a British New Deal for every part of Britain..."

Liberal Democrats

The Lib Dems, who are a strongly pro-European party, announced that they respect the referendum result, but would make remaining in the EU a manifesto pledge at the next election. Leader Tim Farron said that "The British people deserve the chance not to be stuck with the appalling consequences of a leave campaign that stoked that anger with the lies of Farage, Johnson and Gove."

More United

In reaction to the lack of unified pro-EU voice following the referendum, members of the Liberal Democrats and others discussed the launch of a new centre-left political movement. This was officially launched on 24 June as More United, named after a line in the maiden speech of Labour MP Jo Cox, who was killed during the referendum campaign. More United is a cross-party coalition, and will crowdfund candidates from any party who support its goals, which include environmentalism, a market economy with strong public services, and close co-operation with the EU.

UKIP

The UK Independence Party was founded to press for British withdrawal from the EU, and following the referendum its leader Nigel Farage announced, on 4 July, that having succeeded in this goal, he would stand down as leader. Following the resignation of the elected leader Diane James, Farage became the interim party leader on 5 October. Farage's successor Paul Nuttall was elected the party leader on 28 November 2016.

General politics

The government and the civil service is heavily focused on Brexit. Former Head of the Home Civil Service Bob Kerslake has stated that there is a risk that other matters will get insufficient attention until they develop into crises.[936]

A cross party coalition of MP's has been formed to oppose hard Brexit. This group is known as, the all-party parliamentary group on EU relations. Chuka Umunna said that MP's should be active players rather than spectators, he said, "We will be fighting in parliament for a future relationship with the EU that protects our prosperity and rights at work, and which delivers a better and safer world."[937]

Second general election

Under the Fixed-term Parliaments Act 2011, the next general election was scheduled to be held on 7 May 2020.

Following the result of the referendum, many political commentators argued that it might be necessary to hold an early general election before negotiations to leave begin, with, for example, Conservative MP Jacob Rees-Mogg suggesting that a general election could be held in autumn 2016. The final two candidates in the Conservative Party leadership election – Andrea Leadsom and Theresa May – said they would not seek an early general election. However, after Leadsom's withdrawal and with May thus due to become Prime

Minister without any broader vote, there were renewed calls for an early election from commentators[938] and politicians. Tim Farron, leader of the Liberal Democrats, called for an early election shortly after Leadsom's withdrawal.

Despite repeatedly previously ruling out an early General Election, May announced on 18 April 2017 her intention to call an election on 8 June 2017. This required a two-thirds super-majority of the Commons in support of a motion for an early general election, which was agreed on 19 April. May stated that "division in Westminster will risk ability to make a success of Brexit and it will cause damaging uncertainty and instability to the country... We need a general election and we need one now, because we have at this moment a one-off chance to get this done while the European Union agrees its negotiating position and before the detailed talks begin. I have only recently and reluctantly come to this conclusion."

The snap election resulted in an unexpected Hung Parliament with the Conservatives losing their overall majority but remained as the largest party which has led to further political turmoil.

Pressure groups

Numerous pressure groups were established after the referendum to oppose Brexit.[939]

Former Prime Ministers' views

A week after the referendum, Gordon Brown, a former Labour Prime Minister who had signed the Lisbon Treaty in 2007, warned of a danger that in the next decade the country would be refighting the referendum. He wrote that remainers were feeling they must be pessimists to prove that Brexit is unmanageable without catastrophe, while leavers optimistically claim economic risks are exaggerated.

The previous Labour Prime Minister, Tony Blair, in October 2016 called for a second referendum, a decision through parliament or a general election to decide finally if Britain should leave the EU. Former leader of the Conservative Prime Minister John Major argued in November 2016 that parliament will have to ratify whatever deal is negotiated and then, depending on the deal there could be a case for a second referendum.

Withdrawal negotiations

Five British people think the government is handling negotiations badly for every one who approves of the government's negotiations.[940]

Immigration concerns

To what extent free movement of people would or would not be retained in any post-Brexit deal with the EU has emerged as a key political issue. Shortly after the result, the Conservative politician Daniel Hannan, who campaigned for Leave, told the BBC's *Newsnight* that Brexit was likely to change little about the freedom of movement between the UK and the European Union, concluding "We never said there was going to be some radical decline ... we want a measure of control."[941]

Theresa May stated in August 2016 that leaving the EU 'must mean controls on the numbers of people who come to Britain from Europe but also a positive outcome for those who wish to trade goods and services'. According to a Home Office document leaked in September 2017, Britain plans to end the free movement of labour immediately after Brexit and introduce restrictions to deter all but highly skilled EU workers. It proposes offering low-skilled workers residency for a maximum of two years and the highly skilled work permits for three to five years.

Boris Johnson initially argued that restricting freedom of movement was not one of the main reasons why people have voted Leave, but his position was seen as too lax on the issue by other Conservative Party Leave supporters, which may have contributed to Michael Gove's decision to stand for the party's leadership contest. Meanwhile, EU leaders warned that full access to the single market would not be available without retaining free movement of people. Limitations on the free movement of EU citizens within the UK will also have consequences for research and innovation. While campaigning in the Conservative leadership contest, Gove pledged to end the freedom of movement accord with the EU and instead implement an Australian-style points system.

Natasha Bouchard, the Mayor of Calais, suggests that the government of France should renegotiate the Le Touquet treaty, which allows British border guards to check trains, cars and lorries before they cross the Channel from France to Britain and therefore to keep irregular immigrants away from Britain. French government officials doubt that the trilateral agreement (it includes Belgium) would be valid after the UK has officially left the European Union and especially think that it is unlikely that there will be any political motivation to enforce the agreement. However, on 1 July 2016 François Hollande said British border controls would stay in place in France, though France suggested during the referendum campaign they would be scrapped allowing migrants in the "Jungle" camp easy access to Kent.

In late July 2016, discussions were underway that might provide the UK with an exemption from the EU rules on refugees' freedom of movement for up to seven years. Senior UK government sources confirmed to *The Observer* that this was "certainly one of the ideas now on the table". If the discussions led to an agreement, the UK – though not an EU member – would also retain access to the single market but would be required to pay a significant annual contribution to the EU. According to *The Daily Telegraph* the news of this possibility caused a rift in the Conservative Party: "Tory MPs have reacted with fury ... [accusing European leaders of] ... failing to accept the public's decision to sever ties with the 28-member bloc last month."

According to CEP analysis of Labour Force Survey, immigrants in the UK are on average more educated than UK-born citizens. Citizens in the UK are concerned that immigrants are taking over their jobs since most immigrants are highly educated, however, they are actually helping the economy because they too consume goods, and produce jobs. Immigrants to the UK help to mitigate the negative effects of the ageing British labour force and are believed to have an overall net positive fiscal effect. Some have argued that immigration has a dampening effect on wages due to the greater supply of labour. However, other studies suggest that immigration has only a small impact on the average wage of workers. Immigration may have a negative impact on the wages of low-skilled workers but can push up the wages of medium- and highly paid workers.

Status of current EU immigrants and British emigrants

There were about 3.7 million EU citizens (including Irish) living in the UK in 2016 and around 1.2 million British citizens living in other EU countries. The future status of both groups of people and their reciprocal rights are the object of Brexit negotiations. According to the British Office for National Statistics, 623,000 EU citizens came to live in England and Wales before 1981. A further 855,000 arrived before the year 2000. As of 2017, approximately 1.4 million Eastern Europeans were living in Britain, including 916,000 Poles. In May 2004, when the EU welcomed ten new member states from a majority of Central and Eastern European countries, the UK was one of only three EU member states, alongside Sweden and Ireland, to open their labour market immediately to these new EU citizens. In the 12 months following the referendum, the estimated number of EU nationals immigrating to the UK fell from 284,000 to 230,000. In parallel, the number of EU citizens emigrating from the UK increased from an estimated 95,000 in the year before the vote to 123,000. Annual net immigration from the EU to the UK has, thus, fallen to about 100,000.

Theresa May, when candidate for Conservative leader, suggested that the status of EU immigrants currently in the UK could be used in negotiations with other European countries, with the possibility of expelling these people if the EU does not offer favourable exit terms. This position has been strongly rejected by other politicians from both Remain and Leave campaigns. In response to a question by Labour Leave campaigner Gisela Stuart, the Minister for Security and Immigration James Brokenshire said that the Government was unable to make any promises about the status of EU citizens in the UK before the government had set out negotiating positions, and that it would seek reciprocal protection for UK citizens in EU countries.

The Vice-Chancellor of Germany, Sigmar Gabriel, announced that the country would consider easing citizenship requirements for British nationals currently in Germany, to protect their status. The foreign ministry of Ireland stated that the number of applications from UK citizens for Irish passports increased significantly after the announcement of the result of the referendum on the membership in the European Union. The Irish Embassy in London usually receives 200 passport applications a day, which increased to 4,000 a day after the vote to leave. Other EU nations also had increases in requests for passports from British citizens, including France and Belgium.

EU funding

Cornwall voted to leave the EU but Cornwall Council issued a plea for protection of its local economy and to continue receiving subsidies, as it had received millions of pounds in subsidies from the EU.

After the referendum, leading scientists expressed fear of a shortfall in funding for research and science and worried that the UK had become less attractive for scientists. The UK science minister, Jo Johnson said the government would be on the watch for discrimination against UK scientists, after stories circulated about scientists being left out of joint grant proposals with other EU scientists in the aftermath of the referendum. On 15 August 2016, ministers announced that research funding would be matched by the UK government.

In October 2016, government ministers announced that the UK would be investing 220 million pounds ($285 million) in support of the nation's technology industry. The consequences of Brexit for academia will become clearer once negotiations for Britain's post-Brexit relationship with the EU get under way.

The European Union Youth Orchestra announced in October 2017 that, as a result of Brexit, it intends to relocate from London to Italy. It is expected British youth will cease being eligible to participate in the orchestra in future.

British participation in European institutions

As of January 2018, the European Commission had announced that three European agencies would be leaving the UK as a consequence of its withdrawal from the EU: the European Medicines Agency, European Banking Authority and the Galileo Satellite Monitoring Agency.

Republic of Ireland–United Kingdom border

The United Kingdom and the Republic of Ireland are members of the Common Travel Area, which allows free movement between these countries. If the UK negotiates a settlement with the EU that does not involve Freedom of Movement, while the Republic of Ireland remains an EU member, an open border between the Republic and Northern Ireland is likely to become untenable. Martin McGuinness, deputy First Minister of Northern Ireland, said this would "seriously undermine" the Good Friday Agreement that brought an end to the Troubles. David Cameron pledged to do whatever possible to maintain the open border. Since becoming Prime Minister Theresa May has reassured both Northern Ireland and the Republic of Ireland that there will not be a "hard (customs or immigration) border" on the island of Ireland.

Notification of intention to leave the EU (Article 50)

The most likely way that exit from the EU is activated is through Article 50 of the Treaty on European Union. The British government chooses when to invoke, although theoretically the other members of the European Union could refuse to negotiate before invocation.[942] This will be the first time that this article has been invoked. The government can theoretically ignore the result of the referendum.

Although Cameron had previously announced that he would invoke Article 50 on the morning after a Leave vote, he declared during his resignation that the next Prime Minister should activate Article 50 and begin negotiations with the EU. During the Conservative leadership contest, Theresa May expressed that the UK needs a clear negotiating position before triggering Article 50, and that she would not do so in 2016. The other 27 members of the EU issued a joint statement on 26 June 2016 regretting but respecting Britain's decision and asking them to proceed quickly in accordance with Article 50.[943] This was echoed by the EU Economic Affairs Commissioner Pierre Moscovici.[944] However, with the next French presidential election being held in April and May 2017, and the next German federal election likely to be held in autumn 2017, "people close to the E.U. Commission" were reported as saying that the European Commission was at the time working under the assumption that Article 50 notification would not be made before September 2017.

On 27 June 2016, a "Brexit unit" of civil servants were tasked with "intensive work on the issues that will need to be worked through in order to present options and advice to a new Prime Minister and a new Cabinet",[945] while on 14 July, David Davis was appointed to the newly created post of Secretary of State for Exiting the European Union, or "Brexit Secretary", with a remit to oversee the UK's negotiations for withdrawing from the EU. Davis called for a "brisk but measured" approach to negotiations, and suggested the UK should be ready to trigger Article 50 "before or by the start of" 2017, saying "the first order of business" should be to negotiate trade deals with countries outside the European Union. However, Oliver Letwin, a former Minister of State for Europe, warned the UK had no trade negotiators to lead such talks.

Having previously ruled out starting the Article 50 process before 2017, on 15 July 2016, following a meeting with Scottish First Minister Nicola Sturgeon, May said that it would not begin without a coherent "UK approach" to negotiations. Lawyers representing the government in a legal challenge over the Article 50 process said that May would not trigger Article 50 before 2017. However, in September 2016, *The Washington Post* highlighted the lack of coherent strategy following what it described as the "hurricane-strength political wreckage" left by the Brexit vote. It said the public still had no idea what the oft repeated "Brexit means Brexit" meant and there have been nearly as many statements on what the objectives were as there are cabinet ministers.

The Supreme Court ruled in the Miller case in January 2017 that the government needed parliamentary approval to trigger Article 50. After the House of Commons overwhelmingly voted, on 1 February 2017, for the government's bill authorising the prime minister to invoke Article 50, the bill passed into law as the European Union (Notification of Withdrawal) Act 2017. Theresa May signed the letter invoking Article 50 on 28 March 2017, which was delivered on 29 March by Tim Barrow, the UK's ambassador to the EU, to Donald Tusk.

Informal discussions

On 20 July 2016, following her first overseas trip as prime minister, during which she flew to Berlin for talks with German Chancellor Angela Merkel, Theresa May reaffirmed her intention not to trigger Article 50 before 2017, suggesting it would take time for the UK to negotiate a "sensible and orderly departure" from the EU. However, although Merkel said it was right for the UK to "take a moment" before beginning the process, she urged May to provide more clarity on a timetable for negotiations. Shortly before travelling to Berlin, May had also announced that in the wake of the referendum, Britain would relinquish the presidency of the Council of the European Union, which passes between member states every six months on a rotation basis, and that the UK had been scheduled to hold in the second half of 2017.

Geographical variations within the UK, and implications

<templatestyles src="Multiple_image/styles.css" />

Results by country/region (left) and by district/parliamentary constituency (right)

Leave majority

Remain majority

The distribution of Remain and Leave votes varied dramatically across the country. Remain won every single Scottish district, most London boroughs, Gibraltar and the predominantly Catholic parts of Northern Ireland, as well as many English and Welsh cities. Leave by contrast won almost all other English and Welsh districts and most of the predominantly Ulster Protestant districts, and won a majority in Wales as a whole as well as every English region outside London. These results were interpreted by many commentators as revealing a "split" or "divided" country, and exacerbated regional tensions.

Following the referendum result the all-party Constitution Reform Group announced its intention to publish a draft Act of Union bill outlining a proposed federal constitutional structure for the United Kingdom. Among its proposals are the establishment of an English Parliament, replacing the House of Lords with a directly elected chamber, and greater devolution for the English regions, following a similar format to that of the Greater Manchester Combined Authority.

England

Of the constituent countries in the United Kingdom, England voted most in favour of leaving the European Union with 53% of voters choosing to leave compared to 47% of voters who chose to remain. Every region apart from Greater London returned large majority votes in favour of "Leave". The largest regional vote in favour of "Leave" was recorded in the West Midlands which saw 59% of voters chose to leave the EU which was closely followed by the East Midlands which saw 58% of voters opting to leave. The East Midlands also saw the two highest local authority votes in the United Kingdom in favour of leaving the EU which was recorded in the Borough of Boston in Lincolnshire in which 75.6% of voters chose to leave which was closely followed by the neighbouring local authority South Holland which saw 73% of voters there opting to leave.

Scotland

Scotland voted 62% to remain in the European Union, with all 32 council areas returning a majority for remaining (albeit with an extremely narrow margin of 122 votes in Moray). Scottish First Minister Nicola Sturgeon said it was "clear that the people of Scotland see their future as part of the European Union" and that Scotland had "spoken decisively" with a "strong, unequivocal" vote to remain in the European Union. The Scottish Government announced on 24 June 2016 that officials would plan for a "highly likely" second referendum on independence from the United Kingdom and start preparing legislation to that effect. Former First Minister Alex Salmond said the vote was a "significant and material change" in Scotland's position within the United Kingdom, and

Figure 38:
All 32 Scottish council areas returned major-
ity votes in favour of "Remain" in Scotland
Leave
Remain

that he was certain his party would implement its manifesto on holding a second referendum. Sturgeon said she will communicate to all EU member states that "Scotland has voted to stay in the EU and I intend to discuss all options for doing so." An emergency cabinet meeting on 25 June 2016 agreed that the Scottish Government would "begin immediate discussions with the EU institutions and other member states to explore all the possible options to protect Scotland's place in the EU."

On 26 June, First Minister Nicola Sturgeon told the BBC that Scotland could attempt to refuse legislative consent for the UK's exit from the European Union, and on 28 June, established a "standing council" of experts to advise her on how to protect Scotland's relationship with the EU. On the same day she made the following statement: "I want to be clear to parliament that whilst I believe that independence is the best option for Scotland – I don't think that will come as a surprise to anyone – it is not my starting point in these discussions. My starting point is to protect our relationship with the EU." Sturgeon met with EU leaders in Brussels the next day to discuss Scotland remaining in the EU. Afterwards, she said the reception had been "sympathetic", in spite of

France and Spain objecting to negotiations with Scotland, but conceded that she did not underestimate the challenges.

Also on 28 June, Scottish MEP Alyn Smith received standing ovations from the European Parliament for a speech ending *"Scotland did not let you down, do not let Scotland down."* Manfred Weber, the leader of the European People's Party Group and a key ally of Angela Merkel, said Scotland would be welcome to remain a member of the EU. In an earlier *Welt am Sonntag* interview, Gunther Krichbaum, chairman of the Bundestag's European affairs committee, stated that "the EU will still consist of 28 member states, as I expect a new independence referendum in Scotland, which will then be successful," and urged to "respond quickly to an application for admission from the EU-friendly country."

In a note to the US bank's clients, JP Morgan Senior Western Europe economist Malcolm Barr wrote: "Our base case is that Scotland will vote for independence and institute a new currency" by 2019.

On 15 July, following her first official talks with Nicola Sturgeon at Bute House, Theresa May said that she was "willing to listen to options" on Scotland's future relationship with the European Union and wanted the Scottish government to be "fully involved" with discussions, but that Scotland had sent a "very clear message" on independence in 2014. Sturgeon said she was "very pleased" that May would listen to the Scottish Government, but that it would be "completely wrong" to block a referendum if it was wanted by the people of Scotland. Two days later, Sturgeon told the BBC that she would consider holding a referendum for 2017 if the UK began the process of exiting the European Union without Scotland's future being secured. She also suggested it may be possible for Scotland to remain part of the UK while also remaining part of the EU. However, on 20 July, this idea was dismissed by Attorney General Jeremy Wright, who told the House of Commons that no part of the UK had a veto over the Article 50 process.

On 28 March 2017, the Scottish parliament voted 69-59 in favour of holding a new referendum on Scottish Independence, and on 31 March, Nicola Sturgeon wrote to PM May requesting permission to hold a second referendum.

Northern Ireland

<templatestyles src="Multiple_image/styles.css" />

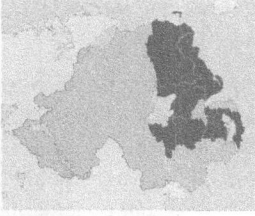

Results in Northern Ireland

Leave

Remain

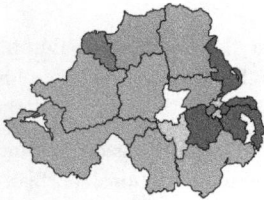

Religious belief in Northern Ireland

More Catholic than Protestant

More Protestant than Catholic

A referendum on Irish unification has been advocated by Sinn Féin, the largest nationalist/republican party in Ireland, which is represented both in the Northern Ireland Assembly and Dáil Éireann in the Republic of Ireland. Northern Ireland's deputy First Minister, Martin McGuinness of Sinn Féin, called for a referendum on the subject following the UK's vote to leave the EU because the majority of the Northern Irish population voted to remain.[946] The First Minister, Arlene Foster of the Democratic Unionist Party, said that Northern Ireland's status remained secure and that the vote had strengthened the union within the United Kingdom. This was echoed by DUP MLA Ian Paisley Jr., who nevertheless recommended that constituents apply for an Irish passport to retain EU rights.

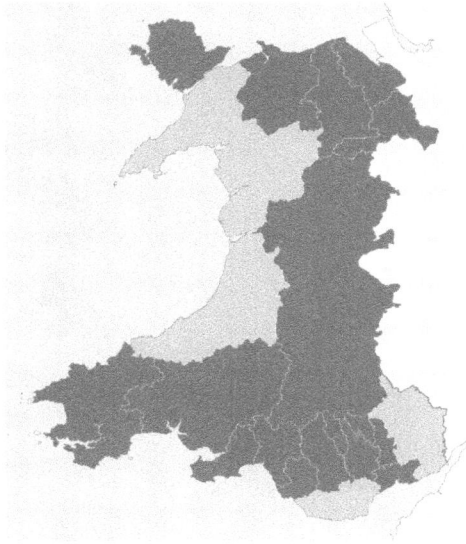

Figure 39:
Wales along with England voted to leave.
Leave
Remain

Wales

Although Wales voted to leave the European Union, Leanne Wood, the leader of Plaid Cymru suggested that the result had "changed everything" and that it was time to begin a debate about independence for Wales. Sources including *The Guardian* have noted that opinion polls tend to put the number in favour of Wales seceding from the United Kingdom at 10%, but Wood suggested in a speech shortly after the referendum that attitudes could change following the result: "The Welsh economy and our constitution face unprecedented challenges. We must explore options that haven't been properly debated until now." On 5 July, a YouGov opinion poll commissioned by ITV Wales indicated that 35% would vote in favour of Welsh independence in the event that it meant Wales could stay in the European Union, but Professor Roger Scully, of Cardiff University's Wales Governance Centre said the poll indicated a "clear majority" against Wales ceasing to be part of the UK: "The overall message appears to be that while Brexit might reopen the discussion on Welsh independence there is little sign that the Leave vote in the EU referendum has yet inclined growing numbers of people to vote Leave in a referendum on Welsh independence from the UK."

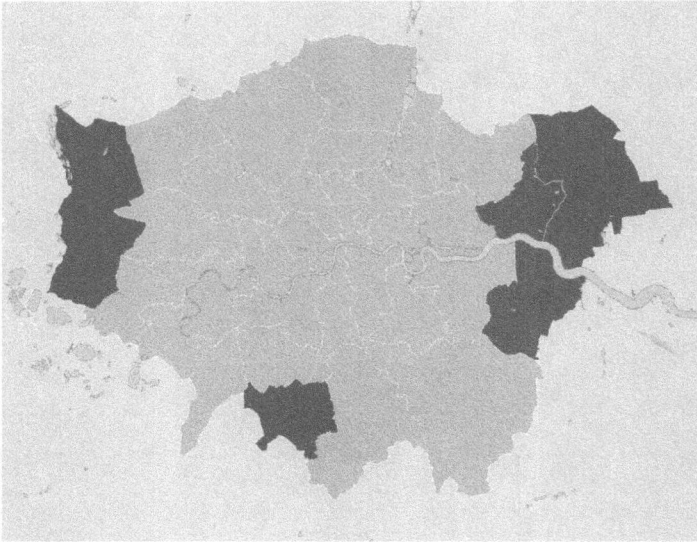

Figure 40:
Voting on the referendum in Greater London
Leave
Remain

Greater London

Greater London voted to remain in the EU, and Scottish First Minister Nicola
Sturgeon said she had spoken to London Mayor Sadiq Khan about the possibility of remaining in the EU and said he shared that objective for London. A
petition calling on Khan to declare London independent from the UK received
tens of thousands of signatures. The BBC reported the petition as tongue-in-
cheek. Supporters of London's independence argued that London's demographic, culture and values are different from the rest of England, and that it
should become a city state similar to Singapore, while remaining an EU member state. Spencer Livermore, Baron Livermore, said that London's independence "should be a goal," arguing that a London city-state would have twice
the GDP of Singapore. Khan said that complete independence was unrealistic,
but demanded devolving more powers and autonomy for London.

Gibraltar

Spain's foreign minister José Manuel García-Margallo said "It's a complete change of outlook that opens up new possibilities on Gibraltar not seen for a very long time. I hope the formula of co-sovereignty – to be clear, the Spanish flag on the Rock – is much closer than before." Gibraltar's Chief Minister Fabian Picardo however immediately dismissed García-Margallo's remarks, stating that "there will be no talks, or even talks about talks, about the sovereignty of Gibraltar", and asked Gibraltar's citizens "to ignore these noises". This is while he was in talks with Nicola Sturgeon, the First Minister of Scotland, to keep Gibraltar in the EU, while remaining British too. He said that "I can imagine a situation where some parts of what is today the member state United Kingdom are stripped out and others remain." Nicola Sturgeon said on the same day that talks were under way with Gibraltar to build a "common cause" on EU membership.

Republic of Ireland

The Republic of Ireland, which shares a land border with the United Kingdom, joined the then European Communities alongside its neighbour on 1 January 1973, and as of 2016, its trade with the UK was worth £840m (€1bn) a week, while as many as 380,000 Irish citizens were employed in the UK. Britain was also a significant contributor towards the 2010 bailout package that was put together in the wake of the banking crisis of the late 2000s. Concerned by the possibility of a UK vote to leave the EU, in 2015, Enda Kenny, the Taoiseach of Ireland, established an office to put together a contingency plan in the event of a Brexit vote.

On 18 July 2016, *Bloomberg News* reported that the UK's vote to leave the EU was having a negative impact on the Republic of Ireland, a country with close economic and cultural ties to the UK. Share prices in Ireland fell after the result, while exporters warned that a weaker UK currency would drive down wages and economic growth in a country still recovering from the effects of the banking crisis. John Bruton, who served as Taoiseach from 1994 to 1997, and later an EU ambassador to the United States, described Britain's vote to leave the European Union as "the most serious, difficult issue facing the country for 50 years". Nick Ashmore, head of the Strategic Banking Corporation of Ireland argued the uncertainty caused by the result had made attracting new business lenders into Ireland more difficult. However, John McGrane, director general of the British Irish Chamber of Commerce, said the organisation had been inundated with enquiries from UK firms wishing to explore the feasibility of basing themselves in a country "with the same language and legal system and with a commitment to staying in the EU".

On 21 July, following talks in Dublin, Kenny and French President Francois Hollande issued a joint statement saying they "looked forward to the notification as soon as possible by the new British government of the UK's intention to withdraw from the Union" because it would "permit orderly negotiations to begin". Hollande also suggested Ireland should secure a "special situation" in discussions with European leaders during the UK's European withdrawal negotiations.

Racist abuse and hate crimes

More than a hundred racist abuse and hate crimes were reported in the immediate aftermath of the referendum with many citing the plan to leave the European Union, with police saying there had been a five-fold increase since the vote. On 24 June, a school in Cambridgeshire was vandalised with a sign reading "Leave the EU. No more Polish vermin." Following the referendum result, similar signs were distributed outside homes and schools in Huntingdon, with some left on the cars of Polish residents collecting their children from school. On 26 June, the London office of the Polish Social and Cultural Association was vandalised with racist graffiti. Both incidents were investigated by the police. Other instances of racism occurred as perceived foreigners were targeted in supermarkets, on buses and on street corners, and told to leave the country immediately. The hate crimes were widely condemned by politicians, the UN and religious groups. MEP Daniel Hannan disputed both the accuracy of reporting and connection to the referendum, in turn receiving criticism for rejecting evidence.

On 8 July 2016, figures released by the National Police Chiefs' Council indicated there were 3,076 reported hate crimes and incidents across England, Wales and Northern Ireland between 16–30 June, compared to 2,161 for the same period in 2015, a 42% increase; the number of incidents peaked on 25 June, when there were 289 reported cases. Assistant Chief Constable Mark Hamilton, the council's lead on hate crime, described the "sharp rise" as unacceptable. The figures were reported to have shown the greatest increase in areas that voted strongly to leave.

Post-referendum campaigning

Petition for a new referendum

Within hours of the result's announcement, a petition, calling for a second referendum to be held in the event that a result was secured with less than 60% of the vote and on a turnout of less than 75%, attracted tens of thousands of new signatures. The petition had been initiated by William Oliver Healey of the English Democrats on 24 May 2016, when the Remain faction had been leading in the polls, and had received 22 signatures prior to the referendum result being declared. On 26 June, Healey said that the petition had actually been started to favour an exit from the EU and that he was a strong supporter of the Vote Leave and Grassroots Out campaigns. Healey also said that the petition had been "hijacked by the remain campaign". English Democrats chairman Robin Tilbrook suggested those who had signed the petition were experiencing "sour grapes" about the result of the referendum.

By late July it had attracted over 4 million signatures, about one quarter of the total number of remain votes in the referendum and over forty times the 100,000 needed for any petition to be considered for debate in Parliament. As many as a thousand signatures per minute were being added during the day after the referendum vote, causing the website to crash on several occasions. Some of the signatories had abstained from voting or had voted leave but regretted their decision, in what the media dubbed "bregret", or "regrexit" at the result.

No previous government petition had attracted as many signatures, but it was reported that the House of Commons Petitions Committee were investigating allegations of fraud. Chair of that committee, Helen Jones, said that the allegations were being taken seriously, and any signatures found to be fraudulent would be removed from the petition: "People adding fraudulent signatures to this petition should know that they undermine the cause they pretend to support." By the afternoon of 26 June the House of Commons' petitions committee said that it had removed "about 77,000 signatures which were added fraudulently" and that it would continue to monitor the petition for "suspicious activity"; almost 40,000 signatures seemed to have come from the Vatican City, which has a population of under 1,000. Hackers from 4chan claimed that they had added the signatures with the use of automated bots, and that it was done as a prank.

<templatestyles src="Template:Quote_box/styles.css" />

As the Prime Minister made clear in his statement to the House of Commons on 27 June, the referendum was one of the biggest democratic exercises in British history with over 33 million people having their say. The Prime Minister and

Government have been clear that this was a once in a generation vote and, as the Prime Minister has said, the decision must be respected. We must now prepare for the process to exit the EU and the Government is committed to ensuring the best possible outcome for the British people in the negotiations.

Email to petition signatories from Foreign and Commonwealth Office, 8 July 2016

On 8 July, the Foreign and Commonwealth Office sent an email to all signatories of the petition setting out the government's position. It rejected calls for a second referendum: "Prime Minister and Government have been clear that this was a once in a generation vote and, as the Prime Minister has said, the decision must be respected." On 12 July the Committee scheduled a debate on the petition for 5 September because of the "huge number" of people who had signed it, but stressed that this did not mean it was backing calls for a second referendum. The debate, held in Westminster Hall, the House of Commons' second chamber, does not have the power to change the law; a spokesman for the Committee said that the debate would not pave the way for Parliament to decide on holding a second referendum. The petition closed on 26 November 2016, having received 4,150,259 signatures.

Backing for a new referendum

The TUC fears that any Brexit deal the government might make could harm workers' interests and lead to workers in many industries losing their jobs. Frances O'Grady of the TUC said that unless the government provides a deal that is good for working people, the TUC will strongly support calls for a second referendum. O'Grady said, "I want to serve notice to the prime minister today that if we don't get the deal that working people need, then the TUC will be throwing our full weight behind a campaign for a popular vote so that people get a say on whether that deal is good enough or not,"[947]

Debate over legitimacy of a second referendum

The petition initiated a debate over the legitimacy of holding a second referendum. BBC political correspondent Iain Watson argued that since the petition requests a piece of retrospective legislation, it is unlikely to be enacted, while David Cameron had previously ruled out holding a second referendum, calling it "a once-in-a-lifetime event". However, Jolyon Maugham QC, a barrister specialising in tax law, argued that a second referendum on EU membership could be triggered by one of two scenarios: following a snap general election won by one or more parties standing on a remain platform, or as a result of parliament deciding that circumstances had changed significantly enough to require a fresh mandate. Maugham cited several instances in which a country's electorate have been asked to reconsider the outcome of a referendum relating to the EU, among them the two Treaty of Lisbon referendums held in Ireland, in 2008 and 2009.

Historian Vernon Bogdanor said that a second referendum would be "highly unlikely", and suggested governments would be cautious about holding referendums in future, but argued it could happen if the EU rethought some of its policies, such as those regarding the free movement of workers. Political scientist John Curtice agreed that a change of circumstances could result in another referendum, but said the petition would have little effect. BBC legal correspondent Clive Coleman argued that a second referendum was "constitutionally possible [but] politically unthinkable. It would take something akin to a revolution and full-blown constitutional crisis for it to happen". Conservative MP Dominic Grieve, a former Attorney General for England and Wales said that although the government should respect the result of the referendum, "it is of course possible that it will become apparent with the passage of time that public opinion has shifted on the matter. If so a second referendum may be justified." Barristers Belinda McRae and Andrew Lodder argued the referendum "is wrongly being treated as a majority vote for the terms of exit that Britain can negotiate [with] the EU" when the public were not asked about the terms of exiting the EU, so a second referendum would be needed on that issue. Richard Dawkins argued that if a second referendum upheld the result of the first, it would "unite the country behind Brexit". However, political scientist Liubomir K. Topaloff argued that a second referendum would "surely destroy the EU" because the resulting anger of Leave supporters in the UK would spread anti-EU sentiment in other countries.

On 26 June, former Prime Minister Tony Blair said the option of holding a second referendum should not be ruled out. A week later he suggested the will of the people could change, and that Parliament should reflect that. Alastair Campbell, the Downing Street Director of Communications under Blair called for a second referendum setting out "the terms on which we leave. And the terms on which we could remain". Labour MP David Lammy commented that, as the referendum was advisory, Parliament should vote on whether to leave the EU. On 1 July, Shadow chancellor John McDonnell outlined Labour's vision for leaving the EU, saying that Britain had to respect the decision that was made in the referendum.[948]

Following the first post-referendum meeting of the Cabinet on 27 June, a spokesman for the Prime Minister said that the possibility of a second referendum was "not remotely on the cards. There was a decisive result [in the EU referendum]. The focus of the Cabinet discussion was how we get on and deliver that." Theresa May also ruled out the possibility at the launch of her campaign to succeed Cameron. On 28 June, Health Secretary Jeremy Hunt raised the possibility of a second referendum, but said that it would be about the terms of the UK's exit from the European Union rather than on the issue of EU membership. Labour MP Geraint Davies also suggested that a second referendum would focus on the terms of an exit plan, with a default of remaining in the EU if it were rejected. Citing a poll published in the week after the referendum that indicated as many as 1.1 million people who voted to leave the EU regretted their decision, he tabled an early day motion calling for an exit package referendum.

On 26 June it was reported that Conservative grandee Michael Heseltine was suggesting that a second referendum should take place after Brexit negotiations, pointing to the overwhelming majority in the House of Commons against leaving the EU. On 13 July, Labour leadership candidate Owen Smith said that he would offer a second referendum on the terms of EU withdrawal if elected to lead the party.

The outcome of the referendum was debated by the Church of England's General Synod on 8 July, where Archbishop of Canterbury Justin Welby ruled out supporting a second referendum. The idea of a second referendum was also rejected by Plaid Cymru leader Leanne Wood, who favoured a general election following negotiations instead. Sammy Wilson, a Democratic Unionist Party MP likened those calling for a second referendum to fascists, saying "They don't wish to have the democratic wishes of the people honoured... They wish to have only their views."

On 8 July, an ORB poll indicated 40% support for a referendum on the terms of withdrawal from the EU. On 16 July, a ComRes poll indicated 57% opposed to a second referendum, with 29% in favour. On 27 July 2018, a YouGov poll indicated a slim majority in favour of a second referendum.

Pro-EU activities

Pro-EU demonstrations took place in the days following the referendum result. On 24 June, protesters gathered in cities across the UK, including London, Edinburgh and Glasgow. At one demonstration in London protesters marched on the headquarters of News UK to protest against "anti-immigration politics". Protesters on bicycles angry at the result attempted to block Boris Johnson's car as he was leaving his home on the morning of 24 June, while campaigners aged 18–25, as well as some teenagers under the age of majority, staged a protest outside Parliament.

On 28 June, up to 50,000 people attended Stand Together, a pro-EU demonstration organised for London's Trafalgar Square, despite the event having been officially cancelled amid safety concerns. The organiser had announced

Figure 41: *A Pro-EU march in London, in March 2017*

the rally on social media, with a view to bringing "20 friends together", but urged people not to attend as the number of people expressing interest reached 50,000. The meeting was addressed by Liberal Democrat leader Tim Farron before protesters made their way to Whitehall. A similar event in Cardiff was addressed by speakers including Plaid Cymru leader Leanne Wood. On 2 July, around 50,000 demonstrators marched in London to show support for the EU and to demand that Britain continues to co-operate with other European states. A similar event was held in Edinburgh outside the Scottish Parliament building.

On 8 July 2016, and in response to the referendum result, *The New European*, was launched with an initial print run of 200,000. This is a national weekly newspaper aimed at people who voted to remain in the EU, which its editor felt had not been represented by the traditional media, and remains in print as of December 2017.

Proposed British Independence Day national holiday

Some Brexit supporters such as David Davies, Steve Double, William Wragg and Sir David Amess called for the Brexit referendum result on 23 June 2016 to be recognised as British Independence Day and be made a public holiday in the United Kingdom. The concept was widely used in social media, with the BBC naming it as one of "Five social media trends after Brexit vote". With support from Conservative MP Nigel Evans, an online petition on the

UK Parliament government website calling for the date to be "designated as Independence Day, and celebrated annually" reached sufficient signatures to trigger a government response, which stated there were "no current plans to create another public holiday".

On 5 September 2017, a number of Conservative MPs backed MP Peter Bone's June Bank Holiday (Creation) Bill in the House of Commons, for the Brexit referendum date to be a UK-wide public holiday. The bill proposes that "June 23 or the subsequent weekday when June 23 falls at a weekend" should serve as a national holiday.

Official investigations into campaigns

On 9 May 2016, Leave.EU was fined £50,000 by the UK Information Commissioner's Office 'for failing to follow the rules about sending marketing messages': they sent people text messages without having first gained their permission to do so.[949,950]

On 4 March 2017, the Information Commissioner's Office also reported that it was 'conducting a wide assessment of the data-protection risks arising from the use of data analytics, including for political purposes' in relation to the Brexit campaign. It was specified that among the organisations to be investigated was Cambridge Analytica and its relationship with the Leave.EU campaign. The findings are expected to be published sometime in 2017.[951,952]

On 21 April 2017, the Electoral Commission announced that it was investigating 'whether one or more donations – including of services – accepted by Leave.EU was impermissible; and whether Leave.EU's spending return was complete', because 'there were reasonable grounds to suspect that potential offences under the law may have occurred'.[953]

Possible Russian and foreign interference

In the run up to the Brexit referendum, Prime Minister David Cameron suggested that Russia "might be happy" with a positive Brexit vote, while the Remain campaign accused the Kremlin of secretly backing a positive Brexit vote.[954] In December 2016, Ben Bradshaw MP claimed in Parliament that Russia had interfered in the Brexit referendum campaign.[955] In February 2017, Bradshaw called on the British intelligence service, Government Communications Headquarters, currently under Boris Johnson as Foreign Secretary, to reveal the information it had on Russian interference.[956]

In April 2017, the House of Commons Public Administration and Constitutional Affairs Committee issued a report stating that Russian and foreign interference in the referendum was probable, including the shut down of the government voter registration website immediately before the vote. In May 2017, it was reported by the *Irish Times* that £425,622 had potentially been donated by sources in Saudi Arabia to the "vote leave" supporting Democratic Unionist Party for spending during the referendum.[957]

External links

- Daily Telegraph – Brexit[958]
- The Independent – Brexit[959]
- BBC News – Brexit[960]
- BBC Radio 4 – A point of view: After the vote (5 episodes)[961]
- LSE Blog – Brexit Vote[962]
- Gov UK - Department for Exiting the European Union[963]
- UK Parliament - Brexit News[964]
- Brexit[965] at Curlie (based on DMOZ)

Russian interference in the Brexit referendum

Russian interference in the 2016 Brexit referendum

Russian interference in the 2016 Brexit referendum concerns the evidence and ongoing investigation by the UK Electoral Commission, the UK Parliament's Culture Select Committee, and the US Senate, on alleged Russian interference in the "Brexit" poll of 23 June 2016.[966] This has raised questions over the legal validity of the Brexit referendum,[967] and multiple criminal charges,[968] including allegations of treason.[969]

Background

After the referendum on the United Kingdom exiting the European Union ("Brexit"), Prime Minister David Cameron suggested that Russia "might be happy" with a positive Brexit vote. The official Remain campaign accused the Kremlin of secretly backing a positive Brexit vote.[970] In March 2016, Philip Hammond, the former Secretary for Defence and Foreign Secretary (later the Chancellor of the Exchequer) stated "the only country who would like us to leave the EU is Russia" at a speech in March 2016.[971]

After the vote

In December 2016, Ben Bradshaw MP claimed in Parliament that Russia had interfered in the Brexit referendum campaign.[972] In February 2017, Bradshaw called on the British intelligence service, Government Communications Headquarters, then under Boris Johnson as Foreign Secretary, to reveal any information it had on Russian interference.[973]

In June 2017, it was reported by *The Guardian* that "Leave" campaigner Nigel Farage was a "person of interest" in the United States Federal Bureau of Investigation into Russian interference in the United States 2016 Presidential election.[974] Farage has called claims that he had any involvement, "What utter baloney, complete and utter baloney." By November 2017 he had yet to be questioned by the FBI.

In October 2017, Members of Parliament in the Culture, Media and Sport Committee demanded that Facebook, Twitter, Google and other social media corporations, to disclose all adverts and details of payments by Russia in the Brexit campaign.[975]

In November 2017 it became public knowledge that Matthew Elliott, the chief executive of Vote Leave, was a founding member of Conservative Friends of Russia, and had been a target asset by someone known to be a Russian spy.[976]

On 12 December 2017, members of the US Congress Ruben Gallego, Eric Swalwell and Gerry Connolly wrote to the Director of National Intelligence requesting information on Russian interference in the Brexit vote.[977] On 13 December 2017, Facebook stated that it found no significant Russian activity during Brexit, but this was immediately rejected by the committee chair, Damian Collins, as being information that was already public after US investigations into Russian interference.[978]

In January 2018, a US Senate minority report suggested possible ways Russia may have influenced the Brexit campaign.[979] It stated,[980]

> The Russian government has sought to influence democracy in the United Kingdom through disinformation, cyber hacking, and corruption. While a complete picture of the scope and nature of Kremlin interference in the UK's June 2016 referendum is still emerging, Prime Minister Theresa May and the UK government have condemned the Kremlin's active measures, and various UK government entities, including the Electoral Commission and parliamentarians, have launched investigations into different aspects of possible Russian government meddling.

In June 2018 it was revealed that Arron Banks, the biggest donor to the campaign for leaving, and co-organiser of Leave.EU received the offer of a Russian gold mine, and had had a series of meetings with the Russian Ambassador. On 14 June 2018, Banks appeared before Parliamentary committee hearing, where he appeared to admit to having lied about his engagements with Russians, and later walked out refusing to answer further questions by citing a luncheon appointment with the Democratic Unionist Party.[981] This has led Vince Cable, former Secretary of State for Business, to publicly state there is the possibility of "treason".[982]WP:NOTRS

In July 2018, the House of Commons Culture, Media and Sport Select Committee, released an interim report on 'Disinformation and 'fake news'', stating that Russia had engaged in "unconventional warfare" through Twitter and other social media against the United Kingdom, designed to amplify support for a "leave" vote in Brexit.[983]

External links

- Bastos, M.T. and Mercea, D. (2017). The Brexit Botnet and User-Generated Hyperpartisan News. Social Science Computer Review[984]
- R Booth et al, 'Russia used hundreds of fake accounts to tweet about Brexit, data shows' (14 November 2017) Guardian[985]
- M Burgess, 'Facebook claims Russia paid for 3 ads around Brexit – costing 73p' (13 December 2017) Wired[986]
- E McGaughey, ' Could Brexit be void?[987] (2018) SSRN, and Verfassungsblog[988]
- House of Commons Culture, Media and Sport Select Committee, 'Disinformation and 'fake news': Interim Report' (July 2018) ch 5, Russian influence in political campaigns[989]
- US Committee on Foreign Relations, Minority Report, 'Putin's Asymmetric Assault on Democracy in Russia and Europe: Implications for U.S. National Security' (2018[990])

Procedure for leaving the EU

United Kingdom invocation of Article 50 of the Treaty on European Union

Part of a series of articles on theUnited Kingdom
in the
European Union

Accession

- 1973 EC enlargement
- 1975 Referendum Act
- 1975 EC membership referendum
- 1972 EC Act
- UK rebate
- 2011 EU Act

Membership

- The Euro
- European Movement UK
- Nationality law
- UK Euroscepticism
  - Maastricht Rebels
- Black Wednesday

- **Officials and bodies**

- EU Committee
- European Scrutiny Committee
- Northern Ireland Executive in Brussels
- EU Representative in London
- Young European Movement UK
- UK European Commissioners
- Permanent EU Representatives

Legislation

- 1972 EC Act
- 1986 EC (Amendment) Act
- 1993 EC (Amendment) Act
- 1998 EC (Amendment) Act
- 2002 EC (Amendment) Act
- 2008 EU (Amendment) Act
- 2011 EU Act

European Parliament Elections

- 1979
- 1984
- 1989
- 1994
- 1999
- 2004
- 2009
- 2014

  - 1973 delegation
  - 1st
  - 2nd
  - 3rd
  - 4th
  - 5th
  - 6th
  - 7th
  - 8th

Withdrawal

- 2004–05 EU Bill
- 2013–14 EU (Referendum) Bill
- 2015–16 EU membership renegotiation
- 2015 EU Referendum Act
- 2016 EU (Referendum) Act (Gibraltar)

- **2016 EU membership referendum**

- Issues
- Endorsements
- Opinion polling
- Results
- Causes

- **Campaigns**

- **Organisations advocating and campaigning for a referendum**

- People's Pledge
- Labour for a Referendum

- **Leave**

- **Vote Leave** (official lead group)
  - Business for Britain
  - Conservatives for Britain
  - Students for Britain
- Labour Leave
- Leave.EU
  - Bpoplive
- Grassroots Out
- Get Britain Out
- The Freedom Association
  - Better Off Out

- **Other anti-EU advocacy organisations**

- Bruges Group
- Campaign for an Independent Britain

- **Remain**

- **Britain Stronger in Europe** (official lead group)
- Labour In for Britain
- European Movement UK

- **Other pro-EU advocacy organisations**

- Britain in Europe
- British Influence
- Business for New Europe
- Nucleus

- **Pejorative term for pro-EU advocacy**

- Project Fear

- **Media coverage**

- *Brexit: The Movie*
- *In or Out*

- **Aftermath**

- International reactions
- Terms of Withdrawal from EU (Referendum) Bills
- 2016 Conservative Party election
- 2016 Labour Party election
- 2017 Liberal Democrats Party election
- Proposed second Scottish independence referendum
- Proposed London independence
- *The New European*
- European Union (Withdrawal) Act 2018 (including meaningful vote)
- European Union (Withdrawal Agreement) Bill 2017-19
- Gibraltar
- 2017 General Election
- EU Withdrawal Agreement (Public Vote) Bill 2017-19
- UK's relations with EU after 2019

- **Triggering of Article 50 & Negotiations**

- *R (Miller) v Secretary of State for Exiting the European Union'*
- EU (Notification of Withdrawal) Act 2017
- UK invocation of Article 50
- Brexit negotiations
- Department for Exiting the EU (Brexit Department)
- Department for International Trade

- **Post-referendum organisations**

- Change Britain
- More United
- Open Britain

Calls for second vote

- European Union Withdrawal Agreement (Public Vote) Bill 2017-19

- **Organisations campaigning**
  for a second vote via People's Vote

- Britain for Europe
- European Movement UK
- For our Future's Sake
- Healthier IN the EU
- Open Britain

- Our Future Our Choice
- Scientists for EU
- **Other organisations campaigning
  for a second vote**
- Best for Britain
- **See also**
- Opposition to Brexit in the United Kingdom
- <u>v</u>
- <u>t</u>
- <u>e</u>[991]

Constitutional documents and events (present & historical) relevant to the status of the United Kingdom and legislative unions of its constituent countries

Treaty of Union	1706
Acts of Union	1707
Wales and Berwick Act	1746
Irish Constitution	1782
Acts of Union	1800
Parliament Act	1911
Government of Ireland Act	1920
Anglo-Irish Treaty	1921
Royal and Parliamentary Titles Act	1927
Statute of Westminster	1931
United Nations Act	1946
Parliament Act	1949
EC Treaty of Accession	1972
NI (Temporary Provisions) Act	1972
European Communities Act	1972
Local Government Act	1972
Local Government (Scotland) Act	1973
NI Border Poll	1973
NI Constitution Act	1973
Referendum Act	1975

EC Membership Referendum	1975
Scotland Act	1978
Wales Act	1978
Scottish Devolution Referendum	1979
Welsh Devolution Referendum	1979
Local Government (Wales) Act	1994
Local Government etc. (Scotland) Act	1994
Referendums (Scotland & Wales) Act	1997
Scottish Devolution Referendum	1997
Welsh Devolution Referendum	1997
Good Friday Agreement	1998
Northern Ireland Act	1998
Government of Wales Act	1998
Human Rights Act	1998
Scotland Act	1998
Government of Wales Act	2006
Northern Ireland Act	2009
Welsh Devolution Referendum	2011
European Union Act	2011
Fixed-term Parliaments Act	2011
Scotland Act	2012
Edinburgh Agreement	2012
Scottish Independence Referendum	2014
Wales Act	2014
European Union Referendum Act	2015
EU Membership Referendum	2016
Scotland Act	2016
Wales Act	2017
EU (Notification of Withdrawal) Act	2017
Invocation of Article 50	2017
European Union (Withdrawal) Act	2018

- v
- t
- e[992]

On 29 March 2017 the United Kingdom (UK) invoked Article 50 of the Treaty on European Union (TEU) which began the member state's withdrawal, commonly known as Brexit, from the European Union (EU). In compliance with the TEU, the UK gave formal notice to the European Council of its intention to withdraw from the EU to allow withdrawal negotiations to begin.

The process of leaving the EU was initiated by a referendum held in June 2016 which favoured British withdrawal from the EU. In October 2016 the UK Prime Minister, Theresa May, announced that Article 50 would be invoked by "the first quarter of 2017". On 24 January 2017 the Supreme Court ruled in the *Miller* case that the process could not be initiated without an authorising act of Parliament, and unanimously ruled against the Scottish government's claim in respect of devolution. Consequently, the European Union (Notification of Withdrawal) Act 2017 empowering the prime minister to invoke Article 50 was enacted in March 2017.

Invocation of Article 50 occurred on 29 March 2017, when Sir Tim Barrow, the Permanent Representative of the United Kingdom to the European Union, formally delivered by hand a letter signed by Prime Minister Theresa May to Donald Tusk, the President of the European Council in Brussels. The letter also contained the United Kingdom's intention to withdraw from the European Atomic Energy Community (EAEC or Euratom). This means that the UK will cease to be a member of the EU on 30 March 2019.

Background

The first ever invocation of Article 50 of the Treaty on European Union was by the United Kingdom, after the Leave vote in the 2016 referendum on the United Kingdom's membership of the European Union.

When David Cameron resigned in June 2016, he stated that the next Prime Minister should activate Article 50 and begin negotiations with the EU.

At the time of the invocation of Article 50 the United Kingdom had been a full member state of the European Communities / European Union since its accession on 1 January 1973 some forty four years earlier.

Views on invocation

Necessity of invoking Article 50

The UK government stated that they would expect a leave vote to be followed by withdrawal, not by a second vote. In a leaflet sent out before the referendum, the UK government stated "This is your decision. The Government will implement what you decide." Although Cameron stated during the campaign that he would invoke Article 50 straight away in the event of a leave victory, he refused to allow the Civil Service to make any contingency plans, something the Foreign Affairs Select Committee later described as "an act of gross negligence."

Unlike the Parliamentary Voting System and Constituencies Act 2011, which contained provisions for an "alternative vote" system which would have become operative only if approved by the voting result in the referendum held under the Act, the European Union Referendum Act 2015 did not state that the government could lawfully invoke Article 50 without a further authorising Act of Parliament.

Following the referendum result Cameron announced before the Conservative Party conference that he would resign by October, and that it would be for the incoming Prime Minister to invoke Article 50. He said that "A negotiation with the European Union will need to begin under a new Prime Minister, and I think it is right that this new Prime Minister takes the decision about when to trigger Article 50 and start the formal and legal process of leaving the EU."

After a court case the government introduced a bill that was passed as the European Union (Notification of Withdrawal) Act 2017.

Article 50 process

Article 50 provides an invocation procedure whereby a member can notify the European Council and there is a negotiation period of up to two years, after which the treaties cease to apply – although a leaving agreement may be agreed by qualified majority voting.[993] In this case, 20[994]</ref> remaining EU countries with a combined population of 65% must agree to the deal. Unless the Council of the European Union unanimously agrees to extensions, the timing for the UK leaving under the article is the mandatory period ending at the second anniversary of the country giving official notice to the EU. The assumption is that new agreements will be negotiated during the mandatory two-year period, but there is no legal requirement that agreements have to be made. Some aspects, such as new trade agreements, may be difficult to negotiate until after the UK has formally left the EU.

Renegotiation of membership terms

Negotiations after invoking Article 50 cannot be used to renegotiate the conditions of future membership as Article 50 does not provide the legal basis of withdrawing a decision to leave.

On the other hand, the constitutional lawyer and retired German Supreme Court judge Udo Di Fabio has stated that

- The Lisbon Treaty does not forbid an exiting country to withdraw its application for leaving, because the Vienna Convention on the Law of Treaties prescribes an initial notification procedure, a kind of period of notice. Before a contract under international law [such as the Lisbon Treaty], which had been agreed without specifying details of giving notice, can be effectively cancelled, it is required that the intention to do so is expressed 12 months in advance: in this matter there exists the principle of preserving existing agreements and international organisations. In this light, the declaration of the intention to leave would itself be, under EU law, not a notice of cancellation.
- Separate negotiations of the EU institutions with pro-EU regions [London, Scotland or Northern Ireland] would constitute a violation of the Lisbon Treaty, according to which the integrity of a member country is explicitly put under protection.

A February 2016 briefing note for the European Parliament stated that a withdrawal from the EU ends, from then on, the application of the EU Treaties in the withdrawing state, although any national acts previously adopted for implementing or transposing EU law would remain valid until amended or repealed, and a withdrawal agreement would need to deal with phasing-out EU financial programmes. The note mentions that a member withdrawing from the EU would need to enact its own new legislation in any field of exclusive EU competence, and that complete isolation of a withdrawing state would be impossible if there is to be a future relationship between the former member and the EU, but that a withdrawal agreement could have transitional provisions for rights deriving from EU citizenship and other rights deriving from EU law that the withdrawal would otherwise extinguish.[995] The Common Fisheries Policy is one of the exclusive competences reserved for the European Union; others concern customs union, competition rules, monetary policy and concluding international agreements.

In oral evidence to a Select Committee of the House of Lords in March 2016, one of the legal experts (Sir David Edward) stated that the German text of Article 50 could be taken to mean that the structure of future relations between the UK and EU will already have been established at the point when withdrawal takes place, which could be taken as a difference from the English text "the Union shall negotiate and conclude an agreement with the withdrawing state setting out the arrangements for its withdrawal and taking account of the framework for its future relationship with the Union".

Arguments for moving slowly

Nicolas J. Firzli of the World Pensions Council (WPC) argued in July 2016 that it could be in Britain's national interest to proceed slowly in the following months; Her Majesty's Government might want to push Brussels to accept the principles of a free trade deal before invoking Article 50, hopefully gaining support from some other member states whose economy is strongly tied to the UK, thus "allowing a more nimble union to focus on the free trade of goods and services without undue bureaucratic burdens, modern antitrust law and stronger external borders, leaving the rest to member states".

Prime Minister Theresa May confirmed that discussions with the EU would not start in 2016. "I want to work with ... the European council in a constructive spirit to make this a sensible and orderly departure", she said. "All of us will need time to prepare for these negotiations and the United Kingdom will not invoke article 50 until our objectives are clear." In a joint press conference with May on 20 July, Germany's Chancellor Angela Merkel supported the UK's position in this respect: "We all have an interest in this matter being carefully prepared, positions being clearly defined and delineated. I think it is absolutely necessary to have a certain time to prepare for that."

Scottish Parliament

In February 2017 the Scottish Parliament voted with overwhelming majority against invoking Article 50.[996] After the UK Government had nevertheless chosen to invoke Article 50, the Scottish Government was formally authorised by the Parliament by a vote of 69 to 59 to seek to hold a second Scottish independence referendum.

Pre-notification negotiations

Prior to the UK Government's invocation of Article 50, the UK stayed a member of the EU, had to continue to fulfill all EU-related treaties including possible future agreements, and was legally treated as a member. The EU has no framework to exclude the UK—or any member—as long as Article 50 was not invoked, and the UK did not violate EU laws. However, if the UK had breached EU law significantly, there were legal venues to discharge the UK from the EU via Article 7, the so-called "nuclear option" which allows the EU to cancel membership of a state that breaches fundamental EU principles, a test that is hard to pass. Article 7 does not allow forced cancellation of membership, only denial of rights such as free trade, free movement and voting rights.

At a meeting of the Heads of Government of the other states in June 2016, leaders decided that they would not start any negotiation before the UK formally invoked Article 50. Consequently, the President of the European Commission, Jean-Claude Juncker, ordered all members of the EU Commission not to engage in any kind of contact with UK parties regarding Brexit. Media statements of various kinds still occurred. For example, on 29 June 2016, European Council president Donald Tusk told the UK that they would not be allowed access to the European Single Market unless they accept its four freedoms of goods, capital, services, and people. Angela Merkel said, "We'll ensure that negotiations don't take place according to the principle of cherry-picking ... It must and will make a noticeable difference whether a country wants to be a member of the family of the European Union or not".

To strike and extend trade agreements between the UK and non-EU states, the Department for International Trade (DIT) was created by Prime Minister Theresa May, shortly after she took office on 13 July 2016. As of February 2017, the DIT employs about 200 trade negotiators[997] and is overseen by Liam Fox, the Secretary of State for International Trade.

Subjects of negotiation

Since Article 50 has been invoked, the United Kingdom will negotiate with the European Union the status of the 1.2 million UK citizens living in the EU, the status of the 3.2 million EU nationals living in the UK. Issues relating to immigration, free trade, the freedom of movement, the Irish border, intelligence-sharing and financial services will also be discussed.

Process

Initial speculation

During the referendum David Cameron pledged to invoke Article 50 on the morning of a Leave vote, and there was speculation that he would do this on the morning with Eurosceptic MPs calling for caution to assess the negotiating position and Jeremy Corbyn calling for immediate invocation. During a 27 June 2016 meeting, the Cabinet decided to establish a unit of civil servants, headed by senior Conservative Oliver Letwin, who would proceed with "intensive work on the issues that will need to be worked through in order to present options and advice to a new Prime Minister and a new Cabinet".

Conservative Party Leadership election

Instead of invoking Article 50 Cameron resigned as Prime Minister, leaving the timing to a successor. There was speculation in the UK that it would be delayed,[998] and the European Commission in July 2016 was under the assumption that Article 50 notification would not be made before September 2017.

Following the referendum result Cameron announced that he would resign before the Conservative party conference in October and that it would be for the incoming Prime Minister to invoke Article 50:

<templatestyles src="Template:Quote/styles.css"/>

> *A negotiation with the European Union will need to begin under a new Prime Minister, and I think it is right that this new Prime Minister takes the decision about when to trigger Article 50 and start the formal and legal process of leaving the EU.*

Cameron made it clear that his successor as Prime Minister should activate Article 50 and begin negotiations with the EU. Among the candidates for the Conservative Party leadership election there were disagreements about when this should be: Theresa May said that the UK needed a clear negotiating position before triggering Article 50, and that she would not do so in 2016, while Andrea Leadsom said that she would trigger it as soon as possible.

EU views

According to EU Economic Affairs Commissioner Pierre Moscovici, Britain had to proceed promptly. In June 2016 he said: "There needs to be a notification by the country concerned of its intention to leave (the EU), hence the request (to British Prime Minister David Cameron) to act quickly." In addition, the remaining EU leaders issued a joint statement on 26 June 2016 regretting but respecting Britain's decision and asking them to proceed quickly in accordance with Article 50. The statement also added: "We stand ready to launch negotiations swiftly with the United Kingdom regarding the terms and conditions of its withdrawal from the European Union. Until this process of negotiations is over, the United Kingdom remains a member of the European Union, with all the rights and obligations that derive from this. According to the Treaties which the United Kingdom has ratified, EU law continues to apply to the full to and in the United Kingdom until it is no longer a Member."

An EU Parliament motion passed on 28 June 2016 called for the UK immediately to trigger Article 50 and start the exit process. There is no mechanism allowing the EU to invoke the article. As long as the UK Government has not invoked Article 50, the UK stays a member of the EU; must continue to fulfil all EU-related treaties, including possible future agreements; and should legally be treated as a member. The EU has no framework to exclude the UK as long as Article 50 is not invoked, and the UK does not violate EU laws. However, if the UK were to breach EU law significantly, there are legal provisions to allow the EU to cancel membership of a state that breaches fundamental EU principles, a test that is hard to pass. These do not allow forced cancellation of membership, only denial of rights such as free trade, free movement and voting rights.

Prime Minister Theresa May made it clear that discussions with the EU would not start in 2016. "I want to work with ... the European Council in a constructive spirit to make this a sensible and orderly departure." she said. "All of us will need time to prepare for these negotiations and the United Kingdom will not invoke article 50 until our objectives are clear." In a joint press conference with May on 20 July 2016, Germany's Chancellor Angela Merkel supported the UK's position in this respect: "We all have an interest in this matter being carefully prepared, positions being clearly defined and delineated. I think it is absolutely necessary to have a certain time to prepare for that."

The Miller Case

The Supreme Court ruled in the Miller case that an explicit Act of Parliament is necessary to authorise the invocation of Article 50.

The Constitution of the United Kingdom is unwritten and it operates on convention and legal precedent: this question is without precedent and so the legal position was thought to be unclear. The Government argued that the use of prerogative powers to enact the referendum result was constitutionally proper and consistent with domestic law whereas the opposing view was that prerogative powers could not be used to set aside rights previously established by Parliament.

<templatestyles src="Template:Quote_box/styles.css" />

"I am writing to give effect to the democratic decision of the people of the United Kingdom. I hereby notify the European Council in accordance with Article 50 (2) of the Treaty on European Union of the United Kingdom's intention to withdraw from the European Union. In addition, in accordance with the same Article 50(2) as applied by Article 106a of the Treaty Establishing the European Atomic Energy Community, I hereby notify the European Council of the United Kingdom's intention to withdraw from the European Atomic Energy Community. References in this letter to the European Union should therefore be taken to include a reference to the European Atomic Energy Community."

Letter from Prime Minister May to EU Council President Tusk, 29 May 2017 (para. 3).[999]

Three distinct groups of citizens – one supported by crowd funding – brought a case before the High Court of England and Wales to challenge the government's interpretation of the law.

On 13 October 2016, the High Court commenced hearing opening arguments. The Government argued that it would be constitutionally impermissible for the court to make a declaration that it [Her Majesty's Government] could not lawfully issue such a notification. The government stated that such a declaration [by the Court] would trespass on proceedings in Parliament, as the Court had ruled previously when rejecting a challenge to the validity of the ratification of the Lisbon Treaty after the passing of the European Union (Amendment) Act 2008 but without a referendum. Opening the case for the Plaintiffs, Lord Pannick QC told the Court that the case "raises an issue of fundamental constitutional importance concerning the limits of the power of the Executive". He argued Mrs May could not use royal prerogative powers to remove rights established by the European Communities Act 1972, which made EU law part of UK law, as it was for Parliament to decide whether or not to maintain those statutory rights.[1000]

On 3 November 2016, the High Court ruled in *R (Miller) v Secretary of State for Exiting the European Union* that only Parliament could make the decision on when or indeed whether to invoke Article 50.[1001] The Government's appeal to the Supreme Court took place on 5–8 December 2016. On 24 January 2017, the Supreme Court upheld the decision of lower court by a majority of eight to three, declaring that the invocation of Article 50 could only come by an Act of Parliament. The case was seen as having constitutional significance in deciding the scope of the royal prerogative in foreign affairs. The Supreme Court also ruled that devolved legislatures in Scotland, Wales and Northern Ireland have no legal right to veto the act.

Other court cases

In January 2017, a claim of several people in legal proceedings against the Secretary of State centred on the UK's links with the European Economic Area.[1002] The following month, the High Court rejected their application for judicial review.[1003]

UK Parliament

On 2 October 2016, the Prime Minister, Theresa May, announced that she intended to invoke Article 50 by the end of March 2017, meaning that the UK would be on a course to leave the EU by the end of March 2019.

On 7 December 2016, the House of Commons approved a non-legally-binding motion supporting Article 50's invocation by 31 March 2017.

As a direct consequence of the Supreme Court ruling the House of Commons voted by a majority of 384 votes (498 to 114) to approve the second reading of the European Union (Notification of Withdrawal) Act 2017 to allow the Prime Minister to invoke Article 50 unconditionally.

On 7 March 2017 the bill passed the House of Lords, though with two amendments. Following further votes in the Commons and the Lords on 13 March 2017, these two amendments did not become part of the bill, so the bill passed its final reading unamended and it received royal assent on 16 March 2017.

Invocation of Artcile 50 has been challenged in the UK courts on the basis that the UK Parliament never voted to leave the EU despite the clear decision of the Supreme Court ruling. Campaigners argue the referendum result was not ratified by an act of Parliament, which they claim means the triggering of Article 50 is invalid.

According to David Davis MP when presenting the European Union (Notification of Withdrawal) Act 2017: "It is not a Bill about whether the UK should leave the European Union or, indeed, about how it should do so; it is simply about Parliament empowering the Government to implement a decision already made – a point of no return already passed", further saying that the Bill was "the beginning of a process to ensure that the decision made by the people last June is honoured."[1004]

Formal notification

In October 2016 the UK Prime Minister, Theresa May, announced that the government would trigger Article 50 by "the first quarter of 2017". Theresa May announced on Monday 20 March 2017 that the UK would formally invoke Article 50 on Wednesday 29 March 2017, meeting her self-imposed deadline. The letter invoking Article 50 was signed by May on 28 March 2017, and was hand delivered on 29 March by Tim Barrow, the Permanent Representative of the United Kingdom to the European Union, to Donald Tusk, the President of the European Council in Brussels. The letter also contained the United Kingdom's intention to withdraw from the European Atomic Energy Community (EAEC or Euratom). On 31 March Tusk sent draft negotiation guidelines to the leaders of the EU to prepare for the upcoming Brexit negotiations.

Reversibility

Differing views have been expressed on whether the UK's invocation of Article 50 can be revoked.

British government lawyers had argued that the Article 50 process could not be stopped.[1005] An Irish court case challenging this view was later abandoned.

Lord Kerr has asserted that the Article 50 notification can be revoked unilaterally.

UK barrister Hugh Mercer QC noted before Article 50 was invoked that: "Though Art. 50 includes no express provision for revocation of the UK notice, it is clearly arguable for example on the grounds of the duties of sincere cooperation between member states (Art. 4(3) of the Treaty on European Union) that, were the UK to feel on mature reflection that leaving the EU and/or the European Economic Area (EEA) is not in the national interest, the notice under Art. 50 could be revoked."

US law professor Jens Dammann argues: "there are strong policy reasons for allowing a Member State to rescind its declaration of withdrawal until the moment that the State's membership in the European Union actually ends" and "there are persuasive doctrinal arguments justifying the recognition of such a right as a matter of black letter law".

EU politicians have said that if the UK changes its mind, they are sure a political formula will be found to reverse article 50, regardless of the technical specifics of the law. According to the influential German finance minister Wolfgang Schäuble, "The British Government has said we will stay with the Brexit. We take the decision as a matter of respect. But if they wanted to change their decision, of course, they would find open doors."

On 29 March 2017, the EU Commission stated "It is up to the United Kingdom to trigger Article 50. But once triggered, it cannot be unilaterally reversed. Notification is a point of no return. Article 50 does not provide for the unilateral withdrawal of notification." Similarly, the European Parliament Brexit committee headed by Guy Verhofstadt has stated that "a revocation of notification [by Article 50] needs to be subject to conditions set by all EU27, so that it cannot be used as a procedural device or abused in an attempt to improve on the current terms of the United Kingdom's membership".

However, in July 2016 former German Supreme Court judge Udo Di Fabio had argued, on the basis of international law, that a triggering of Article 50 can be revoked: "in EU law, the declaration of intention to leave is not itself a notification of withdrawal; rather, at any time and at least until the Treaty becomes inapplicable, it can be retracted or declared to have become redundant".[1006]

In October 2017, barrister Jessica Simor QC of the leading London law firm Matrix Chambers lodged a freedom of information request to the UK Prime Minister for disclosure of legal advice which, she claims, states that the UK government can withdraw the Article 50 application at any time before 29 March 2019; she notes that Article 50 provides only for notification of an intention to withdraw and contends that such intention can be changed at any time before actual withdrawal.

In February 2018, a crowd-funded petition by a cross-party group of Scottish politicians for judicial review of the notice was rejected by Scotland's Court of Session, but in March the Court overturned that decision. The petition will be considered further by the Court.

External links

- *The Brexit Papers*, Bar Council, December 2016[1007]
- *The United Kingdom's exit from and new partnership with the European Union*, February 2017 ("White paper")[1008]
- *Letter from the Prime Minister to President Tusk*, 29 March 2017[1009]
- *Legislating for the United Kingdom's withdrawal from the European Union* (The Great Repeal Bill White Paper), 30 March 2017[1010]

Negotiations

Brexit negotiations

Brexit negotiations (2017–present)

Map of the United Kingdom within the European Union

Type	Withdrawal agreement Transitional agreement Trade agreement
Con-dition	Ratification by all members of the Council of the European Union and the European Parliament, the Parliament of the United Kingdom and the legislatures of all EU member states.
Nego-tia-tors	• 🇬🇧 Theresa May (Prime Minister) • 🇬🇧 Dominic Raab[1011] (Secretary of State for Exiting the European Union) • ⬛ Donald Tusk (Council President) • ⬛ Jean-Claude Juncker (Commission President) • ⬛ Michel Barnier (Commission Chief Negotiator)
Par-ties	• 🇬🇧 United Kingdom • ⬛ European Union

Part of a series of articles on theUnited Kingdom
in the
European Union

Accession

- 1973 EC enlargement
- 1975 Referendum Act
- 1975 EC membership referendum
- 1972 EC Act
- UK rebate
- 2011 EU Act

Membership

- The Euro
- European Movement UK
- Nationality law
- UK Euroscepticism
  - Maastricht Rebels
- Black Wednesday

- **Officials and bodies**

- EU Committee
- European Scrutiny Committee
- Northern Ireland Executive in Brussels
- EU Representative in London
- Young European Movement UK
- UK European Commissioners
- Permanent EU Representatives

Legislation

- 1972 EC Act
- 1986 EC (Amendment) Act
- 1993 EC (Amendment) Act
- 1998 EC (Amendment) Act

- 2002 EC (Amendment) Act
- 2008 EU (Amendment) Act
- 2011 EU Act

European Parliament Elections

- 1979
- 1984
- 1989
- 1994
- 1999
- 2004
- 2009
- 2014

  - 1973 delegation
  - 1st
  - 2nd
  - 3rd
  - 4th
  - 5th
  - 6th
  - 7th
  - 8th

Withdrawal

- 2004–05 EU Bill
- 2013–14 EU (Referendum) Bill
- 2015–16 EU membership renegotiation
- 2015 EU Referendum Act
- 2016 EU (Referendum) Act (Gibraltar)

- **2016 EU membership referendum**

- Issues
- Endorsements
- Opinion polling
- Results
- Causes

- **Campaigns**

- **Organisations advocating and campaigning for a referendum**

- People's Pledge
- Labour for a Referendum

- **Leave**
- **Vote Leave** (official lead group)
  - Business for Britain
  - Conservatives for Britain
  - Students for Britain
- Labour Leave
- Leave.EU
  - Bpoplive
- Grassroots Out
- Get Britain Out
- The Freedom Association
  - Better Off Out

- **Other anti-EU advocacy organisations**

- Bruges Group
- Campaign for an Independent Britain

- **Remain**

- **Britain Stronger in Europe** (official lead group)
- Labour In for Britain
- European Movement UK

- **Other pro-EU advocacy organisations**

- Britain in Europe
- British Influence
- Business for New Europe
- Nucleus

- **Pejorative term for pro-EU advocacy**

- Project Fear

- **Media coverage**

- *Brexit: The Movie*
- *In or Out*

- **Aftermath**

- International reactions
- Terms of Withdrawal from EU (Referendum) Bills
- 2016 Conservative Party election
- 2016 Labour Party election
- 2017 Liberal Democrats Party election
- Proposed second Scottish independence referendum
- Proposed London independence

- *The New European*
- European Union (Withdrawal) Act 2018 (including meaningful vote)
- European Union (Withdrawal Agreement) Bill 2017-19
- Gibraltar
- 2017 General Election
- EU Withdrawal Agreement (Public Vote) Bill 2017-19
- UK's relations with EU after 2019

- **Triggering of Article 50 & Negotiations**

- *R (Miller) v Secretary of State for Exiting the European Union*'
- EU (Notification of Withdrawal) Act 2017
- UK invocation of Article 50
- Brexit negotiations
- Department for Exiting the EU (Brexit Department)
- Department for International Trade

- **Post-referendum organisations**

- Change Britain
- More United
- Open Britain

Calls for second vote

- European Union Withdrawal Agreement (Public Vote) Bill 2017-19

- **Organisations campaigning
  for a second vote via People's Vote**

- Britain for Europe
- European Movement UK
- For our Future's Sake
- Healthier IN the EU
- Open Britain
- Our Future Our Choice
- Scientists for EU

- **Other organisations campaigning
  for a second vote**

- Best for Britain

- **See also**

- Opposition to Brexit in the United Kingdom

- v
- t
- e[1012]

<templatestyles src="Multiple_image/styles.css" />

🏴 Dominic Raab

⬛ Michel Barnier

Lead negotiators for the UK and for the EU

The **Brexit negotiations** are the negotiations currently taking place between the United Kingdom and the European Union for the prospective withdrawal of the United Kingdom from the European Union, following the UK's referendum on EU membership in June 2016.

A negotiating period began on 29 March 2017 when the United Kingdom served the withdrawal notice under Article 50 of the Treaty on European Union. The period for negotiation stated in Article 50 is two years from notification, unless an extension is agreed.

On 19 June 2017, British Secretary of State for Exiting the European Union, David Davis, arrived in Brussels to begin negotiation of the terms of the withdrawal with the Chief Negotiator appointed by the European Commission, Michel Barnier.

The scope of the negotiations could include the withdrawal agreement, a temporary transitional period agreement and another agreement for the post-transitional period.Wikipedia:Attribution needed

Brexit negotiation might also need to address Free Trade Agreement treaties between the European Union and its members (including the UK) for one part and third countries for the other part, and the tariff-rate quota, which might be split or renegotiated.

Background

7th May 2015 United Kingdom General Election

In the Conservative Party's manifesto for the 7th May 2015 United Kingdom General Election, an EU referendum was promised by the end of 2017[1013][1014].

Preparatory work, and intentions

According to the European parliament, "For the moment, it appears that the two sides have different views on the sequencing and scope of the negotiations, and notably the cross-over between the withdrawal agreement and the structure of future relations, and this divergence itself may be one of the first major challenges to overcome."

UK negotiation

- David Davis (until 9 July 2018), Secretary of State for Exiting the European Union.
- Dominic Raab (from 9 July 2018), Secretary of State for Exiting the European Union.
- Sir Tim Barrow, UK Permanent Representative to the EU

- Theresa May, Prime Minister of the United Kingdom
- Oliver Robbins, Europe advisor to the Prime Minister

The Department for Exiting the European Union is responsible for overseeing the negotiations to leave the EU and for establishing the future relationship between the UK and EU.

The proposed principles were set out in the Article 50 notification:

- Constructive discussions
- Citizens first
- Comprehensive agreement
- Minimise disruption

- Ireland/Northern Ireland position
- Technical talks on detailed policy
- Work together on European values

The Prime Minister's formal letter of notification was delivered in Brussels on 29 March 2017. It included withdrawal from the European Atomic Energy Community. The letter recognized that consequences for the UK of leaving the EU included loss of influence over the rules that affect the European economy, and UK companies trading within the EU aligning with rules agreed by institutions of which the UK would no longer be part. It proposed agreeing to seven principles for the conduct of the withdrawal negotiation. These are for:

i. engaging with one another constructively and respectfully, in a spirit of sincere cooperation.

ii. aiming to strike an early agreement about the rights of the many EU citizens living in the United Kingdom, and UK citizens living elsewhere in the European Union.

iii. working towards securing a comprehensive agreement, taking in both economic and security cooperation, and agreeing the terms of our future partnership alongside those of our withdrawal from the EU.

iv. working together to minimise disruption and giving as much certainty as possible, letting people and businesses in the UK and the EU benefit from implementation periods to adjust in an orderly way to new arrangements.

v. in particular, paying attention to the UK's unique relationship with the Republic of Ireland and the importance of the peace process in Northern Ireland.

vi. beginning technical talks on detailed policy areas as soon as possible, including a Free Trade Agreement covering sectors crucial to our linked economies such as financial services and network industries.

vii. continuing to work together to advance and protect our shared liberal, democratic values of Europe, to ensure that Europe remains able to lead in the world, projecting its values and defending itself from security threats.

Role of the countries of the United Kingdom

The constitutional lawyer and retired German Supreme Court judge Udo Di Fabio has stated that separate negotiations of the EU institutions with Scotland or Northern Ireland would constitute a violation of the Lisbon Treaty, according to which the integrity of a member country is explicitly put under protection.

UK general election

The start of negotiations was delayed until after the United Kingdom general election, which took place on 8 June 2017. Antonio Tajani, speaking on 20 April said that the early election should bring stability to the UK, which would have been good for negotiations. In the event, the election led to a hung parliament which is expected to increase instability.

EU27 negotiation

- Michel Barnier, European Commission chief negotiator
- Jean-Claude Juncker, President of the European Commission
- Donald Tusk, President of the European Council
- Guy Verhofstadt, lead negotiator for the European Parliament
- Antonio Tajani, President of the European Parliament

Following the United Kingdom's notification under Article 50, draft guidelines for the negotiations were sent to EU delegations of the 27 other member states (the EU27). The draft, prepared by the President of the European Council, states that the guidelines define the framework for negotiations under Article 50 and set out the overall positions and principles that the Union will pursue throughout the negotiation. It states that in the negotiations the Union's overall objective will be to preserve its interests, those of its Member States, its citizens and its businesses, and that, in the best interest of both sides, the Union will be constructive throughout and strive to find an agreement. The draft sets out two Core Principles:

"1. The European Council will continue to base itself on the principles set out in the statement of Heads of State or Government and of the Presidents of the European Council and the European Commission on 29 June 2016. It reiterates its wish to have the United Kingdom as a close partner in the future. It further reiterates that any agreement with the United Kingdom will have to be based on a balance of rights and obligations, and ensure a level-playing field. Preserving the integrity of the European Single Market excludes participation based on a sector-by-sector approach. A non-member of the Union, that does not live up to the same obligations as a member, cannot have the same rights and enjoy the same benefits as a member. In this context, the European Council welcomes the recognition by the British Government that the four freedoms of the Single Market are indivisible and that there can be no "cherry picking". "

"2. Negotiations under Article 50 TEU (Treaty on European Union) will be conducted as a single package. In accordance with the principle that nothing is agreed until everything is agreed, individual items cannot be settled separately. The Union will approach the negotiations with unified positions, and will engage with the United Kingdom exclusively through the channels set out in these guidelines and in the negotiating directives. So as not to undercut the position of the Union, there will be no separate negotiations between individual Member States and the United Kingdom on matters pertaining to the withdrawal of the United Kingdom from the Union."

According to the European Parliament, the withdrawal agreement and any possible transitional arrangement(s) should enter into force "well before the elections to the European Parliament of May 2019", and the negotiations should focus on:

* The legal status of European Union citizens living or having lived in the United Kingdom and of United Kingdom citizens living or having lived in other Member States, as well as other provisions concerning their rights;
* The settlement of financial obligations between the United Kingdom and the European Union;
* The European Union's external border;
* The clarification of the status of the United Kingdom's international commitments taken as a Member of the European Union, given that the European Union of 27 Member States will be the legal successor of the European Union of 28 Member States;
* Legal certainty for legal entities, including companies;
* The designation of the Court of Justice of the European Union as the competent authority for the interpretation and enforcement of the withdrawal agreement.

On 18 April 2017, a spokesman for Donald Tusk said "We expect to have the Brexit guidelines adopted by the European Council on 29 April and, following that, the Brexit negotiating directives ready on 22 May". On 29 April the EU27 unanimously endorsed the draft guidelines with no debate.

In a speech to a plenary session of the European Committee of the Regions in Brussels on 22 March 2017, Barnier, as EU Chief Negotiator for the Preparation and Conduct of the Negotiations, said that the EU wanted to succeed by reaching a deal with the British, not against them.

On 22 May the European Commission Council, following the approval of negotiating directives which had been adopted by strong qualified majority (72% of the 27 Member States, i.e. 20 Member States representing 65% of the population of the EU27), authorised the opening of Article 50 discussions with the Commission appointed as the negotiator. It further confirmed that all agendas, EU position papers, Non-papers and EU text proposals will be released to the public and published on line.

Intergovernmental organization

Intergovernmental organizations also involved in Brexit uncertainty considerations include the World Trade Organization (WTO) and the International Air Transport Association (IATA). IATA expects an agreement to avoid disruption.

Phases

EU27 guidelines include:

- Agreement on the so-called "divorce bill";
- Agreement on rights of EU citizens living in the UK;
- Agreement on the border between Northern Ireland and the Republic

within the withdrawal phase.

The second phase, covering the post-Brexit relationship between the EU27 and the UK, will begin "as soon as the European Council decides that sufficient progress has been made in the first phase towards reaching a satisfactory agreement on the arrangements for an orderly withdrawal". The earliest opportunity for this decision was 19 October 2017, at a summit of EU leaders. although at that meeting it was agreed to start negotiations during the December meeting.

Negotiation policy

<templatestyles src="Template:Quote_box/styles.css" />

"We recognise how important it is to provide business, the public sector and the public with as much certainty as possible. So ahead of, and throughout the negotiations, we will provide certainty wherever we can. We will provide as much information as we can without undermining the national interest."

"The United Kingdom's exit from and new partnership with the European Union"[1015] (PDF). *UK Government*. February 2017. p. 9.

Some effects of the UK withdrawal could emerge before the UK and the EU27 conclude the Article 50 negotiation, as a result of policies existing when the negotiation begins, or some change of policy later. At the outset policy provisions binding on the EU include principles, aspirations and objectives set out in the TEU (Treaty on European Union) Preamble and Articles, of which

> *Article 3* mentions the promotion of "scientific and technological advance" in a context governed by "The Union's aim is to promote peace, its values and the well-being of its peoples", the Union's internal market, "work for the sustainable development of Europe based on balanced economic growth and price stability, a highly competitive social market economy, aiming at full employment and social progress", and the requirement that "The Union shall pursue its objectives by appropriate means commensurate with the competences which are conferred upon it in the Treaties",

and

Article 4 mentions "competences not conferred upon the Union in the Treaties remain with the Member States".

Policies mentioned in the Preamble include:

– Achieve the strengthening and convergence of Member States' economies and establish an economic and monetary union including a single and stable currency,

– Promote economic and social progress for their peoples, taking into account the principle of sustainable development and within the context of the accomplishment of the internal market and of reinforced cohesion and environmental protection, and implement policies ensuring that advances in economic integration are accompanied by parallel progress in other fields,

– Establish a citizenship common to nationals of their countries,

– Implement a common foreign and security policy including the progressive framing of a common defence policy, thereby reinforcing the European identity and its independence in order to promote peace, security and progress in Europe and in the world,

– Facilitate the free movement of persons, while ensuring the safety and security of their peoples, by establishing an area of freedom, security and justice.

– Continue the process of creating an ever-closer union among the peoples of Europe, in which decisions are taken as closely as possible to the citizen in accordance with the principle of subsidiarity.

UK policy was stated in a white paper published in February 2017: *The United Kingdom's exit from and new partnership with the European Union.* In the white paper, UK negotiating policy was set out as twelve guiding principles:

1. Providing certainty and clarity, including a "Great Repeal Bill" to remove the European Communities Act 1972 from the statute book and convert existing EU law into domestic law.

2. Taking control of the UK statute book and ending the jurisdiction of the Court of Justice of the European Union in the UK.

3. Strengthening the Union of all parts of the Kingdom, and remaining fully committed to the Belfast Agreement and its successors.

4. Working to deliver a practical solution that allows for the maintenance of the Common Travel Area whilst protecting the integrity of the UK immigration system, and which protects the strong ties with Ireland.

5. Controlling the number of EU nationals coming to the UK.

6. Securing the status of EU citizens who are already living in the UK, and that of UK nationals in other Member States.

7. Protecting and enhancing existing workers' rights.

8. Forging a new partnership with the EU, including a wide reaching free trade agreement, and seeking a mutually beneficial new customs agreement with the EU.

9. Forging free trade relationships across the world.

10. Remaining at the vanguard of science and innovation and seeking continued close collaboration with the UK's European partners.

11. Continuing to work with the EU to preserve European security, to fight terrorism, and to uphold justice across Europe.

12. Seeking a phased process of implementation, in which both the UK and the EU institutions and the remaining EU Member States prepare for the new arrangements.

Pre–negotiation meetings

A meeting at 10 Downing Street took place on 6 April 2017 between Theresa May and Donald Tusk to discuss "the way ahead on Brexit". Another meeting took place in London on 20 April 2017, this time between Theresa May and Antonio Tajani to discuss the rights of EU citizens. After the 20 April meeting, Antonio Tajani said that the UK and EU27 timetables fitted well together, with a two-year exit deal negotiation followed by a three-year transition phase. A 10 Downing Street meeting between Theresa May, Michel Barnier and Jean-Claude Juncker took place on 26 April to discuss the withdrawal process. May reiterated the UK's aim for a "deep and special partnership" after Brexit.

At a meeting on 29 April 2017 the EU27 unanimously endorsed the draft guidelines with no debate. A meeting took place between Michel Barnier and both houses of the Irish parliament on 11 May, where Barnier assured members of Dáil Éireann and Seanad Éireann that Europe would "work with you to avoid a hard border". Barnier went on to say that "the Irish border issue would be one of his three priorities in the negotiations," and that "there is always an answer".

The UK retains its full EU rights until Brexit, and the EU is seeking to increase their budget, leading to the possibility that Britain may veto EU budget increases, which in the immediate term amount to 4 billion euros. A continued British veto would have far-reaching consequences and "will hurt us" according to German MEP Jens Geier.

Negotiation phase 1: withdrawal arrangements

June 2017

On 19 June 2017, David Davis arrived in Brussels to start negotiations with
Michel Barnier. Terms of reference were agreed, and dates were set for four-
week cycles, to culminate in a fifth round of negotiations in the week commencing 9 October. Negotiating groups were established for three topics:
citizens' rights, the financial settlement and "other separation issues", with a
separate dialogue on Ireland / Northern Ireland to be led by Barnier and Davis.

July

Four days of talks, largely between officials, were held in Brussels on 17–20
July. Progress was made in understanding each other's positions.

On citizens' rights, a joint paper compared the positions of the two parties in
tabular form. On Irish border issues, both parties stated that they remained
committed to the Good Friday Agreement. Michel Barnier called for clarification from the UK in the August round on the financial settlement, citizens'
rights and Ireland, including on how the UK intends to maintain the Common
Travel Area.

August

Talks were held in Brussels on 28–31 August. Agreement was reached on
points including protecting the rights of frontier workers (those living in one
country and working in another); recognition by the UK of social security
contributions made both before and after exit; and continuation of healthcare
reimbursement for UK citizens who are in the EU27 on exit day and vice versa.
The joint paper comparing the two parties' positions was updated.

Speaking at the conclusion of the talks, Michel Barnier highlighted two areas
of disagreement: the role of the European Court of Justice in enforcing citizens' rights, and the extent of the UK's financial obligations. He stated "Time
is passing quickly" and added that "at the current speed, we are far from being able to recommend to the European Council that there has been sufficient
progress in order to start discussions on the future relationship".

September

On 7 September the EU Task Force published guiding principles for the dialogue on Ireland / Northern Ireland which reiterated and expanded the principles given in 29 April guidelines, in particular the protection of the Good Friday Agreement and the continuation of the Common Travel Area.

The fourth round of talks began on 25 September, having been delayed by one week as Theresa May was due to deliver a speech in Florence on the 22nd. She proposed a transitional "implementation period" of "around two years" and said that the UK "will honour commitments" so as to not make other EU countries pay more or receive less during the current EU budget period.

The programme for the round of talks arranged for meetings between the "Principals" and for three negotiating groups covering citizens' rights, financial settlement and other separation issues, while Northern Ireland issues would be addressed by the "Coordinators", and governance of the withdrawal agreement was also for discussion at technical level.

David Davis repeated Theresa May's request for a time-limited implementation period. The UK offered to incorporate the Withdrawal Agreement into UK law and ensure the UK courts can refer directly to it, but there was no agreement on the role of the European Court of Justice and the standing of future ECJ case law.

Mr Barnier welcomed the UK's commitment regarding payments into the current EU budget plan, but expressed reservations about obligations beyond 2020. Mr Davis said the UK was not yet in a position to quantify its commitments.

There were constructive discussions on the Irish border, but no substantive progress.

The UK accepted the EU's definition of 'citizens lawfully resident before the cut off date', although that date was not agreed. There was agreement on the definitions of permanent and temporary residence. The UK offered a more generous "right of return" (after absence for longer than two consecutive years) than the minimum rights under current EU law. Rights of future family members remains a point of disagreement. The joint paper comparing the two parties' positions was again updated.

October

The fifth round of negotiations was held on 9, 10 and 12 October. There was technical progress on citizens' rights, although divergences remained on aspects of family reunion and the export from the UK of social security benefits. The UK stated an intention to offer a simple process for registration of EU citizens. On the Irish border, work continued to map out current areas of cooperation and build a picture of the future challenges.

On the financial settlement, Michel Barnier welcomed the commitment made by Theresa May in her Florence speech, but no negotiations took place because the UK was not ready to give details of what it would pay. Barnier said this issue had reached an impasse.

This round of talks completed the timetable agreed in June, with no further rounds scheduled.

November

Further talks were held in Brussels on 9 and 10 November. Speaking at the closing press conference, Michel Barnier confirmed that clarification on financial commitments by the UK was required within the next two weeks. If the informal deadline is not met, the next phase of negotiations will not start in December, said Barnier. EU diplomats have described the situation as a "chicken and egg dilemma", as the EU will only start working on transition guidelines if Britain makes progress on financial issues by the end of November 2017. By 17 November, however, Donald Tusk said there was no deadlock in talks between Britain and the EU following a meeting with Theresa May in Gothenburg, Sweden and that he was optimistic that negotiations could move on to the next phase in December.

Discussions on the financial settlement took place later in the month, led by Oliver Robbins for the UK and Sabine Weyand for the EU.

December 2017

Negotiations between officials led to a draft agreement which was expected to be finalised at a meeting between Jean-Claude Juncker and Theresa May in Brussels on 4 December. There was progress on the financial settlement and citizens' rights, but the meeting was abandoned after Northern Ireland's Democratic Unionist Party objected to arrangements for the Irish border; the agreement had earlier received the support of Leo Varadkar, Ireland's Taoiseach (prime minister).

Talks continued on the following days, leading to publication on 8 December of a joint report setting out the commitments to be reflected in the Withdrawal Agreement. "Agreement in principle" was reached on the three areas:

- protecting the rights of Union citizens in the UK and UK citizens in the Union
- the framework for addressing the unique circumstances of Northern Ireland
- the financial settlement.

A joint technical note gave details of the consensus on citizens' rights. Topics postponed to a later phase included:

- rights of UK citizens resident in an EU27 country on the withdrawal date to move to another EU27 country, and their right to return to the UK
- recognition of professional qualifications, beyond those already mutually recognised at the withdrawal date.

Juncker described the agreement as a "breakthrough" Brexit deal. The second phase of negotiations – concerning Britain's post-Brexit trade with the EU – will now be able to take place as a result of the agreement.

January 2018

Discussions on the outstanding issues continued and were described as "low-key".

February 2018

Several meetings took place between the negotiators.

March 2018

Due to the ambivalence of UK on the Irish border question, Tusk declared in March 2018 "We know today that the UK Government rejects a customs and regulatory border down the Irish Sea, the EU single market, and the customs union." Tusk's has said that talks cannot proceed around this issue, that it must be resolved first.

Negotiation phase 2: transitional arrangements

The second phase of the negotiation covers the arrangements for transition towards the UK's withdrawal, together with the framework for the future relationship.

On 15 December 2017, the European Council adopted guidelines for this phase. The document confirmed that progress in the first phase was "sufficient", while stating that commitments made in that phase must be "translated faithfully into legal terms as quickly as possible"; and notes the UK's proposal for a transition period of "around two years". On 20 December, the European Commission published a draft of the negotiating directives stating a transition period should not last beyond 31 December 2020. During the transition the United Kingdom would not be part of agreements the EU made on behalf of its members with third countries, such as CETA.

The European Council adopted and published negotiating directives on 29 January 2018. These state that the whole of the EU acquis (the rights and obligations binding on all member states) will continue to apply to the UK during the transition period. The UK will continue to be within the customs union and the single market, while no longer participating in EU decision-making. The UK's position was outlined in speeches and interviews.

In March 2018 resolution, the MEPs expect an EU-UK agreement which safeguard the framework of existing commercial relationships between the EU and third countries with consistency for keeping a tuned tariff and quota system and rules of origin for products vis-à-vis third and a countries, and also a transitional arrangements fully compatible with WTO obligations to not disrupt trade relations with third countries.

On 19 March 2018, the transition period has been agreed while it can not be considered legally binding until after ratification of a wider agreement on withdrawal: "Nothing is agreed until everything is agreed,".

On 19 March 2018, the document was published; text in green has been agreed. (75% agreed).

- green areas include citizens rights and the financial settlement.
- white areas concern police and judicial cooperation.
- in yellow: The Northern Ireland border representing the agreement struck in December but the lack of clarity on what that could mean in practice.

A curious development with this release was the avoidance of mentioning what will happen with the free movement rights of UK citizens living abroad on the basis of those rights. The section which previously stated that those rights would be removed, article 32, was removed from the agreement, although references to it remain in other parts of the document.

Negotiation phase 3: trade relations with EU after Brexit

The European Union (Withdrawal) Act 2018 that became law in the United Kingdom on 26 June 2018, and two bills that were then progressing through Parliament relating to world and cross-border trade after the withdrawal, allow for various outcomes including no negotiated settlement. The two bills passed from the House of Commons to the House of Lords in July 2018.

On 6 July 2018, the UK Government announced that the May Cabinet had agreed that it should propose a "UK-EU free trade area which establishes a common rule book for industrial goods and agricultural products" [but not services] after Brexit. A few days earlier, senior EU officials had intimated that a proposal for "partial" membership of the European Single Market would not be welcomed. Before the Cabinet meeting at Chequers on 6 July, Barnier stated that the EU would accept a trade agreement with the UK if it does not damage the European Single Market. However, he said the EU would not shift its own red line on the single market, which he said was "not and never should be seen as a big supermarket; it is economic, cultural and social life, it should be developed in all its dimensions". On 10 July 2018, Barnier announced that 80% of the Brexit deal was now complete.

The government's policy for this phase of negotiations was published on 12 July 2018. In response to a statement about it by the Secretary of State, the opposition spokesman said that it was a disgrace that it had been shown to the media from 9 a.m. that morning but it had not been shown to MPs until hours later.

While the President of the United States Donald Trump was on a visit to the United Kingdom on 13 July 2018, his comment – made in an exclusive interview with *The Sun* – that the UK would probably not get a trade deal with the US if the prime minister's plan went ahead, was widely published in the media. Later the same day he stated, in a joint press conference with May at Chequers, that the Prime Minister was "doing a fantastic job" as prime minister, and contrary reports were "fake news", but he only asked for an "even" deal with the UK, and, complaining about EU trade barriers and tariffs on cars, he said that the US lost $151 billion to the EU. *The Sun*, which had conducted the interview with Trump that was the original source of the comment, afterwards denied that it produced fake news and published the interview verbatim.

While the negotiations continued, the UK government confirmed in the House of Commons on 19 July 2018 that the UK would be leaving the EU on 29 March 2019, as stated in the withdrawal act and the white paper. The first meeting of Dominic Raab, the newly appointed UK Secretary of State for

Exiting the European Union, with the EU's chief negotiator, Michel Barnier, was later on the same day (19 July 2018) in Brussels. Raab offered to meet Barnier throughout August to "intensify" talks, while both the UK and EU were insisting that reaching agreement by the autumn on the UK withdrawal in March 2019 was still very much on the cards.

On 20 July 2018, May repeated her opposition to the EU's proposals for the Irish border question during a speech in Belfast, stating that the EU must "evolve" and that there would be no further compromises over the issue. Just hours after the Prime Minister's remarks, Barnier expressed skepticism towards the Chequers plan. On 24 July 2018, May announced that she would now lead the Brexit negotiations with the EU and that Raab was now only "deputizing" on her behalf.

On 26 July, Barnier held another meeting with Raab and both stated afterwards stated in a joint press conference that "sufficient progress" had been made in the trade negotiations. Raab also stated during the joint press conference that "a lot has been achieved." Barnier also stated that both sides wanted a wide-ranging free trade deal and that he would meet again with Raab in mid-August. However, he also acknowledged that obstacles remained due to the White Paper's proposal to allow Britain to collect custom duties on behalf of the EU and that the proposal would never be accepted for any non-member. Barnier also stated that the only other challenge in the trade negotiations was finalizing an agreement between both sides concerning a backstop that guarantees a frictionless border between Ireland and Northern Ireland. Barnier stated that the EU holds "no objections in principle" to the backstop, but has "doubts that it can be done without putting at risk the integrity of our customs union, our common commercial policy, our regulatory policy and our fiscal revenue."

On 2 August 2018, Barnier announced the EU was "ready to improve the EU proposal" on the issue of the Ireland border. Barnier stated that the EU was willing to be flexible on the details of the proposed backstop, but will "not change the substance". The backstop was originally proposed by the EU and has been a source of tension in the negotiations with Britain, which has viewed the backstop as a threat to the union with Northern Ireland. However, Barnier also stated the White Paper's customs proposal still remains an issue.

On 9 August 2018, *The Times* and *Business Insider* said that EU had made concessions and agreed to accept, among other things, a free trade deal which does not include free movement of EU citizens. Under the proposal, the EU would also accept the terms outlined in the White Paper if Britain agreed to abide by the EU's social, environment and customs rules. However, this would also include keeping Britain in the European Single Market for a longer period, which is a matter of concern for the British government. Agreeing to the single market proposal could potentially mean that Britain will be unable to change laws in order to give it a competitive edge against the EU and could hinder any chance of signing additional trade deals.

On 16 August 2018, EU and British officials began two days of talks to resolve the issue concerning the Irish border. However, Barnier and Raab did not attend the talks and both sides indicated there would be little chance of a breakthrough. On 16 August, leaked documents obtained by *Buzzfeed News* showed that May had now set plans for a "no-deal" Brexit for "84 areas of life." The May government intends to start publicly disclosing the plans in the following week as a warning to the EU. On 18 August, *The Daily Telegraph* reported that the first batch of the papers detailing a no-deal Brexit are due to be published on 23 August.

On 21 August 2018, Barnier said that the EU and Britain would not reach a trade deal by the October EU summit and that an emergency summit would have to be held in either November or December. Both sides still disagree over a hard border between Ireland and Northern Ireland. While there is a possibly that there could be a summit in December, this is highly unlikely to occur and November would be the most likely month to hold an emergency summit. Gabriele Zimmer, a leftist German member of the European Parliament who deals with Brexit, told Reuters "we didn't see any concrete proposal that would work on the Irish border issue. November is the last moment. December is already too late for us." Despite the setback, however, Raab and Barnier both agreed to hold "continuous talks" in an effort to resolve the deadlock. Barnier stated that talks had previously been held in "rounds" every few weeks.

The first batch of "no-deal" Brexit advice was published by Raab on 23 August.

On 29 August, Barnier announced in Berlin that the EU would now offer a trade deal which would ensure close ties between the EU and Britain following Brexit. Barnier described the proposed trade deal as a partnership "such as there never has been with any other third country." Though "red lines" still remained between the EU and Britain, Barnier also stated that the EU would also respect Britain's red lines, such as the Northern Ireland border, so long as Britain did not undermine the European Single Market. The same day, Raab announced to a House of Lords committee that a post-Brexit trade deal with the EU was now "within our sights." Raab also stated that a vote at the EU October summit was still possible and that only "a measure of leeway" remained over the precise timetable for the agreement.

On 31 August, Raab and Barnier held a joint press conference in Brussels.[1016,1017] Both stated that progress was made in the negotiations. Raab stated that Britain was now committed to a vote on a Brexit trade deal at the SU October Summit and that he was "stubbornly optimistic that a trade deal was "within reach."[1018] Barnier stated that the EU was also committed to an

October EU Summit vote and that the "building blocks" of a trade deal were now falling into place.[1019] Certain issues are still being worked out.

On 4 September, 2018, Raab stated to other MPs that he was now "confident" that the White Paper's proposals, dubbed the Chequers plan, would serve as the basis of the UK-EU trade deal.[1020,1021] Raab also described the feedback from the EU as "positive." The same day, the cross border trade bill passed its second reading, committee stages and third reading in the House of Lords;[1022] it later became law after receiving Royal Assent on September 13.[1023] On 5 September, German Chancellor Angela Merkel dropped a key demand and announced that Germany would now accept a trade deal that is not fully detailed.[1024,1025] Merkel also stated that Germany would work to preserve good and close relations with Britain following Brexit.[1026] On 5 September EU Commission spokesman Margaritis Schinas stated that the EU saw some "positive element" in the Chequers plan and urged journalists to wait for a transcript to be published before making assumptions about how the EU feels about it.[1027]

On 7 September, it was revealed that Barnier had made a concession to a group of British MPs and stated that the EU will allow the trade agreement to be linked to the Brexit "divorce bill."[1028] The EU Commission had long insisted that any trade agreement between the EU and Britain could not be linked to payment of financial settlements. This bill will amount to approximately £39 billion. During the meeting with the delegation of MPs, which took place in Brussels on 3 September, Barnier described May's White Paper as "useful."[1029] Also on 7 September, British Finance Minister Philip Hammond stated that he was now "sure" that a trade deal would be reached by the original October deadline.[1030]

On 19 September, May reiterated her previous position the EU had to "evolve" its position concerning the Irish border.[1031]

Detailed history of negotiations

On 28 June 2016, five days after the referendum, Chancellor of Germany Angela Merkel announced to the German parliament the forthcoming EU negotiation position: the UK could only remain in the European Single Market (ESM) if the UK accepted EU migrants. There would be no cherrypicking of the ESM's four conditions (free movement of goods, capital, services and labour). While she expected the UK to remain an important NATO partner, the EU's priority was unity and self-preservation. She warned the UK not to delude itself. The next day, Tusk confirmed that the UK would not be allowed access to the ESM unless they accepted its four freedoms of movement for goods, capital, services, and people.

In contrast, at her October 2016 party conference, Prime Minister Theresa May emphasised that ending the jurisdiction of EU law and free movement from Europe were priorities. She wished "to give British companies the maximum freedom to trade with and operate in the Single Market – and let European businesses do the same here", but not at the expense of losing sovereignty.

In November 2016, May proposed that Britain and the other EU countries mutually guarantee the residency rights of the 3.3 million EU immigrants in Britain and those of the 1.2 million British citizens living on the Continent, in order to exclude their fates being bargained during Brexit negotiations. Despite initial approval from a majority of EU states, May's proposal was blocked by European Council President Tusk and German Chancellor Merkel.

In January 2017, the Prime Minister presented 12 negotiating objectives and confirmed that the UK government would not seek permanent single market membership. The European Parliament's lead negotiator Guy Verhofstadt responded that there could be no "cherry-picking" by the UK in the talks.

The statutory period for negotiation began on 29 March 2017, when the letter notifying withdrawal, signed by the British Prime Minister, was handed to the president of the European Council. The letter called for a "deep and special relationship" between the UK and the EU, and warned that failure to reach an agreement would result in EU-UK trade under World Trade Organisation terms, and a weakening of the UK's cooperation in the fight against crime and terrorism. The letter suggested prioritising an early deal on the rights of EU citizens in the UK and vice versa. In the letter, the Prime Minister reasoned that, as the EU leaders did not wish "cherry picking" of the ESM, the UK would not seek to remain within the ESM. Instead, the UK would seek a free trade agreement with the EU. In response, Merkel insisted that the EU would not discuss future cooperation without first settling the divorce, Verhofstadt referred to the letter as "blackmail" with regard to the point on security and terrorism, and EU Commission president Jean-Claude Juncker said the UK's decision to quit the block was a "choice they will regret one day".

On 29 April 2017, immediately after the first round of French presidential elections, the EU27 heads of state accepted, without discussion, negotiating guidelines prepared by the President of the European Council. The guidelines take the view that Article 50 permits a two-phased negotiation, whereby the UK first needs to agree to a financial commitment and to lifelong benefits for EU citizens in Britain, before the EU27 will entertain negotiations on a future relationship. In the requested first phase of the withdrawal negotiation, the EU27 negotiators demand the UK pay a "divorce bill", initially estimated as amounting up to £52bn and then, after additional financial demands from Germany, France, and Poland, amounting to £92bn. Nevertheless, a report of the European Union Committee of the House of Lords published on 4 March

2017 states that if there is no post-Brexit deal at the end of the two-year negotiating period, the UK could withdraw without payment. Similarly, the Prime
Minister insisted to EU Commission President Juncker that talks about the future UK-EU relationship should start early and that Britain did not owe any
money to the EU under the current treaties.

On the EU27 side, unflattering details of a four-way meeting between Prime
Minister Theresa May, Brexit Minister David Davis, EU Commission President Juncker and his chief-of-staff Martin Selmayr were leaked to the German newspaper *Frankfurter Allgemeine Sonntagszeitung*, presumably by Martin Selmayr. According to the leaked description, Juncker claimed that Theresa
May was "living in another galaxy" when suggesting that British and EU migrant rights could be rapidly negotiated and agreed in the course of June 2017.
German Chancellor Angela Merkel concurred the next day by stating that there
were "illusions" on the British side. A few days later, Juncker disclaimed responsibility and called the leak a mistake, *Der Spiegel* magazine reported that
Angela Merkel was annoyed with Juncker for the leak, while European Council
President Tusk admonished participants to use discretion during the negotiations. The background for German nervousness allegedly is the possibility
that Britain may veto EU budget increases, which for example in the immediate term amount to 4 billion euros. A continued British veto would have
far-reaching consequences and "will hurt us" according to German MEP Jens
Geier.

On 22 May 2017, the European Council authorised its negotiators to start the
Brexit talks and it adopted its negotiating directives. The first day of talks took
place on 19 June, where Davis and Barnier agreed to prioritise the question of
residency rights, while Davis conceded that a discussion of the Northern Irish
border would have to await future trade agreements.

On 22 June 2017, Prime Minister May guaranteed, at a European Council
meeting in Brussels, that no EU citizen living legally in the UK would be forced
to leave, and she offered that any EU citizen living in the UK for more than
5 years until an unspecified deadline between March 2017 and March 2019
would enjoy the same rights as a UK citizen, conditional on the EU providing
the same offer to British expatriates living in the EU. The EU leaders did not
immediately reciprocate the offer, with Council President Tusk objecting that
the European Council is not a forum for the Brexit negotiations, and Commission president Juncker stating "I'm not negotiating here."

The Prime Minister detailed her residency proposals in the House of Commons
on 26 June 2017, but drew no concessions from EU negotiators, who had
declined to expedite agreement on expatriates by the end of June 2017, and
who are hoping for European courts to continue to have jurisdiction in the UK

with regards to EU citizens, according to their negotiation aims published in May 2017.

The second round of negotiations began in Brussels in mid-July 2017. It is considered the beginning of substantial negotiations, with 98 UK negotiators and 45 EU27 negotiators. Progress is being made on the Northern Irish border question, whereas UK negotiators have requested a detailed breakdown of the "divorce bill" demand estimated at 65 billion euros, while the EU negotiators criticise the UK's citizenship rights offer. At the concluding press conference, David Davis did not commit to a net payment by the UK to the EU with regards to the requested divorce bill, while Michel Barnier explained that he would not compromise on his demand for the European Court of Justice to have continuing jurisdiction over the rights of EU citizens living in the UK after Brexit, rejecting the compromise proposal of a new international body made up of British and EU judges.

On 16 August 2017, the British government disclosed the first of several papers detailing British ambitions following Brexit, discussing trade and customs arrangements. On 23 August 2017, Prime Minister Theresa May announced that Britain will leave the EU Court of Justice's direct jurisdiction when the Brexit transition period that is planned after March 2019 ends, but that both the British courts and the EU Court of Justice will also keep "half an eye" on each other's rulings afterwards as well. One of the UK government's position papers published in August called for no additional restrictions for goods already on the market in the UK and EU.

The third round of negotiations began in Brussels on 28 August 2017. The European Commission president Juncker criticised the UK's Brexit negotiations, saying none of the papers provided so far were satisfactory and that there would be no trade negotiations between the EU and UK until the divorce bill was settled. He had previously claimed that the UK's Brexit bill could be £55bn (which Theresa May's government ministers consider unacceptable) and EU Budget Commissioner Günther Oettinger voiced the view that the UK should make payments until 2023. The *Irish Times* explained the disagreement as follows: British negotiators referred to the seven-year Multi-annual Financial Framework (MFF or Maff) for the period 2014-2020 agreed by member states and the EU parliament as a "planning tool" for the next period rather than a legally-binding financial obligation on member states. The British case is that the MFF sets ceilings on spending under various headings and is later radically revised during the annual budget process when real legal obligations on each state arises. This contrasts with the EU Commission's methodology for calculating the UK Brexit bill which involves dividing the MFF into the shares historically agreed by each member state. On the Irish border question there was a "breakthrough", with the British side guaranteeing

Figure 42: *The Ambrosetti Forum is held annually in
the Villa d'Este on the shores of Lake Como in Italy.*

free movement of EU citizens within the Common travel area constituting Ireland and the United Kingdom. The BBC's Europe correspondent commented "the British perception of the talks is more positive than the EU's".

At the elite European Ambrosetti Forum on 2 September 2017, Michel Barnier explained his negotiation aims, in that he would "teach the British people and others what leaving the EU means". Although this remark caused controversy in the UK, BBC correspondent Mark Mardell interpreted it in the context of French and Dutch euroscepticism, of the forthcoming German, Austrian and Italian elections, and of the eurosceptic Polish and Hungarian governments.

In a statement to Parliament on 5 September 2017, David Davis said that "concrete progress" had been made over the summer in areas such as protecting the rights of British expats in the EU to access healthcare and over the future of the Irish border, while significant differences over the "divorce bill" remain. He expected that "the money argument will go on for the full duration of the negotiation. The famous European "nothing is agreed until everything is agreed" will apply here absolutely, as anywhere else".

On 6 September 2017, Prime Minister May announced that new immigration controls will be placed on EU nationals when Brexit concludes.

On 9 September 2017, the EU Commission published several negotiating papers, including "Guiding Principles on the Dialogue for Ireland/Northern Ireland". In it, the EU concedes/declares that it is the responsibility of the UK to propose solutions for the post-Brexit Irish border. The paper envisages that a "unique" solution would be permissible here; in other words, any such exceptional Irish solution should not be seen as a template for post-Brexit relationships with the other EU members on border and customs control matters, for example ETIAS.

At the European Council meeting of 19/20 October 2017, the 27 leaders of the EU states were to decide whether or not to start trade negotiations with the UK. However, David Davis has conceded that so soon after the German elections on 24 September, a German coalition government may not be in place in time for making this decision in October, delaying any European Council decision until their December meeting.

On 21 September 2017, Prime Minister May, along with her Cabinet, agreed to a transition deal which would inject 20bn euros to the EU budget over a two-year period. A cabinet source confirmed to the BBC that May's Cabinet was in fact unity around the Prime Minister's two year transition deal.

On 22 September 2017, May announced the details of her Brexit proposal during a speech in Florence, Italy. In addition to offering 20 billion euros over a two-year transition period and continued acceptance of European immigrants, she also offered a "bold new security relationship" with the EU which would be "unprecedented in its depth" and to continue to make "an ongoing contribution" to projects considered greatly to the EU and UK's advantage, such as science and security projects. She also confirmed that the UK would not "stand in the way" of Juncker's proposals for further EU integration. The European Union's Brexit negotiator Michel Barnier welcomed May's proposal as "constructive," but that it also "must be translated into negotiating positions to make meaningful progress;" Similarly, President of France Emmanuel Macron was adamant that the EU would not begin negotiations on future EU-UK relationships until "the regulation of European citizens, the financial terms of the exit, and the questions of Ireland" were "clarified" by the UK, though he also acknowledged that May did give openings in her speech on two of these three points. Ireland Taoiseach Leo Varadkar gave May's proposal a "cautious welcome," saying that while it was good of May to reference the Common Travel Area, the Northern Ireland peace process and that both sides in the negotiations do not want any physical structures at the border, more negotiations were needed for clarification. EU Parliamentary negotiator Guy Verhofstadt responded that "a new registration mechanism for EU citizens going to live and/or work in the UK is out of the question".

EU negotiators have stated that an agreement must be reached between Britain and the EU by October 2018 in order to leave time for national parliaments to endorse Brexit.

On the domestic front, Labour Party MP and Shadow Home Secretary Diane Abbott announced she would back May's proposed negotiation for the Brexit timetable.

The programme for the fourth round of talks beginning on 25 September arranged for meetings between the "Principals" and for three negotiating groups covering citizens' rights, financial settlement and other separation issues, while Northern Ireland issues would be addressed by the "Coordinators", and governance of the withdrawal agreement would be discussed at technical level.

On 16 October, May and European Commission President Jean-Claude Juncker issued a joint statement agreeing Brexit talks should "accelerate over the months to come" following a dinner meeting in Brussels which both described as "constructive and friendly." However, as at a similar dinner earlier in 2017, an unflattering "impressionistic" account of this meeting (between Prime Minister Theresa May, her chief Brexit adviser Olly Robbins, Brexit Minister David Davis, EU Commission President Juncker and the EU's chief negotiator, Michel Barnier) was published in the same German newspaper *Frankfurter Allgemeine Sonntagszeitung*. Again, Juncker's chief-of-staff Martin Selmayr was accused as the source of the publication and of trying to undermine the negotiations. This time however Selmayr denied the accusation, and Chancellor Merkel reportedly denied her involvement.

On 17 October, Brexit Secretary David Davis insisted that there will be no deal for a transition phase without EU cooperation and that Brexit will happen regardless, even if there is what one Conservative MP described as "a bridge to nowhere."

On 19 October, the first day of the two-day European Council meeting in Brussels, May issued a direct message to approximately three million EU citizens living in Britain, promising she will make it as easy as possible for them to stay after Brexit. On 20 October, Tusk described media reports of the deadlock in Brexit talks as "exaggerated."

On 23 October, May announced to the House of Commons that Brexit talks underwent "important progress" during her recent meeting with the European Council and that Britain was now "in touching distance" of a trade deal with EU countries, while also reiterating that no transition phase will take place following the conclusion of Brexit without a trade deal as well. The same day, Juncker denied reports by the German media that May had "begged for help" during their recent dinner meeting.

In the wake of the German elections (23 September 2017), as of 10 November, negotiations were still ongoing to form a coalition government between Frau Merkel's CDU, the sister party CSU, the economically liberal FDP and the German Greens; politicians from all three factions published an appeal to reach a coalition agreement (rather than risk new elections), in the interest of Germany forming a "stable anchor" to unite with France and defend the EU and the euro in the current situation.

During the sixth round of meetings in Brussels between UK and EU negotiators on 9–10 November, Michel Barnier set the UK a deadline of two weeks to specify a divorce bill that the UK would pay, without which the UK would not be permitted to start trade negotiations in December 2017. Meanwhile, David Davis rejected an EU proposal that Northern Ireland could remain in the EU customs union (thereby creating a customs border "down the Irish Sea" with Great Britain).

After more than 2 months of a caretaker German government since the German federal elections in September, on 7 December 2017 new elections were averted when the German socialist party under Martin Schulz agreed to negotiate a coalition government with Angela Merkel's Christian Democrat party, but on condition that a "United States of Europe" be created by 2025, dismissing those EU member states who were unwilling to participate.

The following day (8 December), the UK and EU negotiators agreed on the principle that "nothing is agreed until everything is agreed" and formally announced to proceed immediately to the next phase of talks on a transition period and future trade relationships.

The EU's negotiating position as at 10 November was that a future trade relationship between EU and UK should be made conditional upon requirements which would handicap the UK's freedom to negotiate free trade deals with the rest of the world; and that no free trade deal can be agreed in parallel with the Article 50 withdrawal agreement because each of the 27 EU countries would be expected to veto it if they would otherwise face competition from the UK on tax, employment conditions, safety regulations and relaxation of restrictions on GM crops; and that the EU would require any transitional deal to be signed as part of a withdrawal agreement before any agreement was in place on the UK's future relationship with the EU, so that existing arrangements would continue to apply during any transitional period, with the Single Market, Customs Union and European Court of Justice having the same roles as at present, and preventing the UK having control of EU immigration during that period or having the right to enter into trade deals with other countries.

Legality of and payments by the UK to the EU

Two different but incompatible legal approaches would be considered for the Brexit. The EU approach is top down while the British approach is bottom-up. This difference of approach raises a serious problem of confidence. From Michel Barnier point of view, what was decided by 28 member states, has to be paid by 28 member states till the end.

The issue of payments by the UK to the EU as part of the exit agreement is subject to much conjecture and has been divided into two broad questions. Firstly, whether a leaving state is legally obligated to contribute to the EU budget beyond its membership period or compensate for any financial losses that EU may suffer on account of withdrawal, given that Article 50 does not concern itself with financial ramifications of a withdrawal; and secondly – if the United Kingdom is legally obligated to pay – what should be the due amount.

The leaders of France and Germany have both stated that the UK would need to agree terms regarding the departure before discussing future relationships. This has been reinforced by EU27 guidelines issued to the remaining 27 countries. The UK has signalled that it may consider paying the EU to attain preferential access to the economic Single Market and may offer to pay liabilities, even if not legally obligated, on a moral and co-operative basis to secure a preferential working relationship with the EU.

The highest reported claim by the EU is around €60 billion (£50 billion-Wikipedia:Manual of Style/Dates and numbers#Chronological items). In March 2017 the Bruegel think tank estimated that the UK would need to pay at least €25.4 billion, but the method of calculation is debatable and their calculations using seven different methods produced estimates between €30 and €45 billion. However this £50 billion bill includes the United Kingdom's annual EU contribution (approximately £13 billion annually) for the two years from 2020 and 2021 as agreed in the Multiannual Financial Framework (MFF).Wikipedia:Citation needed The United Kingdom, in accordance with Article 50 and unless otherwise extended, will cease to be a member of the EU from 29 March 2019 and the MFF does have a provision for "unforeseen circumstances".

EU27 is expected to ask the UK to pay its liabilities in euros, including the relocation costs associated with the two EU bodies currently based in London.

Speaking on 20 April, Antonio Tajani said that it was too early to quantify the amount the UK would need to pay and that it was not a bill to leave the EU, it was money needed for farmers and small businesses.

House of Lords report

<templatestyles src="Template:Quote_box/styles.css" />

"27. It may seem intuitive that when the UK leaves the EU, it leaves behind both the responsibilities and benefits of membership. However, this does not take account of the complexity of the UK's participation in the EU, nor of the procedures for agreeing current and future budgets, which involve mutual commitments projected many years into the future. ...33. The range of values in circulation for the UK's potential 'exit bill' indicates that the absolute sum of any posited settlement is hugely speculative. Almost every element is subject to interpretation."

HL Paper 125, 4 March 2017, European Union Committee15th sessional report, *Brexit and the EU budget* , Chapter 3, *Potential demands*.[1032]

A March 2017 House of Lords report acknowledges that the EU may claim for (1) part of the current budget (which runs from 2014 to 2020) post March 2019, because it was approved by the UK (2) part of the EU future commitments which amount to €200 billion and (3) a contribution if the UK is to continue with access to some EU programmes. The report concluded that the UK had no legal obligation to make "exit" payments to the EU if there was no post Brexit deal.

Discussing financial and legal complexities involved in negotiating withdrawal, including settlement of outstanding financial liabilities and division of assets, the report mentions (paragraph 15) that the EU budget is funded by revenue drawn from various sources, governed by the EU's Own Resources Decision (ORD), which was made part of UK law by the European Union (Finance) Act 2015. The revenue includes contributions from import duties and VAT collected by member states. The report also mentions the EU Multiannual Financial Framework for controlling the annual expenditure.

Assets and liabilities

The EU has considerable assets including buildings, equipment and financial instruments, and there is a potential claim by the UK for a portion of these assets. Boris Johnson, the UK's Foreign Secretary, commenting on the Brexit "divorce bill" in May 2017 stated that the valuable EU assets the UK has paid for over the years should be properly valued, and that there were good arguments for including them in the negotiations.

The Bank of England (BoE) has invested in the European Central Bank (ECB) amounting to 13.6743%, representing paid up capital of €55.5 billion. The BoE does not participate in any profits (or losses) of the ECB. The BoE has also made loans to the ECB. The ECB set up the European Financial Stability

Facility in 2010, which has a borrowing facility of €440bn and in addition used a guarantee from the European Commission and the Budget of the European Union as collateral to borrow a further €60bn. The UK withdrawal will affect the ECB.

The EU has a pension liability of €64 billion.

The UK benefits from a rebate which reduces its contribution to the EU budget. The rebate is paid a year in arrears, accordingly the 2019 rebate would be payable in 2020.

Policy paper

The EU drafted a 10-page position document regarding the single bill. This position does not define the final cost of the divorce.

UK citizens elsewhere in the EU and other EU citizens in the UK

Concerns have been raised by UK citizens who live in other EU countries, and by citizens from those countries who live in the UK. In May 2017, Michel Barnier stated: "Currently around 3.2 million EU citizens work and live in the UK, and 1.2 million British citizens work and live in the EU."

Issues include rights of movement, citizenship, abode, education, social support and medical treatment, and the payment of pensions; and the extent to which these rights apply to family members. Considerations for UK citizens resident in an EU27 country include their rights to work or live in a different EU27 country. Beyond the 27 EU countries, workers have certain freedom of movement rights to/from Norway, Iceland, Liechtenstein and Switzerland.

"Associate citizenship", suggested by EU27 negotiator Guy Verhofstadt, would allow UK nationals to volunteer individually for EU citizenship, enabling them to continue to work and live on the continent. Jean-Claude Juncker, president of the European Commission, is not opposed to the idea.

Antonio Tajani spoke after a meeting with Theresa May on 20 April, saying "the issue of reciprocal EU citizen rights should be negotiated 'immediately' with a view to getting an agreement by the end of the year." The European Commission published a position paper on "Essential Principles on Citizens' Rights" on 12 June, proposing that current and future family members of European nationals in the UK would keep their rights to settle in their residence country at any time after Britain's withdrawal. Speaking in advance of publication of the paper, David Davis described the demands as "ridiculously high". The UK government published their policy paper "Safeguarding the position of EU citizens in the UK and UK nationals in the EU" on 26 June. The policy paper proposed that EU citizens living in Britain will be required to apply for inclusion on a "settled status" register if they wish to remain in the country after Brexit.

At end of September progress have been made on several of the 60 points which became green. In the same time there around 13 out of the 60 points which remain red. Three points (points #14, #15, and #16 related to monitoring and CJEU) have to be addressed at governance level. Few points remains to clarify (that is yellow). On this basis European parliament will have to assess if sufficient progress have been made.

Implications

The general rule for losing EU citizenship is that European citizenship is lost if member state nationality is lost, but the automatic loss of EU citizenship as a result of a member state withdrawing from the EU is the subject of debate. The situation of a person acquiring EU citizenship when the UK joined the EU in 1973 compared to a person born in the UK after 1973 and was therefore born into EU citizenship may differ. It may be necessary for the European Court of Justice to rule on these issues.

A 2017 decision of the European Court of Human Rights has ruled that where a child is born in the EU, the parent/s, even if they are both non EU citizens, are entitled to rights of residence. This could have consequential effects for UK residents who have young children and wish to live in the EU27 territory post Brexit.

Immigration and mobility

Until the UK effectively withdraws from the EU in 2019 or at another agreed date, the current system of free movement of labour between the EU27 and the UK remains in place.

The report of the House of Commons Exiting the European Union Committee on *The Government's negotiating objectives*, published in April 2017, proposed (paragraphs 20 and 123) that the future system for EU migration should meet the needs of different sectors of the UK economy, including those employing scientists, bankers, vets, care workers, health service professionals and seasonal agriculture workers.

Theresa May, answering press questions on 5 April 2017, commented that the free movement of labour would not end in March 2019; an implementation period of possibly five years would give business and government time to adjust.

The UK currently charges an annual levy of up to £1,000 for each non-EU citizen employed within the UK. Proposals are under consideration to increase this 'immigration skills charge' to £2,000 p.a. and to implement a similar levy on EU citizens employed in the UK.

According to an unconfirmed newspaper report, a leaked Home Office paper has a proposal that the UK will end the free movement of labour of low-skilled workers immediately after Brexit, focusing on highly skilled EU workers instead. The proposal would limit lower-skilled EU migrants' residency permits to a maximum of two years, and the implementation of a new immigration system ending the right to settle in Britain for most European migrants while placing tough restrictions on their rights to bring over family members. Those in "high-skilled occupations" could be given permission to work in the UK for a period of three to five years.

Immigration

Immigration is one topic requiring partnership between EU and UK, as according to Theresa May, "Mass migration and terrorism are but two examples of the challenges to our shared European interests and values that we can only solve in partnership".

In the context of Brexit, the question of migration might contains two subtopics: on one hand migrations between EU including UK and third countries which might be dealt with at a local level; and on the other hand migration between EU and UK once UK has become a third country which was discussed for the withdrawal agreement.

European Court of Justice

The concept of European Court of Justice competence creates complications. Some pro-Brexiteers believe the Court of Justice might be completely removed from the UK landscape. Various other opinions consider that the Court of Justice or some equivalent should be able to rule on remaining issues after Brexit (for instance between a European and a British stakeholder), at least in respect of the TEU (Treaty on European Union), European Union citizens, or access to the European Single Market.

After the 2017 negotiations, in February 2018 the European Commission Draft Withdrawal Agreement on the withdrawal of the United Kingdom of Great Britain and Northern Ireland from the European Union and the European Atomic Energy Community consider for instance that:

- "The Court of Justice of the European Union shall continue to have jurisdiction for any proceedings brought before it by the United Kingdom or against the United Kingdom before the end of the transition period. That jurisdiction shall extend to all stages of proceedings, including appeal proceedings before the Court of Justice and proceedings before the General Court after a case has been referred back to it."
- "The Court of Justice of the European Union shall continue to have jurisdiction to give preliminary rulings on requests from courts and tribunals of the United Kingdom referred to it before the end of the transition period."

Sectoral issues

Brexit might have impact in various sectors.

Documents setting out how the Brexit will affect parts of the British economy were set up for the government, "the most comprehensive picture of our economy on this issue" containing "excruciating detail" according to Brexit Secretary David Davis. The ministers were reluctant to publish them but in November, a vote in Parliament allowed lawmakers to read them under controlled conditions to avoid news leaks. They were released online on 21 December 2017 but lawmakers were unimpressed: "Most of this could be found on Wikipedia or with a quick Google search," said Labour's David Lammy, "these documents [were made] in a couple of weeks. They look like copy and paste essay crises."

Trade

Without a trade agreement in place, UK trade with the EU would be governed by the World Trade Organization's Bali Package. This would lead to common tariffs and non-tariff barriers being imposed by the EU27 upon the UK's access to the European Single Market, because the Market is also a customs union. However, the UK would then have an opportunity to control immigration as well as develop its own trade regulations.

The UK is not permitted to hold trade talks until after Brexit is concluded, however the UK can do preparatory work with other countries regarding the UK's future trading relationships; this is not to the liking of some EU27 countries. Before Britain leaves the EU, they may put trade agreements in place with non-EU countries.

Only the EU can act in areas where it has exclusive competence, such as the customs union and common commercial policy. In those areas Member States

may not act independently. The UK can still negotiate its own bilateral investment protection treaties subject to Commission authorization.

Strategic controls on military goods are primarily a Member State competence.
As a result, Member States themselves negotiate multilateral or bilateral agreements on the strategic aspects of trade in defense goods.

The EU27 wish to exclude the UK from sitting in on trade negotiations held by
the EU during the period ending March 2019, seeing the UK as a competitor.
Theresa May rejected this idea, saying "While we're members of the European
Union we would expect our obligations but also our rights to be honored in
full."

Regional foods

The Geographical indications and traditional specialties in the European
Union, known as protected designation of origin (PDO) is applied internationally via bilateral agreements. Without an agreement with the EU27, UK
producers of products such as the Cornish pasty, Scotch whisky and Jersey
Royal potatoes are at risk of being copied.

Fisheries

The EU27 have stated that UK fish suppliers could lose tariff-free access to
the continent unless EU countries have continued access to UK waters after
Brexit.

Agriculture

The Irish agricultural sector is heavily dependent on UK markets for its exports.

Financial services

Banks

Investment banks may want to have new or expanded offices up and running
inside the EU27 bloc before the UK's departure in March 2019, with Frank-
furt and Dublin the possible favourites. Ireland's investment arm, IDA Ireland,
witnessed an increase in inquiries from London-based financial groups considering to open up on an office in Dublin by the end of 2016, mostly coming
from North American companies. In May 2017, JP Morgan became the first
major bank to officially choose Dublin to transfer some of its personnel and
operations from its London office.

Insurance

Lloyd's of London have confirmed that they will open a subsidiary in Brussels, hoping to ensure continuation of their continental business which generates 11% of its premiums.

Asset management companies

The situation may be different when it comes to the fund management industry, as British asset owners, notably UK pension funds, often constitute an incommensurate share of total turnover for German, French, Dutch and other Continental European asset managers.

This imbalance could potentially give Britain some negotiating leverage e.g. power of retorsion in case the EU attempts to impose an abrupt cancellation of the mutually-binding obligations and advantages pertaining to the Markets in Financial Instruments Directive 2004 (*"fund passporting"*). Research conducted by the World Pensions Council (WPC) shows that <templatestyles src="Template:Quote/styles.css"/>

> *"Assets owned by UK pension funds are more than 11 times bigger than those of all German and French pension funds put together [...] If need be, at the first hint of threat to the City of London, Her Majesty's Government should be in a position to respond very forcefully."*

Stock exchanges

The London Stock Exchange issued a warning over a proposal by the EU, to allow euro-denominated transactions to be cleared only within the EU eurozone, claiming it would increase business costs by €100bn over 5 years and isolate the euro capital market.

Security

The letter of 29 March 2017 giving the UK's notice of intention to withdraw from the EU stated "In security terms a failure to reach agreement would mean our cooperation in the fight against crime and terrorism would be weakened." This was seen by some as a threat. On 31 March, Boris Johnson, the UK Foreign Secretary, confirmed that the "UK commitment to EU security is unconditional".

The call by the United States to other members of NATO to increase their defence expenditure to the 2% of GDP level coincides in timing with Brexit. The UK is the second largest contributor to NATO defence, one of only five to meet the 2% level and one of only two EU members who have nuclear weapons. The possibility of a new Franco-German partnership to fill the vacuum left by Britain has been raised as a possibility and post Brexit an EU military headquarters, previously vetoed by the UK, may be created. The UK is fully committed to NATO.

Academic research

The UK government's negotiating policy when the negotiating period started on 29 March 2017 included remaining at the vanguard of science and innovation, and seeking continued close collaboration with the UK's European partners.

British Overseas Territories and Crown dependencies

In the Great Repeal Bill white paper published on 30 March 2017, the UK government stated "The Government is committed to engaging with the Crown Dependencies, Gibraltar and the other Overseas Territories as we leave the EU.":ch.5

Overseas territories

Robin Walker MP, a junior minister at the Department for Exiting the European Union, is responsible for managing the relationship between the overseas territories and Parliament in their discussion with the EU27.

Gibraltar

Brexit raised issues around sovereignty for Gibraltar, the only British Overseas Territory in the EU. Gibraltarians voted to stay in the European Union by 96%. Spain claims sovereignty over Gibraltar; however, in 2002 Gibraltarians voted 99% to keep British sovereignty.

The EU27 draft guidelines allow Spain a veto over any effect that the Brexit agreement has as regards Gibraltar. The guidelines state: "After the United Kingdom leaves the Union, no agreement between the EU and the United Kingdom may apply to the territory of Gibraltar without the agreement between the Kingdom of Spain and the United Kingdom."

Crown dependencies

The Crown dependencies are neither part of the EU nor of the UK. They have a unique constitutional relationship both with the UK and, as encapsulated in Protocol 3 to the UK's Treaty of Accession, with the EU. They have no voting rights in EU or UK referenda or elections and no international voice, the UK government having the responsibility to act for the dependencies on foreign matters. Oliver Heald QC MP is responsible for managing the relationship between the Islands and Parliament in their discussion with the EU27.

The "no deal" scenario

If no withdrawal agreement is in place on 30 March 2019 at midnight (European central time) or at 23h on 29 March (British time) (the end of the two-year period under Article 50) the EU Treaties will cease to apply to the UK. It is understood that, should there be "no deal", there will be no transition period and EU law (in particular, the Single Market) will cease to apply to the UK/EU relationship from that date. However, the EU would prefer a Brexit with an agreed deal rather than with no deal. Nonetheless, even in the case of a no withdrawal deal, the Commission believes that UK and EU may soon relaunch trade negotiations.

No deal possibility and likeliness

A Parliamentary inquiry has concluded that "the possibility of 'no deal' is real enough to justify planning for it. The Government has produced no evidence, either to this inquiry or in its White Paper, to indicate that it is giving the possibility of 'no deal' the level of consideration that it deserves, or is contemplating any serious contingency planning. This is all the more urgent if the Government is serious in its assertion that it will walk away from a 'bad' deal."

The UK government has consistently said that it will aim for the "best possible deal" but that "no deal is better than a bad deal". This position was restated in the Conservative Party manifesto for the 2017 general election.[1033] In July, Michel Barnier said that "a fair deal is better than no deal", because "In the case of Brexit, 'no deal' is a return to a distant past".

According to the French Prime Minister Édouard Philippe, "The more we think the worst should be avoided, the more we think it's not impossible it could eventually happen" .

With the British (UK) white paper, both sides are wondering if the *no deal scenario* is more likely rather than possible.

No deal adverse consequences

A "no-deal" Brexit has been described by General Council of the Bar, a lawyers' interest body, as "falling over the cliff-edge". According to the IMF, the no deal Brexit could create economic pain across Europe, with no winner. The most affected country would be UK, according to the IMF: the IMF consider that UK and Ireland could lose 4% of their GDP, while close countries such as the Netherlands, Denmark and Belgium could lose 1% of GDP.

In September 2017 the BBC reported that there was little evidence of UK government preparations for a "No Deal" scenario: "our government is not behaving like it is really preparing for No Deal – and the EU27 can surely see it."

In her 4 October 2017 speech at the Conservative Party Conference, UK Prime Minister Theresa May repeated her position that "no deal is better than a bad deal" and emphasized that "It is our responsibility as a government to prepare for every eventuality. And let me reassure everyone in this hall – that is exactly what we are doing." In her 9 October 2017 statement in the House of Commons, May warned that Britain could operate as an "independent trading nation" after Brexit if no trade deal is reached with the EU.

The *no deal* scenario has been described by Nick Timothy as leaving the EU [with Britain] in "chaos" or not leaving the bloc at all, which he says would be a "national humiliation" on a par with the Suez Crisis.

Sir Martin Donnelly feels that no deal would be dangerous: while no deal makes trade only dependent on World Trade Organisation terms which do not include services—80% of the British economy—he believes that no deal "could mean an awful lot of legal uncertainty and that's very bad for businesses, for jobs, for investment in Britain".

In the Scottish Centre on European Relations paper "Brexit Uncertainty, Scotland and the UK in 2018", a conclusion is reached that the delivery of a no deal Brexit could raise support for a second independence referendum in Scotland.

Nonetheless, according to Shadow Chancellor John McDonnell there are enough people in the House of Commons to prevent some no-agreement exit.

According to Dominic Cummings, campaign director of Vote Leave, "If there's no deal, there will be significant problems that were completely avoidable".

---

* Source, Olivier Wayman report, *La Tribune* pounds have been converted to euros, on 12 March 2018

Aviation would be particularly affected if the European Common Aviation Area and EU–US Open Skies Agreement no longer applied to the UK after a "no-deal" Brexit, since World Trade Organisation rules do not cover that sector, implying that the following day a British plane could not land at an EU airport.

The *no deal scenario* could create a disruption in transport between the United Kingdom and the European Union: for instance, with delays generated by the customs, sanitary and phytosanitary controls for road transport and ports.

The National Police Coordination Centre has warned that no deal would result in civil disorder at the UK's ports and borders, a "real possibility" of calling upon military assistance, a rise in crime (particularly theft and robbery) and widespread illness and disease following food and drug shortages (including NHS supplies). Police officers who are EU nationals may potentially be unable to hold a warrant card (which would leave the Metropolitan Police 750 officers short), and the ability for the police to deal with criminality from non-UK residents would be undermined as the UK "falls out of the various treaties such as the European arrest warrant, Schengen information system and membership of Europol". Sara Thornton of the NPCC said, "Existing EU tools allow us to respond quickly and intelligently to crime and terrorism in the UK and the EU – they make us better at protecting the public. The alternatives we are planning to use, where they exist, are without exception slower, more bureaucratic and ultimately less effective."[1034] Finding out if a suspect has criminal convitions will take much longer.[1035]

Contingency and preparedness

An EU document on *Preparedness* outlines the plans related to various issues (with or without withdrawal agreement), and another on *Contingency* describes measures to answer the consequences of a *No deal*.

To answer the consequences of a no deal Brexit, some players are involved in contingency planning and preparedness (but not panic).

To limit the consequences of a *no deal* scenario, some companies, such as Airbus and Rolls-Royce, are stockpiling spares.

In the Netherlands, around 1,000 customs officials are being recruited to manage the border with UK after the no deal Brexit.

In the UK the need for new customs agents is estimated at 5,000.

In Ireland, the need for new customs agents is estimated at 1,000.

The UK is considering converting some part of the M20 motorway into a parking lot for trucks, to manage a possible 17-mile (around 25-kilometer) line of traffic, as planned by the Dover port authority.

Dominic Raab's department is preparing public detailed plans to make the UK to deal with a no deal scenario for 29 March 2019.

The EU Commission has published 68 notices to help various players to be aware of the Brexit consequences.

The EU Commission is also considering notifying its international partners for international agreements that involved the UK as a member state, in case of no deal.

The UK Treasury department is using "Operation Yellowhammer" for "no-deal" contingency planning.

The deep and special relationship scenario

The UK side has called for a deep and special relationship between UK and EU.

Possibility of an extended transitional period

Most of the major UK political parties support the idea of a two-year period for applying temporary trade arrangements after the end of the membership of the EU single market, customs union and other EU agreements and before a stand-alone UK.

According to Michel Barnier, the EU might have to define the conditions for a transitional period, if the UK requests one. Such a transition period would begin on 30 March 2019 (European time, as Brexit occurs at midnight the day before).

According to Michel Barnier, the transition period is subject to a withdrawal agreement, by law written in Article 50.

Future trade deal between UK and EU

While negotiations between the United Kingdom and the European Union were in progress, Barnier, as the EU's chief negotiator, speaking in Rome to Committees of the Italian Parliament on 21 September 2017, stated that a future trade deal with the United Kingdom is the trade deal which will be negotiated after sufficient progress has been made on the withdrawal deal. Barnier commented that the EU will want to negotiate a future trade deal with the United Kingdom, because trade with the United Kingdom will continue. At the same time Barnier said "the future trade deal with the United Kingdom will be particular, as it will be less about building convergence, and more about controlling future divergence. This is key to establishing fair competition."

The United Kingdom's prime minister, in a speech at the Santa Maria Novella church in Florence on 22 September 2017, proposed an economic partnership between the UK and the EU which respects both the freedoms and principles of the EU, and the wishes of the British people. At the same time she re-affirmed that after the UK leaves the EU a period of implementation would be in their mutual interest, to be agreed under Article 50 for a strictly time-limited period.

The European parliament voted a Brexit resolution (the European Parliament resolution of 14 March 2018 on the framework of the future EU-UK relationship (2018/2573(RSP)) with 544 MEP against 110 (with 51 abstentions). The 14 page document states that an association agreement between EU and UK could be an adequate framework for the future. This resolution proposes that the agreement address four domains: trade, interior security, foreign and defense policy collaboration, and thematic cooperation (for instance for research and innovation). The resolution also urges the UK to present a clear position on all outstanding issues pertaining to its orderly withdrawal.

External links

- UK Parliament – Brexit News[1036]
- Gov.UK – Department for Exiting the European Union[1037]
- UK Government – "Plan for Britain" website[1038]
- Europa (EU official website) – UK – Brexit – overview[1039]
- European Commission – Brexit negotiations website[1040]
- European Commission – list of published negotiating documents[1041]
- European Commission – Preparedness notices[1042]
- *Brexit*, EC, CEU Timeline and list of key documents for Brexit negotiations[1043]
- *The Principle of Loyalty in EU Law*, 2014, by Marcus Klamert, Legal Officer, European Commission[1044]
- Resource page[1045] and commentary by David Allen Green

Post-Article 50 British legislation

European Union (Withdrawal) Act 2018

European Union (Withdrawal) Act 2018

Act of Parliament	
Parliament of the United Kingdom	
Long title	An Act to Repeal the European Communities Act 1972 and make other provision in connection with the withdrawal of the United Kingdom from the EU.
Citation	2018 c.16
Introduced by	• David Davis, Secretary of State for Exiting the European Union • Baroness Evans of Bowes Park (Leader of the House of Lords) • Lord Callanan (Minister of State for Exiting the European Union)
Territorial extent	United Kingdom (England and Wales, Scotland, Northern Ireland) *Directly and indirectly also affects (not part of the territorial extent):* Gibraltar (Although it also provides in Section 24(3): "Regulations under section 8(1) or 23 may make provision which extends to Gibraltar...) The Isle of Man Bailiwick of Jersey Bailiwick of Guernsey
Dates	
Royal assent	26 June 2018

Com-mence-ment	26 June 2018 (partly in force)
Other legislation	
Amends	Finance Act 1973 Interpretation Act 1978 European Economic Area Act 1993 Criminal Procedure (Scotland) Act 1995 Human Rights Act 1998 Scotland Act 1998 Northern Ireland Act 1998 Government of Wales Act 2006 Interpretation and Legislative Reform (Scotland) Act 2010 Small Business, Enterprise and Employment Act 2015
Repeals	• European Communities Act 1972 • European Parliamentary Elections Act 2002 • European Parliament (Representation) Act 2003 • European Union (Amendment) Act 2008 • European Union Act 2011 • European Union (Approval of Treaty Amendment Decision) Act 2012 • European Union (Approvals) Act 2013 • European Union (Approvals) Act 2014 • Serious Crime Act 2015, sections 82 and 88(5)(c) • European Union (Finance) Act 2015 • European Union (Approvals) Act 2015
Relates to	• European Union Referendum Act 2015 • European Union (Notification of Withdrawal) Act 2017 • Nuclear Safeguards Act 2018
Status: Current legislation	
History of passage through Parliament[1046]	
Text of statute as originally enacted[1047]	
Revised text of statute as amended[1048]	

Part of a series of articles on theUnited Kingdom
in the
European Union

Accession

• 1973 EC enlargement
• 1975 Referendum Act
• 1975 EC membership referendum

- 1972 EC Act
- UK rebate
- 2011 EU Act

Membership

- The Euro
- European Movement UK
- Nationality law
- UK Euroscepticism
  - Maastricht Rebels
- Black Wednesday

- **Officials and bodies**

- EU Committee
- European Scrutiny Committee
- Northern Ireland Executive in Brussels
- EU Representative in London
- Young European Movement UK
- UK European Commissioners
- Permanent EU Representatives

Legislation

- 1972 EC Act
- 1986 EC (Amendment) Act
- 1993 EC (Amendment) Act
- 1998 EC (Amendment) Act
- 2002 EC (Amendment) Act
- 2008 EU (Amendment) Act
- 2011 EU Act

European Parliament Elections

- 1979
- 1984
- 1989
- 1994
- 1999
- 2004
- 2009
- 2014

  - 1973 delegation
  - 1st
  - 2nd
  - 3rd

- 4th
- 5th
- 6th
- 7th
- 8th

Withdrawal

- 2004–05 EU Bill
- 2013–14 EU (Referendum) Bill
- 2015–16 EU membership renegotiation
- 2015 EU Referendum Act
- 2016 EU (Referendum) Act (Gibraltar)

- **2016 EU membership referendum**

- Issues
- Endorsements
- Opinion polling
- Results
- Causes

- **Campaigns**

- **Organisations advocating and campaigning for a referendum**

- People's Pledge
- Labour for a Referendum

- **Leave**

- **Vote Leave** (official lead group)
  - Business for Britain
  - Conservatives for Britain
  - Students for Britain
- Labour Leave
- Leave.EU
  - Bpoplive
- Grassroots Out
- Get Britain Out
- The Freedom Association
  - Better Off Out

- **Other anti-EU advocacy organisations**

- Bruges Group
- Campaign for an Independent Britain

- **Remain**

- **Britain Stronger in Europe** (official lead group)
- Labour In for Britain
- European Movement UK

- **Other pro-EU advocacy organisations**

- Britain in Europe
- British Influence
- Business for New Europe
- Nucleus

- **Pejorative term for pro-EU advocacy**

- Project Fear

- **Media coverage**

- *Brexit: The Movie*
- *In or Out*

- **Aftermath**

- International reactions
- Terms of Withdrawal from EU (Referendum) Bills
- 2016 Conservative Party election
- 2016 Labour Party election
- 2017 Liberal Democrats Party election
- Proposed second Scottish independence referendum
- Proposed London independence
- *The New European*
- European Union (Withdrawal) Act 2018 (including meaningful vote)
- European Union (Withdrawal Agreement) Bill 2017-19
- Gibraltar
- 2017 General Election
- EU Withdrawal Agreement (Public Vote) Bill 2017-19
- UK's relations with EU after 2019

- **Triggering of Article 50 & Negotiations**

- *R (Miller) v Secretary of State for Exiting the European Union*'
- EU (Notification of Withdrawal) Act 2017
- UK invocation of Article 50
- Brexit negotiations
- Department for Exiting the EU (Brexit Department)
- Department for International Trade

- **Post-referendum organisations**

- Change Britain
- More United

- Open Britain

Calls for second vote

- European Union Withdrawal Agreement (Public Vote) Bill 2017-19

- **Organisations campaigning
  for a second vote via People's Vote**

- Britain for Europe
- European Movement UK
- For our Future's Sake
- Healthier IN the EU
- Open Britain
- Our Future Our Choice
- Scientists for EU

- **Other organisations campaigning
  for a second vote**

- Best for Britain

- **See also**

- Opposition to Brexit in the United Kingdom

- <u>v</u>
- <u>t</u>
- <u>e</u>[1049]

Constitutional documents and events (present & historical) relevant to the status of the United Kingdom and legislative unions of its constituent countries

Treaty of Union	1706
Acts of Union	1707
Wales and Berwick Act	1746
Irish Constitution	1782
Acts of Union	1800
Parliament Act	1911
Government of Ireland Act	1920
Anglo-Irish Treaty	1921
Royal and Parliamentary Titles Act	1927

Statute of Westminster	1931
United Nations Act	1946
Parliament Act	1949
EC Treaty of Accession	1972
NI (Temporary Provisions) Act	1972
European Communities Act	1972
Local Government Act	1972
Local Government (Scotland) Act	1973
NI Border Poll	1973
NI Constitution Act	1973
Referendum Act	1975
EC Membership Referendum	1975
Scotland Act	1978
Wales Act	1978
Scottish Devolution Referendum	1979
Welsh Devolution Referendum	1979
Local Government (Wales) Act	1994
Local Government etc. (Scotland) Act	1994
Referendums (Scotland & Wales) Act	1997
Scottish Devolution Referendum	1997
Welsh Devolution Referendum	1997
Good Friday Agreement	1998
Northern Ireland Act	1998
Government of Wales Act	1998
Human Rights Act	1998
Scotland Act	1998
Government of Wales Act	2006
Northern Ireland Act	2009
Welsh Devolution Referendum	2011
European Union Act	2011
Fixed-term Parliaments Act	2011
Scotland Act	2012
Edinburgh Agreement	2012
Scottish Independence Referendum	2014
Wales Act	2014
European Union Referendum Act	2015
EU Membership Referendum	2016

Scotland Act	2016
EU (Notification of Withdrawal) Act	2017
Wales Act	2017
Invocation of Article 50	2017
European Union (Withdrawal) Act	2018

- v
- t
- e[1050]

The **European Union (Withdrawal) Act 2018** (c. 16) is an Act of the Parliament of the United Kingdom that provides for repealing the European Communities Act 1972, and for Parliamentary approval of the withdrawal agreement being negotiated between HM Government and the European Union.

This will enable the "cutting off the source of EU law in the UK... and remove the competence of EU institutions to legislate for the UK."[1051] As such, It is the most significant constitutional legislation that has been introduced by the Government since the European Communities Act itself in 1972.

To provide legal continuity, it will enable the transposition of directly-applicable already-existing EU law into UK law, and so "create a new category of domestic law for the United Kingdom: retained EU law." It will also give the government some restricted power to adapt and remove laws that are no longer relevant.

The bill's passage through both Houses of Parliament was completed on 20 June 2018 and it became law by Royal Assent on 26 June. It makes future ratification of the withdrawal agreement as a treaty between the UK and EU depend upon the prior enactment of another act of Parliament for approving the final terms of withdrawal when the current Brexit negotiations are completed; and fixes 21 January 2019, at the latest, when the government must decide on how to proceed if the negotiations have not reached agreement in principle on both the withdrawal arrangements and the framework for the future relationship between the UK and EU, for Parliamentary debate.

The act is one of a number of current and projected pieces of legislation affecting international transactions and control of borders, including movement of goods.[1052]

The Act

For repealing ECA 1972 and ratifying withdrawal agreement

The Act is made in connection with the withdrawal of the United Kingdom from the European Union on 29 March 2019, the second anniversary of notice of withdrawal under Article 50 (2) of the Treaty on European Union. The Act provides for ratifying and implementing the agreement setting out the withdrawal arrangements. The mandatory period for negotiating the agreement is stated in the EU negotiating directives as ending "at the latest on 30 March 2019 at 00:00 (Brussels time)," —i.e. Central European Time— "unless the European Council, in agreement with the United Kingdom, unanimously decides to extend this period in accordance with Article 50(3) of the Treaty on European Union".

The Act legislates for the following:

- repeal of the European Communities Act 1972.
- fixing "exit day", naming the hour for this as 11.00 p.m. on 29 March 2019.
- formal incorporation and adaptation ("copying") of up to 20,000 pieces of EU law onto the UK statute book by:
  - conversion of directly-applicable EU law (EU regulations) into UK law.
  - preservation of all laws that have been made in the UK to implement EU obligations.
  - continuing to make available in UK law the rights in EU treaties, that are relied on directly in court by an individual.
  - ending the supremacy of EU law in the United Kingdom.:ch.2
- creating powers to make commencement orders and other secondary legislation:ch.3 under statutory instrument procedures.
- Parliamentary approval of the outcome of the government's negotiations with the EU under Article 50(2) of the Treaty on European Union.

Parliamentary approval: section 13

The Act's section 13 contains a set of mandatory procedures for Parliament's approval to the various possible outcomes of the government's negotiations with the EU. One outcome is that there will be an agreement between the United Kingdom and the EU under Article 50 of the Treaty on European Union which sets out the arrangements for the United Kingdom's withdrawal from the EU. In the Act the agreement is called the withdrawal agreement. The Act provides (*section 13*) that before the withdrawal agreement can be ratified, as a treaty between the United Kingdom and the European Union, an act of Parliament must have been passed which provides for its implementation. The

Act allows (*section 9*) regulations to be made and in force on or before exit day for the purpose of implementing the withdrawal agreement, but only if by then an act of Parliament has been enacted "approving the final terms of withdrawal of the United Kingdom from the EU."

An analysis of the process set out in the Act published by the Institute for Government discusses the procedure for approving treaties that is set out in the Constitutional Reform and Governance Act 2010 (CRAG) which may apply to the withdrawal agreement and the framework agreement for future relations, depending on what they contain. The procedure could prevent ratification, but in exceptional cases a government may ratify a treaty without consulting Parliament.

Alternatively (*section 13 (10)*), if by Monday 21 January 2019 – less than eleven weeks before the mandatory negotiating period ends on Friday 29 March – there is no agreement in principle in the negotiations on the substance of the withdrawal arrangements and the framework for the future relationship between the EU and the United Kingdom, the government must publish a statement setting out how the government proposes to proceed, and must arrange for debate about that in Parliament within days.

<templatestyles src="Template:Quote_box/styles.css" />

"Under the Standing Orders of the House of Commons it will be for the Speaker to determine whether a motion when it is introduced by the Government under the European Union (Withdrawal) Bill is or is not in fact cast in neutral terms and hence whether the motion is or is not amendable. The Government recognises that it is open for Ministers and members of the House of Commons to table motions on and debate matters of concern and that, as is the convention, parliamentary time will be provided for this."

Ministerial Statement HCWS781, 21 June 2018

The approval provisions use certain words in special ways:

- "a motion in neutral terms" is used three times in section 13 and is not defined in the Act, but a document dated 21 June 2018 setting out the government's undertsanding stated "Under the Standing Orders of the House of Commons it will be for the Speaker to determine whether a motion when it is introduced by the Government under the European Union (Withdrawal) Bill is or is not in fact cast in neutral terms and hence whether the motion is or is not amendable. The Government recognises that it is open for Ministers and members of the House of Commons to table motions on and debate matters of concern and that, as is the convention, parliamentary time will be provided for this."

- "a statement that political agreement has been reached" is used three times in section 13, and defined (*section 13 (16)*) as a Minister's written statement that, in the Minister's opinion, "an ageement in principle has been reached in negotiations under Article 50(2) of the Treaty on European Union on the substance of (i) the arrangements for the United Kingdom's withdrawal from the EU, and (ii) the framework for the future relationship between the EU and the United Kingdom after withdrawal".

Coming into force: section 25

The sections of the Act that came into force immediately when the Act passed into law on 26 June 2018, as listed in section 25 (1), include:

- 8 Dealing with deficiencies arising from withdrawal
- 9 Implementing the withdrawal agreement
- 10 Continuation of North-South co-operation in Ireland and the prevention of new border arrangements
- 11 Powers involving devolved authorities corresponding to sections 8 and 9
- 16 Maintenance of environmental principles etc.
- 17 Family unity for those seeking asylum or other protection in Europe
- 18 Customs arrangement as part of the framework for the future relationship
- 20 Interpretation
- 21 Index of defined expressions
- 22 Regulations
- 23 Consequential and transitional provision, except subsection (5)
- 24 Extent.
- 25 Commencement and short title.

Subsections (2) and (3) relate to the devolved administrations of Northern Ireland, Scotland and Wales. Subsection (4) provides for bringing into force by regulation the remaining provisions of the Act, including:

- 1 Repeal of the European Communities Act 1972
- 2 Saving for EU-derived domestic legislation
- 3 Incorporation of direct EU legislation
- 4 Saving for rights etc. under section 2(1) of the ECA
- 5 Exceptions to savings and incorporation
- 6 Interpretation of retained EU law
- 7 Status of retained EU law
- 13 Parliamentary approval of the outcome of negotiations with the EU
- 14 Financial provision
- 15 Publication and rules of evidence

- 19 Future interaction with the law and agencies of the EU.

No regulation for bringing any of those provisions into force was made before the end of June 2018.

Post-act events

The Democratic Unionist Party, whose support the government needs to have a majority in key Commons votes, said on 2 July 2018 it would not support any deal which did not give the UK full control over its borders.

After a meeting to discuss the latest development of the negotiations, when the European Union's chief negotiator Michel Barnier repeatedly told the Prime Minister the EU would not agree to discuss trade until an agreement was found on the terms of withdrawal, the prime minister informed the House of Commons on 2 July 2018 that she warned EU leaders that she did not think Parliament will approve the withdrawal agreement in the autumn "unless we have clarity about our future relationship alongside it." This was followed by a decision at a Cabinet meeting at Chequers on 6 July that continuing preparations for potential outcomes included the 'no deal' possibility.

David Davis, who as Secretary of State for Exiting the European Union had introduced the Act as a bill in Parliament, and who had attended the Cabinet meeting at Chequers on 6 July, resigned on 8 July. saying in his resignation letter, "In my view the inevitable consequence of the proposed policies will be to make the supposed control by Parliament illusory rather than real." The next day, the prime minister appointed Dominic Raab as Brexit Secretary. Later in the day, the resignation of the Foreign Secretary, Boris Johnson, who had also attended the Chequers Cabinet meeting, was made public. Within hours, the prime minister appointed Jeremy Hunt as the next Foreign Secretary.

The government's policy on the future relationship between the United Kingdom and the European Union that the Cabinet had discussed at Chequers was published as a White Paper on 12 July 2018 for debate in the House of Commons the following week.

While the President of the United States was on a visit to the United Kingdom on 13 July 2018, his comment, that the UK would probably not get a trade deal with the US if the prime minister's plan went ahead, was widely published in the media.

The government confirmed in the House of Commons on 19 July 2018 that the UK would be leaving the EU on 29 March 2019, as stated in the Withdrawal Act and the White Paper. The first meeting of Dominic Raab, the newly appointed UK Secretary of State, with the EU's chief negotiator, Michel Barnier, was in Brussels later on the same day (19 July 2018). Raab offered to meet

Barnier throughout August to "intensify" talks, while both the UK and EU were insisting that reaching agreement by the autumn on the UK withdrawal in March 2019 was still very much on the cards.

Connected legislation: world and cross-border trade

Two bills that allow for various outcomes including no negotiated settlement, that were introduced in the House of Commons in November 2017, completed all stages there in July 2018 and passed from the Commons to the House of Lords: the Taxation (Cross-border Trade) Bill on 16 July, and the Trade Bill on 17 July. The government stated that the Haulage Permits and Trailer Registration Act 2018, which became law on 19 July 2018,[1053] would apply to a permit scheme for international road haulage and was made in connection with the government's aim in the negotiations to develop the existing international access for commercial road haulage.[1054] On September 4, 2018, the Taxation (Cross-Border Trade) Bill passed its second reading, committee stages and third reading in the House of Lords and later became law after receiving Royal Assent on September 13.[1055,1056,1057]

Impact on devolution

The government published in March 2018 a provisional analysis about the devolved administrations receiving new powers as the UK leaves the EU.

In devolved administrations, the powers currently exercised by the EU in relation to common policy frameworks would return to the UK, allowing the rules to be set in the UK by Westminster representatives. Ministers of devolved administrations would be given the power to amend devolved legislation to correct law that would not operate appropriately following Brexit.[:ch.4] However, the bill also prevents devolved administrations from making changes that are "inconsistent" with those made by the UK government.[:sch.2, pt.3(2)] This significantly limits the power of the devolved governments by making it impossible for them to, for example, choose to retain a piece of EU law that has been modified by the UK government.

To prepare Welsh law for Brexit the National Assembly for Wales passed an EU Continuity Act – formally the "Law Derived from the European Union (Wales) Act 2018 – that became law on 6 June 2018.

The Scottish Parliament passed an EU Continuity Bill (formally the "UK Withdrawal from the European Union (Legal Continuity) (Scotland) Bill 2018") on 21 March 2018, to prepare Scots law for Brexit, but it has been referred for scrutiny to the Supreme Court under section 33 of the Scotland Act 1998, to determine whether the Parliament had legislative competence to pass such a bill, and thus Royal Assent is still pending, as of June 2018.[1058] The Supreme Court hearing is due to start on 24 July 2018.

As the Northern Ireland Assembly has been suspended and the province has been without devolved government since 9 January 2017 — before the passage of the European Union (Notification of Withdrawal) Act 2017 — it has not been possible for the assembly to consider any equivalent continuity powers. Without an Assembly or Executive, the province is governed by the Secretary of State for Northern Ireland and their junior ministers; these would be the same ministers responsible for making or amending continuity orders under the Withdrawal Act.

EU case law

At present, case law emanating from the Court of Justice of the European Union (CJEU, formerly and still commonly known as the ECJ) is binding on UK courts. The Act will have ECJ case law retained as part of the law, but it will no longer be binding on the courts and tribunals of the United Kingdom. The legislation permits courts to depart from ECJ caselaw after applying the same test as they would apply in deciding whether to depart from their own case law.

Human rights laws

The Act makes explicit in section 5 that the Charter of Fundamental Rights of the European Union will cease to be a part of UK law after Brexit.

Additional repeals

Repeal of other Acts include:

- European Communities (Greek Accession) Act 1979
- European Communities (Spanish and Portuguese Accession) Act 1985
- European Union (Accessions) Act 1994
- European Union (Accessions) Act 2003
- European Union (Accessions) Act 2006
- European Union (Croatian Accession and Irish Protocol) Act 2013
- European Parliamentary Elections Act 2002
- European Parliament (Representation) Act 2003
- European Union (Amendment) Act 2008
- European Union Act 2011
- European Union (Approval of Treaty Amendment Decision) Act 2012
- European Union (Approvals) Act 2013
- European Union (Approvals) Act 2014
- European Union (Approvals) Act 2015

- European Union (Approvals) Act 2017
- European Union (Finance) Act 2015
- European Union Referendum Act 2015
- Sections 82 and 88(5)(c) of the Serious Crime Act 2015

Amendments

Amendments to other Acts include:

- Finance Act 1973
- Interpretation Act 1978
- European Economic Area Act 1993
- Criminal Procedure (Scotland) Act 1995
- Human Rights Act 1998
- Scotland Act 1998
- Northern Ireland Act 1998
- Government of Wales Act 2006
- Interpretation and Legislative Reform (Scotland) Act 2010
- Small Business, Enterprise and Employment Act 2015

EU response

After the Act became law on 26 June 2018 the European Council decided on 29 June to renew its call on Member States and Union institutions to step up their work on preparedness at all levels and for all outcomes.

Legislative history

In October 2016 the Prime Minister, Theresa May, promised a "Great Repeal Bill", which would repeal the European Communities Act 1972 and restate in UK law all enactments previously in force under EU law. It would smooth the transition by ensuring that all laws remain in force until specifically repealed.

Henry VIII clauses

In March 2017, a report by Thomson Reuters identified 52,741 pieces of legislation that have been passed since 1990. Transferring European legislation into British law is the quickest way to ensure continuity. Because these may refer to EU institutions that the UK will no longer belong to, or use phrasing assuming that the UK is an EU member state, they cannot simply be directly converted into law. Redrafting all of the tens of thousands of laws affected and voting on them through Parliament would be an impossibly time-consuming process, so the bill included provisions, informally known as Henry VIII clauses,

which would allow ministers to make secondary legislation to amend or remove these laws (both primary and secondary legislation) to resolve "deficiencies" by making statutory instruments.

In the bill, the powers were divided between two clauses. Clause 7 made provision for ministers to correct "deficiencies" in law (including references to
EU institutions that the UK is no longer a member of, EU treaties that are no
longer relevant, and redundancies), expiring two years after the UK leaves the
EU. These proposed powers could not be used to make secondary legislation
for

- Imposing or increasing taxation.
- Making retrospective provision.
- Creating a criminal offence with a maximum sentence greater than impris-
  onment for two years.
- Amending, repealing or revoking the Human Rights Act 1998 or any
  subordinate legislation made under it.
- Amending or repealing the Northern Ireland Act 1998 (with some limited
  exceptions).[§7]

Clause 9 of the bill offered ministers unusually broad powers to make changes
to legislation. Although some safeguards were included to limit the situa-
tions in which law can be modified, for instance with the inclusion of sun-
set clauses, the provisions granting these powers were criticised for being too
wide-ranging.

House of Commons First and Second Readings

On 13 July 2017, David Davis, the Secretary of State for Exiting the European
Union, introduced the bill in the House of Commons. As a government bill,
this first reading was pro forma, with the first debate taking place on the second
reading.

The second reading and debate on the bill began on 7 September 2017. The
debate and second reading resumed on 11 September. Shortly after midnight
on 12 September, the second reading passed by a margin of 326 to 290, a
majority of 36 votes, after an amendment proposed by the Labour Party was
rejected by a margin of 318 to 296. A motion to put the Bill under eight days
of Committee scrutiny passed 318 to 301.

House of Commons Committee Stage

The Committee stage was originally scheduled to take place after MPs returned to Parliament following the conclusion, in October, of their respective party conferences. However, House of Commons leader Andrea Leadsom announced on 26 October that the committee stage was to begin on 14 November. Committee stage began as scheduled on 14 November as a Committee of the Whole House, and completed on 20 December 2017.

MPs tabled more than 470 amendments to the bill, and one of these provided Theresa May's government with its first defeat on government business, as MPs voted by 309 to 305 to give Parliament a legal guarantee of a vote on the final Brexit deal struck with Brussels. The government had originally suggested that as the bill will be a major focus of the parliamentary debate on Brexit as a whole, it would provide an alternative to a vote on the deal agreed in the Brexit negotiations. However, on 13 November 2017 the government announced that it would introduce a separate Withdrawal Agreement and Implementation Bill to deal separately with examining an agreement from the negotiations between the UK and EU, if any is reached, which would provide Parliament with a vote, but this did not prevent the amendment to the bill being passed.

The repeal was planned to be enacted during the Brexit negotiations, but to come into force on 'exit day'. As originally tabled, the bill did not give a date for 'exit day', but said that " 'exit day' means such day as a Minister of the Crown may by regulations appoint". If no time is specified, it was to be "the beginning of that day". However, the government tabled an amendment in Committee Stage so the bill then said " 'exit day' means 29 March 2019 at 11.00 p.m". To avoid a second possible defeat, the government accepted a further amendment that "A Minister of the Crown may by regulations amend the definition of 'exit day' ", allowing for flexibility in the event of a transitional deal, or extra time being needed in the negotiations.

There was a total of 40 divisions during Committee Stage. Proposed amendments that were not passed include:

- An amendment to exclude the section of the bill which states that the Charter of Fundamental Rights of the European Union will not be part of domestic law after exit day, was defeated by 311 votes to 301. On 5 December the Government had published an analysis setting out how each article of the charter will be reflected in UK law after Brexit.
- An amendment to allow the UK to remain in the EU Customs Union was defeated by 320 votes to 114.
- An amendment to hold a referendum on whether to: (1) accept the final exit deal agreed with the EU; or (2) remain in the EU, was defeated by 319 votes to 23.

House of Commons Report Stage and Third Reading

The Report Stage and Third Reading happened on 16 and 17 January 2018. The bill passed Third Reading by 324 votes to 295.

House of Lords First and Second Readings and Committee Stage

The bill had its First Reading in the Lords on 18 January 2018, and Second Reading on 30 and 31 January 2018, and committed to a Committee of the Whole House. This lasted for eleven days between 21 February and 28 March.

House of Lords Report Stage

As part of the Lords Report Stage, a number of amendments were passed, of which 170 were proposed by the Government, and 14 were defeats for the Government, including:

- Amendment 1: A proposal requiring ministers to report on the Government's efforts to negotiate a continued customs union between the EU and the UK was passed by 348 to 225 – a majority of 123.
- Amendment 11: A proposal that certain areas of retained EU Law cannot be amended or repealed after Exit by Ministers, but only through primary legislation (i.e. an Act of Parliament), was passed by 314 to 217 – a majority of 97. These areas of retained EU Law are: (a) employment entitlements, rights and protection; (b) equality entitlements, rights and protection; (c) health and safety entitlements, rights and protection; (d) consumer standards; and (e) environmental standards and protection. Even technical changes to the retained EU Law in these areas can only be made with approval of both Houses of Parliament, and following 'an enhanced scrutiny procedure'.
- Amendment 15: One of the few pieces of EU Law the bill proposed to repeal, rather than transpose into UK Law, was the Charter of Fundamental Rights of the European Union, but an amendment to keep the Charter part of UK Law after Exit was passed by 316 to 245, majority 71.
- Amendment 18: A proposal which allows individuals to retain the right to challenge the validity of EU law post-Brexit was passed by 285 to 235 – a majority of 50.
- Amendment 19: A proposal which limits ministerial powers to alter EU law when it is incorporated into UK law post-Brexit was passed by 280 to 223 – a majority of 57.

- Amendment 31: A proposal to amend a clause that originally gave ministers power to make 'appropriate' changes to legislation, to instead give them power to make 'necessary' changes, was passed by 349 votes to 221 – a majority of 128, 25 April 2018.

- Amendment 49: A proposal that means parliament must approve the withdrawal agreement and transitional measures in an act of parliament, before the European parliament has debated and voted on this, and also gives the Commons the power to decide the next steps for the government if the deal is rejected (dubbed the 'meaningful vote') was passed by 335 to 244 – a majority of 91.

- Amendment 51: A proposed change giving parliament a say on future negotiations on the UK's future relationship with the EU was passed by 270 to 233 – a majority of 37.

- Amendment 59: A proposed change requiring the government to reunite unaccompanied child refugees with relatives in the UK was passed by 205 to 181 – a majority of 24.

- Amendment 70: A proposal to create a parliamentary committee to sift certain regulations introduced under the legislation to recommend whether they require further scrutiny of Brexit statutory instruments was passed by 225 to 194 – a majority of 31.

- Amendment 88: The Lords voted in favour of inserting a new clause regarding the continuation of North-South co-operation and the prevention of new border arrangements between Northern Ireland and the Republic of Ireland, 309 votes to 242 – a majority of 67.

- Amendment 93: A proposal to allow the Government to replicate any EU law in domestic law and to continue to participate in EU agencies (such as European Atomic Energy Community (Euratom)) after Brexit was passed by 298 to 227 – a majority of 71.

- Amendment 95: A proposal to remove the exit day of 29 March 2019 from the face of the Bill was passed by 311 to 233 – a majority of 78.

- Amendment 110A: A proposal to mandate the Government to negotiate continued membership of the European Economic Area was passed by 245 to 218 – a majority of 27.

On 30 April, a proposal to advance a second EU Referendum (amendment 50) was rejected by the Lords 260 votes to 202 – a majority of 58.[1059]

House of Lords Third Reading

During the Third Reading on 16 May 2018, the Government suffered its 15th defeat in the Lords which, including the Commons Committee defeat, meant 16 defeats overall. The bill then passed the Third Reading.

Consideration of Amendments

The Commons debated the amendments proposed by the Lords on 12 and 13 June. A majority voted to reject 14 of the 15 Lords amendments and accepted only one, which pertained to preservation of relations with the EU. The government also agreed to accept an amendment encouraging the negotiation of a customs arrangement with the EU and further compromised with amendments concerning the issues of Northern Ireland, scrutiny, the environment and unaccompanied child migrants. A government-backed amendment allowing legal challenges on the basis of EU law for the three-year period following Brexit also passed. It was also agreed that any withdrawal agreement with the EU would not be implemented without Parliament approval and if there was no such approval, a minister will make a statement setting out how the Government "proposes to proceed" within 28 days, as contained in section 13 of the Act as passed.

On 18 June the House of Lords passed another "meaningful vote" amendment similar to the one rejected by the House of Commons which allows a parliament vote on Brexit in case no UK-EU Brexit deal was reached, this time reworded so it wouldn't involve only a "neutral motion." This amendment was later defeated by the Commons on 20 June in a 319-303 vote. The same day, the Lords agreed to accept the government's EU Withdrawal Bill, thus paving the way for it to become law upon royal assent.

Royal Assent and Commencement

The bill became law as an Act on 26 June 2018. Section 1 states that the European Communities Act 1972 is repealed on exit day, defined in another section as 29 March 2019 at 11.00 p.m. Section 25 subsection (1) sets out the provisions of the Act that commenced on 26 June 2018, subsections (2) and (3) set out the provisions of the Act that commenced on that day for certain purposes, and subsection (4) states that the remaining provisions will come into force on the day or days appointed by regulations.

External links

- European Union (Withdrawal) Act 2018[1060]
- Explanatory Notes on the European Union (Withdrawal) Act 2018 prepared by the Department for Exiting the European Union[1061]
- UK government's *Frameworks analysis: breakdown of areas of EU law that intersect with devolved competence in Scotland, Wales and Northern Ireland*[1062]
- Law Derived from the European Union (Wales) Act 2018 (anaw 3, 6 June 2018)[1063]

- *Brexit: new guidelines on the framework for future EU-UK relations*, April 2018[1064]
- Statement from HM Government on the future relationship, Chequers, 6 July 2018[1065]
- Davis' resignation letter and May's reply in full, BBC News 9 July 2018[1066]

Legislative history

- Progress of the Bill and royal assent[1067]
- Hansard References for each stage of the Act's passage through Parliament[1061]
- Explanatory Notes, 13 July 2017 , published with the European Union (Withdrawal) Bill[1068]
- Select Committee on the Constitution[1069] European Union (Withdrawal) Bill: interim report] (published 7 September 2017)
- *Legislating for the United Kingdom's withdrawal from the European Union* (The Great Repeal Bill White Paper), 30 March 2017 (Accessible web version)[1070] (Print version)[1071]
- Briefing paper[1072], House of Commons Library, 1 September 2017
- UK Government – "Plan for Britain" website[1073]

Economic effects

Economic effects of Brexit

The **economic effects of Brexit** were a major area of debate during the Referendum on UK membership of the European Union, and the debate continues after the Leave vote. There is a broad consensus among economists and in the economic literature that Brexit will likely reduce the UK's real per-capita income level.

Supporters of remaining, including the UK treasury, argued that being in the EU has a strong positive effect on trade and as a result the UK's trade would be worse off if it left the EU. Supporters of withdrawal from the EU have argued that the cessation of net contributions to the EU would allow for some cuts to taxes or increase in government spending.[1074]

Contributions to the EU

Supporters of withdrawal argued that ending net contributions to the EU would allow for tax cuts or government spending increases. On the basis of Treasury figures, in 2014 the United Kingdom's *gross* national contribution (ignoring the rebate) was £18.8 billion, about 1% of GDP, or £350 million a week. Because the UK receives (per capita) less EU spending than other member states, a rebate was negotiated; net of this rebate, the contribution was £14.4 billion, approximately 0.8% of GDP, or £275 million a week. If EU spending in Britain is also taken into account, the average *net* contribution for the next five years is estimated at about £8 billion a year, which is about 0.4% of national income, or £150 million per week. The Institute for Fiscal Studies noted that the majority of forecasts of the impact of Brexit on the UK economy indicated that the government would have less money to spend even if it no longer had to pay into the EU.

Single market

According to Paul Krugman, Brexiteers' assertions that leaving the single market and customs union might increase UK exports to the rest of the world are wrong. He considers the costs of Brexit might be around 2 per cent of GDP.

Effect on trade and the economy

Most economists, including the UK Treasury, argue that being in the EU has a strong positive effect on trade and as a result the UK's trade would be worse off if it left the EU. Surveys of leading economists show overwhelming agreement that Brexit will likely reduce the UK's real per-capita income level. A 2017 survey of existing academic literature found "the research literature displays a broad consensus that in the long run Brexit will make the United Kingdom poorer because it will create new barriers to trade, foreign direct investment, and immigration. However, there is substantial uncertainty over how large the effect will be, with plausible estimates of the cost ranging between 1 and 10 percent of the UK's income per capita." These estimates differ depending on whether the UK stays in the European Single Market (for instance, by joining the EEA), makes a free trade agreement with the EU, or reverts to the trade rules that govern relations between all World Trade Organization members. Prior to the referendum, the UK treasury estimated that leaving the EU would be bad for the UK's trade.

On 10 August the Institute for Fiscal Studies published a report funded by the Economic and Social Research Council which warned that Britain faced some very difficult choices as it couldn't retain the benefits of full EU membership whilst restricting EU migration. The IFS claimed the cost of reduced economic growth would cost the UK around £70 billion, more than the £8 billion savings in membership fees. It did not expect new trade deals to make up the difference.

On 5 January 2017, Andy Haldane, the Chief Economist and the Executive Director of Monetary Analysis and Statistics at the Bank of England, said that the BoE's own forecast predicting an immediate economic downturn due to the referendum result was inaccurate and noted strong market performance immediately after the referendum, although some have pointed to prices rising faster than wages.[1075] Haldane said the forecast was only inaccurate in its near-term assessment, and that over time, Brexit would harm economic growth. London School of Economics economist Thomas Sampson notes that it is hard to assess the impact that the transition process to Brexit will have.

A report by the London School of Economics suggests that food prices, notably prices of dairy products could rise and food supplies could become less secure if Britain leaves the EU under WTO trading arrangements.[1076]

Foreign direct investment

European experts from the World Pensions Council (WPC) and the University of Bath have argued that, beyond short-lived market volatility, the long term economic prospects of Britain remain high, notably in terms of country attractiveness and foreign direct investment (FDI): "Country risk experts we spoke to are confident the UK's economy will remain robust in the event of an exit from the EU. 'The economic attractiveness of Britain will not go down and a trade war with London is in no one's interest,' says M Nicolas Firzli, director-general of the World Pensions Council (WPC) and advisory board member for the World Bank Global Infrastructure Facility [...] Bruce Morley, lecturer in economics at the University of Bath, goes further to suggest that the long-term benefits to the UK of leaving the Union, such as less regulation and more control over Britain's trade policy, could outweigh the short-term uncertainty observed in the [country risk] scores."

The mooted importance of the UK's membership of the EU as a lure for FDI has long been stressed by supporters of the UK's continued involvement in the EU. In this view, foreign firms see the UK as a gateway to other EU markets, with the UK economy benefiting from its resulting attractiveness as a location for activity. The UK is certainly a major recipient of FDI. In 2014, it held the second largest stock of inward investment in the world, amounting to just over £1 trillion or almost 7% of the global total. This was more than double the 3% accounted for by Germany and France. On a per capita basis, the UK is the clear front-runner among major economies with a stock of FDI around three times larger than the level in other major European economies and 50% larger than in the US.

Property market

The BBC reported on 28 April 2017 that property investment firm JLL (company) data shows Asian investors accounted for 28% of the transactions in the UK property market in 2016, up from the 17% the year before — indicating that Brexit is not dissuading Asian property investors. The BBC also cited Chinese international property portal Juwai.com, which reported a 60% increase in enquiries into UK property in the prior 12 months. Property firm CBRE Group said in January 2017 that Brexit has increased risk in UK property markets by creating new uncertainties.

Stock markets and currencies

When the London Stock Exchange opened on Friday 24 June, the FTSE 100 fell from 6338.10 to 5806.13 in the first ten minutes of trading. It recovered to 6091.27 after a further 90 minutes before further recovering to 6162.97 by the end of the day's trading. This equated to a fall of 3% by the close of trading. When the markets reopened the following Monday, the FTSE 100 showed a steady decline, losing over 2% by mid-afternoon. Upon opening later on the Friday after the referendum, the US Dow Jones Industrial Average dropped nearly 450 points or about 2.5% in less than half an hour. The Associated Press called the sudden worldwide stock market decline a stock market crash. Internationally, more than US$2 trillion of wealth in equities markets was wiped out in the highest one-day sell-off in recorded history, in absolute terms. The stock market losses amounted to a total of 3 trillion US dollars by 27 June; up to the same date, the FTSE 100 index had lost £85 billion. Near the close of trading on 27 June, the domestically-focused FTSE 250 Index was down approximately 14% compared to the day before the referendum results were published.

However, by 1 July the FTSE 100 had risen above pre-referendum levels, to a ten-month high. Taking the previous fall into account, this represented the index's largest single-week rise since 2011. On 11 July, it officially entered bull market territory, having risen by more than 20% from its February low. The FTSE 250 moved above its pre-referendum level on 27 July. In the US, the S&P 500, a broader market than the Dow Jones, reached an all-time high on 11 July.

On the morning of 24 June, the pound sterling fell to its lowest level against the US dollar since 1985, marking the pound down 10% against the US dollar and 7% against the euro. The drop from $1.50 to $1.37 was the biggest move for the currency in any two-hour period in history. The pound remained low, and on 8 July became the worst performing currency of the year, against 31 other major currencies, performing worse than the Argentine peso, the previous lowest currency. By contrast, the pound's trade-weighted index is only back at levels seen in the period 2008–2013.

The referendum result also had an immediate economic effect on a number of other countries. The South African rand experienced its largest single-day decline since 2008, dropping in value by over 8% against the US dollar. Other countries negatively affected included Canada, whose stock exchange fell 1.70%, Nigeria, and Kenya. This was partly due to a general global financial shift out of currencies seen as risky and into the US dollar, and partly due to concerns over how the UK's withdrawal from the EU would affect the economies and trade relations of countries with close economic links to the United Kingdom.

However, by September 2016 British media had reported that ignoring so-called 'Project Fear' scaremongering had rewarded those shareholders who ignored the associated pessimism, after the FTSE250 broke all records in the months following the referendum.

On 5 January 2017, Andy Haldane, the Chief Economist and the Executive Director of Monetary Analysis and Statistics at the Bank of England, admitted that forecasts predicting an economic downturn due to the referendum have so far been inaccurate and noted strong market performance since the referendum.

Economy and business

On 27 June, Chancellor of the Exchequer George Osborne attempted to reassure financial markets that the UK economy was not in serious trouble. This came after media reports that a survey by the Institute of Directors suggested that two-thirds of businesses believed that the outcome of the referendum would produce negative results as well as falls in the value of sterling and the FTSE 100. Some British businesses had also predicted that investment cuts, hiring freezes and redundancies would be necessary to cope with the results of the referendum. Osborne indicated that Britain was facing the future "from a position of strength" and there was no current need for an emergency Budget. "No-one should doubt our resolve to maintain the fiscal stability we have delivered for this country .... And to companies, large and small, I would say this: the British economy is fundamentally strong, highly competitive and we are open for business."

On 14 July Philip Hammond, Osborne's successor as Chancellor, told BBC News the referendum result had caused uncertainty for businesses, and that it was important to send "signals of reassurance" to encourage investment and spending. He also confirmed there would not be an emergency budget: "We will want to work closely with the governor of the Bank of England and others through the summer to prepare for the Autumn Statement, when we will signal and set out the plans for the economy going forward in what are very different circumstances that we now face, and then those plans will be implemented in the Budget in the spring in the usual way."

It was expected that the weaker pound would also benefit aerospace and defence firms, pharmaceutical companies, and professional services companies; the share prices of these companies were boosted after the EU referendum.[1077]

On 12 July, the global investment management company BlackRock predicted the UK would experience a recession in late 2016 or early 2017 as a result of the vote to leave the EU, and that economic growth would slow down for at least five years because of a reduction in investment. On 18 July, the UK-based economic forecasting group EY ITEM club suggested the country would experience a "short shallow recession" as the economy suffered "severe confidence effects on spending and business"; it also cut its economic growth forecasts for the UK from 2.6% to 0.4% in 2017, and 2.4% to 1.4% for 2018. The group's chief economic adviser, Peter Soencer, also argued there would be more long-term implications, and that the UK "may have to adjust to a permanent reduction in the size of the economy, compared to the trend that seemed possible prior to the vote". Senior City investor Richard Buxton also argued there would be a "mild recession". On 19 July, the International Monetary Fund (IMF) reduced its 2017 economic growth forecast for the UK from 2.2% to 1.3%, but still expected Britain to be the second fastest growing economy in the G7 during 2016; the IMF also reduced its forecasts for world economic growth by 0.1% to 3.1% in 2016 and 3.4% in 2017, as a result of the referendum, which it said had "thrown a spanner in the works" of global recovery.

On 20 July, a report released by the Bank of England said that although uncertainty had risen "markedly" since the referendum, it was yet to see evidence of a sharp economic decline as a consequence. However, around a third of contacts surveyed for the report expected there to be "some negative impact" over the following year.

In September 2016, following three months of positive economic data after the referendum, commentators suggested that many of the negative statements and predictions promoted from within the "remain" camp had failed to materialise, but by December, analysis began to show that Brexit was having an effect on inflation.

Financial institutions

On the day after the referendum, Bank of England Governor Mark Carney told a press conference:

The capital requirements of our largest banks are now 10 times higher than before the financial crisis. The Bank of England has stress-tested those banks against scenarios far more severe than our country currently faces. As a result of these actions UK banks have raised over a £130bn of new capital and now have more than £600bn of high quality liquid assets. That substantial capital and huge liquidity gives banks the flexibility they need to continue to lend to UK businesses and households even during challenging times.
Moreover, as a backstop to support the functioning of the markets the Bank of England stands ready to provide more than £250bn of additional

funds through its normal market operations. The Bank of England is also able to provide substantial liquidity in foreign currency if required. We expect institutions to draw on this funding if and when appropriate.

It will take some time for the UK to establish a new relationship with Europe and the rest of the world. So some market and economic volatility can be expected as this process unfolds, but we are well prepared for this. Her Majesty's Treasury and the Bank of England have engaged in extensive contingency planning and the chancellor and I have remained in close contact including through the night and this morning. The Bank of England will not hesitate to take additional measure as required, as markets adjust.

Nonetheless, share prices of the five largest British banks fell an average of 21% on the morning after the referendum. Shares in many other non-UK banks also fell by more than 10%. By the end of Friday's trading, both HSBC and Standard Chartered had fully recovered, while Lloyds, RBS Group and Barclays remained more than 10% down. All of the Big Three credit rating agencies reacted negatively to the vote: Standard & Poor's cut the UK credit rating from AAA to AA, Fitch Group cut from AA+ to AA, and Moody's cut the UK's outlook to "negative".

To increase financial stability, on 5 July the Bank of England released £150 billion in lending by reducing the countercyclical capital buffers that banks are required to hold.

Fears of a fall in commercial property values led investors to begin redeeming investments in property funds, prompting Standard Life to bar withdrawals on 4 July, and Aviva followed suit the next day. Other investment companies including Henderson Group and M&G Investments cut the amount that investors cashing in their funds would receive. In the following weeks, the suspension of redemptions by several companies was lifted, replaced by exit penalties, and the exit penalties were successively reduced.

On 4 October 2016, the *Financial Times* assessed the potential effect of Brexit on banking. The City of London is world leading in financial services, especially in foreign exchange currency transactions, including euros.[1078,1079] This position is enabled by the EU-wide "passporting" agreement for financial products. Should the passporting agreement expire in the event of a Brexit, the British financial service industry might lose up to 35,000 of its 1 million jobs, and the Treasury might lose 5 billion pounds annually in tax revenue. Indirect effects could increase these numbers to 71,000 job losses and 10 billion pounds of tax annually. The latter would correspond to about 2% of annual British tax revenue.

By July 2016 the Senate of Berlin had sent invitation letters encouraging UK-based start-ups to re-locate to Berlin. According to Anthony Browne of the

British Banking Association, many major and minor banks may relocate outside the UK.

Asset management companies

But the situation may be different when it comes to the fund management industry, as British asset owners, notably UK pension funds, often constitute an incommensurate share of total turnover for German, French, Dutch and other Continental European asset managers.

This imbalance could potentially give Britain some negotiating leverage e.g. power of retorsion in case the EU attempts to impose an abrupt cancellation of the mutually-binding obligations and advantages pertaining to the Markets in Financial Instruments Directive 2004 (*'fund passporting'*). Research conducted by the World Pensions Council (WPC) shows that <templatestyles src="Template:Quote/styles.css"/>

> *"Assets owned by UK pension funds are more than 11 times bigger than those of all German and French pension funds put together [...] If need be, at the first hint of threat to the City of London, Her Majesty's Government should be in a position to respond very forcefully."*

International Monetary Fund

In late July 2016, the IMF released a report warning that "'Brexit' marks the materialisation of an important downside risk to global growth," and that considering the current uncertainty as to how the UK would leave the EU, there was "still very much unfolding, more negative outcomes are a distinct possibility". In September 2018 the IMF stated that Brexit would probably, "entail costs", but a disorderly leaving could result in, "a significantly worse outcome". Christine Lagarde said, "Any deal will not be as good as the smooth process under which goods, services, people and capital move around between the EU and the UK without impediments and obstacles." Lagarde said, "Our projections assume a timely agreement with the EU on a broad free-trade pact and a relatively smooth Brexit process after that. A more disruptive departure will have a much worse outcome. Let me be clear: compared with today's smooth single market, all the likely Brexit scenarios will have costs for the UK economy, and to a lesser extent for the EU as well. The larger the impediments to trade in the new relationship, the costlier it will be. This should be obvious but it seems that sometimes it is not." Lagarde also said a, "disorderly" or "crash" Brexit would have many results, including cuts to growth, a worsened deficit and depreciation of sterling, causing the size of the UK economy to be reduced. She added, "The larger the impediments to trade in the new relationship, the costlier it will be." She stated countries tended to trade chiefly with their neighbours and added, "I think geography talks very loudly." Lagarde was asked if she predicted any positives from Brexit, Lagarde said, "I see a lot of negatives. If all the uncertainties were removed it would be better. It is bad for the economy to have this amount of uncertainty."[1080,1081]

G20 finance ministers

Held in late July 2016 in Chengdu, China this summit of finance ministers of 20 major economies warned that the UK's planned departure from the European Union was adding to uncertainty in the global economy and urged that the UK should remain a "close partner" with the European Union to reduce turmoil. While the G20 agreed that other world factors, including terrorist acts, were creating problems, Brexit was at the forefront of their concerns.

In interviews while attending the G20 Summit, Philip Hammond, the UK's recently appointed Chancellor of the Exchequer, said the country would attempt to minimise uncertainty by explaining in the near future "more clearly the kind of arrangement we envisage going forward with the European Union". He emphasised that "the uncertainty will only end when the deal is done" but hoped that the UK and the EU would be able to announce some agreement by late 2016 as to how the exit would be staged. Hammond also reiterated previous Government comments indicating that steps would be taken to stimulate the economy including tax cuts or increased spending, though without specifics. The UK was also planning to increase bilateral trade with China, he told the BBC. "Once we are out of the European Union then I have no doubt on both sides we will want to cement that relationship into a firmer structure in a bilateral way that's appropriate."

Although he was not addressing only the UK's departure from the EU, Mark Carney, chair of the Financial Stability Board (and Governor of the Bank of England), sent a letter in late July 2016 to Finance Ministers attending the G20 Summit and to Central Bank Governors about the difficulties the global economy had weathered (including the effects of Brexit) and the steps the FSB was taking. The letter indicated that the financial system had "continued to function effectively" in spite of the "spikes in uncertainty and risk aversion", confirming that "this resilience in the face of stress demonstrates the enduring benefits of G20 post-crisis reforms." He emphasised the value of specific reforms that had been implemented by the Financial Stability Board stating that these had "dampened aftershocks from these events [world crises] rather than amplifying them". He expressed confidence in the FSB's strategies: "This resilience in the face of stress demonstrates the enduring benefits of G20 post-crisis reforms."

Impact of Brexit on bilateral UK relations

Continuing United Kingdom relationship with the European Union

Part of a series of articles on the
United Kingdom in the European Union

Accession

- 1973 EC enlargement
- 1975 Referendum Act
- 1975 EC membership referendum
- 1972 EC Act
- UK rebate
- 2011 EU Act

Membership

- The Euro
- European Movement UK
- Nationality law
- UK Euroscepticism
  - Maastricht Rebels
- Black Wednesday
- **Officials and bodies**
- EU Committee
- European Scrutiny Committee
- Northern Ireland Executive in Brussels
- EU Representative in London
- Young European Movement UK
- UK European Commissioners
- Permanent EU Representatives

Legislation

- 1972 EC Act
- 1986 EC (Amendment) Act
- 1993 EC (Amendment) Act
- 1998 EC (Amendment) Act
- 2002 EC (Amendment) Act
- 2008 EU (Amendment) Act
- 2011 EU Act

European Parliament Elections

- 1979
- 1984
- 1989
- 1994
- 1999
- 2004
- 2009
- 2014

  - 1973 delegation
  - 1st
  - 2nd
  - 3rd
  - 4th
  - 5th
  - 6th
  - 7th
  - 8th

Withdrawal

- 2004–05 EU Bill
- 2013–14 EU (Referendum) Bill
- 2015–16 EU membership renegotiation
- 2015 EU Referendum Act
- 2016 EU (Referendum) Act (Gibraltar)
- **2016 EU membership referendum**
- Issues
- Endorsements
- Opinion polling
- Results
- Causes
- **Campaigns**
- **Organisations advocating and campaigning for a referendum**
- People's Pledge
- Labour for a Referendum
- **Leave**
- **Vote Leave** (official lead group)
  - Business for Britain
  - Conservatives for Britain
  - Students for Britain
- Labour Leave
- Leave.EU
  - Bpoplive
- Grassroots Out
- Get Britain Out
- The Freedom Association
  - Better Off Out
- **Other anti-EU advocacy organisations**
- Bruges Group
- Campaign for an Independent Britain
- **Remain**
- **Britain Stronger in Europe** (official lead group)
- Labour In for Britain
- European Movement UK
- **Other pro-EU advocacy organisations**
- Britain in Europe
- British Influence
- Business for New Europe
- Nucleus
- **Pejorative term for pro-EU advocacy**
- Project Fear
- **Media coverage**
- *Brexit: The Movie*
- *In or Out*
- **Aftermath**
- International reactions
- Terms of Withdrawal from EU (Referendum) Bills
- 2016 Conservative Party election
- 2016 Labour Party election
- 2017 Liberal Democrats Party election
- Proposed second Scottish independence referendum
- Proposed London independence
- *The New European*
- European Union (Withdrawal) Act 2018 (including meaningful vote)
- European Union (Withdrawal Agreement) Bill 2017-19
- Gibraltar
- 2017 General Election
- EU Withdrawal Agreement (Public Vote) Bill 2017-19
- UK's relations with EU after 2019
- **Triggering of Article 50 & Negotiations**
- *R (Miller) v Secretary of State for Exiting the European Union*'
- EU (Notification of Withdrawal) Act 2017
- UK invocation of Article 50
- Brexit negotiations
- Department for Exiting the EU (Brexit Department)
- Department for International Trade

Calls for second vote
- European Union Withdrawal Agreement (Public Vote) Bill 2017-19
- **Organisations campaigning**
  for a second vote via People's Vote
- Britain for Europe
- European Movement UK
- For our Future's Sake
- Healthier IN the EU
- Open Britain
- Our Future Our Choice
- Scientists for EU
- **Other organisations campaigning**
  for a second vote
- Best for Britain
- **See also**
- Opposition to Brexit in the United Kingdom

- $\underline{v}$
- $\underline{t}$
- $\underline{e}^{1082}$

The **United Kingdom's post-Brexit relationship with the remaining European Union members** could take several forms. A research paper presented to the UK Parliament in July 2013 proposed a number of alternatives to membership which would continue to allow access to the EU internal market. These include remaining in the European Economic Area (EEA) as a European Free Trade Association (EFTA) member (alongside Iceland, Liechtenstein, and Norway), or seeking to negotiate bilateral terms more akin to the Swiss model with a series of interdependent sectoral agreements. The exit from the EU without EEA membership or a trade agreement is known as the WTO option.

A transitional arrangement may apply between the time the UK leaves the EU and the coming into force of the final relationship. The report from the first phase of Brexit negotiations (June to December 2017) mentioned the possibility of agreeing a transitional arrangement during the second phase.

UK membership of the European Economic Area

The UK could seek to continue to be a member of the European Economic Area as a member of EFTA. In January 2017, Theresa May, the British Prime Minister, announced a 12-point plan of negotiating objectives and said that the UK government would not seek continued membership in the single market. EEA membership would mean being under existing EU internal market legislation that is part of the EEA Agreement. Some EU law originates from various international bodies on which non-EU EEA countries have a seat. EFTA members are free to set their own policies in areas such as agriculture, fisheries, Customs Union, trade, the Common Foreign and Security Policy, direct and indirect taxation and criminal matters. EEA countries are required to contribute to the EU Budget in exchange for access to the internal market. The

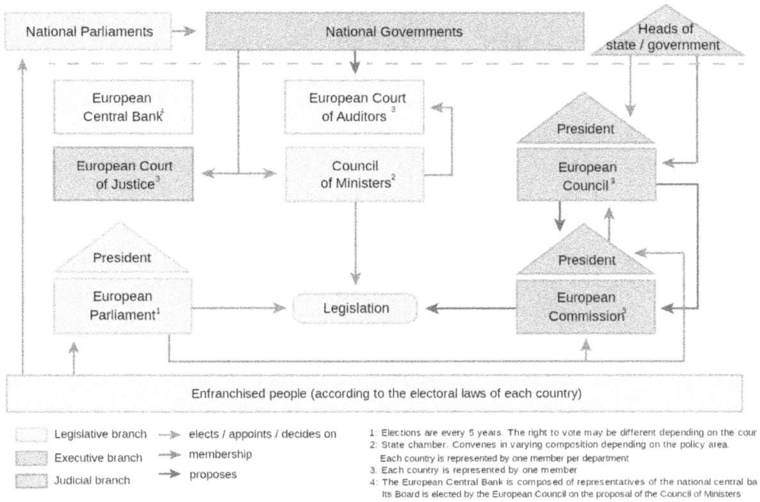

National Parliaments → National Governments   Heads of state / government

European Central Bank⁴

European Court of Auditors ³

President

European Court of Justice³

Council of Ministers²

European Council ³

President

European Parliament¹

Legislation

President

European Commission³

Enfranchised people (according to the electoral laws of each country)

Legislative branch → elects / appoints / decides on
Executive branch → membership
Judicial branch → proposes

1: Elections are every 5 years. The right to vote may be different depending on the cour
2: State chamber. Convenes in varying composition depending on the policy area.
   Each country is represented by one member per department
3: Each country is represented by one member
4: The European Central Bank is composed of representatives of the national central ba
   Its Board is elected by the European Council on the proposal of the Council of Ministers

Figure 43: *Political system of the European Union*

UK would be subject to the EFTA Court rather than the European Court of Justice.[1083]

Bilateral deals

Seeking to negotiate bilateral terms more along the Swiss model with a series of interdependent sectoral agreements. Britain has not negotiated a trade agreement since before 1973, and the government is looking to the private sector for assistance.

WTO option

The WTO option would involve the United Kingdom leaving the European Union without any Free Trade Agreement and relying on the trading rules set by the World Trade Organization.

Immigration

The EEA Agreement and the agreement with Switzerland cover free movement of goods, and free movement of people.[1084,1085] Many supporters of Brexit want to restrict freedom of movement;[1086] Liechtenstein has a de facto permanent limit on the free movement of persons, though the EEA Joint Committee said this was because of Liechtenstein's specific geographical situation. Also, an EEA Agreement would include free movement for EU and EEA citizens, although the EEA Agreement allows EEA EFTA states to suspend it temporarily due to serious economic, societal or environmental difficulties.[1087] Passport systems allow EEA institutions to access markets in EU Member States, for the most part, without having to establish subsidiaries in each EU Member State and incur the costs of full authorisation in those jurisdiction. OthersWikipedia:Manual of Style/Words to watch#Unsupported attributions present ideas of a Swiss solution, that is tailor-made agreements between the UK and the EU, but EU representatives have claimed they would not support such a solution.Wikipedia:Citation needed The Swiss agreements contain free movement for EU citizens. (The Swiss immigration referendum, February 2014 voted narrowly in favour of an end to the 'free movement' agreement, by February 2017. However, the bilateral treaties between Switzerland and the European Union are all co-dependent: if one is terminated then all are terminated. Consequently, should Switzerland choose unilaterally to cancel the 'free movement' agreement then all its agreements with the EU will lapse unless a compromise is found. A compromise was reached in December 2016, effectively canceling quotas on EU citizens but still allowing for favorable treatment of Swiss-based job applicants c).[1088]

Several thousand British citizens resident in other EU countries have after the referendum applied for citizenship where they live, since they fear losing the right to work there.

Governance

An EU position paper stated: "The Withdrawal Agreement should establish institutional arrangements to ensure the effective management, implementation and enforcement of the Agreement. It should include appropriate dispute settlement mechanisms regarding the application and interpretation of the Withdrawal Agreement. The Withdrawal Agreement should respect the Union's autonomy. The Withdrawal Agreement should provide that both The Union and the United Kingdom supervise the implementation of the Withdrawal Agreement."

Effect of Brexit on Gibraltar

The **effect of Brexit on Gibraltar** concerns the status of Gibraltar after the withdrawal of the United Kingdom from the European Union. The UK voted to leave the EU in the 2016 referendum and formally notified the EU of its intention to withdraw in March 2017. Gibraltar is not part of the UK but, as a British Overseas Territory, participated in the referendum and will, by default, cease to be a part of the EU upon the UK's withdrawal.

Gibraltar's position during the process of UK withdrawal from the European Union presents unique issues during the negotiations. Gibraltar voted strongly to remain in the European Union during the referendum, and its unique situation could lead to difficulties in Brexit negotiations due to the Spanish claim on Gibraltar, the large contribution of on-line gambling, offshore banking and duty-free shopping, to the Gibraltar economy, and the possibility that Gibraltar will cease to be a part of the single market. With the British government's initiation of the official EU withdrawal process on 29 March 2017, Gibraltar's participation of the United Kingdom's European Union membership will cease to exist by 30 March 2019 (unless all parties to the negotiations agree otherwise).

History

Gibraltar's status in EU elections

Gibraltar did not participate in the 1975 UK European Communities membership referendum even though the result directly impacted on its membership and did not participate in any European Parliamentary Elections between 1979 and 1999 but in 2002 legislation was passed by the British Parliament which allowed Gibraltar to formally take part in the 2004 European Parliament election as part of the South West European Parliament constituency in all subsequent European elections. Following the surprise election victory by the Conservatives in May 2015 it was announced that Gibraltar would fully participate in the proposed referendum on continuing EU membership and was legislated for in the European Union Referendum Act 2015. This meant that Gibraltar was the only British Overseas Territory in the European Union (EU) and uniquely it has the right to vote in EU elections and in referenda.

Pre referendum

In 2015, Chief Minister of Gibraltar Fabian Picardo suggested that Gibraltar would attempt to remain part of the EU in the event the UK voted to leave, but reaffirmed that, regardless of the result, the territory would remain a British overseas territory In a letter to the UK Foreign Affairs Select Committee, he requested that Gibraltar be considered in negotiations post-Brexit.

Before the referendum, José García-Margallo, the Spanish minister of foreign affairs at the time stated that in case of Brexit, Gibraltar would not have access to the single market unless a formula giving Spain co-sovereignty were agreed for a transitional period; after the referendum, he saw the result as increasing the chance of a Spanish flag on Gibraltar. He also said Spain would seek talks on Gibraltar, whose status is disputed, the "very next day" after a British exit from the EU.

Referendum

United Kingdom European Union membership referendum, 2016 Gibraltar		
Choice	**Votes**	**%**
Remain a member of the European Union	**19,322**	**95.91%**
Leave the European Union	823	4.09%
Registered voters and turnout	24,119	83.64%
Source: Electoral Commission[1089]		

The European Union (Referendum) Act 2016 (Gibraltar),[1090] was passed by the Gibraltar Parliament and implemented in Gibraltar after the European Union Referendum Act 2015 was passed by the UK Parliament.

During the campaign leading up to the United Kingdom's national referendum on whether to leave the European Union (known as "Brexit") the Spanish government warned that if the UK chose to leave, Spain would push to reclaim control over Gibraltar. The Chief Minister of Gibraltar Fabian Picardo warned the UK of the threat to Gibraltar's safety posed by Brexit. All three parties represented in the legislature supported remaining in the EU during the Referendum and the Remain campaign was known as Gibraltar Stronger in Europe.

The referendum result within Gibraltar was declared early on Friday 24 June 2016 by the counting officer and Clerk to the Gibraltar Parliament Paul Martinez at the University of Gibraltar at 0040 CEST making it the first of the

382 voting areas to declare and its result was fed into the South West England regional count and then the overall national count. The result saw the single biggest "Remain" vote of all the 382 voting areas with only 4% of Gibraltarian voters opting to leave on a very high turnout of 84% with large queues reported at the Polling stations. Overall the United Kingdom voted narrowly by 51.9% to 48.1% to leave the European Union. Despite the overwhelming vote to remain in the European Union Gibraltar will be leaving the European Union as it was a popular vote of the whole of the United Kingdom.Wikipedia:Citation needed

Gibraltar in the Brexit negotiations

Gibraltar has no direct say in the negotiations between the UK and the 27 remaining countries of the European Union (EU27); the duty and responsibility of dealing with foreign affairs rest with the UK, as do the duties of defence and internal security in Gibraltar.[11]

Robin Walker MP Parliamentary Under-Secretary of State for Department for Exiting the European Union visited Gibraltar in March 2017 to discuss Brexit with Fabian Picardo Chief Minister of Gibraltar and Joseph Garcia Deputy Chief Minister of Gibraltar.

With the impending Brexit negotiations, the House of Lords produced a report entitled "Brexit: Gibraltar".

The European Council released a series of guidelines for the EU27 on negotiations for withdrawal. Within these guidelines, core principle number 22 stated that "After the United Kingdom leaves the Union, no agreement between the EU and the United Kingdom may apply to the territory of Gibraltar without the agreement between the Kingdom of Spain and the United Kingdom". Pro-Brexit conservative M.P. Jack Lopresti thought it shameful that the EU would attempt to allow Spain an effective veto over the future of British sovereign territory, ignoring the will of the people of Gibraltar. Foreign minister Boris Johnson re-iterated the United Kingdom's commitment to Gibraltar.

Esteban González Pons, a Spanish MEP and chairman of the Brexit working group of the European People's Party, met with Ireland's Minister for European affairs Dara Murphy in May, when he (Pons) called Gibraltar a "colony" and pushed for support for the Spanish position that the status of the Rock is a bilateral issue solely for the UK and Spain to resolve. Ireland recognises that the issue is a bilateral one but wishes to avoid parallels being drawn with the status of Northern Ireland. Murphy stated that "Ireland will address issues regarding the nature of the relationship of Gibraltar with the European Union post-Brexit as and when they arise in the course of negotiations on the future relationship of the UK with the European Union."

On April 2017, former director of operational capability at the UK Ministry of Defence, Rear Admiral Chris Parry said, "We could cripple Spain in the medium term and I think the Americans would probably support us too.[1091]

Key issues

Sovereignty

The day after the result Spain's acting Foreign Minister, José Manuel García-Margallo, renewed calls for joint Spanish–British control of the peninsula. These calls were strongly rebuffed by Gibraltar's Chief Minister. After the result Spain reiterated its position that it wanted to jointly govern Gibraltar with the United Kingdom and said it would seek to block Gibraltar from participating in talks over future deals between the UK and EU.

In April 2017, Theresa May reiterated that "the UK would seek the best possible deal for Gibraltar as the UK exits the EU, and there would be no negotiation on the sovereignty of Gibraltar without the consent of its people."

In April 2018, Spanish Foreign Minister Alfonso Dastis announced that Spain hopes to sign off on a bilateral agreement with Britain over Gibraltar before October so as not to hinder a Brexit transition deal. Talks between London and Madrid had progressed well. While reiterating the Spanish long-term aim of "recovering" Gibraltar, he said that Spain would not hold Gibraltar as a "hostage" to the EU negotiations.

Movement over the border

Questions were raised over the future of free-flowing traffic at the Gibraltar–Spain border.

People

Gibraltar, like Britain, is outside the Schengen Area. All people crossing the border to/from Spain have therefore always been required to go through British and Spanish border controls. 10,000 people living in La Línea, in Spain, cross the border every day to work in Gibraltar. La Línea has an unemployment rate of 35% whereas Gibraltar has a 1% unemployment rate.

Goods

Gibraltar is not part of the EU's customs union, so there are more detailed checks on goods moving over the Spanish-Gibraltar border.

Air travel

A Spanish diplomat has indicated that any agreement on airline landing rights agreed during Brexit negotiations would not apply to the Gibraltar International Airport.

Finance industry

Finance Centre Director James Tipping told a European Parliament committee in May that the finance industry in Gibraltar is essential to the economy of the Rock. The industry was resigned to a loss of access to the EU market but had been given firm assurances that Gibraltar would have greater access to UK markets which will bring opportunities.

Impact of Brexit on the European Union

European Union

This article is part of a series on the
**politics and government of
the European Union**

European Union portal

- Other countries
- Atlas

- v
- t
- e[1092]

The **impact of Brexit on the European Union** (EU) will result in economic changes to the Union, but also longer term political and institutional shifts. The nature be extent of these effects remain somewhat speculative until the precise terms of the United Kingdom's post-Brexit relationship with the EU become clear. However Brexit has been cited already as a factor leading to the establishment of the PESCO initiative (cooperation between the armed forces of 25 member states) and to the prospect of a decrease in the voting blocs which favour economic liberalism.

Size and Wealth

As of 2016[1093], the UK has the fifth highest [absolute] GDP in the world and the second largest in the EU.

Comparison	Population	Area (km²)	GDP (PPP) (Trillions of US$)
European Union (with the United Kingdom)	511,805,088	4,475,757	20.9
European Union (without the United Kingdom)	445,996,515	4,232,147	18.28

Budget

The UK's contribution to the EU budget in 2016, after accounting for its rebate, was €19.4 billion. After removing about €7 billion that the UK receives in EU subsidies, the loss to the EU budget comes to about 5% of the total. Unless the budget is reduced, Germany [already the largest net contributor] seems likely to be asked to provide the largest share of the cash, its share estimated at about 2.5 billion euros.[1094]

To help fill the gap, the European Commission has looked at reductions in regional spending of up to 30%, which has concerned some of the poorer member states which rely heavily on the regional funds. However the EU has been under-spending on regional funds to the extent that €7.7 billion of unpaid funds was paid back to member states in 2017 (in addition to several billion more that came in due to cartel and anti-trust fines). The result may be that most of the savings in the EU budget could be located in regional funds which are being under-spent regardless.[1095]

Policy changes

<templatestyles src="Template:Quote_box/styles.css" />

The years are over when Europe cannot follow a course because the British will object. Now the British are going, Europe can find a new élan.

Christine Lagarde, Director of the IMF,

The UK has been a major player in the EU which has both been an asset to the Union, but also a hindrance to those who supported a direction firmly opposed by the British government.

Ideological shift

As the EU's third most populous state, with over 12% of the Union's population, the UK is an influential player in the European Parliament and the Council of the European Union. Its absence will impact the ideological balance within the EU institutions.[1096]

In the Council, during the UK membership there have been two blocs, each capable of forming a blocking minority against the other; the protectionist bloc of mainly southern states and the liberalist bloc of mainly northern states. As a member of the latter, the UK's departure would weaken the liberalist bloc as the UK has been a sizeable and fervent proponent of an economically liberal Europe, larger trade deals with third countries and of further EU enlargement. While weakening the liberal bloc, it would also strengthen Germany's individual position in the Council through the loss of a key counterweight. Despite this, Germany remains uneasy about this role lest other countries uneasy about German dominance may be more tempted to ally against it.

Similarly, a majority of the UK's representatives sit with right-leaning groups, namely the European Conservatives and Reformists and the Europe of Freedom and Direct Democracy, both of which are built around, and led by members of, the British Conservative Party and UKIP. The Progressive Alliance of Socialists and Democrats would also lose its members from the UK's Labour Party, but on the whole would be left strengthened by the greater loss to the right, and thus able to form majorities without seeking support from the (conservative) European People's Party. This may lead to a Parliament which may:

- be more willing to pass extra regulations;
- have less support for strong copyright protection;
- pass a smaller budget, but with increased member-state contributions;
- support tax harmonisation and a financial transaction tax (taxation is outwith current treaties);
- give less support to nuclear energy and shale gas in favour of renewable energy sources.

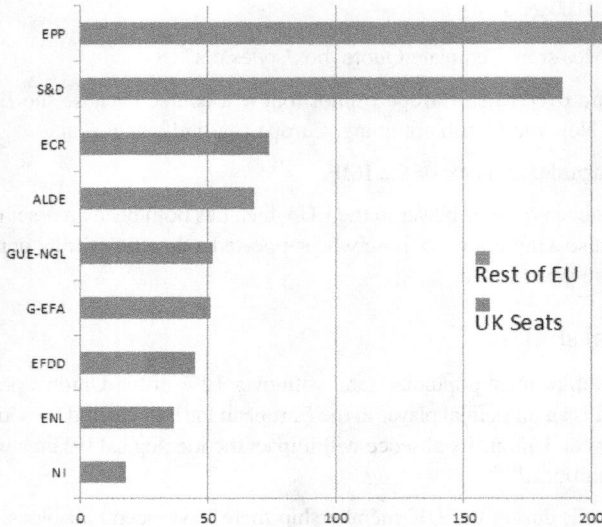

Figure 44: *UK seats in EP groups highlighted in red*
(seat numbers based on EP groups in December 2017

Defence and foreign affairs

The UK has been a key asset for the EU in the fields of foreign affairs and
defence given that the UK is (with France) one of the EU's two major military
powers, has significant intelligence capabilities, soft power and a far reaching
diplomatic network. Without the UK, EU foreign policy could be less influential. The US saw the UK as a bridge between the US and Europe, and the
UK helped align the EU positions to the US and provide tougher responses to
Russia.[1097]

However Brexit also produced new opportunities for European defence cooperation, as the UK has consistently vetoed moves in this direction, arguing it
would undermine NATO. It attempted to do so again – even after its withdrawal referendum, in relation to the establishment of a military HQ.[1098] With
the UK's withdrawal and a feeling that the US under Donald J. Trump may
not honour NATO commitments, the European Council has put defence co-
operation as a major project in its [post-Brexit vote] Bratislava and Rome declarations and moved forward with setting up a European Defence Fund and
activating Permanent Structured Cooperation (a defence clause in the Lisbon
Treaty).[1099,1100]

Eurozone

EU GDP by currency group

Eurozone (72.9%)

Non-Eurozone (Minus UK) (12%)

United Kingdom (15.1%)

The relationship between euro and non-euro states has been on debate both during the UK's membership (as a large opt-out state) and in light of its planned withdrawal from the EU. The question is how Brexit might impact the balance of power between those in and out of the euro; namely avoiding a eurozone caucus out-voting non-euro states. The UK had called for the EU treaties to be amended to declare the EU to be a "multicurrency union", which sparked concerns that to do so might undermine the progress of euro adoption in remaining countries.[1101,1102,1103,1104]

Simon Hix contends that Brexit would strengthen the Eurozone, which may well replace the single market as the EU's core and driving force. Tim Oliver agrees, stating that Brexit would allow the Eurozone and the EU to 'more neatly align'. In the pre-referendum negotiation, David Cameron emphasised the importance (in his view) of keeping the Eurozone clearly distinct from the EU. Following a British withdrawal, such pressure may well dissipate.

Economic impacts

Trade with UK

While the trade impact of Brexit on the UK is likely to be significantly negative, its impact on the EU is also expected to be negative, but small. The UK and the EU would become each other's largest trading partner but some states, notably Belgium, Cyprus, Ireland, Germany and the Netherlands, are more exposed to a Brexit-induced economic shock. The economy of the Republic of Ireland is particularly sensitive due to its common land border with the United Kingdom and its close agribusines integration with Northern Ireland[1105] The reintroduction of a customs border would be economically and politically damaging to both sides,[1106,1107] particularly because of the risk to

the Northern Ireland peace process that a physical border presents.[1108] Despite
protestations of good will on both sides, it is not obvious how border controls can be avoided unless the UK has a Customs Union with the EU.[1109,1110]
Arising from the agreements made at the Phase 1 negotiations (after the DUP
intervention), any arrangements to be made to facilitate cross-border trade in
Ireland will apply equally to cross-Channel trade but the details remain unclear.[1111]

The sectors across the EU that would be most hit by the UK's withdrawal are
motor vehicles and parts (the UK is a large manufacturer and depends on an EU
chain of supply for parts), electronics equipment and processed foods. Export
of raw materials from the Ruhr valley would also be impacted.

Migration

The UK's aim is to have as much access to the EU market without accepting
free movement. The impact of this would be felt most on eastern European
member states who have approximately 1.2 million workers in the UK by the
end of 2015; the largest groups from Poland (853,000), Romania (175,000)
and Lithuania (155,000). A year after the Brexit vote, net annual immigration
to the UK fell by 106,000 with most attributed to EU citizens leaving for other
states, with the biggest drop among those from the western European states.[1112]

The Polish government is encouraging its young emigrant workforce to return
to Poland, but due to regulatory or political reasons many would either stay
in the UK or move to other western cities such as Amsterdam or Berlin.[1113]
Other western European member states may see much of the flow coming
from eastern states in future. The influx of workers from the east would be
economically beneficial to countries such as Germany, but may be politically
problematic.

Institutional changes

Agencies located in the UK

In 2017, the UK was currently hosting the European Medicines Agency and
the European Banking Authority. As an EU agency could not be located outside the Union, the Council began a process to identify new host cities for the
agencies. Hosting an agency is seen as a valuable prize for a city, so the process was hotly contested by nearly two dozen cities not just on the objective
criteria, but on political grounds. By November 2017, it was agreed that they
would relocated to Amsterdam and Paris.[1114]

The backup data centre for the security behind the Galileo satellite navigation
system was also relocated from the UK to Spain due to Brexit.[1115]

European Parliament seats

The UK is allotted 73 seats in the 751 seat European Parliament, which are likely to become vacant just before the 2019 elections. Under normal procedures, these seats would be re-distributed between the remaining members according to the standard formula, but there have been a number of alternative proposals. The Parliament has proposed that 22 seats would be redistributed and the remaining 50 would be reserved either for new members, or an additional trans-national list of MEPs which would be elected across the Union in an effort to deepen a direct democratic link. This has been a long-standing proposal, notably supported by the European Green Party and French President Emmanuel Macron. However, due to the legal uncertainty around Brexit, any bold moves are opposed by constitutional affairs committee chair Danuta Huebner.[1116,1117]

Computations were proposed in "THE COMPOSITION OF THE EUROPEAN PARLIAMENT WORKSHOP" paper on 30 January 2017.[1118]

Public opinion

Eurosceptics expected that the Brexit vote could strengthen anti-EU movements across the Union.

In the wake of the UK's vote to withdraw, opinion polls showed that support for the EU surged across Europe – including in the UK.[1119,1120,1121]

Euroscepticism across Europe has increased heralded by a 'wave of populism'[1122] notably during the campaign of Marine Le Pen in the French presidential election, 2017. In the Italian general election, 2018, the populist Five Star Movement and the right wing Lega Nord, both Eurosceptic, received 32% and 17% respectively.

Languages

Danuta Hübner, the head of the European Parliament Committee on Constitutional Affairs, has argued that after Brexit, English would no longer be an official EU language: "We have a regulation … where every EU country has the right to notify one official language. The Irish have notified Gaelic, and the Maltese have notified Maltese, so you have only the U.K. notifying English … If we don't have the U.K., we don't have English."[1123]

However, this statement has been contradicted by the European Commission Representation in Ireland, whose spokesperson argued that changing the current language regime would require a unanimous vote by the Council,[1124] as well as by President Jean-Claude Juncker in an answer to a Parliamentary

Question on 9 August 2017.[1125] However Jean-Claude Juncker has also stated that despite this, in the wake of Brexit English is losing its importance in Europe[1126] and members of the German Bundestag have called on staff in EU institutions to use German more often.[1127]

When the United Kingdom and Ireland joined the EU's predecessor in 1973, French was the dominant language of the institutions. With the addition of Sweden and Finland in the 1990s, and the Eastern European states in the 2000s, English slowly supplanted French as the dominant working language of the institutions. In 2015, it was estimated that 80% of legislative proposals were drafted first in English. The role of English as a lingua franca is believed to be likely to continue, given how heavily staff rely on it,[1128] and that in European schools, 97% of children learn English as an additional language, compared with 34% learning French and 23% learning German.[1129]

It has also been suggested by an academic paper by Dr Marko Modiano, of Gavle University in Sweden that the "Euro English" variant of English, already present in Brussels, could become codified in the same way as American English or Australian English and taught in schools if English is retained as a common lingua franca. The multilingual community in the institutions was already developing a distinct way of speaking English and could adopt American spellings. It includes words with adjusted meanings, such as "eventual" becoming a synonym for "possibly" and adjusted grammar that is common not just in Brussels, but in the way continental Europeans speak English. With the absence of the considerable number of British native-English speakers in Brussels to police language use, it is believed Euro-English could "take on a life of its own".[1130,1131]

Language rules are currently covered, amongst others, by: Article 55 of the Treaty on European Union (TEU) (which lists the 24 "Treaty languages" in which the Treaty is drawn up);[1132] Articles 20 and 24 of the Treaty on the Functioning of the European Union (TFEU), which lay down the rights of citizens to petition the European Parliament and to address the institutions in any of the Treaty languages and to obtain a reply in the same language, and Article 342 TFEU, which states that "the rules governing the languages of the institutions of the Union shall, without prejudice to the provisions contained in the Statute of the Court of Justice of the European Union, be determined by the Council, acting unanimously by means of regulations";[1133] and Council Regulation No 1/1958,[1134] which lists the 24 official languages.

Appendix

References

[1] //en.wikipedia.org/w/index.php?title=Template:United_Kingdom_in_the_European_Union&action=edit

[2] //en.wikipedia.org/w/index.php?title=Template:History_of_the_United_Kingdom&action=edit

[3] The "i" newspaper, 27 June 2018

[4] //en.wikipedia.org/w/index.php?title=Brexit&action=edit

[5] "Brexit, n." OED Online. Oxford University Press, March 2017. Web. 9 May 2017.

[6] Alex May, *Britain and Europe since 1945* (1999).

[7] the Shetland Islands and the Outer Hebrides

[8] Election 2015: Conservative manifesto at-a-glance (15th April 2015) https://www.bbc.co.uk/news/election-2015-32302062

[9] Conservatives election manifesto 2015 - the key points (14th April 2015) https://www.theguardian.com/politics/2015/apr/14/conservatives-election-manifesto-2015-the-key-points

[10] *New Open Europe/ComRes poll: Failure to win key reforms could swing UK's EU referendum vote* http://openeurope.org.uk/today/blog/new-open-europecomres-poll-failure-to-win-key-reforms-could-swing-uks-eu-referendum-vote openeurope.org, 16 December 2015.

[11] Other major campaign groups included Grassroots Out, Get Britain Out and Better Off Out.

[12] Electoral Commission http//www.electoralcommission.org.uk, 'Report of an investigation' (July 2018)

[13] House of Commons Culture, Media and Sport Select Committee, *Disinformation and 'fake news': Interim Report* (July 2018). ch 5, Russian influence in political campaigns https://publications.parliament.uk/pa/cm201719/cmselect/cmcumeds/363/36308.htm#_idTextAnchor033

[14] 'Grounds for Judicial Review' in *Wilson v Prime Minister*, 13 August 2018.http://www.croftsolicitors.com/wp-content/uploads/2018/08/239484-Grounds-for-Judicial-Review-and-Statement-of-Facts.pdf

[15] Court rejects application for judicial review as "Totally Without Merit", *R (Webster) v Secretary of State for Exiting the EU* 12 June 2018, para.10.https://drive.google.com/file/d/16ylKxZqL-QoBdVfz547-rEFaL6yW-8po/view

[16] Article 50(3) of the Treaty on European Union.

[17] In a leaflet sent out before the referendum, the UK government stated "This is your decision. The Government will implement what you decide."

[18] "a revocation of notification [by Article 50] needs to be subject to conditions set by all EU27, so that it cannot be used as a procedural device or abused in an attempt to improve on the current terms of the United Kingdom's membership"

[19] "Divorce settlement or leaving the club? A breakdown of the Brexit bill" March 2017, A breakdown of the Brexit bill (2017) http://bruegel.org/wp-content/uploads/2017/03/WP_2017_03-.pdf

[20] BBC News, 4 March 2017, "Brexit: UK 'not obliged' to pay divorce bill say peers".https://www.bbc.co.uk/news/uk-politics-39154218

[21] "Brexit: UK caves in to EU demand to agree divorce bill before trade talks" https://www.theguardian.com/politics/2017/jun/19/uk-caves-in-to-eu-demand-to-agree-divorce-bill-before-trade-talks, *The Guardian*, 19 June 2017. Retrieved 20 June 2017

[22] Conclusions adopted by the European Council (Art. 50), 29 June 2018 http://www.consilium.europa.eu/media/35966/29-euco-art50-conclusions-en.pdf

[23] Hannah White and Jill Rutter, "Legislating Brexit: The Great Repeal Bill and the wider legislative challenge", Institute for Government, 20 March 2017, p.9 https://www.instituteforgovernment.org.uk/sites/default/files/publications/IFGJ5347-Legislating-Brexit-IFG-Analysis-032017-WEB.pdf

[24] https://www.publications.parliament.uk/pa/ld201617/ldselect/ldeucom/72/72.pdf

[25] https://www.publications.parliament.uk/pa/ld201617/ldselect/ldeucom/76/76.pdf

[26] https://www.publications.parliament.uk/pa/ld201617/ldselect/ldeucom/77/77.pdf

[27] https://www.publications.parliament.uk/pa/ld201617/ldselect/ldeucom/78/78.pdf

[28] https://www.publications.parliament.uk/pa/ld201617/ldselect/ldeucom/109/109.pdf

[29] https://www.publications.parliament.uk/pa/ld201617/ldselect/ldeucom/136/136.pdf

[30] https://www.publications.parliament.uk/pa/ld201617/ldselect/ldeucom/134/134.pdf

[31] https://www.publications.parliament.uk/pa/ld201617/ldselect/ldeucom/135/135.pdf

[32] See:<ref>

[33] "The Brexit vote is starting to have major negative consequences' – experts debate the data https://www.theguardian.com/politics/2017/mar/24/brexit-vote-experts-data-bank-of-england *The Guardian*

[34] Between 2007–2013 the UK received €8.8 billion from the EU for research while contributing €5.4 billion to the EU's research budget.

[35] Around 11% of the research income of British universities came from the EU in 2014–2015

[36] "It is likely that the UK would wish to remain an associated member of the European Research Area, like Norway and Iceland, in order to continue participating in the EU framework programmes."

[37] Brexit: the unexpected threat to peace in Northern Ireland https://edition.cnn.com/2018/04/06/opinions/20-years-good-friday-agreement-northern-ireland-nic-r-intl/index.html Nic Robertson, CNN, 6 April 2018

[38] George Mitchell: UK and Ireland need to realise what's at stake in Brexit talks. https://www.belfasttelegraph.co.uk/news/northern-ireland/george-mitchell-uk-and-ireland-need-to-realise-whats-at-stake-in-brexit-talks-36785893.html *Belfast Telegraph*, 8 April 2018

[39] Brexit threatens Good Friday agreement, Irish PM warns. https://www.theguardian.com/world/2018/mar/14/brexit-threatens-good-friday-agreement-irish-pm-warns David Smith, The Guardian, 14 March 2018

[40] "the UK would seek the best possible deal for Gibraltar as the UK exits the EU, and there would be no negotiation on the sovereignty of Gibraltar without the consent of its people." Theresa May, 6 April 2017,

[41] ' Sir Joe slams EU's 'disgraceful' stance on Brexit and Gibraltar http://chronicle.gi/2018/02/sir-joe-slams-eus-disgraceful-stance-on-brexit-and-gibraltar/': *The Gibraltar Chronicle*, 2 February 2018

[42] https://www.express.co.uk/news/politics/856874/Brexit-news-Australian-senator-James-Paterson-CANZUK-UK-EU-exit

[43] https://www.express.co.uk/news/world/806280/commonwealth-visa-free-UK-australia-canada-new-zealand

[44] https://www.express.co.uk/news/uk/909657/UK-Australia-New-Zealand-Canada-Brexit-plans-free-movement-visa-petition-CANZUK

[45] "A two-speed post-Brexit Europe is best avoided" https://www.ft.com/content/e0051162-1ee0-11e7-b7d3-163f5a7f229c

[46] Trading places / Negotiating post-Brexit deals. Economist, 4–10 February 2017, page 25

[47] https://d25d2506sfb94s.cloudfront.net/cumulus_uploads/document/2req6g7z50/Internal_180905_Brexit_W.pdf

[48] https://d25d2506sfb94s.cloudfront.net/cumulus_uploads/document/j73mcdcj1w/Times_180904_VI_Trackers_W.pdf

[49] https://d25d2506sfb94s.cloudfront.net/cumulus_uploads/document/64h0v3epuv/Times_180829_VI_Trackers.pdf

[50] http://d25d2506sfb94s.cloudfront.net/cumulus_uploads/document/7xksricmrw/TimesResults_180821_VI_Trackers_w.pdf

[51] https://d25d2506sfb94s.cloudfront.net/cumulus_uploads/document/aapy92s0pl/InternalResults_180814_VI_Trackers_Website.pdf

[52] https://d25d2506sfb94s.cloudfront.net/cumulus_uploads/document/8dvhq299ql/TimesResults_180809_VI_Trackers_w.pdf

[53] https://d25d2506sfb94s.cloudfront.net/cumulus_uploads/document/eswcvhvq60/TimesResults_180723_VI_Trackers_w.pdf

[54] https://d25d2506sfb94s.cloudfront.net/cumulus_uploads/document/j26n4y534f/
TimesResults_180717_VI_Trackers_w.pdf

[55] http://d25d2506sfb94s.cloudfront.net/cumulus_uploads/document/phvyn092lg/TimesResults_
180711_VI_Brexit.pdf

[56] https://d25d2506sfb94s.cloudfront.net/cumulus_uploads/document/71kfwwcl1a/
TimesResults_18_07_09_VI_Trackers_w.pdf

[57] https://d25d2506sfb94s.cloudfront.net/cumulus_uploads/document/hogkt4gv80/
TimesResults_180704_VI_Trackers.pdf

[58] https://d25d2506sfb94s.cloudfront.net/cumulus_uploads/document/h3j0yxq1jf/TimesResults_
180626_VI_Trackers_w.pdf

[59] https://d25d2506sfb94s.cloudfront.net/cumulus_uploads/document/3flpkaywfj/
InternalResults_180620_Brexit_w.pdf

[60] https://d25d2506sfb94s.cloudfront.net/cumulus_uploads/document/xi51ey4b6h/
TimesResults_180619_VI_Trackers_w.pdf

[61] https://d25d2506sfb94s.cloudfront.net/cumulus_uploads/document/qzm7srmkvi/
TimesResults_180612_VI_Trackers_w.pdf

[62] https://d25d2506sfb94s.cloudfront.net/cumulus_uploads/document/z1w1jcj6s9/
TimesResults_180605_VI_Trackers_w.pdf

[63] https://d25d2506sfb94s.cloudfront.net/cumulus_uploads/document/v0m1echerf/
TimesResults_180529_VI_Trackers.pdf

[64] http://d25d2506sfb94s.cloudfront.net/cumulus_uploads/document/8vbs3n6auc/TimesResults_
180521_VI_Trackers.pdf

[65] http://d25d2506sfb94s.cloudfront.net/cumulus_uploads/document/fhgs8okigo/TimesResults_
180514_VI_Trackers_w.pdf

[66] http://d25d2506sfb94s.cloudfront.net/cumulus_uploads/document/gkdmvglevl/TimesResults_
180509_VI_Trackers.pdf

[67] https://d25d2506sfb94s.cloudfront.net/cumulus_uploads/document/0322e6admo/
TimesResults_180501_VI_Trackers.pdf

[68] https://d25d2506sfb94s.cloudfront.net/cumulus_uploads/document/tmi4jdgt4o/TimesResults_
180425_VI_Trackers.pdf

[69] https://d25d2506sfb94s.cloudfront.net/cumulus_uploads/document/ck1l2ze60y/
TimesResults_180417_VI_Trackers.pdf

[70] https://d25d2506sfb94s.cloudfront.net/cumulus_uploads/document/jfvhk2jlbk/TimesResults_
180410_VI_Trackers.pdf

[71] https://d25d2506sfb94s.cloudfront.net/cumulus_uploads/document/o3oayi8z58/
TimesResults_180327_VI_Trackers_W.pdf

[72] https://d25d2506sfb94s.cloudfront.net/cumulus_uploads/document/1daln9otjj/TimesResults_
180305_VI_Trackers_w.pdf

[73] https://d25d2506sfb94s.cloudfront.net/cumulus_uploads/document/qi8qzf33xl/TimesResults_
180227_VI_Trackers_w.pdf

[74] https://d25d2506sfb94s.cloudfront.net/cumulus_uploads/document/um02uga2au/
TimesResults_180220_VI_Trackers.pdf

[75] https://d25d2506sfb94s.cloudfront.net/cumulus_uploads/document/8d28iz3x5j/
TimesResults_180213_VI_Trackers.pdf

[76] https://d25d2506sfb94s.cloudfront.net/cumulus_uploads/document/fb1csi9qjl/TimesResults_
180205_VI_Trackers.pdf

[77] https://d25d2506sfb94s.cloudfront.net/cumulus_uploads/document/yzgd1a3wr0/
TimesResults_180129_Trackers_VI.pdf

[78] https://d25d2506sfb94s.cloudfront.net/cumulus_uploads/document/srb6u4hbl6/
TimesResults_180117_VI_Trackers.pdf

[79] https://d25d2506sfb94s.cloudfront.net/cumulus_uploads/document/9xj0batl27/TimesResults_
180108_VI_Trackers_w.pdf

[80] https://d25d2506sfb94s.cloudfront.net/cumulus_uploads/document/3l97nvvr78/
TimesResults_171220_VI_Trackers_w.pdf

[81] https://d25d2506sfb94s.cloudfront.net/cumulus_uploads/document/5tu7akhw6z/
TimesResults_171211_VI_Trackers_w.pdf

[82] https://d25d2506sfb94s.cloudfront.net/cumulus_uploads/document/b22zrk1yft/TimesResults_171205_VI_Trackers_w.pdf

[83] http://d25d2506sfb94s.cloudfront.net/cumulus_uploads/document/t7a4lpcsdh/TimesResults_171108_VI_Trackers.pdf

[84] http://d25d2506sfb94s.cloudfront.net/cumulus_uploads/document/4y1e1sdlwa/InternalResults_171024_VI.pdf

[85] https://d25d2506sfb94s.cloudfront.net/cumulus_uploads/document/mg654q435f/TimesResults_171019_VI_Trackers.pdf

[86] https://d25d2506sfb94s.cloudfront.net/cumulus_uploads/document/ptmrf0v5kz/Timesresults_171011_VI_Trackers.pdf

[87] https://d25d2506sfb94s.cloudfront.net/cumulus_uploads/document/xdlp14v0de/TimesResults_170922_VI_Trackers_W.pdf

[88] https://d25d2506sfb94s.cloudfront.net/cumulus_uploads/document/zc2c6t9xh2/TimesResults_170831_VI_Trackers_W.pdf

[89] https://d25d2506sfb94s.cloudfront.net/cumulus_uploads/document/hm2d5c6net/TimesResults_170822_VI_Trackers_W.pdf

[90] https://d25d2506sfb94s.cloudfront.net/cumulus_uploads/document/qwyuvkvik4/TimesResults_170801_VI_Trackers_W.pdf

[91] https://d25d2506sfb94s.cloudfront.net/cumulus_uploads/document/o6jgxxwn5k/TimesResults_170719_VI_Trackers_W.pdf

[92] https://d25d2506sfb94s.cloudfront.net/cumulus_uploads/document/3gnej2eb9r/TimesResults_170711_VI_Trackers_W.pdf

[93] http://d25d2506sfb94s.cloudfront.net/cumulus_uploads/document/hrngg4b5a8/TimesResults_170622_Trackers_W.pdf

[94] https://d25d2506sfb94s.cloudfront.net/cumulus_uploads/document/9pum7c5c4j/AnthonyResults_170613_Brexit_W.pdf

[95] https://d25d2506sfb94s.cloudfront.net/cumulus_uploads/document/d8zsb99eyd/TimesResults_FINAL%20CALL_GB_June2017_W.pdf

[96] https://d25d2506sfb94s.cloudfront.net/cumulus_uploads/document/imdk9bjaff/TimesResults_170531_VI_Trackers_W.pdf

[97] https://d25d2506sfb94s.cloudfront.net/cumulus_uploads/document/dcfgflapq2/TimesResults_170525_VI_Trackers_Terrorism_W.pdf

[98] https://d25d2506sfb94s.cloudfront.net/cumulus_uploads/document/txtodyx8bk/TimesResults_170517_VI_Trackers_W.pdf

[99] http//www.gfk.com

[100] https://d25d2506sfb94s.cloudfront.net/cumulus_uploads/document/fko52um47n/TimesResults_170510_VI_Trackers_W.pdf

[101] https://d25d2506sfb94s.cloudfront.net/cumulus_uploads/document/dpzz1r8u3o/TimesResults_170503_VI_Trackers_with_Slogans_W.pdf

[102] https://d25d2506sfb94s.cloudfront.net/cumulus_uploads/document/8nchxu7nac/TimesResults_170426_VI_Trackers_W.pdf

[103] https://d25d2506sfb94s.cloudfront.net/cumulus_uploads/document/hxfn0j417w/SundayTimesResults_170421_VI_W.pdf

[104] https://d25d2506sfb94s.cloudfront.net/cumulus_uploads/document/04xxn42p3e/TimesResults_170419_VI_Trackers_GE_W.pdf

[105] https://d25d2506sfb94s.cloudfront.net/cumulus_uploads/document/zs2ifb9u3g/TimesResults_170413_VI_Trackers.pdf

[106] https://d25d2506sfb94s.cloudfront.net/cumulus_uploads/document/x4597y9nuj/TimesResults_170406_VI_Trackers_W.pdf

[107] https://d25d2506sfb94s.cloudfront.net/cumulus_uploads/document/glo3xaqerh/InternalResults_170327_AnthonyBrexitQs_W.pdf

[108] https://d25d2506sfb94s.cloudfront.net/cumulus_uploads/document/tksnufybtn/TimesResultsResults_170321_VI_Immigration_W.pdf

[109] http://www.gfk.com/en-gb/insights/press-release/new-gfk-political-poll-shows-jeremy-corbyn-as-unpopular-as-president-trump-among-gb-adults/

[110] https://d25d2506sfb94s.cloudfront.net/cumulus_uploads/document/f2a3lpb26v/TimesResults_170314_VI_ScottishIndy_W.pdf

[111] http://opinium.co.uk/wp-content/uploads/2017/03/Polling-Matters-100317-Tables.xlsx

[112] https://d25d2506sfb94s.cloudfront.net/cumulus_uploads/document/z1elxz48n9/TimesResults_170228_VI_Trackers_W.pdf

[113] https://d25d2506sfb94s.cloudfront.net/cumulus_uploads/document/2jolkn11ps/TimesResults_170222_VI_Trackers_W.pdf

[114] https://d25d2506sfb94s.cloudfront.net/cumulus_uploads/document/auuihsqsjz/TimesResults_170213_VI_Trackers_W.pdf

[115] https://d25d2506sfb94s.cloudfront.net/cumulus_uploads/document/3hy4qn55vq/TimesResults_170131_VI_Trackers_W.pdf

[116] https://d25d2506sfb94s.cloudfront.net/cumulus_uploads/document/xalfiwu0ed/TimesResults_170118_VI_Trackers_MaySpeech_W.pdf

[117] http://opinium.co.uk/wp-content/uploads/2017/01/Polling-Matters-200117-Tables.xlsx

[118] https://d25d2506sfb94s.cloudfront.net/cumulus_uploads/document/17ahuih4ja/TimesResults_170110_VI_Trackers_W.pdf

[119] https://d25d2506sfb94s.cloudfront.net/cumulus_uploads/document/ipnfdlzlvq/TimesResults_170104_VI_Trackers_W.pdf

[120] https://d25d2506sfb94s.cloudfront.net/cumulus_uploads/document/upts71m2pt/TimesResults_161219_VI_Trackers_EndofYear_W.pdf

[121] https://d25d2506sfb94s.cloudfront.net/cumulus_uploads/document/bg3iahmaw8/TimesResults_161205_VI_Trackers_W.pdf

[122] https://d25d2506sfb94s.cloudfront.net/cumulus_uploads/document/wemnebeo20/TimesResults_161129_VI_Trackers_W.pdf

[123] https://d25d2506sfb94s.cloudfront.net/cumulus_uploads/document/j91v52gjon/YGArchive-171116-VotingIntention.pdf

[124] https://d25d2506sfb94s.cloudfront.net/cumulus_uploads/document/qq4bax70w5/InternalResults_161020_Brexit_W.pdf

[125] https://d25d2506sfb94s.cloudfront.net/cumulus_uploads/document/vohvzlss3c/TimesResults_161012_VI_Trackers_W.pdf

[126] https://d25d2506sfb94s.cloudfront.net/cumulus_uploads/document/36cem5h375/TimesResults_160914_VI_Trackers_W.pdf

[127] https://d25d2506sfb94s.cloudfront.net/cumulus_uploads/document/jb4y2me4q0/TimesResults_160831_VI_Trackers_W.pdf

[128] https://d25d2506sfb94s.cloudfront.net/cumulus_uploads/document/ocn4lf00me/TimesResults_160823_VI_Trackers_W.pdf

[129] https://d25d2506sfb94s.cloudfront.net/cumulus_uploads/document/jmwlsfmd1k/TimesResults_160817_VI_Trackers.pdf

[130] https://d25d2506sfb94s.cloudfront.net/cumulus_uploads/document/5yng128b6c/TimesResults_160809_VI_Trackers_Website.pdf

[131] //en.wikipedia.org/w/index.php?title=Template:Brexit/Post-referendum_opinion_polling:_Right-Wrong&action=edit

[132] https://d3n8a8pro7vhmx.cloudfront.net/in/pages/15665/attachments/original/1537174959/Under_25s_180911_(1).xls?1537174959

[133] https://www.survation.com/boris-johnson-theresa-may-leadership-survation-for-daily-mail-september-8th/

[134] https://d25d2506sfb94s.cloudfront.net/cumulus_uploads/document/zr7v0xtbbl/180905_GMB%20publish.pdf

[135] https://d25d2506sfb94s.cloudfront.net/cumulus_uploads/document/fnzvd8ui1k/180905_Unison%20publish.pdf

[136] https://d25d2506sfb94s.cloudfront.net/cumulus_uploads/document/gv8pa368st/180905_Unite%20publish.pdf

[137] https://d25d2506sfb94s.cloudfront.net/cumulus_uploads/document/dx1qnnwoym/PeoplesVoteResults_180914_Merge_Newspapers.pdf

[138] https://d25d2506sfb94s.cloudfront.net/cumulus_uploads/document/30tafmcnkc/PeoplesVote_LondonMerge_180905_w.pdf

[139] https://www.survation.com/wp-content/uploads/2018/09/Final-Tables-1.pdf#page=9

[140] https://d25d2506sfb94s.cloudfront.net/cumulus_uploads/document/tu6k2mk5wu/PeoplesVoteResults_Wave2_180821_GB_website.pdf

[141] https://d3n8a8pro7vhmx.cloudfront.net/in/pages/15508/attachments/original/1535728901/Gender_tracker_poll.xls?1535728901

[142] https://d25d2506sfb94s.cloudfront.net/cumulus_uploads/document/zbgd2452w0/NE%20final%20180822%20published.pdf

[143] https://d25d2506sfb94s.cloudfront.net/cumulus_uploads/document/92ofbq76tq/PeoplesVoteResults_180824_Wales_w.pdf

[144] https://d25d2506sfb94s.cloudfront.net/cumulus_uploads/document/tulxamz6op/PeoplesVote_Scotland_180814_w.pdf

[145] http://www.tns-bmrb.co.uk/sites/tns-bmrb/files/Brexit%20Barometer%20tables%20-%20Aug%202018.pdf#page=15

[146] http://www.bmgresearch.co.uk/wp-content/uploads/2018/08/EU-VOTE-INTENTION_BMG-RESREACH_200818.xlsx

[147] https://d25d2506sfb94s.cloudfront.net/cumulus_uploads/document/4e1ciqwvua/Copy%20of%20PV%20results%20180807%20day%20one_w.pdf#page=1

[148] https://d25d2506sfb94s.cloudfront.net/cumulus_uploads/document/zl36ojndti/Brexit%20SW%20180807_w.pdf

[149] https://d25d2506sfb94s.cloudfront.net/cumulus_uploads/document/h8fq3xim2u/TimesResults_180726_SecondReferendum_w.pdf

[150] https://d25d2506sfb94s.cloudfront.net/cumulus_uploads/document/7fjrhub42v/Eurotrack_180724_w.pdf

[151] https://d25d2506sfb94s.cloudfront.net/cumulus_uploads/document/vxuhlu27eg/SundayTimesResults_180720_for_web.pdf#page=11

[152] http://www.deltapoll.co.uk/wp-content/uploads/2018/07/SunSunday_Brexit_Deltapoll180714.pdf#page=26

[153] http://www.tns-bmrb.co.uk/sites/tns-bmrb/files/July%202018%20-%20Brexit%20barometer.pdf#page=7

[154] https://survation.com/wp-content/uploads/2018/07/MoS-final-tables.pdf#page=16

[155] https://d25d2506sfb94s.cloudfront.net/cumulus_uploads/document/htfwdi02df/WelshBarometer_June18_w.pdf#page=11

[156] https://d25d2506sfb94s.cloudfront.net/cumulus_uploads/document/07kprp1z3i/Results_180627_representedbyparty_w.pdf#page=5

[157] https://survation.com/wp-content/uploads/2018/06/GMB-Final-Tables.pdf#page=10

[158] http://d25d2506sfb94s.cloudfront.net/cumulus_uploads/document/hit82jf794/HandelsblattResults_June18_Topline_client_w.pdf

[159] http://survation.com/wp-content/uploads/2018/06/VI-Tables-8-June.xlsx

[160] http://www.deltapoll.co.uk/wp-content/uploads/2018/06/Brext-Trade-180601_FT.pdf#page=1

[161] https://survation.com/wp-content/uploads/2018/05/VI-Tables-May-11th-2.xlsx

[162] https://d25d2506sfb94s.cloudfront.net/cumulus_uploads/document/d2armsga9e/Eurotrack_April18.pdf

[163] https://survation.com/wp-content/uploads/2018/04/Foreign-Affairs-Poll-MoS-140418.pdf#page=12

[164] https://www.icmunlimited.com/wp-content/uploads/2018/04/Voting-9thApr18_pv-only-BPC.pdf

[165] https://d25d2506sfb94s.cloudfront.net/cumulus_uploads/document/cqvaei0d1b/BestForBritain_Results_180406_w.pdf

[166] http://www.bmgresearch.co.uk/wp-content/uploads/2018/03/CONFIDENTIAL-BMG-INDEPENDENT-POLL-26MAR18.xlsx

[167] https://d25d2506sfb94s.cloudfront.net/cumulus_uploads/document/xrtsizcs11/WelshBarometer_March18_w.pdf#page=9

[168] https://www.orb-international.com/wp-content/uploads/2018/03/ORB-International-Website-11-Mar.pdf#page=1

169 http://www.comresglobal.com/wp-content/uploads/2018/03/Sunday-Mirror_Feb-2018_Brexit-poll-006.pdf#page=21
170 https://d25d2506sfb94s.cloudfront.net/cumulus_uploads/document/zck4tfs6qs/HandelsblattResults_Feb18_Topline_client_w.pdf#page=2
171 https://interactive.news.sky.com/Feb2018_MainTabs.pdf#page=12
172 https://survation.com/wp-content/uploads/2018/02/Full-Voting-Intention-Tables-310118.pdf#page=10
173 https://d25d2506sfb94s.cloudfront.net/cumulus_uploads/document/28wjbaqogx/Eurotrack_January2018_w.pdf
174 https://interactive.news.sky.com/Jan2018_MainTabs.pdf
175 https://www.icmunlimited.com/wp-content/uploads/2018/01/ICM-Guardian-Brexit-Questions-BPC-Regions.pdf#page=12
176 http://www.comresglobal.com/wp-content/uploads/2018/01/Daily-Mirror_January-2018-poll_EURef-1.pdf
177 https://www.icmunlimited.com/wp-content/uploads/2017/12/Voting-11thDec17_pv-only-BPC-1.pdf
178 http://www.bmgresearch.co.uk/independent-poll-shift-toward-remain-at-height-of-brexit-negotiation-tensions/
179 http://survation.com/wp-content/uploads/2017/12/Final-MoS-041217.pdf
180 https://d25d2506sfb94s.cloudfront.net/cumulus_uploads/document/0aof66rdfs/WelshBarometerResults_November17_w.pdf#page=9
181 https://d25d2506sfb94s.cloudfront.net/cumulus_uploads/document/rm6tlufhf4/HandelsblattResults_Topline_Nov2017_w.pdf
182 http://d25d2506sfb94s.cloudfront.net/cumulus_uploads/document/kvc16fv4mg/Eurotrack_Oct2017_topline.pdf
183 http://opinium.co.uk/wp-content/uploads/2017/10/OP9180-Observer-Brexit-Tables.xlsx
184 http://survation.com/wp-content/uploads/2017/10/Final-survation-VI-2c0d4h7.pdf
185 http://survation.com/wp-content/uploads/2017/09/Mail-On-Sunday-September-23rd-Data-Tables-1.pdf
186 http://opinium.co.uk/wp-content/uploads/2017/09/VI-19-09-17-Tables.xls
187 http://survation.com/wp-content/uploads/2017/09/Labour-Party-Conference-Poll-2017.pdf
188 http://www.bmgresearch.co.uk/wp-content/uploads/2017/09/BMG-Independent-EU-Referendum-VI-22092017.xlsx
189 http://opinium.co.uk/wp-content/uploads/2017/09/VI-12-09-2017-Tables.xls
190 https://d25d2506sfb94s.cloudfront.net/cumulus_uploads/document/lh9i9z3rmj/WelshBarometerResults_170907_W2.pdf#page=9
191 http://opinium.co.uk/wp-content/uploads/2017/07/VI-15-08-2017.xls
192 http://www.bmgresearch.co.uk/independentbmg-poll-public-remain-split-latest-eu-referendum-poll/
193 https://d25d2506sfb94s.cloudfront.net/cumulus_uploads/document/tjhnf4nw4u/Eurotrack_July2017_1W.pdf
194 http://survation.com/wp-content/uploads/2017/07/Final-MoS-Brexit-Poll-Tables-140717GOCH-1c0d2h4.pdf
195 http://survation.com/wp-content/uploads/2017/07/Final-Survation-UK-Attitudes-Tracker-280617MMDLLMTDC-1c0d1h7-chd.pdf
196 https://d25d2506sfb94s.cloudfront.net/cumulus_uploads/document/gd8a4jt3m3/Eurotrack_June17_1W.pdf
197 http://www.panelbase.com/media/polls/W10470w8tablesforpublication260617.pdf
198 https://survation.com/wp-content/uploads/2017/06/Final-Post-Election-GMB-Tables-160617TOCH-1c0d0h5.pdf#page=10
199 http://survation.com/wp-content/uploads/2017/06/Post-Election_Poll_June10.pdf
200 http://www.panelbase.com/media/polls/W10470w7tablesforpublication.pdf
201 http://www.panelbase.com/media/polls/W10470w6tablesforpublication010617.pdf
202 https://d25d2506sfb94s.cloudfront.net/cumulus_uploads/document/jfwm990f42/WelshBarometer_May31st_W.pdf

[203] http://www.tns-bmrb.co.uk/sites/tns-bmrb/files/KPUK%20-%20final%20tables%20-%2031.5.2017.pdf

[204] https://d25d2506sfb94s.cloudfront.net/cumulus_uploads/document/345h3a4u4f/WelshBarometer_May21st_wellsagenew_w.pdf#page=5

[205] http://www.panelbase.com/media/polls/W10470w4tablesforpublication150517.pdf

[206] http://www.panelbase.com/media/polls/W10407w3tablesforpublication090517.pdf

[207] https://d25d2506sfb94s.cloudfront.net/cumulus_uploads/document/dcj280pkfd/WelshBarometer_May7th_WestminsterVI_agenew.pdf#page=2

[208] https://www.drg.global/wp-content/uploads/2018/01/W10470w2tablesforpublication020517.pdf#page=5

[209] https://www.drg.global/wp-content/uploads/2018/01/W10470maintablesforpublication240417.pdf#page=3

[210] https://d25d2506sfb94s.cloudfront.net/cumulus_uploads/document/a7ywnfqqk9/WelshBarometerResults_April17_WestminsterVI_W_wellsagenew.pdf#page=2

[211] https://d25d2506sfb94s.cloudfront.net/cumulus_uploads/document/q70yr6i56a/Eurotrack_March_Trackers_W.pdf

[212] https://d25d2506sfb94s.cloudfront.net/cumulus_uploads/document/di1fktb0k8/January_Eurotrack_W.pdf

[213] https://d25d2506sfb94s.cloudfront.net/cumulus_uploads/document/s289nens6c/Eurotrack_December_Website.pdf

[214] http://www.comresglobal.com/wp-content/uploads/2016/11/DailyMirror_Poll_Tables-281116.pdf#page=5

[215] https://d25d2506sfb94s.cloudfront.net/cumulus_uploads/document/8e293lt9rf/Eurotrack_October_Trackers_Website.pdf

[216] http://www.bmgresearch.co.uk/wp-content/uploads/2016/11/CONFIDENTIAL-BMG-POLL-OCTOBER-data-tables-031116.pdf#page=21

[217] http://survation.com/wp-content/uploads/2016/10/Final-Brexit-Tables-101016JMDLL-1c0d0h2.pdf#page=4

[218] https://d25d2506sfb94s.cloudfront.net/cumulus_uploads/document/n8t7herkqe/Eurotrack_Results_September_Website.pdf#page=2

[219] https://d25d2506sfb94s.cloudfront.net/cumulus_uploads/document/smow6e2p43/MegaEurotrackerResults_AugustSeptember2016_Toplines.pdf#page=17

[220] https://d25d2506sfb94s.cloudfront.net/cumulus_uploads/document/eokci16bwr/Eurotrack_July_Website.pdf

[221] https://d25d2506sfb94s.cloudfront.net/cumulus_uploads/document/zei5f6pxt4/GB_Results_Full_Website.pdf#page=2

[222] http://www.bmgresearch.co.uk/wp-content/uploads/2016/07/CONFIDENTIAL-BMG-EVENING-STANDARD-POST-BREXIT-RECONTACT-SURVEY_1.pdf#page=15

[223] http://ourinsight.opinium.co.uk/sites/ourinsight.opinium.co.uk/files/vi_28_06_2016_v2.pdf#page=218

[224] //en.wikipedia.org/w/index.php?title=Template:Brexit/Post-referendum_opinion_polling:_Remain-Leave&action=edit

[225] https://d25d2506sfb94s.cloudfront.net/cumulus_uploads/document/yu0hckb8v4/PV%20results%20180807%20day%20one_w.pdf#page=7

[226] https://interactive.news.sky.com/brexitshifttabs.pdf#page=5

[227] https://d25d2506sfb94s.cloudfront.net/cumulus_uploads/document/kgfdyeogty/SundayTimesResults_180720_for_web.pdf#page=12

[228] https://d25d2506sfb94s.cloudfront.net/cumulus_uploads/document/vv29cv0a94/TimesResults_SecondRef_180717_w.pdf#page=3

[229] //en.wikipedia.org/w/index.php?title=Template:Brexit/Post-referendum_opinion_polling:_Three_options&action=edit

[230] https://d25d2506sfb94s.cloudfront.net/cumulus_uploads/document/2req6g7z50/Internal_180905_Brexit_W.pdf#page=5

[231] https://d25d2506sfb94s.cloudfront.net/cumulus_uploads/document/zr7v0xtbbl/180905_GMB%20publish.pdf#page=6

[232] https://d25d2506sfb94s.cloudfront.net/cumulus_uploads/document/fnzvd8ui1k/180905_ Unison%20publish.pdf#page=6

[233] https://d25d2506sfb94s.cloudfront.net/cumulus_uploads/document/gv8pa368st/180905_ Unite%20publish.pdf#page=6

[234] https://d25d2506sfb94s.cloudfront.net/cumulus_uploads/document/dx1qnnwoym/ PeoplesVoteResults_180914_Merge_Newspapers.pdf#page=16

[235] https://d25d2506sfb94s.cloudfront.net/cumulus_uploads/document/30tafmcnkc/PeoplesVote_ LondonMerge_180905_w.pdf#page=5

[236] https://d25d2506sfb94s.cloudfront.net/cumulus_uploads/document/wre3lp7die/JeremyVine_ Results_180901_website.pdf

[237] https://d25d2506sfb94s.cloudfront.net/cumulus_uploads/document/92ofbq76tq/ PeoplesVoteResults_180824_Wales_w.pdf#page=4

[238] https://d25d2506sfb94s.cloudfront.net/cumulus_uploads/document/vv29cv0a94/ TimesResults_SecondRef_180717_w.pdf

[239] https://d25d2506sfb94s.cloudfront.net/cumulus_uploads/document/phvyn092lg/ TimesResults_180711_VI_Brexit.pdf#page=8

[240] https://d25d2506sfb94s.cloudfront.net/cumulus_uploads/document/sfiq16wfpm/ ConservativeMemberResults_180709_w.pdf#page=19

[241] https://d25d2506sfb94s.cloudfront.net/cumulus_uploads/document/wb96oamqk2/ OpenBritainResults_180630_UniteMembers.pdf

[242] https://d25d2506sfb94s.cloudfront.net/cumulus_uploads/document/fhgs8okigo/ TimesResults_180514_VI_Trackers_w.pdf#page=6

[243] https://www.opinium.co.uk/wp-content/uploads/2018/05/VI-01-05-2018-Tables-Website.xlsx

[244] https://www.opinium.co.uk/wp-content/uploads/2018/04/OP10067-Open-Britain-Europe-Tracker-Online-Tables.xlsx

[245] https://d25d2506sfb94s.cloudfront.net/cumulus_uploads/document/jfvhk2jlbk/TimesResults_ 180410_VI_Trackers.pdf#page=6

[246] https://d25d2506sfb94s.cloudfront.net/cumulus_uploads/document/onal3cjvfu/ InternalResults_180327_BrexitQuestions_for_website.pdf#page=10

[247] https://d25d2506sfb94s.cloudfront.net/cumulus_uploads/document/1daln9otjj/TimesResults_ 180305_VI_Trackers_w.pdf#page=8

[248] https://www.icmunlimited.com/wp-content/uploads/2018/01/ICM-Guardian-Brexit-Questions-BPC-Regions.pdf#page=22

[249] https://d25d2506sfb94s.cloudfront.net/cumulus_uploads/document/sty43olvol/ TimesResultss_180110_SecondReferendum_w.pdf

[250] https://d25d2506sfb94s.cloudfront.net/cumulus_uploads/document/5tu7akhw6z/ TimesResults_171211_VI_Trackers_w.pdf#page=5

[251] https://survation.com/wp-content/uploads/2017/12/Final-MoS-041217.pdf#page=15

[252] https://d25d2506sfb94s.cloudfront.net/cumulus_uploads/document/4y1e1sdlwa/ InternalResults_171024_VI.pdf#page=6

[253] https://d25d2506sfb94s.cloudfront.net/cumulus_uploads/document/xdlp14v0de/ TimesResults_170922_VI_Trackers_W.pdf#page=5

[254] https://d25d2506sfb94s.cloudfront.net/cumulus_uploads/document/ndu320grio/TheTimes_ 170913_BrexitQs_W.pdf#page=5

[255] https://d25d2506sfb94s.cloudfront.net/cumulus_uploads/document/lh9i9z3rmj/ WelshBarometerResults_170907_W2.pdf#page=7

[256] https://survation.com/wp-content/uploads/2017/07/Final-MoS-Brexit-Poll-Tables-140717GOCH-1c0d2h4.pdf#page=27

[257] https://www.opinium.co.uk/wp-content/uploads/2017/07/Time-Series-of-Second-EU-Referendum-Polling.xlsx

[258] https://survation.com/wp-content/uploads/2017/07/Final-Survation-UK-Attitudes-Tracker-280617MMDLLMTDC-1c0d1h7-chd.pdf#page=19

[259] https://survation.com/wp-content/uploads/2017/06/Final-MoS-Brexit-Tables-1c0d0h5.pdf#page=5

[260] https://survation.com/wp-content/uploads/2017/06/Final-Post-Election-GMB-Tables-160617TOCH-1c0d0h5.pdf#page=17

[261] https://d25d2506sfb94s.cloudfront.net/cumulus_uploads/document/zebfsayat4/SundayTimesResults_170428_W.pdf#page=8

[262] https://d25d2506sfb94s.cloudfront.net/cumulus_uploads/document/tz9dxy8t29/SundayTimesResults_170421_VI_W.pdf#page=8

[263] http://www.bmgresearch.co.uk/wp-content/uploads/2016/07/CONFIDENTIAL-BMG-EVENING-STANDARD-POST-BREXIT-RECONTACT-SURVEY_1.pdf#page=9

[264] Poll finds that 60% of Britons want to keep their EU citizenship https://www.theguardian.com/politics/2017/jul/01/poll-european-eu-rights-brexit *The Guardian*

[265] Mia Jankowicz, "Britain's thriving art scene strangled by Brexit chaos" in *Politics.co.uk,* 20 March 2017: Online Link http://www.politics.co.uk/comment-analysis/2017/03/20/britain-s-thriving-art-scene-strangled-by-brexit-chaos

[266] Hannah Ellis-Petersen, "Banksy Brexit mural of man chipping away at EU flag appears in Dover" in *The Guardian* (UK newspaper), 8 May 2017

[267] Mick Brown, "Grayson Perry: What I learnt from my Brexit tour around Britain", in *The Daily Telegraph* (UK newspaper), 27 May 2017

[268] Did Daphne du Maurier predict Brexit? - BBC News https://www.bbc.co.uk/news/uk-england-36904536 Retrieved 6 September 2018.

[269] Michael Paraskos, *Rabbitman* (London: Friction Fiction, 2017)

[270] Mark Billingham, *Love Like Blood*, (London: Little Brown Books, 2017)

[271] David Boyle, *Remains of the Day* (London: Real Press, 2017)

[272] Amanda Craig, *The Lie of the Land* (London: Little Brown Books, 2017)

[273] Douglas Board, *Time of Lies* (London: Lightning Books, 2017)

[274] Katie Spencer, "Literature goes Brexit: EU vote prompts writers to tackle issue", Sky News report, 19 March 2017 Click for Link http://news.sky.com/story/literature-goes-brexit-eu-vote-prompts-writers-to-tackle-issue-10807458

[275] Kettle, Martin (10 March 2017) "Brexit stage left: how theatre became the best way to understand today's Britain" *The Guardian.*

[276] Cavendish, Dominic (11 March 2017) "The National Theatre takes on Brexit in My Country, a work in progress". *The Daily Telegraph.*

[277] https://dx.doi.org/10.1080/13501763.2016.1225785

[278] //doi.org/10.1080/13501763.2016.1225785

[279] //www.worldcat.org/issn/1350-1763

[280] //www.worldcat.org/oclc/917161408

[281] https://www.giga-hamburg.de/en/publication/brexit-beyond-the-uks-borders-what-it-means-for-africa

[282] https://www.gov.uk/government/brexit

[283] https://www.gov.uk/government/collections/article-50-and-negotiations-with-the-eu

[284] https://ec.europa.eu/commission/brexit-negotiations/negotiating-documents-article-50-negotiations-united-kingdom_en

[285] http://www.parliament.uk/business/news/european-union

[286] https://researchbriefings.parliament.uk/ResearchBriefing/Summary/CBP-7912

[287] https://researchbriefings.parliament.uk/ResearchBriefing/Summary/CBP-7815

[288] http://www.gov.uk/government/organisations/department-for-exiting-the-european-union

[289] https://www.bbc.co.uk/news/uk-politics-37507129

[290] http://www.barcouncil.org.uk/media/508513/the_brexit_papers.pdf

[291] https://www.gov.uk/government/speeches/the-governments-negotiating-objectives-for-exiting-the-eu-pm-speech

[292] https://www.gov.uk/government/uploads/system/uploads/attachment_data/file/588948/The_United_Kingdoms_exit_from_and_partnership_with_the_EU_Web.pdf

[293] https://curlie.org/Regional/Europe/United_Kingdom/Society_and_Culture/Issues/European_Union/Brexit

[294] http://quotes.euronews.com/topic/brexit

[295] http://www.consilium.europa.eu/en/press/press-releases/2017/04/29-euco-brexit-guidelines

296 http://www.oxfordscholarship.com/view/10.1093/acprof:oso/9780199683123.001.0001/acprof-9780199683123

297 http://www.bailii.org/uk/cases/UKSC/2017/5.html

298 //en.wikipedia.org/w/index.php?title=Template:United_Kingdom_in_the_European_Union&action=edit

299 FCO 30/1048, *Legal and constitutional implications of UK entry into EEC* (open from 1 January 2002 under the Thirty-year rule).http://discovery.nationalarchives.gov.uk/details/r/C11018818

300 Alex May, *Britain and Europe since 1945* (1999).

301 http://news.bbc.co.uk/onthisday/hi/dates/stories/april/26/newsid_2503000/2503155.stm

302 *New Open Europe/ComRes poll: Failure to win key reforms could swing UK's EU referendum vote* http://openeurope.org.uk/today/blog/new-open-europecomres-poll-failure-to-win-key-reforms-could-swing-uks-eu-referendum-vote openeurope.org, 16 December 2015.

303 //en.wikipedia.org/w/index.php?title=Opinion_polling_for_the_United_Kingdom_European_Union_membership_referendum&action=edit

304 //en.wikipedia.org/w/index.php?title=Template:United_Kingdom_in_the_European_Union&action=edit

305 https://d25d2506sfb94s.cloudfront.net/cumulus_uploads/document/640yx5m0rx/On_the_Day_FINAL_poll_forwebsite.pdf

306 https://www.independent.co.uk/news/uk/politics/eu-referendum-poll-brexit-remain-vote-leave-live-latest-who-will-win-results-populus-a7097261.html

307 https://d25d2506sfb94s.cloudfront.net/cumulus_uploads/document/atmwrgevvj/TimesResults_160622_EVEOFPOLL.pdf

308 https://www.ipsos.com/sites/default/files/migrations/en-uk/files/Assets/Docs/Polls/eu-referendum-charts-23-june-2016.pdf

309 https://www.independent.co.uk/news/uk/politics/eu-referendum-final-opinium-poll-shows-leave-ahead-by-one-point-a7095811.html

310 http://www.comres.co.uk/wp-content/uploads/2016/06/Daily-Mail-ITV-News_EU-Referendum-Survey_22nd-June-2016_61021xh5.pdf

311 https://uk.reuters.com/article/uk-britain-eu-tns-poll-idUKKCN0Z824K

312 http://survation.com/wp-content/uploads/2016/06/IG-Tables-21st-June.pdf

313 https://d25d2506sfb94s.cloudfront.net/cumulus_uploads/document/it82go26iz/TimesResults_160620_EUReferendum_W.pdf

314 https://web.archive.org/web/20160705025318/http://www.opinion.co.uk/perch/resources/poll-190616-tables-weighted-v4.pdf

315 http://survation.com/wp-content/uploads/2016/06/Final-18-June-Mos-EU-poll-Tables-part-1.pdf

316 https://d25d2506sfb94s.cloudfront.net/cumulus_uploads/document/2t6fjf3032/SundayTimeslResults_160617_EUReferendum_W.pdf

317 http://uk.reuters.com/article/us-britain-eu-opinium-idUKKCN0Z40OY

318 https://d25d2506sfb94s.cloudfront.net/cumulus_uploads/document/lvxwtdus18/GMBResults_160616_EURef_Website.pdf

319 http://survation.com/wp-content/uploads/2016/06/Final-IG-June-Tables-150616RSDLL-1c1d0h4.pdf

320 http://www.bmgresearch.co.uk/wp-content/uploads/2016/06/CONFIDENTIAL-BMG-HERALD-EU-REFERENDUM-POLL-ONLINE-160616-V1.pdf

321 http://www.bmgresearch.co.uk/bmgherald-final-eu-referendum-poll/

322 https://www.ipsos-mori.com/Assets/Docs/Polls/pm-16-june-2016-tables.pdf

323 http://d25d2506sfb94s.cloudfront.net/cumulus_uploads/document/4ko8mpylq7/TimesResults_160613_EUReferendum_W_Headline.pdf

324 https://www.icmunlimited.com/wp-content/uploads/2016/06/13-Jun.pdf

325 http://www.comres.co.uk/wp-content/uploads/2016/06/The-Sun_EU-Referendum-Poll_June-2016-1.pdf

326 http://www.tns-bmrb.co.uk/press-release/leave-campaign-ahead-laN/A-tns-poll

327 https://web.archive.org/web/20160705085036/http://www.opinion.co.uk/perch/resources/orb-international-daily-telegraph-14th-june-tables.pdf

[328] https://www.reuters.com/article/us-britain-eu-polls-idUSKCN0Z62JT

[329] https://d25d2506sfb94s.cloudfront.net/cumulus_uploads/document/qi3olqsp2n/
SundayTimesResults_160610_EUReferendum.pdf

[330] http://ourinsight.opinium.co.uk/sites/ourinsight.opinium.co.uk/files/vi_07_06_16_new_0.pdf

[331] https://web.archive.org/web/20160611014049/http://www.opinion.co.uk/perch/resources/
orbindependent-friday-10th-june-final-data-tables.pdf

[332] https://d25d2506sfb94s.cloudfront.net/cumulus_uploads/document/0ofltfa592/Times_
Results_160606_EU_Final_Website.pdf

[333] https://www.icmunlimited.com/wp-content/uploads/2016/06/Voting-06thJun16_pv-only-
FOR-WEBSITE-1.pdf

[334] http://www.opinion.co.uk/article.phpN/As=daily-telegraph-poll-2nd-5th-june

[335] https://d25d2506sfb94s.cloudfront.net/cumulus_uploads/document/hkfno5n9fo/GMB_
Results_160603_UndecidedVoters_Website.pdf

[336] http://ourinsight.opinium.co.uk/sites/ourinsight.opinium.co.uk/files/vi_31_05_16.pdf

[337] https://d25d2506sfb94s.cloudfront.net/cumulus_uploads/document/5410is51bi/TimesResults_
160531_EURef&HousePrices_W.pdf

[338] https://www.icmunlimited.com/wp-content/uploads/2016/05/27-29-May-2016-CATI-and-
online-polls.pdf

[339] http://www.opinion.co.uk/article.phpN/As=daily-telegraph-poll-25th-29th-may

[340] http://www.bmgresearch.co.uk/wp-content/uploads/2016/05/CONFIDENTIAL-BMG-
ONLINE-EU-REF-TRACKER-MAY16-250516.pdf

[341] http://survation.com/wp-content/uploads/2016/05/Full-IG-EU-Poll-Tables-230516RSDLL-
1c0d1h3.pdf

[342] http://d25d2506sfb94s.cloudfront.net/cumulus_uploads/document/8j6845m5qq/
TimesResults_160524_EURef&ToryLeadership_W.pdf

[343] http://www2.tnsglobal.com/l/36112/2016-06-05/m28r4f/36112/188168/Tables_for_
publication___06.06.2016.pdf

[344] https://www.icmunlimited.com/wp-content/uploads/2016/05/23-May-2016-v2.pdf

[345] http://www.opinion.co.uk/article.phpN/As=daily-telegraph-poll-18th-22nd-may

[346] https://www.theguardian.com/politics/2016/may/21/tory-eu-referendum-voters-switching-
remain-opinium-observer-poll

[347] http://d25d2506sfb94s.cloudfront.net/cumulus_uploads/document/31mkuwrwz2/
TimesResults_160517_EU_W.pdf

[348] http://www.comres.co.uk/polls/itv-news-daily-mail-eu-referendum-poll-may-2016/

[349] https//www.ipsos-mori.com

[350] https://www.icmunlimited.com/wp-content/uploads/2016/05/2016_guard_may_mode_N/A.
pdf

[351] https://web.archive.org/web/20160603142305/http://www.opinion.co.uk/perch/resources/
daily-telegraph-poll-11th-15th-may.pdf

[352] http://www.tns-bmrb.co.uk/press-release/one-five-voters-still-undecided-eu-referendum

[353] https://yougov.co.uk/news/2016/05/20/revealed-evidence-greater-skews-phone-polls/

[354] http://uk.reuters.com/article/uk-britain-eu-poll-icm-idUKKCN0Y01OM

[355] https://d25d2506sfb94s.cloudfront.net/cumulus_uploads/document/o7f6u41miv/GMB_
Results_160506_UndecidedVoters_Webstie.pdf

[356] https://www.icmunlimited.com/wp-content/uploads/2016/05/3-May-2016.pdf

[357] http://www.cityam.com/240066/eu-referendum-polls-at-odds-on-outcome-of-junes-vote

[358] https://www.theguardian.com/politics/2016/apr/30/referendum-poll-boost-remain-campaign-
economic-argument

[359] https//www.independent.co.uk

[360] http://www.tns-bmrb.co.uk/press-release/eu-referendum-remain-maintains-lead-following-
obama-intervention

[361] https://d25d2506sfb94s.cloudfront.net/cumulus_uploads/document/ieuepajv7k/TimesResults_
160424_EURef_W.pdf

[362] http://survation.com/wp-content/uploads/2016/04/Final-IG-April-Tables-250416RSDLL-
1c0d0h3.pdf

[363] http://us11.campaign-archive2.com/N/Au=7fc68042ca102c052ac0e0f61&id=97dfd0786a

[364] https://www.icmunlimited.com/wp-content/uploads/2016/04/25-April.pdf
[365] https://web.archive.org/web/20160512235539/http://www.opinion.co.uk/perch/resources/orb-poll-eu-referendum-20-24-april.pdf
[366] http://www.comres.co.uk/wp-content/uploads/2016/04/Daily-Mail-ITV-News_EU-Referendum-Poll_April-2016.pdf
[367] https://www.ipsos-mori.com/Assets/Docs/Polls/pm-april-2016-charts.pdf
[368] https://www.icmunlimited.com/wp-content/uploads/2016/04/2016_guardian_april_modeN/A.pdf
[369] https://web.archive.org/web/20160508225216/http://www.opinion.co.uk/perch/resources/orb-daily-telegraph-poll-13-17-april.pdf
[370] http://uk.reuters.com/article/uk-britain-eu-poll-idUKKCN0XH0FKN/A
[371] https://d25d2506sfb94s.cloudfront.net/cumulus_uploads/document/0e8rm3xhr2/GMB_Results_160414_UndecidedVoters_Website.pdf
[372] https://d25d2506sfb94s.cloudfront.net/cumulus_uploads/document/ugdbpjyfyn/TimesResults_160412_VI&EURef_W.pdf
[373] http://www2.tnsglobal.com/l/36112/2016-04-11/kblr37/36112/167346/Brexit_March16_DataTables.pdf
[374] http://www.comres.co.uk/wp-content/uploads/2016/04/The-Sun_EU-Referendum-Survey_April-2016_General-Public.pdf
[375] https://www.icmunlimited.com/wp-content/uploads/2016/04/11_April.pdf
[376] http://d25d2506sfb94s.cloudfront.net/cumulus_uploads/document/gje3eztefm/InternalResults_1600407_EUPolicies_W.pdf
[377] https://d25d2506sfb94s.cloudfront.net/cumulus_uploads/document/0ql1u2e30p/InternalResults_160405_EU_W.pdf
[378] https://www.icmunlimited.com/wp-content/uploads/2016/04/Voting-04thApr16_pv-only-2.pdf
[379] https://web.archive.org/web/20160419093109/http://www.opinion.co.uk/perch/resources/orb-telegraph-poll-april-2016.pdf
[380] https://www.theguardian.com/politics/2016/apr/02/eu-referendum-young-voters-brexit-leave
[381] http://www2.tnsglobal.com/l/36112/2016-03-30/kblr37/36112/167346/Brexit_March16_DataTables.pdf
[382] https://web.archive.org/web/20160414165752/http://www.opinion.co.uk/perch/resources/orb-eu-poll-march-2016.pdf
[383] https://web.archive.org/web/20160405160055/http://www.icmunlimited.com/media-centre/media-center/eu-referendum-introducing-turnout-weighting
[384] https://www.ipsos-mori.com/Assets/Docs/Polls/pm-march-2016-europe-topline.pdf
[385] http://d25d2506sfb94s.cloudfront.net/cumulus_uploads/document/vmzx106mva/Eurotrack_March_Trackers_Website.pdf
[386] http://www.comres.co.uk/wp-content/uploads/2016/03/ComRes_ITVNews_EURef_March2016.pdf
[387] https://www.icmunlimited.com/wp-content/uploads/2016/04/Voting-21stMar16.pdf
[388] http://survation.com/wp-content/uploads/2016/03/EUREFPOLL2.pdf
[389] https://web.archive.org/web/20160316011251/http://www.opinion.co.uk/perch/resources/marchdt.pdf
[390] https://www.icmunlimited.com/wp-content/uploads/2016/03/Voting-14thMar16_pv.pdf
[391] https://gqrr.box.com/shared/static/duyes2adqsjocyt7cdo4dz3p5qv5vws6.pdf
[392] http://www.ncpolitics.uk/2016/03/new-polls-apart.html/
[393] https://www.icmunlimited.com/wp-content/uploads/2016/03/Voting-07thMar16.pdf
[394] https://d25d2506sfb94s.cloudfront.net/cumulus_uploads/document/rzgxjhbyun/InternalResults_160303_EU.pdf
[395] https://d25d2506sfb94s.cloudfront.net/cumulus_uploads/document/cu64v5kd31/InternalResults_160302_EU.pdf
[396] https://d25d2506sfb94s.cloudfront.net/cumulus_uploads/document/e492lvhidi/InternalResults_160301_EU.pdf
[397] https://www.icmunlimited.com/wp-content/uploads/2016/03/Voting-29thFeb16_pv.pdf

398 https://web.archive.org/web/20160307004637/http://www.opinion.co.uk/perch/resources/datatablesfeb2016.pdf

399 https://d25d2506sfb94s.cloudfront.net/cumulus_uploads/document/p3tomelhgo/TimesResults_160223_EUReferendum_Tuesday_Release.pdf

400 http://www.bmgresearch.co.uk/wp-content/uploads/2016/02/CONFIDENTIAL-BMG-POLL-FOR-EVENING-STANDARD-EU-250216.pdf

401 https://www.icmunlimited.com/wp-content/uploads/2016/04/Voting-22ndFeb16_pv.pdf

402 http://www.comres.co.uk/polls/daily-mail-political-poll-february-2016/

403 http://survation.com/wp-content/uploads/2016/02/EU-Renegotiation-Poll-Tables.pdf

404 https://www.theguardian.com/politics/2016/mar/20/britons-on-europe-survey-results-opinium-poll-referendum

405 https://web.archive.org/web/20160311002753/https://www.ipsos-mori.com/Assets/Docs/Polls/political-monitor-feb-2016-tables.pdf

406 http://www.tnsglobal.co.uk/sites/tns-uk/files/EU%20referendum%20tables%2019.02.2016.pdf

407 https://web.archive.org/web/20160324145755/http://www.icmunlimited.com/media-centre/media-center/eu-referendum-tracker-18

408 http://www.comres.co.uk/wp-content/uploads/2016/02/ITV-News_EU-Referendum-Poll_15-February-2016.pdf

409 https://www.icmunlimited.com/wp-content/uploads/2016/04/Voting-08thFeb16_pv.pdf

410 http://d25d2506sfb94s.cloudfront.net/cumulus_uploads/document/4mzy46afe7/TimesResults_160204_EUReferendumDay1.pdf

411 https://www.icmunlimited.com/wp-content/uploads/2016/04/Voting-31jan1616_pv.pdf

412 http://d25d2506sfb94s.cloudfront.net/cumulus_uploads/document/mg7825gzxs/InternalResults_160128_EURef_Website.pdf

413 https://www.ipsos-mori.com/Assets/Docs/Polls/political-monitor-jan-2016-tables.pdf

414 http://www.bmgresearch.co.uk/wp-content/uploads/2016/02/BMG-UK-Poll-EU-Referendum-060216.pdf

415 http://www.comres.co.uk/wp-content/uploads/2016/01/Daily-Mail_Political-Poll_25th-Jan-2016.pdf

416 https://www.icmunlimited.com/wp-content/uploads/2016/04/Voting-25thJan16_pv.pdf

417 http://www.opinion.co.uk/perch/resources/omjanuarypoll.pdf

418 https://gallery.mailchimp.com/fbcf81e4dd2761d48aba0b6da/files/Voting_18thJan16_pv.pdf

419 http://survation.com/wp-content/uploads/2016/01/MoS-EU-Poll-150116SWCH-1c0d1h7.pdf

420 http://panelbase.com/media/polls/CombinedGBtablesforpublicationv2180116.pdf

421 https://www.icmunlimited.com/wp-content/uploads/2016/04/Voting-11thJan16_pv.pdf

422 https://d25d2506sfb94s.cloudfront.net/cumulus_uploads/document/pw2zwai9dn/Times_Results_151218-Website.pdf

423 https://www.ipsos-mori.com/Assets/Docs/Polls/political-monitor-december-2015-topline.pdf

424 http://www.comres.co.uk/wp-content/uploads/2015/12/Open-Europe_EU-renegotiation-poll_Dec15_tables.pdf

425 http://www.icmunlimited.com/data/media/pdf/Voting_14thDec15_pv.pdf

426 https://gallery.mailchimp.com/fbcf81e4dd2761d48aba0b6da/files/Voting_07thDec15_pv.pdf

427 http://www.opinion.co.uk/perch/resources/we-tabs-final-incl.-romania.pdf

428 http://survation.com/wp-content/uploads/2015/12/ADDE-Tables-for-Release.pdf

429 https://d25d2506sfb94s.cloudfront.net/cumulus_uploads/document/1d6iphzuxx/EUResults_November2015-WebsiteV2.pdf

430 http://d25d2506sfb94s.cloudfront.net/cumulus_uploads/document/hdfr2e6nua/Copy%20of%20November_Eurotrack.pdf

431 https://gallery.mailchimp.com/fbcf81e4dd2761d48aba0b6da/files/23_Nov.pdf

432 http://www.opinion.co.uk/perch/resources/omnovemberpoll.pdf

433 http://survation.com/wp-content/uploads/2015/11/Final-Leave.EU-Tables-161115CBLCH-1c5d4h6.pdf

434 http://www.bmgresearch.co.uk/wp-content/uploads/2015/11/CONFIDENTIAL-BMG-Evening-Standard-Opinion-Poll-261115.pdf

435 http://www.icmunlimited.com/data/media/pdf/16_Nov.pdf

[436] http://survation.com/wp-content/uploads/2015/11/Final-Tables-with-cover-091115CBLCH-1-27.pdf

[437] https://gallery.mailchimp.com/fbcf81e4dd2761d48aba0b6da/files/9_Nov.pdf

[438] http://www.icmunlimited.com/data/media/pdf/2%20Nov.pdf

[439] http://d25d2506sfb94s.cloudfront.net/cumulus_uploads/document/4xz4yiikwo/PeterResults_19_10_15_EU_W.pdf

[440] https://d25d2506sfb94s.cloudfront.net/cumulus_uploads/document/82cc6m777i/Eurotrack_October_Trackers_website.pdf

[441] http://www.icmunlimited.com/data/media/pdf/Oct%2026th.pdf

[442] http://www.opinion.co.uk/perch/resources/october-2015poll.pdf

[443] https://d25d2506sfb94s.cloudfront.net/cumulus_uploads/document/5tpjjeedww/Peter_Results_151023_EU_W.pdf

[444] http://d25d2506sfb94s.cloudfront.net/cumulus_uploads/document/ftriq02603/PeterResults_151020_EU_W.pdf

[445] https://www.ipsos-mori.com/Assets/Docs/Polls/polmon_oct15_topline_EU.pdf

[446] https://gqrr.app.box.com/s/lpha0zg5y4k1t4sa2czfuczv7dw0h3wb

[447] https://gallery.mailchimp.com/fbcf81e4dd2761d48aba0b6da/files/Oct_19th_01.pdf

[448] http://www.icmunlimited.com/data/media/pdf/Final%20data-region.pdf

[449] http://comres.co.uk/wp-content/uploads/2015/10/Daily-Mail_EU-Poll.pdf

[450] http://www.icmunlimited.com/data/media/pdf/Voting-28thSep15_pv.pdf

[451] https://d25d2506sfb94s.cloudfront.net/cumulus_uploads/document/n4ocj2dlet/September_Eurotrack_Website.pdf

[452] https://d25d2506sfb94s.cloudfront.net/cumulus_uploads/document/zvlyhdkq2h/Con_and_Lab_Supporters_150928_EU_w.pdf

[453] http://www.icmunlimited.com/data/media/pdf/2015-150915-inouttracker%20(SEPT%202015).pdf

[454] http://survation.com/wp-content/uploads/2015/09/Final-MoS-September-Tables-1c0d0h4.pdf

[455] https://d25d2506sfb94s.cloudfront.net/cumulus_uploads/document/t3aybmity2/Copy%20of%20InternalResults_150819_Europe_W_1.PDF

[456] https://d25d2506sfb94s.cloudfront.net/cumulus_uploads/document/yllngwksjn/EuropeResults_18-Sep-2015_formatted.pdf

[457] https://d25d2506sfb94s.cloudfront.net/cumulus_uploads/document/snt40xcq9c/Eurotrack_July_Website_V1.pdf

[458] http://survation.com/wp-content/uploads/2015/07/Europoll-Tables-for-Release.pdf

[459] https://d25d2506sfb94s.cloudfront.net/cumulus_uploads/document/wlni3f3cyc/YG-Archive-150625-Eurotrack.pdf

[460] http://www.opinion.co.uk/perch/resources/europedata.pdf

[461] https://web.archive.org/web/20150618173649/https://www.ipsos-mori.com/Assets/Docs/Polls/Polmon_June15_lableaders_topline2.pdf

[462] http://d25d2506sfb94s.cloudfront.net/cumulus_uploads/document/pkmgvmnprr/InternalResults_150612_EU_referendum_Website.pdf

[463] https://d25d2506sfb94s.cloudfront.net/cumulus_uploads/document/q32gumm58k/ProspectResults_150602_EU.pdf

[464] https://d25d2506sfb94s.cloudfront.net/cumulus_uploads/document/sok5r12sbw/StephanResults_150608_Europe_W.pdf

[465] http://www.comres.co.uk/wp-content/uploads/2015/06/DailyMail-Political-Poll-May-20152.pdf

[466] http://www.icmunlimited.com/data/media/pdf/EU%20referendum%20wording%20-%20Tables.pdf

[467] http://d25d2506sfb94s.cloudfront.net/cumulus_uploads/document/2g0umt985b/SundayTimesResults_150522_Website.pdf

[468] http://survation.com/wp-content/uploads/2015/06/Full-Second-Release-Tables.pdf

[469] http://www.pewglobal.org/files/2015/06/Pew-Research-Center-European-Union-TOPLINE-FOR-RELEASE-June-2-2015.pdf

[470] https://d25d2506sfb94s.cloudfront.net/cumulus_uploads/document/xla59zgzc5/YG-Archive-Pol-Sunday-Times-results-090515.pdf

471 http://survation.com/wp-content/uploads/2015/05/Final-MoS-Post-election-poll-1c0d2h7.pdf

472 http://www.comres.co.uk/wp-content/uploads/2015/05/ITV-News-Daily-Mail-Political-Poll-5th-May-2015-6527.pdf

473 https://d25d2506sfb94s.cloudfront.net/cumulus_uploads/document/avpu0igaec/YG-Archive-Pol-Sun-results-040515.pdf

474 http://d25d2506sfb94s.cloudfront.net/cumulus_uploads/document/vr8lu4uorp/TimesRedBoxResults_150429_important_issues_EU_referendum_W.pdf

475 https://d25d2506sfb94s.cloudfront.net/cumulus_uploads/document/mupexfsgu3/Eurotrack_April_Website.pdf

476 http://cdn.yougov.com/cumulus_uploads/document/rvj1k0mcpp/YG-Archive-Pol-Sun-results-200415.pdf

477 http://www.populus.co.uk/wp-content/uploads/OmFT-Poll.pdf

478 http://ourinsight.opinium.co.uk/sites/ourinsight.opinium.co.uk/files/vi_08_04_2015_tables.pdf

479 http://storage.pardot.com/36112/86876/BIF_datatables_31Mar2015.pdf

480 http://www.panelbase.com/media/polls/W6836w1poll.pdf

481 https://d25d2506sfb94s.cloudfront.net/cumulus_uploads/document/8h6hq2m8mr/March_Eurotrack_Website.pdf

482 http://cdn.yougov.com/cumulus_uploads/document/fwlih2uar3/YG-Archive-Pol-Sun-results-230315.pdf

483 https://d25d2506sfb94s.cloudfront.net/cumulus_uploads/document/wwqytvw1lq/YG-Archive-150325-TheTimes.pdf

484 http://d25d2506sfb94s.cloudfront.net/cumulus_uploads/document/ozjokr0b37/YG-Archive-150307-Eurotrack.pdf

485 http://cdn.yougov.com/cumulus_uploads/document/2i11ywuxs2/YG-Archive-Pol-Sun-results-230215.pdf

486 http://ourinsight.opinium.co.uk/sites/ourinsight.opinium.co.uk/files/vi_17_02_2015_final_tables.pdf

487 http://cdn.yougov.com/cumulus_uploads/document/tdn54hn4rd/YG-Archive-Pol-Sun-results-260115.pdf

488 https://d25d2506sfb94s.cloudfront.net/cumulus_uploads/document/tscgkeooir/BritishInfluenceResults_150119_Europe_Website.pdf

489 http://www2.tnsglobal.com/l/36112/2015-01-22/32zr5f/36112/72376/BIF_datatables_22Jan2015.pdf

490 http://www2.tnsglobal.com/l/36112/2015-01-15/2yj4th/36112/71176/BIF_datatables_16Jan2015.pdf

491 https://d25d2506sfb94s.cloudfront.net/cumulus_uploads/document/gb2s5b76rk/YG-Archive-Pol-Sun-results-151214.pdf

492 http://cdn.yougov.com/cumulus_uploads/document/wbz4pttdol/YG-Archive-Pol-Sun-results-011214.pdf

493 https://d25d2506sfb94s.cloudfront.net/cumulus_uploads/document/dpm8pminx9/November_Eurotrack_EU_Website.pdf

494 http://www.comres.co.uk/wp-content/uploads/2015/04/ITV_News_Index_28th_November_2014.pdf

495 https://d25d2506sfb94s.cloudfront.net/cumulus_uploads/document/6au4g3f66s/YG-Archive-Pol-Sunday-Times-results-211114.pdf

496 http://cdn.yougov.com/cumulus_uploads/document/q4rrapo5ra/SunOnSundayResults_141121_whole_sample_Website.pdf

497 https://d25d2506sfb94s.cloudfront.net/cumulus_uploads/document/kocfpy6y21/YG-Archive-Pol-Sun-results-171114.pdf

498 http://survation.com/wp-content/uploads/2014/11/MoS-Labour-Leadership-poll-pt1.pdf

499 https://d25d2506sfb94s.cloudfront.net/cumulus_uploads/document/79dheq09yb/YG-Archive-Pol-Sun-results-031114.pdf

500 http://survation.com/wp-content/uploads/2014/12/Final-TFA-Data-Tables.pdf

501 http://cdn.yougov.com/cumulus_uploads/document/n965i9mzb8/YG-Archive-Pol-Sunday-Times-results-311014.pdf

[502] http://cdn.yougov.com/cumulus_uploads/document/e94v83thrn/RedBoxResults_141028_EU_referendum_immigration-Website.pdf

[503] https://d25d2506sfb94s.cloudfront.net/cumulus_uploads/document/tg001pwhwn/YG-Archive-Pol-Sunday-Times-results-241014.pdf

[504] https://d25d2506sfb94s.cloudfront.net/cumulus_uploads/document/u021h6mva9/YG-Archive-Pol-Sun-results-201014.pdf

[505] https://www.ipsos-mori.com/Assets/Docs/Polls/October%202014%20Political%20Monitor%20Topline%20-%20EU.pdf

[506] https://d25d2506sfb94s.cloudfront.net/cumulus_uploads/document/db1174l98f/YG-Archive-Pol-Sun-results-220914-F.pdf

[507] https://d25d2506sfb94s.cloudfront.net/cumulus_uploads/document/ylfpbtmctf/YG-Archive-Pol-Sun-results-260814.pdf

[508] https://d25d2506sfb94s.cloudfront.net/cumulus_uploads/document/uo5xionluj/YG-Archive-Pol-Sun-results-110814.pdf

[509] https://d25d2506sfb94s.cloudfront.net/cumulus_uploads/document/hohs9sk704/YG-Archive-Pol-Sun-results-140714.pdf

[510] https://d25d2506sfb94s.cloudfront.net/cumulus_uploads/document/ie1bqvkbkp/YG-Archive-Pol-Sun-results-300614.pdf

[511] http://www.comres.co.uk/wp-content/themes/comres/poll/ITV_News_Index_EU__30th_June_2014.pdf

[512] http://survation.com/wp-content/uploads/2014/06/Jean-Claude-Juncker-Poll-MoS.pdf

[513] http://cdn.yougov.com/cumulus_uploads/document/s703u4qd5l/YG-Archive-Pol-Sunday-Times-results-270614.pdf

[514] http://cdn.yougov.com/cumulus_uploads/document/mjjvoa38px/YG-Archive-Pol-Sunday-Times-results-200614.pdf

[515] http://ourinsight.opinium.co.uk/sites/ourinsight.opinium.co.uk/files/vi_17_06_2014.pdf

[516] http://cdn.yougov.com/cumulus_uploads/document/65qzen2gxe/YG-Archive-Pol-Sun-results-160614.pdf

[517] http://www.comres.co.uk/wp-content/themes/comres/poll/ITV_News_Index_5th_June_2014.pdf

[518] https://d25d2506sfb94s.cloudfront.net/cumulus_uploads/document/8fglspvdzl/YG-Archive-Pol-Sunday-Times-results-140530.pdf

[519] https://d25d2506sfb94s.cloudfront.net/cumulus_uploads/document/2mve1n75l7/Full_EU_Poll_Final_for_Sun_Times_website.pdf

[520] http://cdn.yougov.com/cumulus_uploads/document/19xw44td80/YG-Archive-Pol-Sun-results-190514.pdf

[521] http://www.ipsos-mori.com/Assets/Docs/Publications/sri-politicalmonitor-may2014-tables-TR-2.pdf

[522] https://d25d2506sfb94s.cloudfront.net/cumulus_uploads/document/nleftko4lu/YouGov-EuroTrack-Results-May-2014-EU-Elections-140512.pdf

[523] http://survation.com/wp-content/uploads/2014/05/Political-attitudes-poll-Mirror.pdf

[524] http://www.tnsglobal.com/uk/press-release/public-opinion-monitor-public-have-low-confidence-uk-government's-ability-renegotiate-

[525] https://d25d2506sfb94s.cloudfront.net/cumulus_uploads/document/pjvdg1r9fz/YG-Archive-Pol-Sunday-Times-results-140525.pdf

[526] https://d25d2506sfb94s.cloudfront.net/cumulus_uploads/document/zvvptj27x4/YG-Archive-Pol-Sun-results-220414.pdf

[527] http://d25d2506sfb94s.cloudfront.net/cumulus_uploads/document/52pydxm3qk/YG-Archive-Pol-Sunday-Times-results-140404.pdf

[528] https://d25d2506sfb94s.cloudfront.net/cumulus_uploads/document/yxi0qcxhxl/YG-Archive-Pol-Sunday-Times-results-140328.pdf

[529] https://d25d2506sfb94s.cloudfront.net/cumulus_uploads/document/xczor908qu/YG-Archive-Pol-Sun-results-240314_2.pdf

[530] http://cdn.yougov.com/cumulus_uploads/document/b6654v2muw/YG-Archive-Pol-Sun-results-100314.pdf

[531] http://d25d2506sfb94s.cloudfront.net/cumulus_uploads/document/9wqnovujf1/YG-Archive-Pol-Sun-results-100214.pdf

[532] http://lordashcroftpolls.com/wp-content/uploads/2014/03/Europe-on-Trial-poll-Full-tables.pdf

[533] http://d25d2506sfb94s.cloudfront.net/cumulus_uploads/document/ud4n712kak/YG-Archive-Pol-Sun-results-130114.pdf

[534] https://d25d2506sfb94s.cloudfront.net/cumulus_uploads/document/oqhuuatt8g/YG-Archive-September-Eurotrack-results-270913.pdf

[535] http://ourinsight.opinium.co.uk/sites/ourinsight.opinium.co.uk/files/VI_06_08_2013.pdf

[536] http://cdn.yougov.com/cumulus_uploads/document/zg7t63xa2p/YG-Archive-Eurotrack-July-results-240713-European-Union-English.pdf

[537] https//web.archive.org

[538] http://survation.com/wp-content/uploads/2014/04/Europe-Poll-Data-Tables.pdf

[539] http://cdn.yougov.com/cumulus_uploads/document/wfk7o4dbz5/YG-Archive-London-Omnibus-full-results-280513.pdf

[540] http://survation.com/wp-content/uploads/2013/05/Survation_May_Voting_Intentions_Poll_Tables_20th-May.pdf

[541] http://cdn.yougov.com/cumulus_uploads/document/lu4hu1in3u/YG-Archive-Pol-Sunday-Times-results-170513.pdf

[542] http://www.comres.co.uk/polls/IoS_SM_Political_Poll_May_2013.pdf

[543] https://www.telegraph.co.uk/active/10066273/Lets-quit-EU-say-46-per-cent-of-voters-in-poll.html

[544] http://cdn.yougov.com/cumulus_uploads/document/tb4puhe9cy/YG-Archive-Pol-Sun-results-130513.pdf

[545] https://www.theguardian.com/politics/2013/may/13/ukip-surge-polls-unprecedented

[546] http://cdn.yougov.com/cumulus_uploads/document/2chabiz0nj/YG-Archive-Pol-Sunday-Times-results-100513.pdf

[547] http://d25d2506sfb94s.cloudfront.net/cumulus_uploads/document/fgxlo89myr/YG-Archive-Times-results-070513-Europe.pdf

[548] http://cdn.yougov.com/cumulus_uploads/document/3jediflroz/YG-Archive-Pol-Sun-results-080413.pdf

[549] http://www.pewglobal.org/files/2013/05/Pew-Research-Center-Global-Attitudes-Project-European-Union-Report-FINAL-FOR-PRINT-May-13-2013.pdf

[550] http://cdn.yougov.com/cumulus_uploads/document/dz4ejczj7f/YG-Archive-Pol-Sun-results-180213.pdf

[551] http://www.tns-bmrb.co.uk/assets-uploaded/documents/pomjan13_1360081203.pdf

[552] http://www.ft.com/cms/s/0/cb2057fc-7917-11e2-b4df-00144feabdc0.html#axzz2LCm5Tdxj

[553] http://survation.com/wp-content/uploads/2013/01/Referendum_Pledge-Poll_Weighted-tables_25-01-2013.pdf

[554] http://cdn.yougov.com/cumulus_uploads/document/2dyt3nf221/YG-Archive-Pol-Sunday-Times-results-25-270113.pdf

[555] http://www.itv.com/news/update/2013-01-24/poll-most-voters-would-want-britain-to-leave-eu/

[556] http://d25d2506sfb94s.cloudfront.net/cumulus_uploads/document/nqf0ycudkh/YG-Archives-Pol-Trackers-Europe-220113.pdf

[557] http://d25d2506sfb94s.cloudfront.net/cumulus_uploads/document/1ix1a52xzw/YG-Archive-Pol-Sunday-Times-results-18-200113.pdf

[558] http://d25d2506sfb94s.cloudfront.net/cumulus_uploads/document/27rl48uusq/YG-Archive-Pol-Sunday-Times-results-11-130113.pdf

[559] http://survation.com/wp-content/uploads/2013/01/New-Year-Issues-Poll-5th-Jan-2013.pdf

[560] https://www.theguardian.com/politics/2012/nov/17/eu-referendum-poll

[561] http://d25d2506sfb94s.cloudfront.net/cumulus_uploads/document/92415ml14e/UniofCardiff_FoES_England.pdf

[562] http://www.panelbase.com/media/polls/W7181stn.pdf

[563] http://d25d2506sfb94s.cloudfront.net/cumulus_uploads/document/bcpps63ha9/EveningStandard_EUReferendum_160606_W.pdf

[564] https://www.standard.co.uk/news/london/eu-referendum-london-backs-remain-vote-poll-shows-a3256001.html

[565] http://d25d2506sfb94s.cloudfront.net/cumulus_uploads/document/6npv0yq1wf/LBCResults_London_Boris_EUReferendum_ISISterroristattack_160106_W2.pdf

[566] https://d25d2506sfb94s.cloudfront.net/cumulus_uploads/document/m936j3qhqi/EveningStandard_EU_141119_Website.pdf

[567] https://d25d2506sfb94s.cloudfront.net/cumulus_uploads/document/gp3bxnpwlr/YG-Archive-London-Omnibus-results-250613.pdf

[568] https//www.ipsos-mori.com

[569] http://storage.pardot.com/36112/187064/TNS___EU_Referendum_Poll__Scotland____2_June_2016.pdf

[570] https://www.icmunlimited.com/wp-content/uploads/2016/06/ICM_Scotland-Poll_May-2016-v2.pdf

[571] http://survation.com/wp-content/uploads/2016/05/Final-DR-Scomnibus-010516DCCH-1c0d2h4-ltv.pdf

[572] http://www.panelbase.com/media/polls/W7181w6tablesforpublication280416.pdf

[573] https://www.ipsos-mori.com/researchpublications/researcharchive/3730/SNP-set-to-win-election-while-Conservatives-and-Greens-make-progress.aspx

[574] http://www.tns-bmrb.co.uk/press-release/fall-snp-support-still-dominant-holyrood-election-approaches

[575] http://survation.com/wp-content/uploads/2016/04/Scomnibus-IV-15661626471-140416DCCH-1c0d0h5.pdf

[576] http://www.bmgresearch.co.uk/wp-content/uploads/2016/04/CONFIDENTIAL-BMG-Poll-The-Herald-180416.xlsx

[577] https://web.archive.org/web/20160513130808/http://panelbase.com/media/polls/W7181w5ScottishSundayTimesApril2016PolltablesForPublication150416.pdf

[578] http://www.tns-bmrb.co.uk/press-release/large-preference-scotland-remaining-eu-many-still-unsure

[579] http://survation.com/wp-content/uploads/2016/03/Full-Scomnibus-III-Tables-100316DCCH-1c0d5h1-1803.pdf

[580] https://d25d2506sfb94s.cloudfront.net/cumulus_uploads/document/0a9038zv4u/TimesResults_160310_Scotland_DayOne.pdf

[581] http://survation.com/wp-content/uploads/2016/02/Final-Scomnibus-II-110216DCCH-Tables-1c0d0h6-1702.pdf

[582] https://www.ipsos-mori.com/Assets/Docs/Scotland/scottish-monitor-feb-2016-tables.pdf

[583] http://d25d2506sfb94s.cloudfront.net/cumulus_uploads/document/xqh3y5ghb2/TimesResults_JanFeb16_ScotlandVI_Leaders_Tax_Fracking_Refugees_Website.pdf

[584] http://www.tnsglobal.co.uk/press-release/scottish-voters-favour-staying-eu-gap-narrowing

[585] http://survation.com/wp-content/uploads/2016/01/Final-Scomnibus-I-Tables-DR-1c0d2h9-51.pdf

[586] https://www.ipsos-mori.com/Assets/Docs/Scotland/scotland-opinion-monitor-november-2015-tables.pdf

[587] http://d25d2506sfb94s.cloudfront.net/cumulus_uploads/document/jl4e6xiy7z/TimesResults_October15_ScotlandVI_leaders_parties_tax_fracking_issues_w2.pdf

[588] http://www.tnsglobal.co.uk/press-release/snp-maintains-strong-lead-new-leaders-fail-boost-labour-support

[589] http://d25d2506sfb94s.cloudfront.net/cumulus_uploads/document/b35cuttugk/UniofCardiff_FoES_Scotland.pdf

[590] http://survation.com/wp-content/uploads/2015/09/Independence-Referendum-Anniversary-Poll-Scottish-Daily-Mail.pdf

[591] http://storage.pardot.com/36112/102592/TNS_Holyrood_Voting_Intention_Poll___9th_June_2015.pdf

[592] http://www.snp.org/media-centre/news/2015/may/snp-welcome-eu-poll

[593] http://d25d2506sfb94s.cloudfront.net/cumulus_uploads/document/a7awj68e8x/Final_Times_Results_150202_Website.pdf

[594] http://www.panelbase.com/media/polls/F6581wings.pdf

[595] http://survation.com/wp-content/uploads/2014/11/Scottish-Attitudes-November-Tables_1_46.pdf

[596] http://www.panelbase.com/media/polls/F6356tables.pdf

[597] https://www.ipsos-mori.com/Assets/Docs/Polls/scotland-attitudes-towards-EU-membership-2013-tables.pdf

[598] https://d25d2506sfb94s.cloudfront.net/cumulus_uploads/document/gapliwnrt9/WelshBarometer_June2016_w.pdf

[599] http://d25d2506sfb94s.cloudfront.net/cumulus_uploads/document/1dtezrp6mr/WelshBarometerPoll_April11th2016_w.pdf

[600] http://d25d2506sfb94s.cloudfront.net/cumulus_uploads/document/ld4xrymvff/ITVWales_Feb16_VI_and_EU_w.pdf

[601] http://d25d2506sfb94s.cloudfront.net/cumulus_uploads/document/z9rgsqjwg5/UniofCardiff_FoES_Wales.pdf

[602] http://blogs.cardiff.ac.uk/electionsinwales/wp-content/uploads/sites/100/2013/07/May2015.pdf

[603] http://d25d2506sfb94s.cloudfront.net/cumulus_uploads/document/e7erxqlrz8/ITVWalesResults_150327_March_Website.pdf

[604] http://blogs.cardiff.ac.uk/electionsinwales/wp-content/uploads/sites/100/2013/07/March-2015.pdf

[605] http://www.icmunlimited.com/data/media/pdf/2015_bbcwales_march_poll.pdf

[606] https://d25d2506sfb94s.cloudfront.net/cumulus_uploads/document/yooqei4d9h/ITVWales_January15_w.pdf

[607] https://d25d2506sfb94s.cloudfront.net/cumulus_uploads/document/6zuj63gt5x/ITVWalesResults_Dec14_Website.pdf

[608] http://d25d2506sfb94s.cloudfront.net/cumulus_uploads/document/2kgidh3rfa/ITVWalesResults_Sept14_Website.pdf

[609] http://d25d2506sfb94s.cloudfront.net/cumulus_uploads/document/yyeygksd82/ITV_Wales_Results_140701_website.pdf

[610] https://www.bbc.com/news/uk-wales-26378274

[611] http://www.walesonline.co.uk/news/wales-news/eu-referendum-more-people-wales-5076490

[612] http://chronicle.gi/2016/06/support-for-remain-strengthens-in-gibraltar-poll/

[613] http://chronicle.gi/2016/04/gibraltar-will-vote-to-remain-in-eu-poll/

[614] https://d25d2506sfb94s.cloudfront.net/cumulus_uploads/document/2req6g7z50/Internal_180905_Brexit_W.pdf

[615] https://d25d2506sfb94s.cloudfront.net/cumulus_uploads/document/j73mcdcj1w/Times_180904_VI_Trackers_W.pdf

[616] https://d25d2506sfb94s.cloudfront.net/cumulus_uploads/document/64h0v3epuv/Times_180829_VI_Trackers.pdf

[617] http://d25d2506sfb94s.cloudfront.net/cumulus_uploads/document/7xksricmrw/TimesResults_180821_VI_Trackers_w.pdf

[618] https://d25d2506sfb94s.cloudfront.net/cumulus_uploads/document/aapy92s0pl/InternalResults_180814_VI_Trackers_Website.pdf

[619] https://d25d2506sfb94s.cloudfront.net/cumulus_uploads/document/8dvhq299ql/TimesResults_180809_VI_Trackers_w.pdf

[620] https://d25d2506sfb94s.cloudfront.net/cumulus_uploads/document/eswcvhvq60/TimesResults_180723_VI_Trackers_w.pdf

[621] https://d25d2506sfb94s.cloudfront.net/cumulus_uploads/document/j26n4y534f/TimesResults_180717_VI_Trackers_w.pdf

[622] http://d25d2506sfb94s.cloudfront.net/cumulus_uploads/document/phvyn092lg/TimesResults_180711_VI_Brexit.pdf

[623] https://d25d2506sfb94s.cloudfront.net/cumulus_uploads/document/71kfwwcl1a/TimesResults_18_07_09_VI_Trackers_w.pdf

[624] https://d25d2506sfb94s.cloudfront.net/cumulus_uploads/document/hogkt4gv80/TimesResults_180704_VI_Trackers.pdf

[625] https://d25d2506sfb94s.cloudfront.net/cumulus_uploads/document/h3j0yxq1jf/TimesResults_180626_VI_Trackers_w.pdf

626 https://d25d2506sfb94s.cloudfront.net/cumulus_uploads/document/3flpkaywfj/InternalResults_180620_Brexit_w.pdf

627 https://d25d2506sfb94s.cloudfront.net/cumulus_uploads/document/xi51ey4b6h/TimesResults_180619_VI_Trackers_w.pdf

628 https://d25d2506sfb94s.cloudfront.net/cumulus_uploads/document/qzm7srmkvi/TimesResults_180612_VI_Trackers_w.pdf

629 https://d25d2506sfb94s.cloudfront.net/cumulus_uploads/document/z1w1jcj6s9/TimesResults_180605_VI_Trackers_w.pdf

630 https://d25d2506sfb94s.cloudfront.net/cumulus_uploads/document/v0m1echerf/TimesResults_180529_VI_Trackers.pdf

631 http://d25d2506sfb94s.cloudfront.net/cumulus_uploads/document/8vbs3n6auc/TimesResults_180521_VI_Trackers.pdf

632 http://d25d2506sfb94s.cloudfront.net/cumulus_uploads/document/fhgs8okigo/TimesResults_180514_VI_Trackers_w.pdf

633 http://d25d2506sfb94s.cloudfront.net/cumulus_uploads/document/gkdmvglevl/TimesResults_180509_VI_Trackers.pdf

634 https://d25d2506sfb94s.cloudfront.net/cumulus_uploads/document/0322e6admo/TimesResults_180501_VI_Trackers.pdf

635 https://d25d2506sfb94s.cloudfront.net/cumulus_uploads/document/tmi4jdgt4o/TimesResults_180425_VI_Trackers.pdf

636 https://d25d2506sfb94s.cloudfront.net/cumulus_uploads/document/ck1l2ze60y/TimesResults_180417_VI_Trackers.pdf

637 https://d25d2506sfb94s.cloudfront.net/cumulus_uploads/document/jfvhk2jlbk/TimesResults_180410_VI_Trackers.pdf

638 https://d25d2506sfb94s.cloudfront.net/cumulus_uploads/document/o3oayi8z58/TimesResults_180327_VI_Trackers_W.pdf

639 https://d25d2506sfb94s.cloudfront.net/cumulus_uploads/document/1daln9otjj/TimesResults_180305_VI_Trackers_w.pdf

640 https://d25d2506sfb94s.cloudfront.net/cumulus_uploads/document/qi8qzf33xl/TimesResults_180227_VI_Trackers_w.pdf

641 https://d25d2506sfb94s.cloudfront.net/cumulus_uploads/document/um02uga2au/TimesResults_180220_VI_Trackers.pdf

642 https://d25d2506sfb94s.cloudfront.net/cumulus_uploads/document/8d28iz3x5j/TimesResults_180213_VI_Trackers.pdf

643 https://d25d2506sfb94s.cloudfront.net/cumulus_uploads/document/fb1csi9qjl/TimesResults_180205_VI_Trackers.pdf

644 https://d25d2506sfb94s.cloudfront.net/cumulus_uploads/document/yzgd1a3wr0/TimesResults_180129_Trackers_VI.pdf

645 https://d25d2506sfb94s.cloudfront.net/cumulus_uploads/document/srb6u4hbl6/TimesResults_180117_VI_Trackers.pdf

646 https://d25d2506sfb94s.cloudfront.net/cumulus_uploads/document/9xj0batl27/TimesResults_180108_VI_Trackers_w.pdf

647 https://d25d2506sfb94s.cloudfront.net/cumulus_uploads/document/3l97nvvr78/TimesResults_171220_VI_Trackers_w.pdf

648 https://d25d2506sfb94s.cloudfront.net/cumulus_uploads/document/5tu7akhw6z/TimesResults_171211_VI_Trackers_w.pdf

649 https://d25d2506sfb94s.cloudfront.net/cumulus_uploads/document/b22zrk1yft/TimesResults_171205_VI_Trackers_w.pdf

650 http://d25d2506sfb94s.cloudfront.net/cumulus_uploads/document/t7a4lpcsdh/TimesResults_171108_VI_Trackers.pdf

651 http://d25d2506sfb94s.cloudfront.net/cumulus_uploads/document/4y1e1sdlwa/InternalResults_171024_VI.pdf

652 https://d25d2506sfb94s.cloudfront.net/cumulus_uploads/document/mg654q435f/TimesResults_171019_VI_Trackers.pdf

653 https://d25d2506sfb94s.cloudfront.net/cumulus_uploads/document/ptmrf0v5kz/Timesresults_171011_VI_Trackers.pdf

[654] https://d25d2506sfb94s.cloudfront.net/cumulus_uploads/document/xdlp14v0de/
TimesResults_170922_VI_Trackers_W.pdf
[655] https://d25d2506sfb94s.cloudfront.net/cumulus_uploads/document/zc2c6t9xh2/
TimesResults_170831_VI_Trackers_W.pdf
[656] https://d25d2506sfb94s.cloudfront.net/cumulus_uploads/document/hm2d5c6net/
TimesResults_170822_VI_Trackers_W.pdf
[657] https://d25d2506sfb94s.cloudfront.net/cumulus_uploads/document/qwyuvkvik4/
TimesResults_170801_VI_Trackers_W.pdf
[658] https://d25d2506sfb94s.cloudfront.net/cumulus_uploads/document/o6jgxxwn5k/
TimesResults_170719_VI_Trackers_W.pdf
[659] https://d25d2506sfb94s.cloudfront.net/cumulus_uploads/document/3gnej2eb9r/
TimesResults_170711_VI_Trackers_W.pdf
[660] http://d25d2506sfb94s.cloudfront.net/cumulus_uploads/document/hrngg4b5a8/TimesResults_
170622_Trackers_W.pdf
[661] https://d25d2506sfb94s.cloudfront.net/cumulus_uploads/document/9pum7c5c4j/
AnthonyResults_170613_Brexit_W.pdf
[662] https://d25d2506sfb94s.cloudfront.net/cumulus_uploads/document/d8zsb99eyd/
TimesResults_FINAL%20CALL_GB_June2017_W.pdf
[663] https://d25d2506sfb94s.cloudfront.net/cumulus_uploads/document/imdk9bjaff/TimesResults_
170531_VI_Trackers_W.pdf
[664] https://d25d2506sfb94s.cloudfront.net/cumulus_uploads/document/dcfgflapq2/TimesResults_
170525_VI_Trackers_Terrorism_W.pdf
[665] https://d25d2506sfb94s.cloudfront.net/cumulus_uploads/document/txtodyx8bk/
TimesResults_170517_VI_Trackers_W.pdf
[666] http//www.gfk.com
[667] https://d25d2506sfb94s.cloudfront.net/cumulus_uploads/document/fko52um47n/
TimesResults_170510_VI_Trackers_W.pdf
[668] https://d25d2506sfb94s.cloudfront.net/cumulus_uploads/document/dpzz1r8u3o/
TimesResults_170503_VI_Trackers_with_Slogans_W.pdf
[669] https://d25d2506sfb94s.cloudfront.net/cumulus_uploads/document/8nchxu7nac/
TimesResults_170426_VI_Trackers_W.pdf
[670] https://d25d2506sfb94s.cloudfront.net/cumulus_uploads/document/hxfn0j417w/
SundayTimesResults_170421_VI_W.pdf
[671] https://d25d2506sfb94s.cloudfront.net/cumulus_uploads/document/04xxn42p3e/
TimesResults_170419_VI_Trackers_GE_W.pdf
[672] https://d25d2506sfb94s.cloudfront.net/cumulus_uploads/document/zs2ifb9u3g/TimesResults_
170413_VI_Trackers.pdf
[673] https://d25d2506sfb94s.cloudfront.net/cumulus_uploads/document/x4597y9nuj/
TimesResults_170406_VI_Trackers_W.pdf
[674] https://d25d2506sfb94s.cloudfront.net/cumulus_uploads/document/glo3xaqerh/
InternalResults_170327_AnthonyBrexitQs_W.pdf
[675] https://d25d2506sfb94s.cloudfront.net/cumulus_uploads/document/tksnufybtn/
TimesResultsResults_170321_VI_Immigration_W.pdf
[676] http://www.gfk.com/en-gb/insights/press-release/new-gfk-political-poll-shows-jeremy-
corbyn-as-unpopular-as-president-trump-among-gb-adults/
[677] https://d25d2506sfb94s.cloudfront.net/cumulus_uploads/document/f2a3lpb26v/
TimesResults_170314_VI_ScottishIndy_W.pdf
[678] http://opinium.co.uk/wp-content/uploads/2017/03/Polling-Matters-100317-Tables.xlsx
[679] https://d25d2506sfb94s.cloudfront.net/cumulus_uploads/document/z1elxz48n9/
TimesResults_170228_VI_Trackers_W.pdf
[680] https://d25d2506sfb94s.cloudfront.net/cumulus_uploads/document/2jolkn11ps/TimesResults_
170222_VI_Trackers_W.pdf
[681] https://d25d2506sfb94s.cloudfront.net/cumulus_uploads/document/auuihsqsjz/TimesResults_
170213_VI_Trackers_W.pdf
[682] https://d25d2506sfb94s.cloudfront.net/cumulus_uploads/document/3hy4qn55vq/
TimesResults_170131_VI_Trackers_W.pdf

[683] https://d25d2506sfb94s.cloudfront.net/cumulus_uploads/document/xalfiwu0ed/
TimesResults_170118_VI_Trackers_MaySpeech_W.pdf

[684] http://opinium.co.uk/wp-content/uploads/2017/01/Polling-Matters-200117-Tables.xlsx

[685] https://d25d2506sfb94s.cloudfront.net/cumulus_uploads/document/17ahuih4ja/TimesResults_
170110_VI_Trackers_W.pdf

[686] https://d25d2506sfb94s.cloudfront.net/cumulus_uploads/document/ipnfdlzlvq/TimesResults_
170104_VI_Trackers_W.pdf

[687] https://d25d2506sfb94s.cloudfront.net/cumulus_uploads/document/upts71m2pt/
TimesResults_161219_VI_Trackers_EndofYear_W.pdf

[688] https://d25d2506sfb94s.cloudfront.net/cumulus_uploads/document/bg3iahmaw8/
TimesResults_161205_VI_Trackers_W.pdf

[689] https://d25d2506sfb94s.cloudfront.net/cumulus_uploads/document/wemnebeo20/
TimesResults_161129_VI_Trackers_W.pdf

[690] https://d25d2506sfb94s.cloudfront.net/cumulus_uploads/document/j91v52gjon/YGArchive-
171116-VotingIntention.pdf

[691] https://d25d2506sfb94s.cloudfront.net/cumulus_uploads/document/qq4bax70w5/
InternalResults_161020_Brexit_W.pdf

[692] https://d25d2506sfb94s.cloudfront.net/cumulus_uploads/document/vohvzlss3c/TimesResults_
161012_VI_Trackers_W.pdf

[693] https://d25d2506sfb94s.cloudfront.net/cumulus_uploads/document/36cem5h375/
TimesResults_160914_VI_Trackers_W.pdf

[694] https://d25d2506sfb94s.cloudfront.net/cumulus_uploads/document/jb4y2me4q0/
TimesResults_160831_VI_Trackers_W.pdf

[695] https://d25d2506sfb94s.cloudfront.net/cumulus_uploads/document/ocn4lf00me/
TimesResults_160823_VI_Trackers_W.pdf

[696] https://d25d2506sfb94s.cloudfront.net/cumulus_uploads/document/jmwlsfmd1k/
TimesResults_160817_VI_Trackers.pdf

[697] https://d25d2506sfb94s.cloudfront.net/cumulus_uploads/document/5yng128b6c/
TimesResults_160809_VI_Trackers_Website.pdf

[698] //en.wikipedia.org/w/index.php?title=Template:Brexit/Post-referendum_opinion_polling:
_Right-Wrong&action=edit

[699] https://d3n8a8pro7vhmx.cloudfront.net/in/pages/15665/attachments/original/1537174959/
Under_25s_180911_(1).xls?1537174959

[700] https://www.survation.com/boris-johnson-theresa-may-leadership-survation-for-daily-mail-
september-8th/

[701] https://d25d2506sfb94s.cloudfront.net/cumulus_uploads/document/zr7v0xtbbl/180905_
GMB%20publish.pdf

[702] https://d25d2506sfb94s.cloudfront.net/cumulus_uploads/document/fnzvd8ui1k/180905_
Unison%20publish.pdf

[703] https://d25d2506sfb94s.cloudfront.net/cumulus_uploads/document/gv8pa368st/180905_
Unite%20publish.pdf

[704] https://d25d2506sfb94s.cloudfront.net/cumulus_uploads/document/dx1qnnwoym/
PeoplesVoteResults_180914_Merge_Newspapers.pdf

[705] https://d25d2506sfb94s.cloudfront.net/cumulus_uploads/document/30tafmcnkc/PeoplesVote_
LondonMerge_180905_w.pdf

[706] https://www.survation.com/wp-content/uploads/2018/09/Final-Tables-1.pdf#page=9

[707] https://d25d2506sfb94s.cloudfront.net/cumulus_uploads/document/tu6k2mk5wu/
PeoplesVoteResults_Wave2_180821_GB_website.pdf

[708] https://d3n8a8pro7vhmx.cloudfront.net/in/pages/15508/attachments/original/1535728901/
Gender_tracker_poll.xls?1535728901

[709] https://d25d2506sfb94s.cloudfront.net/cumulus_uploads/document/zbgd2452w0/NE%
20final%20180822%20published.pdf

[710] https://d25d2506sfb94s.cloudfront.net/cumulus_uploads/document/92ofbq76tq/
PeoplesVoteResults_180824_Wales_w.pdf

[711] https://d25d2506sfb94s.cloudfront.net/cumulus_uploads/document/tulxamz6op/PeoplesVote_
Scotland_180814_w.pdf

[712] http://www.tns-bmrb.co.uk/sites/tns-bmrb/files/Brexit%20Barometer%20tables%20-%20Aug%202018.pdf#page=15

[713] http://www.bmgresearch.co.uk/wp-content/uploads/2018/08/EU-VOTE-INTENTION_BMG-RESREACH_200818.xlsx

[714] https://d25d2506sfb94s.cloudfront.net/cumulus_uploads/document/4e1ciqwvua/Copy%20of%20PV%20results%20180807%20day%20one_w.pdf#page=1

[715] https://d25d2506sfb94s.cloudfront.net/cumulus_uploads/document/zl36ojndti/Brexit%20SW%20180807_w.pdf

[716] https://d25d2506sfb94s.cloudfront.net/cumulus_uploads/document/h8fq3xim2u/TimesResults_180726_SecondReferendum_w.pdf

[717] https://d25d2506sfb94s.cloudfront.net/cumulus_uploads/document/7fjrhub42v/Eurotrack_180724_w.pdf

[718] https://d25d2506sfb94s.cloudfront.net/cumulus_uploads/document/vxuhlu27eg/SundayTimesResults_180720_for_web.pdf#page=11

[719] http://www.deltapoll.co.uk/wp-content/uploads/2018/07/SunSunday_Brexit_Deltapoll180714.pdf#page=26

[720] http://www.tns-bmrb.co.uk/sites/tns-bmrb/files/July%202018%20-%20Brexit%20barometer.pdf#page=7

[721] https://survation.com/wp-content/uploads/2018/07/MoS-final-tables.pdf#page=16

[722] https://d25d2506sfb94s.cloudfront.net/cumulus_uploads/document/htfwdi02df/WelshBarometer_June18_w.pdf#page=11

[723] https://d25d2506sfb94s.cloudfront.net/cumulus_uploads/document/07kprp1z3i/Results_180627_representedbyparty_w.pdf#page=5

[724] https://survation.com/wp-content/uploads/2018/06/GMB-Final-Tables.pdf#page=10

[725] http://d25d2506sfb94s.cloudfront.net/cumulus_uploads/document/hit82jf794/HandelsblattResults_June18_Topline_client_w.pdf

[726] http://survation.com/wp-content/uploads/2018/06/VI-Tables-8-June.xlsx

[727] http://www.deltapoll.co.uk/wp-content/uploads/2018/06/Brext-Trade-180601_FT.pdf#page=1

[728] https://survation.com/wp-content/uploads/2018/05/VI-Tables-May-11th-2.xlsx

[729] https://d25d2506sfb94s.cloudfront.net/cumulus_uploads/document/d2armsga9e/Eurotrack_April18.pdf

[730] https://survation.com/wp-content/uploads/2018/04/Foreign-Affairs-Poll-MoS-140418.pdf#page=12

[731] https://www.icmunlimited.com/wp-content/uploads/2018/04/Voting-9thApr18_pv-only-BPC.pdf

[732] https://d25d2506sfb94s.cloudfront.net/cumulus_uploads/document/cqvaei0d1b/BestForBritain_Results_180406_w.pdf

[733] http://www.bmgresearch.co.uk/wp-content/uploads/2018/03/CONFIDENTIAL-BMG-INDEPENDENT-POLL-26MAR18.xlsx

[734] https://d25d2506sfb94s.cloudfront.net/cumulus_uploads/document/xrtsizcs11/WelshBarometer_March18_w.pdf#page=9

[735] https://www.orb-international.com/wp-content/uploads/2018/03/ORB-International-Website-11-Mar.pdf#page=1

[736] http://www.comresglobal.com/wp-content/uploads/2018/03/Sunday-Mirror_Feb-2018_Brexit-poll-006.pdf#page=21

[737] https://d25d2506sfb94s.cloudfront.net/cumulus_uploads/document/zck4tfs6qs/HandelsblattResults_Feb18_Topline_client_w.pdf#page=2

[738] https://interactive.news.sky.com/Feb2018_MainTabs.pdf#page=12

[739] https://survation.com/wp-content/uploads/2018/02/Full-Voting-Intention-Tables-310118.pdf#page=10

[740] https://d25d2506sfb94s.cloudfront.net/cumulus_uploads/document/28wjbaqogx/Eurotrack_January2018_w.pdf

[741] https://interactive.news.sky.com/Jan2018_MainTabs.pdf

[742] https://www.icmunlimited.com/wp-content/uploads/2018/01/ICM-Guardian-Brexit-Questions-BPC-Regions.pdf#page=12

743 http://www.comresglobal.com/wp-content/uploads/2018/01/Daily-Mirror_January-2018-poll_EURef-1.pdf

744 https://www.icmunlimited.com/wp-content/uploads/2017/12/Voting-11thDec17_pv-only-BPC-1.pdf

745 http://www.bmgresearch.co.uk/independent-poll-shift-toward-remain-at-height-of-brexit-negotiation-tensions/

746 http://survation.com/wp-content/uploads/2017/12/Final-MoS-041217.pdf

747 https://d25d2506sfb94s.cloudfront.net/cumulus_uploads/document/0aof66rdfs/WelshBarometerResults_November17_w.pdf#page=9

748 https://d25d2506sfb94s.cloudfront.net/cumulus_uploads/document/rm6tlufhf4/HandelsblattResults_Topline_Nov2017_w.pdf

749 http://d25d2506sfb94s.cloudfront.net/cumulus_uploads/document/kvc16fv4mg/Eurotrack_Oct2017_topline.pdf

750 http://opinium.co.uk/wp-content/uploads/2017/10/OP9180-Observer-Brexit-Tables.xlsx

751 http://survation.com/wp-content/uploads/2017/10/Final-survation-VI-2c0d4h7.pdf

752 http://survation.com/wp-content/uploads/2017/09/Mail-On-Sunday-September-23rd-Data-Tables-1.pdf

753 http://opinium.co.uk/wp-content/uploads/2017/09/VI-19-09-17-Tables.xls

754 http://survation.com/wp-content/uploads/2017/09/Labour-Party-Conference-Poll-2017.pdf

755 http://www.bmgresearch.co.uk/wp-content/uploads/2017/09/BMG-Independent-EU-Referendum-VI-22092017.xlsx

756 http://opinium.co.uk/wp-content/uploads/2017/09/VI-12-09-2017-Tables.xls

757 https://d25d2506sfb94s.cloudfront.net/cumulus_uploads/document/lh9i9z3rmj/WelshBarometerResults_170907_W2.pdf#page=9

758 http://opinium.co.uk/wp-content/uploads/2017/07/VI-15-08-2017.xls

759 http://www.bmgresearch.co.uk/independentbmg-poll-public-remain-split-latest-eu-referendum-poll/

760 https://d25d2506sfb94s.cloudfront.net/cumulus_uploads/document/tjhnf4nw4u/Eurotrack_July2017_1W.pdf

761 http://survation.com/wp-content/uploads/2017/07/Final-MoS-Brexit-Poll-Tables-140717GOCH-1c0d2h4.pdf

762 http://survation.com/wp-content/uploads/2017/07/Final-Survation-UK-Attitudes-Tracker-280617MMDLLMTDC-1c0d1h7-chd.pdf

763 https://d25d2506sfb94s.cloudfront.net/cumulus_uploads/document/gd8a4jt3m3/Eurotrack_June17_1W.pdf

764 http://www.panelbase.com/media/polls/W10470w8tablesforpublication260617.pdf

765 https://survation.com/wp-content/uploads/2017/06/Final-Post-Election-GMB-Tables-160617TOCH-1c0d0h5.pdf#page=10

766 http://survation.com/wp-content/uploads/2017/06/Post-Election_Poll_June10.pdf

767 http://www.panelbase.com/media/polls/W10470w7tablesforpublication.pdf

768 http://www.panelbase.com/media/polls/W10470w6tablesforpublication010617.pdf

769 https://d25d2506sfb94s.cloudfront.net/cumulus_uploads/document/jfwm990f42/WelshBarometer_May31st_W.pdf

770 http://www.tns-bmrb.co.uk/sites/tns-bmrb/files/KPUK%20-%20final%20tables%20-%2031.5.2017.pdf

771 https://d25d2506sfb94s.cloudfront.net/cumulus_uploads/document/345h3a4u4f/WelshBarometer_May21st_wellsagenew_w.pdf#page=5

772 http://www.panelbase.com/media/polls/W10470w4tablesforpublication150517.pdf

773 http://www.panelbase.com/media/polls/W10407w3tablesforpublication090517.pdf

774 https://d25d2506sfb94s.cloudfront.net/cumulus_uploads/document/dcj280pkfd/WelshBarometer_May7th_WestminsterVI_agenew.pdf#page=2

775 https://www.drg.global/wp-content/uploads/2018/01/W10470w2tablesforpublication020517.pdf#page=5

776 https://www.drg.global/wp-content/uploads/2018/01/W10470maintablesforpublication240417.pdf#page=3

[777] https://d25d2506sfb94s.cloudfront.net/cumulus_uploads/document/a7ywnfqqk9/
WelshBarometerResults_April17_WestminsterVI_W_wellsagenew.pdf#page=2

[778] https://d25d2506sfb94s.cloudfront.net/cumulus_uploads/document/q70yr6i56a/Eurotrack_
March_Trackers_W.pdf

[779] https://d25d2506sfb94s.cloudfront.net/cumulus_uploads/document/di1fktb0k8/January_
Eurotrack_W.pdf

[780] https://d25d2506sfb94s.cloudfront.net/cumulus_uploads/document/s289nens6c/Eurotrack_
December_Website.pdf

[781] http://www.comresglobal.com/wp-content/uploads/2016/11/DailyMirror_Poll_Tables-
281116.pdf#page=5

[782] https://d25d2506sfb94s.cloudfront.net/cumulus_uploads/document/8e293lt9rf/Eurotrack_
October_Trackers_Website.pdf

[783] http://www.bmgresearch.co.uk/wp-content/uploads/2016/11/CONFIDENTIAL-BMG-POLL-
OCTOBER-data-tables-031116.pdf#page=21

[784] http://survation.com/wp-content/uploads/2016/10/Final-Brexit-Tables-101016JMDLL-
1c0d0h2.pdf#page=4

[785] https://d25d2506sfb94s.cloudfront.net/cumulus_uploads/document/n8t7herkqe/Eurotrack_
Results_September_Website.pdf#page=2

[786] https://d25d2506sfb94s.cloudfront.net/cumulus_uploads/document/smow6e2p43/
MegaEurotrackerResults_AugustSeptember2016_Toplines.pdf#page=17

[787] https://d25d2506sfb94s.cloudfront.net/cumulus_uploads/document/eokci16bwr/Eurotrack_
July_Website.pdf

[788] https://d25d2506sfb94s.cloudfront.net/cumulus_uploads/document/zei5f6pxt4/GB_Results_
Full_Website.pdf#page=2

[789] http://www.bmgresearch.co.uk/wp-content/uploads/2016/07/CONFIDENTIAL-BMG-
EVENING-STANDARD-POST-BREXIT-RECONTACT-SURVEY_1.pdf#page=15

[790] http://ourinsight.opinium.co.uk/sites/ourinsight.opinium.co.uk/files/vi_28_06_2016_v2.pdf#
page=218

[791] //en.wikipedia.org/w/index.php?title=Template:Brexit/Post-referendum_opinion_polling:
_Remain-Leave&action=edit

[792] https://d25d2506sfb94s.cloudfront.net/cumulus_uploads/document/yu0hckb8v4/PV%
20results%20180807%20day%20one_w.pdf#page=7

[793] https://interactive.news.sky.com/brexitshifttabs.pdf#page=5

[794] https://d25d2506sfb94s.cloudfront.net/cumulus_uploads/document/kgfdyeogty/
SundayTimesResults_180720_for_web.pdf#page=12

[795] https://d25d2506sfb94s.cloudfront.net/cumulus_uploads/document/vv29cv0a94/
TimesResults_SecondRef_180717_w.pdf#page=3

[796] //en.wikipedia.org/w/index.php?title=Template:Brexit/Post-referendum_opinion_polling:
_Three_options&action=edit

[797] https://www.ncpolitics.uk/wp-content/uploads/2018/04/bloomberg-Brexit-2018-04-18.pdf

[798] https://d25d2506sfb94s.cloudfront.net/cumulus_uploads/document/2req6g7z50/Internal_
180905_Brexit_W.pdf#page=5

[799] https://d25d2506sfb94s.cloudfront.net/cumulus_uploads/document/zr7v0xtbbl/180905_
GMB%20publish.pdf#page=6

[800] https://d25d2506sfb94s.cloudfront.net/cumulus_uploads/document/fnzvd8ui1k/180905_
Unison%20publish.pdf#page=6

[801] https://d25d2506sfb94s.cloudfront.net/cumulus_uploads/document/gv8pa368st/180905_
Unite%20publish.pdf#page=6

[802] https://d25d2506sfb94s.cloudfront.net/cumulus_uploads/document/dx1qnnwoym/
PeoplesVoteResults_180914_Merge_Newspapers.pdf#page=16

[803] https://d25d2506sfb94s.cloudfront.net/cumulus_uploads/document/30tafmcnkc/PeoplesVote_
LondonMerge_180905_w.pdf#page=5

[804] https://d25d2506sfb94s.cloudfront.net/cumulus_uploads/document/wre3lp7die/JeremyVine_
Results_180901_website.pdf

[805] https://d25d2506sfb94s.cloudfront.net/cumulus_uploads/document/92ofbq76tq/
PeoplesVoteResults_180824_Wales_w.pdf#page=4

[806] https://d25d2506sfb94s.cloudfront.net/cumulus_uploads/document/vv29cv0a94/TimesResults_SecondRef_180717_w.pdf

[807] https://d25d2506sfb94s.cloudfront.net/cumulus_uploads/document/phvyn092lg/TimesResults_180711_VI_Brexit.pdf#page=8

[808] https://d25d2506sfb94s.cloudfront.net/cumulus_uploads/document/sfiq16wfpm/ConservativeMemberResults_180709_w.pdf#page=19

[809] https://d25d2506sfb94s.cloudfront.net/cumulus_uploads/document/wb96oamqk2/OpenBritainResults_180630_UniteMembers.pdf

[810] https://d25d2506sfb94s.cloudfront.net/cumulus_uploads/document/fhgs8okigo/TimesResults_180514_VI_Trackers_w.pdf#page=6

[811] https://www.opinium.co.uk/wp-content/uploads/2018/05/VI-01-05-2018-Tables-Website.xlsx

[812] https://www.opinium.co.uk/wp-content/uploads/2018/04/OP10067-Open-Britain-Europe-Tracker-Online-Tables.xlsx

[813] https://d25d2506sfb94s.cloudfront.net/cumulus_uploads/document/jfvhk2jlbk/TimesResults_180410_VI_Trackers.pdf#page=6

[814] https://d25d2506sfb94s.cloudfront.net/cumulus_uploads/document/onal3cjvfu/InternalResults_180327_BrexitQuestions_for_website.pdf#page=10

[815] https://d25d2506sfb94s.cloudfront.net/cumulus_uploads/document/1daln9otjj/TimesResults_180305_VI_Trackers_w.pdf#page=8

[816] https://www.icmunlimited.com/wp-content/uploads/2018/01/ICM-Guardian-Brexit-Questions-BPC-Regions.pdf#page=22

[817] https://d25d2506sfb94s.cloudfront.net/cumulus_uploads/document/sty43olvol/TimesResultss_180110_SecondReferendum_w.pdf

[818] https://d25d2506sfb94s.cloudfront.net/cumulus_uploads/document/5tu7akhw6z/TimesResults_171211_VI_Trackers_w.pdf#page=5

[819] https://survation.com/wp-content/uploads/2017/12/Final-MoS-041217.pdf#page=15

[820] https://d25d2506sfb94s.cloudfront.net/cumulus_uploads/document/4y1e1sdlwa/InternalResults_171024_VI.pdf#page=6

[821] https://d25d2506sfb94s.cloudfront.net/cumulus_uploads/document/xdlp14v0de/TimesResults_170922_VI_Trackers_W.pdf#page=5

[822] https://d25d2506sfb94s.cloudfront.net/cumulus_uploads/document/ndu320grio/TheTimes_170913_BrexitQs_W.pdf#page=5

[823] https://d25d2506sfb94s.cloudfront.net/cumulus_uploads/document/lh9i9z3rmj/WelshBarometerResults_170907_W2.pdf#page=7

[824] https://survation.com/wp-content/uploads/2017/07/Final-MoS-Brexit-Poll-Tables-140717GOCH-1c0d2h4.pdf#page=27

[825] https://www.opinium.co.uk/wp-content/uploads/2017/07/Time-Series-of-Second-EU-Referendum-Polling.xlsx

[826] https://survation.com/wp-content/uploads/2017/07/Final-Survation-UK-Attitudes-Tracker-280617MMDLLMTDC-1c0d1h7-chd.pdf#page=19

[827] https://survation.com/wp-content/uploads/2017/06/Final-MoS-Brexit-Tables-1c0d0h5.pdf#page=5

[828] https://survation.com/wp-content/uploads/2017/06/Final-Post-Election-GMB-Tables-160617TOCH-1c0d0h5.pdf#page=17

[829] https://d25d2506sfb94s.cloudfront.net/cumulus_uploads/document/zebfsayat4/SundayTimesResults_170428_W.pdf#page=8

[830] https://d25d2506sfb94s.cloudfront.net/cumulus_uploads/document/tz9dxy8t29/SundayTimesResults_170421_VI_W.pdf#page=8

[831] http://www.bmgresearch.co.uk/wp-content/uploads/2016/07/CONFIDENTIAL-BMG-EVENING-STANDARD-POST-BREXIT-RECONTACT-SURVEY_1.pdf#page=9

[832] https://ig.ft.com/sites/brexit-polling/

[833] https://www.bbc.co.uk/news/uk-politics-eu-referendum-36271589

[834] https://www.telegraph.co.uk/news/2016/03/23/eu-referendum-poll-tracker-and-odds/

[835] http://whatukthinks.org/eu/opinion-polls/poll-of-polls/

[836] //en.wikipedia.org/w/index.php?title=Template:United_Kingdom_in_the_European_Union&action=edit

[837] http://www.express.co.uk/news/politics/647200/EU-referendum-MEPs-European-Parliament-Britain-no-second-renegotiation-Boris-Johnson

[838] //en.wikipedia.org/w/index.php?title=Template:UK_Referendums&action=edit

[839] //en.wikipedia.org/w/index.php?title=Template:United_Kingdom_constitutional_formation&action=edit

[840] //en.wikipedia.org/w/index.php?title=Template:United_Kingdom_in_the_European_Union&action=edit

[841] European Union (Referendum) Bill, Bill 11 of 2013–14 Research Paper 13/41 (page 1), 28 June 2013; accessdate 5 July 2014.

[842] "Yes to an EU Referendum: Green MP Calls for Chance to Build a Better Europe" https//web.archive.org. Green Party of England and Wales. Retrieved 26 April 2014.

[843] DUP manifesto, 2015 http://dev.mydup.com/images/uploads/publications/DUP_Manifesto_2015_LR.pdf, mydup.com. Retrieved 28 May 2016.

[844] "The EU" http://www.respectparty.org/the-eu . Respect Party. Retrieved 26 April 2014.

[845] European Union Referendum Act 2015 http://www.bailii.org/uk/legis/num_act/2015/ukpga_201536_en_1.html in BAILII.

[846] Act No. 2016-01 (Legislation Number (L.N.) 2016/034, as amended by L.N. 2016/035, L.N. 2016/082 and L.N. 2016/120.

[847] House of Commons Library BRIEFING PAPER Number 07212, 3 June 2015. This content is released under the Open Parliament Licence v3.0.

[848] *R (Miller) v Brexit Secretary* EWHC 2768 (Admin) http://www.bailii.org/ew/cases/EWHC/Admin/2016/2768.html#para105 at para. 106.

[849] //en.wikipedia.org/w/index.php?title=United_Kingdom_European_Union_membership_referendum,_2016&action=edit

[850] Sir James Dyson: 'So if we leave the EU no one will trade with us? Cobblers...' https://www.telegraph.co.uk/men/thinking-man/sir-james-dyson-so-if-we-leave-the-eu-no-one-will-trade-with-us/ A. Pearson, *The Daily Telegraph* (London), 10 June 2016

[851] P. Spence, Pound falls below $1.39 as economists warn Brexit could hammer households https://www.telegraph.co.uk/business/2016/02/24/pound-falls-below-139-as-economists-warn-brexit-could-hammer-hou, *The Daily Telegraph*, Finance, 24 February 2016.

[852] M. Holehouse, "Czech Republic 'will follow Britain out of EU'" https://www.telegraph.co.uk/news/worldnews/europe/czechrepublic/12170994/Czechs-will-follow-Britain-out-of-EU.html, *The Daily Telegraph*, 23 February 2016

[853] " Exclusive: Britain 'could liberate Europe again' by voting for Brexit and sparking populist revolution https://www.telegraph.co.uk/news/2016/05/21/britain-could-liberate-europe-again-by-voting-for-brexit-and-spa/". *The Daily Telegraph* (London). 22 May 2016.

[854] EU referendum: Swedish foreign minister warns Brexit 'could cause break-up of European Union' https//www.independent.co.uk L. Dearden, *The Independent* (London), 11 June 2016

[855] Staying in EU 'best hope' for UK's future say ex-US Treasury secretaries https://www.bbc.com/news/uk-politics-eu-referendum-36087583, BBC News (20 April 2016).

[856] P. Spence, Bank of England can make Brexit work, says Mark Carney https://www.telegraph.co.uk/finance/bank-of-england/11987883/Bank-of-England-can-make-Brexit-work-says-Mark-Carney.html, *The Daily Telegraph*, 11 November 2015.

[857] Mark Carney: EU exit is 'biggest domestic risk' https://www.bbc.co.uk/news/business-35751919 BBC News, 8 March 2016

[858] The impact of immigration on occupational wages: evidence from Britain http://www.bankofengland.co.uk/research/Documents/workingpapers/2015/swp574.pdf S. Nickell and J. Saleheen, Staff Working Paper No. 574, Bank of England (2015)

[859] EU referendum: UK could be better off leaving if TTIP passes, Joseph Stiglitz says https://www.independent.co.uk/news/business/news/eu-referendum-joseph-stiglitz-ttip-labour-transatlantic-trade-investment-partnership-a6907806.html, H. Sheffield, *The Independent*, 2 March 2016

[860] https://d25d2506sfb94s.cloudfront.net/cumulus_uploads/document/640yx5m0rx/On_the_Day_FINAL_poll_forwebsite.pdf

[861] EU Referendum: Record number of migrants arrive in UK without jobs, as Boris Johnson accuses David Cameron of "deeply damaging" faith in democracy https://www.telegraph.co.uk/news/2016/05/26/eu-referendum-lord-ashcroft-poll-finds-nearly-two-thirds-of-vote/ L. Hughes, *The Daily Telegraph* (London), 26 May 2016

[862] Migration Statistics Quarterly Report: May 2016 https://www.ons.gov.uk/peoplepopulationandcommunity/populationandmigration/internationalmigration/bulletins/migrationstatisticsquarterlyreport/may2016 ONS, 26 May 2016

[863] NHS could be part-privatised if UK and EU agree controversial TTIP trade deal, expert warns https//www.independent.co.uk I. Johnston, *The Independent* (London), 21 February 2016

[864] TTIP: Government caves in to cross-party alliance of Eurosceptic MPs demanding NHS is protected from controversial deal https//www.independent.co.uk O. Wright, *The Independent* (London), 19 May 2016

[865] EU referendum: 25 Tory rebels plot to vote down Queen's Speech as Labour MP caught calling voter 'horrible racist' on campaign trail https://www.telegraph.co.uk/news/2016/05/19/downing-street-accused-of-vicious-briefings-against-brexit-campa/ L. Hughes, *The Daily Telegraph*, 19 May 2016

[866] TTIP symbolises the worst of global capitalism. Cameron pushes it at his peril https://www.theguardian.com/commentisfree/2016/may/20/david-cameron-support-ttip N. Dearden, *The Guardian*, 20 May 2016

[867] Jeremy Corbyn Vows To Veto 'TTIP' EU-US Free Trade Deal Amid Privatisation Fears http://www.huffingtonpost.co.uk/entry/jeremy-corbyn-ttip-free-trade-deal-eu-us-eu-referendum-brexit_uk_57500b9ce4b040e3e8190ef3 P. Waugh, *The Huffington Post*, 2 June 2016

[868] The EU Referendum Pits Big Business Against Working People – That's Why I'm Voting 'Leave' http://www.huffingtonpost.co.uk/john-mills/eu-referendum-vote-leave_b_10391536.html J. Mills, *The Huffington Post*, 10 June 2016

[869] European Referendum Act 2015 http://www.legislation.gov.uk/ukpga/2015/36/section/11/ enacted Section 11.

[870] http//www.electoralcommission.org.uk

[871] Give Britain another Brexit referendum, says Sadiq Khan https://www.theguardian.com/politics/2018/sep/15/sadiq-khan-new-referendum-peoples-vote-labour-corbyn *The Observer*

[872] ' DATA PROTECTION ACT 1998 SUPERVISORY POWERS OF THE INFORMATION COMMISSIONER MONETARY PENALTY NOTICE https://ico.org.uk/media/action-weve-taken/mpns/1624135/mpn-better-for-the-country-20160509.pdf (9 May 2016).

[873] ' EU campaign firm fined for sending spam texts https://ico.org.uk/about-the-ico/news-and-events/news-and-blogs/2016/05/eu-campaign-firm-fined-for-sending-spam-texts/' (11 May 2016).

[874] Jamie Doward, Carole Cadwalladr and Alice Gibbs, ' Watchdog to launch inquiry into misuse of data in politics https://www.theguardian.com/technology/2017/mar/04/cambridge-analytics-data-brexit-trump', *The Observer* (4 March 2017).

[875] Carole Cadwalladr, ' The great British Brexit robbery: how our democracy was hijacked https://www.theguardian.com/technology/2017/may/07/the-great-british-brexit-robbery-hijacked-democracy', *The Observer* (Sunday 7 May 2017).

[876] Steve Rosenberg, EU referendum: What does Russia gain from Brexit?' https://www.bbc.co.uk/news/world-europe-36629146, BBC News (26 June 2016).

[877] Joe Watts, Highly probable' that Russia interfered in Brexit referendum, Labour MP says https://www.independent.co.uk/news/uk/politics/russian-interference-brexit-highly-probable-referendum-hacking-putin-a7472706.html, *Independent* (13 December 2016).

[878] Jake Kanter & Adam Bienkov, Labour MPs think the government is hiding info about Russia interfering with Brexit http://uk.businessinsider.com/labour-mp-ben-bradshaw-suspicious-russian-interference-brexit-2017-2?op=1, 'Business Insider *(23 February 2016)*.

[879] Rajeev Syal, Brexit: foreign states may have interfered in vote, report says https://www.theguardian.com/politics/2017/apr/12/foreign-states-may-have-interfered-in-brexit-vote-report-says, *Guardian* (12 April 2017).

[880] David D. Kirkpatrick, Parliament Asks Twitter About Russian Meddling in Brexit Vote https://www.nytimes.com/2017/11/03/world/europe/uk-twitter-russia-brexit.html, *New York Times* (3 November 2017).

[881] 13,500-strong Twitter bot army disappeared shortly after EU referendum, research reveals https://www.city.ac.uk/news/2017/october/13,500-strong-twitterbot-army-disappeared-shortly-after-eu-referendum,-research-reveals, City, University of London (20 October 2017).

[882] Oliver Wright, Lucy Fisher & Sean O'Neill, Watchdog starts inquiry into Russia Brexit links https://www.thetimes.co.uk/article/watchdog-starts-inquiry-into-russia-brexit-links-lnf7h86t0, *The Times* (2 November 2017).

[883] Election watchdog probes spending by EU referendum campaign groups https://www.telegraph.co.uk/news/2017/02/24/election-watchdog-probes-spending-eu-referendum-campaign-groups/, *The Daily Telegraph* (24 February 2017).

[884] Electoral Commission statement on investigation into Leave.EU http//www.electoralcommission.org.uk, Electoral Commission (21 April 2017).

[885] O'Toole, Fintan (16 May 2017) "What connects Brexit, the DUP, dark money and a Saudi prince?" https://www.irishtimes.com/opinion/what-connects-brexit-the-dup-dark-money-and-a-saudi-prince-1.3083586. *The Irish Times*.

[886] Henry Mance, Brexit-backer Arron Banks to be investigated over campaign spending https://www.ft.com/content/308043a6-c026-382a-9e4a-5e694a89dd72, *Financial Times* (1 November 2017).

[887] Holly Watt, Electoral Commission to investigate Arron Banks' Brexit donations: Watchdog to consider whether leave campaigner broke campaign finance rules in run-up to EU referendum https://www.theguardian.com/politics/2017/nov/01/electoral-commission-to-investigate-arron-banks-brexit-donations-eu-referendum, *The Guardian* (1 November 2017).

[888] Henry Mance, Arron Banks investigated for Brexit campaign spending https://www.ft.com/content/8d532c46-beff-11e7-b8a3-38a6e068f464, *Financial Times* (1 November 2017).

[889] Maidment, Jack (19 December 2017) "Liberal Democrats fined £18,000 for breaching campaign finance rules relating to EU referendum" https://www.telegraph.co.uk/news/2017/12/19/liberal-democrats-fined-18000-breaching-campaign-finance-rules/amp/. *The Daily Telegraph*.

[890] " What role did Cambridge Analytica play in the Brexit vote? http://www.dw.com/en/what-role-did-cambridge-analytica-play-in-the-brexit-vote/a-43151460". *Deutsche Welle*. 27 March 2018.

[891] "Campaigners and political parties fined for breaching political finance rules" https//www.electoralcommission.org.uk. The Electoral Commission. 15 May 2018

[892] https://dx.doi.org/10.1080/07036330008429077

[893] //doi.org/10.1080/07036330008429077

[894] https://dx.doi.org/10.1080/07036330601144177

[895] //doi.org/10.1080/07036330601144177

[896] http://archive.intereconomics.eu/year/2016/2/the-economics-of-a-brexit/

[897] //doi.org/10.1007/s10272-016-0574-2

[898] https://digital.library.lse.ac.uk/collections/brexit/2016

[899] https://curlie.org/Society/Government/Multilateral/Regional/European_Union/

[900] http://aboutmyvote.co.uk/uk-voters

[901] https://www.bbc.co.uk/news/politics/eu_referendum

[902] http://www.bbc.co.uk/programmes/b07k08xd

[903] http://www.bbc.co.uk/programmes/b07pgw3k

[904] //en.wikipedia.org/w/index.php?title=Template:United_Kingdom_in_the_European_Union&action=edit

[905] Lead EU referendum campaigns named https://www.bbc.co.uk/news/uk-politics-36038672 BBC, 13 April 2016

[906] http://www.electoralcommission.org.uk/__data/assets/pdf_file/0004/200857/designation-summary-of-assessment-scores-for-leave-outcome.pdf

[907] https://digital.library.lse.ac.uk/collections/brexit/organisation

[908] https://www.theguardian.com/politics/2017/may/06/brexit-donor-peter-hargreaves-rights-eu-nationals-theresa-may

[909] http://www.mandyboylett.co.uk/

438

[910,] DATA PROTECTION ACT 1998 SUPERVISORY POWERS OF THE INFORMATION COMMISSIONER MONETARY PENALTY NOTICE https://ico.org.uk/media/action-weve-taken/mpns/1624135/mpn-better-for-the-country-20160509.pdf (9 May 2016).

[911,] ' EU campaign firm fined for sending spam texts https://ico.org.uk/about-the-ico/news-and-events/news-and-blogs/2016/05/eu-campaign-firm-fined-for-sending-spam-texts/' (11 May 2016).

[912] Jamie Doward, Carole Cadwalladr and Alice Gibbs, ' Watchdog to launch inquiry into misuse of data in politics https://www.theguardian.com/technology/2017/mar/04/cambridge-analytics-data-brexit-trump', *The Observer* (4 March 2017).

[913] Carole Cadwalladr, ' The great British Brexit robbery: how our democracy was hijacked https://www.theguardian.com/technology/2017/may/07/the-great-british-brexit-robbery-hijacked-democracy', *The Observer* (Sunday 7 May 2017).

[914] Electoral Commission statement on investigation into Leave.EU http//www.electoralcommission.org.uk (21 April 2017).

[915] //en.wikipedia.org/w/index.php?title=Template:United_Kingdom_in_the_European_Union&action=edit

[916] European Referendum Act 2015 http://www.legislation.gov.uk/ukpga/2015/36/section/11/ enacted Section 11.

[917] Electoral Commission http//www.electoralcommission.org.uk, 'Report of an investigation' (July 2018)

[918] Information Commissioner's Office, 'Investigation into the use of data analytics in political campaigns: Investigation Update' (10 July 2018 https://ico.org.uk/media/action-weve-taken/2259371/investigation-into-data-analytics-for-political-purposes-update.pdf)

[919] House of Commons Culture, Media and Sport Select Committee, 'Disinformation and 'fake news': Interim Report' (July 2018) ch 5, Russian influence in political campaigns https://publications.parliament.uk/pa/cm201719/cmselect/cmcumeds/363/36308.htm#_idTextAnchor033.

[920] 'Grounds for Judicial Review' in *Wilson v Prime Minister* (2018 http://www.croftsolicitors.com/wp-content/uploads/2018/08/239484-Grounds-for-Judicial-Review-and-Statement-of-Facts.pdf). See further, E McGaughey, ' Could Brexit be void? https//poseidon01.ssrn.com (2018) SSRN, also summarised on ' Verfassungsblog https://verfassungsblog.de/if-vote-leave-broke-the-law-could-brexit-be-void/

[921] EU referendum results http//www.electoralcommission.org.uk Electoral Commission

[922] http//www.electoralcommission.org.uk

[923] Vote totals for Belfast are based on the returns from the four parliamentary constituencies in Belfast. These include areas in districts outside the City of Belfast

[924] https://moderngov.lambeth.gov.uk/documents/s82579/EUREFResultsforLambeth.pdf?platform=hootsuite

[925] https://www.cambridge.gov.uk/sites/default/files/cambridge_turnout_totals_-_june_2016.pdf

[926] http://www.stockport.gov.uk/2013/2986/59933/1244950/eureferendum-results2016

[927] Electoral Commission http//www.electoralcommission.org.uk, 'Report of an investigation' (July 2018)

[928] Information Commissioner's Office, 'Investigation into the use of data analytics in political campaigns: Investigation Update' (10 July 2018 https://ico.org.uk/media/action-weve-taken/2259371/investigation-into-data-analytics-for-political-purposes-update.pdf)

[929] House of Commons Culture, Media and Sport Select Committee, 'Disinformation and 'fake news': Interim Report' (July 2018) (July 2018) ch 5, Russian influence in political campaigns https://publications.parliament.uk/pa/cm201719/cmselect/cmcumeds/363/36308.htm#_idTextAnchor033.

[930] 'Grounds for Judicial Review' in *Wilson v Prime Minister* (2018 http://www.croftsolicitors.com/wp-content/uploads/2018/08/239484-Grounds-for-Judicial-Review-and-Statement-of-Facts.pdf). See further, E McGaughey, ' Could Brexit be void? https//poseidon01.ssrn.com (2018) SSRN, also summarised on ' Verfassungsblog https://verfassungsblog.de/if-vote-leave-broke-the-law-could-brexit-be-void/

931 "We need to take back control": Brexit whistleblower Shahmir Sanni on why there must be a new EU referendum https://www.newstatesman.com/politics/uk/2018/03/we-need-take-back-control-brexit-whistleblower-shahmir-sanni-why-there-must-be *New Statesman*

932 //en.wikipedia.org/w/index.php?title=Template:United_Kingdom_in_the_European_Union&action=edit

933 The end of British austerity starts with Brexit https://www.theguardian.com/commentisfree/2016/apr/14/british-austerity-brexit-budget-nhs-disability-benefits-property J. Redwood, *The Guardian*, 14 April 2016

934 Brexit: Here are the three major winners from a weak pound right now http://www.ibtimes.co.uk/brexit-fallout-rolls-royce-glaxosmithkline-experian-are-big-winners-weak-pound-1569154 E. Shing, International Business Times, 6 July 2016

935 'The Brexit vote is starting to have major negative consequences' – experts debate the data https://www.theguardian.com/politics/2017/mar/24/brexit-vote-experts-data-bank-of-england *The Guardian*

936 Crisis looms for social policy agenda as Brexit preoccupies Whitehall https://www.theguardian.com/global/2017/apr/09/focus-brexit-obliterates-social-policy-agenda *The Guardian*

937 Rebel MPs form cross-party group to oppose hard Brexit https://www.theguardian.com/politics/2017/jul/10/rebel-mps-form-cross-party-group-to-oppose-hard-brexit *The Guardian*

938 *Daily Politics*, BBC2, 11 July 2016

939 The Brexit resistance: 'It's getting bigger all the time' https://www.theguardian.com/politics/2017/jan/10/brexit-resistance-getting-bigger-pro-europe-eu-referendum-organising-groups *The Guardian*

940 What British people think about Brexit now https://www.bbc.co.uk/news/uk-45520517 *BBC*

941 "Frankly, if people watching think that they have voted and there is now going to be zero immigration from the EU, they are going to be disappointed ... you will look in vain for anything that the Leave campaign said at any point that ever suggested there would ever be any kind of border closure or drawing up of the drawbridge."

942 "It is entirely up to the departing member state to trigger article 50, by issuing formal notification of intention to leave: no one, in Brussels, Berlin or Paris, can force it to. But equally, there is nothing in article 50 that obliges the EU to start talks – including the informal talks the Brexit leaders want – before formal notification has been made. 'There is no mechanism to compel a state to withdraw from the European Union,' said Kenneth Armstrong, professor of European law at Cambridge University.... 'The notification of article 50 is a formal act and has to be done by the British government to the European council,' an EU official told Reuters."

943 The statement also added: "We stand ready to launch negotiations swiftly with the United Kingdom regarding the terms and conditions of its withdrawal from the European Union. Until this process of negotiations is over, the United Kingdom remains a member of the European Union, with all the rights and obligations that derive from this. According to the Treaties which the United Kingdom has ratified, EU law continues to apply to the full to and in the United Kingdom until it is no longer a Member."

944 "There needs to be a notification by the country concerned of its intention to leave (the EU), hence the request (to British Prime Minister David Cameron) to act quickly."

945 Quote from the PM's spokesperson Originally headed by Oliver Letwin for the first eight days

946 " EU referendum result: Sinn Fein's Martin McGuinness calls for border poll on united Ireland after Brexit https//www.independent.co.uk". *The Independent*. 24 June 2016.

947 Brexit: TUC issues new EU referendum warning to May https://www.bbc.co.uk/news/uk-politics-45464115 *BBC*

948 EU referendum result must be respected, says John McDonnell https://www.bbc.co.uk/news/uk-politics-36680463 BBC News, 1 July 2016

949 ' DATA PROTECTION ACT 1998 SUPERVISORY POWERS OF THE INFORMATION COMMISSIONER MONETARY PENALTY NOTICE https://ico.org.uk/media/action-weve-taken/mpns/1624135/mpn-better-for-the-country-20160509.pdf (9 May 2016).

950 ' EU campaign firm fined for sending spam texts https://ico.org.uk/about-the-ico/news-and-events/news-and-blogs/2016/05/eu-campaign-firm-fined-for-sending-spam-texts/' (11 May 2016).

[951] Jamie Doward, Carole Cadwalladr and Alice Gibbs, ' Watchdog to launch inquiry into misuse of data in politics https://www.theguardian.com/technology/2017/mar/04/cambridge-analytics-data-brexit-trump', *The Observer* (4 March 2017).

[952] Carole Cadwalladr, ' The great British Brexit robbery: how our democracy was hijacked https://www.theguardian.com/technology/2017/may/07/the-great-british-brexit-robbery-hijacked-democracy', *The Observer* (Sunday 7 May 2017).

[953] Electoral Commission statement on investigation into Leave.EU http//www.electoralcommission.org.uk (21 April 2017).

[954] S Rosenberg, 'EU referendum: What does Russia gain from Brexit?' (26 June 2016) BBC News https://www.bbc.co.uk/news/world-europe-36629146

[955] *Highly probable' that Russia interfered in Brexit referendum, Labour MP says' (13 December 2016) Independent https://www.independent.co.uk/news/uk/politics/russian-interference-brexit-highly-probable-referendum-hacking-putin-a7472706.html*

[956] J Kanter and A Bienkov, 'Labour MPs think the government is hiding info about Russia interfering with Brexit' (23 February 2016) Business Insider http://uk.businessinsider.com/labour-mp-ben-bradshaw-suspicious-russian-interference-brexit-2017-2?op=1

[957] F O'Toole, 'What connects Brexit, the DUP, dark money and a Saudi prince?' (16 May 2017) *Irish Times*

[958] https://www.telegraph.co.uk/brexit

[959] https://www.independent.co.uk/topic/brexit

[960] https://www.bbc.co.uk/news/politics/uk_leaves_the_eu

[961] http://www.bbc.co.uk/programmes/b006qng8/episodes/player

[962] http://blogs.lse.ac.uk/brexitvote

[963] http://www.gov.uk/government/organisations/department-for-exiting-the-european-union

[964] http://www.parliament.uk/business/news/european-union

[965] https://curlie.org/Regional/Europe/United_Kingdom/Society_and_Culture/Issues/European_Union/Brexit

[966] 'UK investigates Brexit campaign funding amid speculation of Russian meddling' (1 November 2017) Reuters https://www.reuters.com/article/us-britain-eu-investigation/uk-investigates-brexit-campaign-funding-amid-speculation-of-russian-meddling-idUSKBN1D157I. 'The UK's election watchdog has now questioned Google over Russian meddling in Brexit' (28 November 2017) Business Insider http://www.businessinsider.de/electoral-commission-probe-google-over-russian-meddling-in-brexit-2017-11?r=UK&IR=T. P Wintour, 'Russian bid to influence Brexit vote detailed in new US Senate report' (10 January 2018) Guardian https://www.theguardian.com/world/2018/jan/10/russian-influence-brexit-vote-detailed-us-senate-report

[967] E McGaughey, ' Could Brexit be void? http//poseidon01.ssrn.com (2018) SSRN, also ' Verfassungsblog https://verfassungsblog.de/if-vote-leave-broke-the-law-could-brexit-be-void/

[968] C Montgomery, H Mountfield, B Silverstone, IN THE MATTER OF THE POLITICAL PARTIES, ELECTIONS AND REFERENDUMS ACT 2000 AND THE EUROPEAN UNION REFERENDUM ACT 2015 AND IN THE MATTER OF REFERENDUM EXPENSES https://drive.google.com/file/d/1jGir3IvUt9te6EMYwurBSHP9sWQFagxY/view (20 March 2018)

[969] Vince Cable MP: [https://twitter.com/vincecable/status/1008369953752469504 Twitter Account, 17 June 2018, 8:25 am. "Powerful piece by @carolecadwalla in the @observer on how treason has been quietly accepted because implications are too big. #Brexit not just a mess but fundamentally illegitimate."

[970] S Rosenberg, 'EU referendum: What does Russia gain from Brexit?' (26 June 2016) BBC News https://www.bbc.co.uk/news/world-europe-36629146

[971] P Hammond, Alternatives to EU Membership https://www.gov.uk/government/speeches/alternatives-to-eu-membership (2 March 2016) "the EU already either has, or is negotiating, trade deals with all the biggest Commonwealth countries, and none of our allies wants us to leave the EU. Not Australia, not New Zealand, not Canada, not the US. In fact, the only country who would like us to leave the EU is Russia. That should tell us all we need to know."

972 *Highly probable' that Russia interfered in Brexit referendum, Labour MP says' (13 December 2016) Independent https://www.independent.co.uk/news/uk/politics/russian-interference-brexit-highly-probable-referendum-hacking-putin-a7472706.html*

973 J Kanter and A Bienkov, 'Labour MPs think the government is hiding info about Russia interfering with Brexit' (23 February 2016) *Business Insider* http://uk.businessinsider.com/labour-mp-ben-bradshaw-suspicious-russian-interference-brexit-2017-2?op=1

974 ' Nigel Farage is 'person of interest' in FBI investigation into Trump and Russia https://www.theguardian.com/politics/2017/jun/01/nigel-farage-is-person-of-interest-in-fbi-investigation-into-trump-and-russia' (2 June 2017) *The Guardian*

975 'MPs order Facebook to hand over evidence of Russian election meddling' (24 October 2017) Telegraph https://www.telegraph.co.uk/technology/2017/10/24/mps-order-facebook-hand-evidence-russian-election-meddling/

976 T Snyder, *The Road to Unfreedom: Russia, Europe, America* (Penguin Random House 2018) 105. C Cadwalladr, 'Brexit, the ministers, the professor and the spy: how Russia pulls strings in UK' (4 Nov 2017) Guardian https://www.theguardian.com/politics/2017/nov/04/brexit-ministers-spy-russia-uk-brexit. S Walters, 'Putin's link to Boris and Gove's Brexit 'coup' revealed: Tycoon who netted millions from Russian gas deal funds think tank that helped write the ministers letter demanding May take a tougher stance on leaving the EU' (25 November 2017) Mail on Sunday http://www.dailymail.co.uk/news/article-5117547/Putins-link-Boris-Goves-Brexit-coup-revealed.html

977 Democratic Congressmen request information about possible Russian interference in "Brexit" vote https://rubengallego.house.gov/media-center/press-releases/democratic-congressmen-request-information-about-possible-russian (12 December 2017)

978 M Burgess, 'Facebook claims Russia paid for 3 ads around Brexit – costing 73p' (13 December 2017) Wired https://www.wired.co.uk/article/russia-brexit-parliamentary-inquiry-damian-collins

979 P Wintour, 'Russian bid to influence Brexit vote detailed in new US Senate report' (10 January 2018) Guardian https://www.theguardian.com/world/2018/jan/10/russian-influence-brexit-vote-detailed-us-senate-report

980 US Committee on Foreign Relations, Minority Report, 'Putin's Asymmetric Assault on Democracy in Russia and Europe: Implications for U.S. National Security' (2018 https://www.foreign.senate.gov/imo/media/doc/FinalRR.pdf)

981 C Cadwalladr, 'Arron Banks 'met Russian officials multiple times before Brexit vote'' (9 June 2018) Guardian. C Cadwalladr and P Jukes, ' Leave.EU faces new questions over contacts with Russia https://www.theguardian.com/uk-news/2018/jun/16/leave-eu-russia-arron-banks-andy-wigmore' (16 June 2018) Guardian. C Cadwalladr, ' Arron Banks, Brexit and the Russia connection https://www.theguardian.com/uk-news/2018/jun/16/arron-banks-nigel-farage-leave-brexit-russia-connection' (16 June 2018) *The Observer*.

982 [https://twitter.com/vincecable/status/1008369953752469504 Vince Cable Twitter Account, 17 June 2018, 8:25 am. "Powerful piece by @carolecadwalla in the @observer on how treason has been quietly accepted because implications are too big. #Brexit not just a mess but fundamentally illegitimate."

983 House of Commons Culture, Media and Sport Select Committee, 'Disinformation and 'fake news': Interim Report' (July 2018) (July 2018) ch 5, Russian influence in political campaigns https://publications.parliament.uk/pa/cm201719/cmselect/cmcumeds/363/36308.htm#_idTextAnchor033. See also, E McGaughey, ' Could Brexit be void? https//poseidon01.ssrn.com (2018) SSRN

984 http://openaccess.city.ac.uk/18143/1/SSRN-id3034051.pdf

985 https://www.theguardian.com/world/2017/nov/14/how-400-russia-run-fake-accounts-posted-bogus-brexit-tweets

986 https://www.wired.co.uk/article/russia-brexit-parliamentary-inquiry-damian-collins

987 https//poseidon01.ssrn.com

988 https://verfassungsblog.de/if-vote-leave-broke-the-law-could-brexit-be-void/

989 https://publications.parliament.uk/pa/cm201719/cmselect/cmcumeds/363/36308.htm#_idTextAnchor033

990 https://www.foreign.senate.gov/imo/media/doc/FinalRR.pdf

991 //en.wikipedia.org/w/index.php?title=Template:United_Kingdom_in_the_European_ Union&action=edit

992 //en.wikipedia.org/w/index.php?title=Template:United_Kingdom_constitutional_ formation&action=edit

993 Article 50(3) of the Treaty on European Union.

994 72% of remaining member states are required for the agreement to pass the Council of the European Union, rather than the usual 55%, as the proposal does not come from the Commission or the high representative.<ref>

995 Eva-Maria Poptcheva, *Article 50 TEU: Withdrawal of a Member State from the EU*, Briefing Note for European Parliament.(Note: "The content of this document is the sole responsibility of the author and any opinions expressed therein do not necessarily represent the official position of the European Parliament.")http://www.europarl.europa.eu/RegData/etudes/BRIE/2016/ 577971/EPRS_BRI(2016)577971_EN.pdf

996 Scottish parliament rejects Brexit in non-binding vote http://www.dw.com/en/scottish-parliament-rejects-brexit-in-non-binding-vote/a-37448650, *DW*, 7 February 2017

997 Trading places / Negotiating post-Brexit deals. Economist, 4–10 February 2017, page 25

998 "there is a growing consensus that [...] the government should delay invoking Article 50 of the Lisbon Treaty, starting the clock on a maximum two-year divorce negotiation, until early 2017 at the earliest. That is provoking alarm in many European capitals, where there is an equally clear consensus that Article 50 should be invoked as soon as possible."

999 https//www.gov.uk

1000 Government cannot trigger Brexit without MPs' backing, court told https://www.theguardian. com/politics/2016/oct/13/government-cannot-trigger-brexit-without-mps-backing-court-told-article-50 *The Guardian*, 13 October 2016

1001 Setback for Theresa May as high court says MPs must approve Brexit https://www.theguardian. com/politics/2016/nov/03/parliament-must-trigger-brexit-high-court-rules *The Guardian*, 3 November 2016

1002 "Fresh Brexit challenge in high court over leaving single market and EEA" https://www. theguardian.com/politics/2016/dec/29/fresh-brexit-challenge-high-court-leaving-single-market-eea, *The Guardian*, 29 December 2016

1003 "Brexit legal challenge: High Court throws out new case over single market vote for MPs" https://www.telegraph.co.uk/news/2017/02/03/brexit-legal-challenge-high-court-throws-new-case-single-market/. *The Daily Telegraph*. 3 February 2017

1004 House of Commons Hansard "European Union (Notification of Withdrawal) Bill debate" https://hansard.parliament.uk/Commons/2017-01-31/debates/C2852E15-21D3-4F03-B8C3-F7E05F2276B0/EuropeanUnion(NotificationOfWithdrawal)Bill

1005 Reuters: Irish court to consider Brexit reversibility case on May 31 https://www.reuters.com/ article/us-britain-eu-reverse-idUSKBN17Q1TG

1006 Original: "die Erklärung über die Absicht eines Austritts im Unionsrecht noch selbst gar keine Kündigung wäre, sondern jederzeit bis längstens zur Unanwendbarkeit der Verträge widerrufen oder für gegenstandslos erklärt werden kann".

1007 http://www.barcouncil.org.uk/media/508513/the_brexit_papers.pdf

1008 https://www.gov.uk/government/uploads/system/uploads/attachment_data/file/588948/The_ United_Kingdoms_exit_from_and_partnership_with_the_EU_Web.pdf

1009 https://www.gov.uk/government/uploads/system/uploads/attachment_data/file/604079/Prime_ Ministers_letter_to_European_Council_President_Donald_Tusk.pdf

1010 https://www.gov.uk/government/publications/the-great-repeal-bill-white-paper

1011 Dominic Raab was appointed as Secretary of State for Exiting the European Union on 9 July 2018. The position was previously held by David Davis.

1012 //en.wikipedia.org/w/index.php?title=Template:United_Kingdom_in_the_European_ Union&action=edit

1013 Election 2015: Conservative manifesto at-a-glance (15th April 2015) https://www.bbc.co.uk/ news/election-2015-32302062

1014 Conservatives election manifesto 2015 - the key points (14th April 2015) https://www. theguardian.com/politics/2015/apr/14/conservatives-election-manifesto-2015-the-key-points

[1015] https://www.gov.uk/government/uploads/system/uploads/attachment_data/file/589191/The_United_Kingdoms_exit_from_and_partnership_with_the_EU_Web.pdf

[1016] https://www.bbc.com/news/uk-politics-45363827

[1017] http://www.euronews.com/2018/08/31/both-sides-in-brexit-say-they-are-determined-to-reach-a-deal-this-autumn

[1018]

[1019]

[1020] https://www.ft.com/content/6cb2ca28-b053-11e8-99ca-68cf89602132

[1021] https://www.bbc.com/news/uk-politics-45396475

[1022] https://services.parliament.uk/Bills/2017-19/taxationcrossbordertrade/stages.html

[1023] https://services.parliament.uk/bills/2017-19/taxationcrossbordertrade.html

[1024] https://www.bloomberg.com/news/articles/2018-09-05/germany-u-k-said-to-drop-key-brexit-ask-easing-path-to-deal

[1025] https://www.thesun.co.uk/news/7186474/pound-soars-as-angela-merkel-opens-the-door-to-a-brexit-deal-by-backing-down-on-europes-red-lines/

[1026] https://www.reuters.com/article/uk-germany-czech-brexit/merkel-says-eu-britain-must-negotiate-brexit-to-ensure-close-ties-idUSKCN1LL1MN

[1027] https://www.bbc.com/news/uk-politics-45427669

[1028] https://www.telegraph.co.uk/politics/2018/09/07/michel-barnier-concedes-brexit-bill-could-linked-uk-eu-trade/

[1029] https://www.bloomberg.com/news/articles/2018-09-07/barnier-puts-positive-spin-on-may-s-brexit-plan-pound-rises

[1030] https://www.reuters.com/article/uk-britain-eu-hammond/britains-hammond-says-he-is-sure-brexit-deal-will-be-reached-by-october-deadline-idUSKCN1LN1X4

[1031] https://www.bbc.com/news/uk-politics-45566205

[1032] https://www.publications.parliament.uk/pa/ld201617/ldselect/ldeucom/125/12506.htm#_idTextAnchor024

[1033] *Conservative and Unionist Party Manifesto 2017*. 18 May 2017. pp35-36. "The negotiations will undoubtedly be tough, and there will be give and take on both sides, but we continue to believe that no deal is better than a bad deal for the UK. But we will enter the negotiations in a spirit of sincere cooperation and committed to getting the best deal for Britain."

[1034] Police chiefs: no-deal Brexit would mean loss of crime-fighting tools https://www.theguardian.com/uk-news/2018/sep/18/police-chiefs-no-deal-brexit-would-mean-loss-crime-fighting-tools *The Guardian*

[1035] No-deal Brexit 'could make policing harder' https://www.bbc.co.uk/news/uk-45561527 *BBC*

[1036] http://www.parliament.uk/business/news/european-union

[1037] http://www.gov.uk/government/organisations/department-for-exiting-the-european-union

[1038] http://www.planforbritain.gov.uk

[1039] http://europa.eu/european-union/about-eu/countries/member-countries/unitedkingdom_en#brexit

[1040] https://ec.europa.eu/commission/brexit-negotiations_en

[1041] https://ec.europa.eu/commission/brexit-negotiations/negotiating-documents-article-50-negotiations-united-kingdom_en

[1042] https://ec.europa.eu/info/brexit/brexit-preparedness/preparedness-notices_en

[1043] http://www.consilium.europa.eu/en/policies/eu-uk-after-referendum/

[1044] http://www.oxfordscholarship.com/view/10.1093/acprof:oso/9780199683123.001.0001/acprof-9780199683123

[1045] http://jackofkent.com/brexit-negotiations-resource-page/

[1046] https://services.parliament.uk/Bills/2017-19/europeanunionwithdrawal.html

[1047] https://www.legislation.gov.uk/ukpga/2018/16/enacted

[1048] https://www.legislation.gov.uk/ukpga/2018/16

[1049] //en.wikipedia.org/w/index.php?title=Template:United_Kingdom_in_the_European_Union&action=edit

[1050] //en.wikipedia.org/w/index.php?title=Template:United_Kingdom_constitutional_formation&action=edit

[1051] Summary https://researchbriefings.parliament.uk/ResearchBriefing/Summary/CBP-8079.

[1052] *Factbox - Britain's Brexit legislation: What is left to do ahead of EU exit?* Reuters, 17 April 2018.https://uk.reuters.com/article/uk-britain-eu-factbox/factbox-britains-brexit-legislation-what-is-left-to-do-ahead-of-eu-exit-idUKKBN1HO2SA

[1053] Haulage Permits and Trailer Registration Act 2018 http://www.legislation.gov.uk/ukpga/2018/19/contents/enacted/data.htm

[1054] "Haulage permits and trailer registration", Department for Transport, 16 May 2018.https://www.gov.uk/government/consultations/haulage-permits-and-trailer-registration

[1055] https://services.parliament.uk/Bills/2017-19/taxationcrossbordertrade/stages.html

[1056] https://services.parliament.uk/bills/2017-19/taxationcrossbordertrade.html

[1057] https://services.parliament.uk/bills/2017-19/taxationcrossbordertrade.html

[1058] //en.wikipedia.org/w/index.php?title=European_Union_(Withdrawal)_Act_2018&action=edit

[1059] *Citations*:

[1060] http://www.legislation.gov.uk/ukpga/2018/16/contents/enacted/data.htm

[1061] http://www.legislation.gov.uk/ukpga/2018/16/pdfs/ukpgaen_20180016_en.pdf

[1062] https//assets.publishing.service.gov.uk

[1063] http://www.legislation.gov.uk/anaw/2018/3/enacted

[1064] https://researchbriefings.parliament.uk/ResearchBriefing/Summary/CBP-8289

[1065] https://www.gov.uk/government/publications/government-statement-following-cabinet-away-day-at-chequers

[1066] https://www.bbc.co.uk/news/uk-politics-44761416

[1067] https://services.parliament.uk/bills/2017-19/europeanunionwithdrawal.html

[1068] https://publications.parliament.uk/pa/bills/cbill/2017-2019/0005/en/18005en.pdf

[1069] https://publications.parliament.uk/pa/ld201719/ldselect/ldconst/19/1902.htm

[1070] https://www.gov.uk/government/uploads/system/uploads/attachment_data/file/604516/Great_repeal_bill_white_paper_accessible.pdf

[1071] https://www.gov.uk/government/uploads/system/uploads/attachment_data/file/604514/Great_repeal_bill_white_paper_print.pdf

[1072] https://researchbriefings.parliament.uk/ResearchBriefing/Summary/CBP-8079

[1073] https://www.planforbritain.gov.uk/

[1074] The end of British austerity starts with Brexit https://www.theguardian.com/commentisfree/2016/apr/14/british-austerity-brexit-budget-nhs-disability-benefits-property J. Redwood, *The Guardian*, 14 April 2016

[1075] "The Brexit vote is starting to have major negative consequences' – experts debate the data https://www.theguardian.com/politics/2017/mar/24/brexit-vote-experts-data-bank-of-england *The Guardian*

[1076] Dairy products 'may become luxuries' after UK leaves EU https://www.theguardian.com/politics/2018/jul/18/dairy-products-may-become-luxuries-after-uk-leaves-eu *The Guardian*

[1077] Brexit: Here are the three major winners from a weak pound right now http://www.ibtimes.co.uk/brexit-fallout-rolls-royce-glaxosmithkline-experian-are-big-winners-weak-pound-1569154 E. Shing, International Business Times, 6 July 2016

[1078] European Central Bank (July 2017) "The international role of the euro" https://www.ecb.europa.eu/pub/pdf/other/ecb.euro-international-role-201707.pdf?5155295783d0b744ab5aa5a85d8674c1. European Central Bank. p. 28.

[1079] Chatsworth Communications (April 6, 2016) "London's leading position as a USD 2.2 trillion hub for FX trading would be harmed by a Brexit, according to poll of currency market professionals" http//www.chatsworthcommunications.com. Chatsworth Communications.

[1080] No-deal Brexit would hit UK economy, says IMF https://www.bbc.co.uk/news/business-45546785 *BBC*

[1081] IMF chief highlights recession risk of no-deal Brexit https://www.theguardian.com/business/2018/sep/17/imf-christine-lagarde-theresa-may-no-deal-brexit-uk-economy *The Guardian*

[1082] //en.wikipedia.org/w/index.php?title=Template:United_Kingdom_in_the_European_Union&action=edit

[1083] http://www.allenovery.com/Brexit-Law/Documents/Macro/EU/AO_BrexitLaw_-_EEA_Membership_Jul_2016.PDF "A&O Legal Opinion on EEA membership"

[1084] "Free Movement of Capital" http://www.efta.int/eea/policy-areas/capital, "EFTA". Retrieved 24 June 2016.

[1085] "Free Movement of Persons" http://www.efta.int/eea/policy-areas/persons, "EFTA". Retrieved 24 June 2016.

[1086] Grose, Thomas. "Anger at Immigration Fuels the UK's Brexit Movement" https://www.usnews.com/news/best-countries/articles/2016-06-16/anger-at-immigration-fuels-the-uks-brexit-movement, *U.S. News & World Report*, Washington, D.C., 16 June 2016. Retrieved 24 June 2016.

[1087] http://www.allenovery.com/Brexit-Law/Documents/Macro/EU/AO_BrexitLaw_-_EEA_Membership_Jul_2016.PDF

[1088] EU and Switzerland agree on free movement https://euobserver.com/justice/136398 *EUobserver*, 22 December 2016

[1089] http//www.electoralcommission.org.uk

[1090] Act No. 2016-01 (Legislation Number (L.N.) 2016/034, as amended by L.N. 2016/035, L.N. 2016/082 and L.N. 2016/120.

[1091] https://www.express.co.uk/news/uk/787061/britain-could-cripple-spain-rear-admiral-chris-parry-gibraltar-royal-navy-commander

[1092] //en.wikipedia.org/w/index.php?title=Template:Politics_of_the_European_Union&action=edit

[1093] //en.wikipedia.org/w/index.php?title=Impact_of_Brexit_on_the_European_Union&action=edit

[1094] From trade to migration - how Brexit may hit the EU economy https://uk.reuters.com/article/uk-britain-eu-economy-europe/from-trade-to-migration-how-brexit-may-hit-the-eu-economy-idUKKCN0ZA0KE, Reuters 24 June 2016

[1095] Brexit's (minimal) impact on the EU budget https://www.politico.eu/article/eu-budget-barnier-davis-brexits-minimal-impact/, Politico Europe, 23 November 2017

[1096]

[1097]

[1098] UK to veto EU 'defence union' https://euobserver.com/institutional/135134, EUObserver 17 September 2016

[1099] Time for the Sleeping Beauty to wake http://www.ecfr.eu/article/commentary_time_for_the_sleeping_beauty_to_wake, ECFR 15/NOV/17

[1100] Angela Merkel: EU cannot completely rely on US and Britain any more https://www.theguardian.com/world/2017/may/28/merkel-says-eu-cannot-completely-rely-on-us-and-britain-any-more-g7-talks, theguardian 28 May 2017

[1101] UK call for 'multicurrency' EU triggers ECB alarm https://www.ft.com/content/4ada3ce0-9aaa-11e5-be4f-0abd1978acaa, Financial Times 4 December 2015

[1102] The Great British Euro Conundrum https://global.handelsblatt.com/opinion/the-great-british-euro-conundrum-544800, Handelsblatt 20 June 2016

[1103] What a fair relationship between 'euro ins' and 'euro outs' could look like http://blogs.lse.ac.uk/europpblog/2016/01/26/what-a-fair-relationship-between-euro-ins-and-euro-outs-could-look-like/, London School of Economics 26 January 2016

[1104]

[1105] Ireland: The forgotten frontier of Brexit https://www.telegraph.co.uk/business/2017/03/04/ireland-forgotten-frontier-brexit/ Peter Foster, Europe Editor, The Daily Telegraph, 4 March 2017

[1106] The Economic Impact of Brexit on UK and EU Trade https://medium.com/@rchen8/the-economic-impact-of-brexit-on-uk-and-eu-trade-464dd090f92e, Richard Chen 14 June 2017

[1107] Brexit: the impact on the UK and the EU https://www.global-counsel.co.uk/sites/default/files/special-reports/downloads/Global_Counsel_Impact_of_Brexit.pdf, Global Counsel 23 June 2015

[1108] Brexit 'puts NI peace process at risk' - Hain https://www.bbc.co.uk/news/uk-northern-ireland-41150206 Mark Devenport BBC News NI Political Editor, 5 September 2017

[1109] What are the options for the Irish border after Brexit? https://www.channel4.com/news/factcheck/factcheck-what-are-the-options-for-the-irish-border-after-brexit, Georgina Lee, Channel 4, 29 Nov 2017

[1110] Brexit: Customs union would solve Irish border, Carwyn Jones says https://www.bbc.co.uk/news/av/uk-wales-politics-42230485/brexit-customs-union-would-solve-irish-border-carwyn-jones-says First Minister of Wales, Carwyn Jones, speaking to BBC Wales, 04 Dec 2017

[1111] Brexit deal allows for three different types of Irish Border https://www.irishtimes.com/news/ireland/irish-news/brexit-deal-allows-for-three-different-types-of-irish-border-1.3320497 Katy Hayward, The Irish Times, 8 Dec 2017

[1112] UK immigration latest: Net migration falls by more than 106,000 after Brexit vote as EU citizens flee https//www.independent.co.uk, BBC 30 November 2017

[1113] Poland hopes Brexit guides star natives home https://www.politico.eu/article/poland-hopes-brexit-will-lead-its-native-stars-home/, Politico 2 January 2018

[1114] EU agencies: The road to 'douze points' https://euobserver.com/europe-in-review/139716, EUObserver 28 December 2017

[1115] UK loses space data center to Spain amid post-Brexit security concerns https://www.politico.eu/article/uk-loses-space-data-center-to-spain-amid-post-brexit-security-concerns/, Politico 18 January 2018

[1116] MEPs want to reduce the size of the European Parliament http://www.europarl.europa.eu/news/en/press-room/20170911IPR83572/meps-want-to-reduce-the-size-of-the-european-parliament, European Parliament 12 September 2017

[1117] EU parliament wary of pan-European lists https://euobserver.com/institutional/138970, EU Observer 12 September 2017

[1118] http://www.europarl.europa.eu/RegData/etudes/IDAN/2017/583117/IPOL_IDA%282017%29583117_EN.pdf

[1119] Support for the EU on the rise since Brexit vote ... even in the UK https://www.theguardian.com/world/2016/nov/21/support-for-the-eu-on-the-rise-since-brexit-vote-even-in-the-uk, The Guardian 21 November 2016

[1120] European support for EU surges in wake of Brexit vote https://www.ft.com/content/78b4ded6-51ce-11e7-bfb8-997009366969, Financial Times 15 June 2017

[1121]

[1122] https://www.washingtonpost.com/news/monkey-cage/wp/2016/03/11/its-not-just-trump-authoritarian-populism-is-rising-across-the-west-heres-why/, Washington Post 11 March 2016

[1123] English will not be an official EU language after Brexit, says senior MEP https://www.politico.eu/article/english-will-not-be-an-official-eu-language-after-brexit-senior-mep/, Politico Europe 27 June 2016

[1124] English language will NOT be banned from EU after Brexit, despite claims https://www.independent.ie/irish-news/english-language-will-not-be-banned-from-eu-after-brexit-despite-claims-34840768.html, independent.ie 28 June 2016

[1125] Parliamentary Questions: Language in the EU, 31 May 2017 http://www.europarl.europa.eu/sides/getDoc.do?type=WQ&reference=E-2017-003658&language=EN

[1126] Brexit: English is losing its importance in Europe, says Juncker https://www.theguardian.com/politics/2017/may/05/brexit-english-is-losing-its-importance-in-europe-says-juncker, The Guardian 5 May 2017

[1127] Bundestag MPs want EU staff to use German more after Brexit http://www.euractiv.com/section/uk-europe/news/bundestag-mps-want-eu-staff-to-use-german-more-after-brexit/, Euractiv 10 August 2017

[1128] English will remain the working language of the EU after Brexit https://www.irishtimes.com/opinion/english-will-remain-the-working-language-of-the-eu-after-brexit-1.2725840, The Irish Times 18 July 2016

[1129] Britain is leaving the EU, but its language will stay https://www.economist.com/news/europe/21721861-despite-jean-claude-junckers-joke-anglophones-should-rest-easy-britain-leaving-eu-its, The Economist 13 May 2017

[1130] English in a post-Brexit European Union http://onlinelibrary.wiley.com/doi/10.1111/weng.12264/full by Marko Modiano, World Englishes 19 September 2017

[1131] Brexit could create a new 'language' – Euro-English https://www.independent.co.uk/news/science/brexit-latest-news-language-euro-english-uk-leave-eu-european-union-a7957001.html, The Independent 20 September 2017

[1132] Consolidated version of the Treaty on European Union http://eur-lex.europa.eu/legal-content/EN/TXT/?uri=celex%3A12012M%2FTXT, Eurlex

[1133] Consolidated version of the Treaty on the Functioning of the European Union http://eur-lex.europa.eu/legal-content/EN/TXT/?uri=celex%3A12012E%2FTXT, Eurlex

[1134] Regulation No 1 determining the languages to be used by the European Economic Community http://eur-lex.europa.eu/legal-content/EN/TXT/PDF/?uri=CELEX:01958R0001-20130701&qid=1408533709461&from=EN, Official Journal of the European Union

Article Sources and Contributors

The sources listed for each article provide more detailed licensing information including the copyright status, the copyright owner, and the license conditions.

Brexit *Source:* https://en.wikipedia.org/w/index.php?oldid=860344338 *License:* Creative Commons Attribution-Share Alike 3.0 *Contributors:* 3142, Absolutelypuremilk, Ajfweb, AlphaMikeOmega, Another Believer, Arrivisto, Attributed to an attribute, BIL, Bajoscanal, Bishonen, Blue Edits, Blue-Haired Lawyer, Boson, Broadwaygenius, BubbleEngineer, Bungler91, C.Fred, Calisthenis, CambridgeBayWeather, Carbon Caryatid, Citizen Canine, ClueBot NG, Cnbrb, Coreybchapman, DanBron, DeFacto, Dean3000, Deku-shrub, Dewritech, Dr. British12, DragonflySixtyseven, Dtellett, E-Soter, Emir of Wikipedia, Entranced98, EosaphOScollain, Esszet, Everything Is Numbers, Exiguity, Felviper, François Robere, Frenchmalawi, G0mx, Galobtter, Ghmyrtle, GhostOfDanGurney, GoodDay, Graham kent, GrahamHardy, Gravuritas, Ham II, Harfarhs, Hazhk, Hijiri88, Hogweard, Hydrox, Iffy, Illegitimate Barrister, Indy beetle, Inowen, InterestingCircle, Ira Leviton, Iridescent, Irishpolitical, JASpencer, JFG, JMS Old Al, Javert2113, John Maynard Friedman, John a s, John of Reading, Jscampbell.05, Kaiketsu, Kashmiri, KeanuGreen, Keith D, Kind Tennis Fan, Kurt213, L293D, LahmacunKebab, Layzeeboi, Lessogg, Luxofluxo, MOTORAL1987, Maczkopeti, MarnetteD, Massimociccare, Materialscientist, McSly, Mervyn, Michihiro Yumoto Soga, Mikeblas, Mmitchell10, Mozart834428196, MrDemeanour, Munci, Nimbles31, Notthebestusername, Nua eire, Nyttend, Ondewelle, Oska, PlanetDeadwing, Prisencolin, Proxima Centauri, Qexigator, QubecMan, RaviC, Red King, Rfl0216, Rjwilmsi, Rodw, Ross UK, Santashark15, SemiHypercube, Sheila1988, Smeat75, Snooganssnoogans, Speed74, Ssolbergj, St170e, Svick, Taras, The Mighty Glen, The Vintage Feminist, Timrollpickering, Tobby72, Ttk371, Two clusters, Vgy7ujm, Volunteer Marek, Wikidea, Wire723, Wtmitchell, XL5, Xover, ZarhanFastfire, Zin92, 70 anonymous edits 1

History of European Union–United Kingdom relations *Source:* https://en.wikipedia.org/w/index.php?oldid=856844317 *License:* Creative Commons Attribution-Share Alike 3.0 *Contributors:* JASpencer, Lacunae, Neutrality, Neveselbert, RaviC, Snooganssnoogans, The Mighty Glen, TheFreeWorld, 4 anonymous edits 59

Opinion polling for the United Kingdom European Union membership referendum *Source:* https://en.wikipedia.org/w/index.php?oldid=858844639 *License:* Creative Commons Attribution-Share Alike 3.0 *Contributors:* 22merlin, Absolutelypuremilk, Acenditcantu, AlphaMikeOmega, Antiochus the Great, Armandomvb, AusLondonder, BU Rob13, Baldeneye, Beebuzbar, Blue-Haired Lawyer, Bondegezou, Brianclog, BrownHairedGirl, Brythones, Budapesthappy, BurritoBazooka, Cahk, Calvin999, Charles Essie, Chris the speller, ClueBot NG, Clyde1998, Colinmotox11, Create account Opinion polling for the United Kingdom EU membership referendum, Cricketfan21, Danpi3141, De wafelenbak, Dewritech, DrArsenal, Dweller, Editing Opinion polling for the United Kingdom European Union membership referendum, Editing Opinion polling for the United Kingdom European membership referendum, Elbbiw, Elephantwood, Epson Salts, EternalNomad, ExcelExcel, Firebrace, Galloglass, GermanJoe, Hammerfrog, HandsomeFella, Harumphy, Histogenea22, Hsinghsarao, Huddsblue, I don't know enough about the clippers' collapse, Isseubnida, JDuggan101, James Brian Ellis, Jayjayla, Jcc, Jehorn, Jim1138, JimKillock, Jmorrison230582, John Maynard Friedman, Jonneeo, Jrc14, Jujutsuan, JustBerry, Jw2036, Kaobear, Kwekubo, Lessogg, LordHello1, Lukeuser, Marko801, Mirrorme22, Moncrief, Mrwho00tm, Mykums, Mélencron, NeilN, Niceguyedc, NightShadow23, Number 57, Oddbodz, Odnailro, Ohconfucius, Ondewelle, Oneoffedit, Paul1337, Pinkshrimp, Poems of borns, Praline97, Quattrostagioni, Rafe87, Rami R, Red Jay, Rgcarr, Ribbet32, Rickya 23, Rjwilmsi, Ross UK, Rwendland, Sangjinhwa, Smurrayinchester, SpacemanSpiff, St170e, Stevo1000, Sujith, T.seppelt, TheFreeWorld, There'sNoTime, This account has been locked indefinitely blocked on the English Wikipedia, Timrollpickering, Tom-s13igh, TorbenTT, Turnless, UAIED, Voidxor, W.carter, Wikipedian555, Xanderale54, Zhu Haifeng, Zolarketh, 71 anonymous edits 67

United Kingdom renegotiation of European Union membership, 2015–16 *Source:* https://en.wikipedia.org/w/index.php?oldid=858187416 *License:* Creative Commons Attribution-Share Alike 3.0 *Contributors:* Adam.james870, Ajfweb, Andrew Gray, AndrewTeal, EddieHugh, Gilo1969, Ground Zero, Issues in the United Kingdom European Union membership referendum, 2016, Jaredjeya, John Maynard Friedman, Jujutsuan, LilHelpa, MOTORAL1987, MartinPoulter, Mervyn, Neveselbert, Pseudoskepsis, Queens1798, Robin S. Taylor, Sport and politics, Tabletop, The C of E, Vpab15, Wallacal, Whizz40, Wikidea, Wire723, Zzuuzz, 39 anonymous edits 115

United Kingdom European Union membership referendum, 2016 *Source:* https://en.wikipedia.org/w/index.php?oldid=859812748 *License:* Creative Commons Attribution-Share Alike 3.0 *Contributors:* Absolutelypuremilk, Alaexis, Bentogoa, Blue-Haired Lawyer, Boy.bowen, BrownHairedGirl, BullRangifer, CD rtoiletman7's lorry, Charlesdrakew, Chris the speller, Chupa tus huevos, ClueBot NG, CommonsDelinker, DNA Cowboy, DeFacto, Dlohcierekim, Dtellett, E-Soter, EU explained, EddieHugh, Favonian, FourthLineGoon, Ghmyrtle, Gilliam, Golfsco, GoodDay, Goodreg3, Grandma-redactrice, Harfarhs, Helper201, Hunterm267, I dream of horses, Impru20, JFG, JRRobinson, Jasonanaggie, Johannes Podgorica, John Maynard Friedman, Jon Kolbert, Julian.h.stacey, KAMiKAZOW, KH-1, KTo288, Kahastok, Keith D, Kind Tennis Fan, LilHelpa, LisaCrux, Lkingscott, Loffe, Loopy30, Luxofluxo, MB190417, MFlet1, MOTORAL1987, Magioladitis, MarnetteD, Michael Hucker, N-HH, Neutrality, Neveselbert, Nick.mon, Number 57, Numbermaniac, Octavio espinosa campodonico, Oiygg, Orenburg1, Philip Stevens, Proxima Centauri, RFBailey, RaviC, Risegate2017, Rubinered40, Sambaines555, SepulchreBrit, Tentinator, TheFreeWorld, This is Paul, Timrollpickering, Tobby72, Tommcgowan, Unreal7, Walterdb, Wbm1058, Wellington1850, Widr, Wikiain, Wikidea, Wikitigresito, Xwoodsterchinx, Yaris678, Ycleymans, 166 anonymous edits 125

Campaigning in the United Kingdom European Union membership referendum, 2016 *Source:* https://en.wikipedia.org/w/index.php?oldid=849310390 *License:* Creative Commons Attribution-Share Alike 3.0 *Contributors:* Adam.james870, Alarichall, AusLondonder, Bensoniensis, BrownHairedGirl, Cae prince, Crisbbacon, Deku-shrub, EU explained, EddieHugh, Editing Opinion polling for the United Kingdom European Union membership referendum, Frietjes, Good Olfactory, Has been blacklisted from creation, IronGargoyle, Issues in the United Kingdom European Union membership referendum, 2016, JASpencer, JFG, Jarble, John Maynard Friedman, Jujutsuan, Just a guy from the KP, LavaBaron, Lklundin, MOTORAL1987, Magioladitis, MartinPoulter, MatiW97, Mike Peel, NeilN, Nick Moyes, Ohconfucius, Ost316, Philafrenzy, Philip Stevens, Politicscurator, Polly Tunnel, ReusGang, RobinCarmody, RoverTheBendInSussex, Roy Bateman, Second planet in size, Smalljim, Smurrayinchester, SpacemanSpiff, Srednuas Lenoroc, This account has been locked indefinitely blocked on the English Wikipedia, Tim!, Timrollpickering, TineWiki, Total Dynamic, Varavour, WereSpielChequers, Woodlot, Zzuuzz, 45 anonymous edits 174

Results of the United Kingdom European Union membership referendum, 2016 *Source:* https://en.wikipedia.org/w/index.php?oldid=860089395 *License:* Creative Commons Attribution-Share Alike 3.0 *Contributors:* 17A Africa, AuditorGeneral, AusLondonder, BrownHairedGirl, Brythones, CeliaCarfra, Certes, ClueBot NG, Crouch, Swale, Dlohcierekim, F7154, Flooded with them hundreds, FriendlyDataNerdV2, GiantSnowman, JC7V7DC5768, JSLove39, John of Reading, Kaihsu, Kayzia, Keith D, MOTORAL1987, Maltrópa, MarnetteD, Mauls, Narky Blert, Number 57, Onel5969, Paianni, PlanetDeadwing, R'n'B, RFBailey, RaviC, RevivesDarks, Ryan76el, Shakescene, Snipkin, StAnselm, Tassedethe, The Banner, The Vintage Feminist, The-, TheFrog001, Tim!, Timrollpickering, ToastButterToast, Unreal7, Valenciano, Vicbijay, Wereon, Wikidea, Zbase4, 213 anonymous edits 183

Aftermath of the United Kingdom European Union membership referendum, 2016 *Source:* https://en.wikipedia.org/w/index.php?oldid=860157677 *License:* Creative Commons Attribution-Share Alike 3.0 *Contributors:* 1990'sguy, 72, A D Monroe III, Alarichall, Alfie Gandon, Anarcho-authoritarian, Arjayay, AusLondonder, Azerty82, Bondegezou, Boson, Britannic124, BrownHairedGirl, BubbleEngineer, Captain Cornwall, CaradhrasAiguo, Charlesdrakew, Deku-shrub, DrStrauss, Drofthec, EddieHugh, Elmeter, FirefoxLSD, Floatjon, Frietjes, Frodar, Gapfall, George Ho, GermanJoe, Ghmyrtle, GiantSnowman, Govindaharihari, Gravuritas, GünniX, Howard Alexander, I dream of horses, Imminent77, Iridescent, JASpencer, JFG, JRPG, Jdcooper, JimVC3, John of Reading, Jon Kolbert, Juniperjen, JzG, KSci, Keith D, Kind Tennis Fan, LahmacunKebab, MOTORAL1987, Magioladitis, Marcocapelle, Marianna251, MatthewJAFields, Mdmadden, Mhockey, Mutt Lunker, Niceguyedc, Ohconfucius, Oshwah, Peter K Burian, Polly Tunnel, Proxima Centauri, Robertgombos, Rodw, Selous Guide, Slashmire, Smurrayinchester, Spleodrach, Sport and politics, Stephenmann22, Sunflower174, Susan Schneegans, T0mpr1c3, The Vintage Feminist, TheFreeWorld, This is Paul, Tiller54, Twobells, Unreal7, Wbm1058, Widefox, Wiki15071, Wikidea, Zigzig20s, Ânes-pur-sàng, 64 anonymous edits 260

Russian interference in the 2016 Brexit referendum *Source:* https://en.wikipedia.org/w/index.php?oldid=858088219 *License:* Creative Commons Attribution-Share Alike 3.0 *Contributors:* Anythingyouwant, EdmundT, Gciriani, Internet Informant, JFG, Jo-Jo Eumerus, Kind Tennis Fan, Slatersteven, The Anome, Tpbradbury, Volunteer Marek, Wikidea, 3 anonymous edits 293

United Kingdom invocation of Article 50 of the Treaty on European Union *Source:* https://en.wikipedia.org/w/index.php?oldid=857932500 *License:* Creative Commons Attribution-Share Alike 3.0 *Contributors:* A3nm, Absolutelypuremilk, Ajfweb, AlexiusHoratius, Aliveness Cascade, Andrew Davidson, Boson, Brandmeister, C. Trifle, Charlesdrakew, Cheeseskates, Closeapple, Coffee, Continentaleurope, Danlaycock, Dr.K., DylanMcKaneWiki, Elmidae, Esszet, Evans1982, FallingGravity, Fixuture, G1729, Gavinayling, George Ho, Ghmyrtle, Graham11, Greenshed, Greggydude, Haakonsson, Ham II, Hameltion, HandsomeFella, HapHaxion, HelgaStick, Hosgeorges, IngenieroLoco, Iridescent, Is Chewbacca racist?, J 1982, JASpencer, Jayron32, John Maynard Friedman, Jusdafax, JustBerry, KTo288, Kaihsu, Kashmiri, Kusma, Lessogg, Lizard the Wizard, Lklundin, LordDimwit, Lugnuts, M1chaeljack, MOTORAL1987, MRD2014, Mattflaschen, Medeis, Mervyn, Mhockey, Mx. Granger, Mythlike-Cell, Ohconfucius, Pol098, Polly Tunnel, Primefac, Qexigator, RaviC, Rwv37, SUM1, Samrp45, Seagull123, Shellwood, Simpatico qa, Slowfun, Smurrayinchester, SquarePeg, Sumorsǣte, Tarheru, Tataral, Tigerboy1966, Tim!, Trappist the monk, Unreal7, Vpab15, Waggers, Wikiain, Wire723, Xevious, YechezkelZilber, You have no idea who I am, Zigzig20s, Zythe, Ânes-pur-sàng, Вечный подмастерье, 96 anonymous edits 297

Brexit negotiations *Source:* https://en.wikipedia.org/w/index.php?oldid=860316207 *License:* Creative Commons Attribution-Share Alike 3.0 *Contributors:* Aisteco, Alpha3031, Arjayay, BIL, Bangalamania, Bennv3771, Bilorv, Boson, BowlAndSpoon, Brexitfighter, Cap1988, Catlemur, CentreLeftRight, Classicwiki, Clyde1998, Comp.arch, Comuna de Paris, Corn cheese, Danski454, Dawkeye, Dawn Bard, Dewritech, Djm-leighpark, Dl2000, ELPEN62, EdmundT, Ghmyrtle, GiovanniSidwell, Govindaharihari, Headbomb, InterestingCircle, JASpencer, Jamacfarlane, John Maynard Friedman, John of Reading, Julesd, K347, Kaldari, Kimsey0, Kind Tennis Fan, Lazeroptyx, Legendiii, Mais oui!, Marc Lacoste, Meters, Mild Bill Hiccup, Moscow Mule,

Image Sources, Licenses and Contributors

The sources listed for each image provide more detailed licensing information including the copyright status, the copyright owner, and the license conditions.

Image *Source:* https://en.wikipedia.org/w/index.php?title=File:Padlock-silver.svg *Contributors:* AzaToth, BotMultichill, BotMultichillT, Gurch, Jarekt, Kallerna, Multichill, Perhelion, Rd232, Riana, Sarang, Siebrand, Steinsplitter, 4 anonymous edits ... 1

Image *Source:* https://en.wikipedia.org/w/index.php?title=File:UK_location_in_the_EU_2016.svg *License:* GNU Free Documentation License *Contributors:* Bazonka, De728631, Furfur, Koavf, OgreBot 2, RaviC, Royal Export, Sarang, Steinsplitter, ThiefOfBagdad, Turnless ... 1

Image *Source:* https://en.wikipedia.org/w/index.php?title=File:A_new_map_of_Great_Britain_according_to_the_newest_and_most_exact_observations_(8342715024).jpg *License:* Creative Commons Attribution 2.0 *Contributors:* http://maps.bpl.org ... 4

Image *Source:* https://en.wikipedia.org/w/index.php?title=File:Flag_of_the_United_Kingdom.svg *License:* Public Domain *Contributors:* Anomie, Good Olfactory, Jo-Jo Eumerus, MSGJ, Mifter ... 4

Figure 1 *Source:* https//en.wikipedia.org *Contributors:* User:Brythones, User:Mirrorme22, User:MrPenguin20, User:Nilfanion, User:RaviC, User:Sting, User:TUBS ... 8

Figure 2 *Source:* https://en.wikipedia.org/w/index.php?title=File:Vote_Leave_poster,_Omagh.jpg *License:* Creative Commons Attribution-Share Alike 2.0 Generic *Contributors:* Kenneth Allen ... 10

Image *Source:* https://en.wikipedia.org/w/index.php?title=File:United_Kingdom_EU_referendum_2016_voting_regions_results.svg *License:* GNU Free Documentation License *Contributors:* User:Furfur, User:NordNordWest ... 12

Image *Source:* https://en.wikipedia.org/w/index.php?title=File:United_Kingdom_EU_referendum_2016_area_results_2-tone.svg *License:* Creative Commons Attribution-Sharealike 3.0 *Contributors:* Cranberry Products, JayCoop, Nilfanion, Sarang, Schmarrnintelligenz, Vivaelcelta ... 12

Image *Source:* https://en.wikipedia.org/w/index.php?title=File:Wikisource-logo.svg *License:* Creative Commons Attribution-Sharealike 3.0 *Contributors:* ChrisiPK, Guillom, INeverCry, Jarekt, JuTa, Leyo, Lokal Profil, MichaelMaggs, NielsF, Rei-artur, Rocket000, Romaine, Steinsplitter ... 15

Figure 3 *Source:* https://en.wikipedia.org/w/index.php?title=File:The_Border_on_Killeen_School_Road_-_geograph.org.uk_-_446719.jpg *License:* Creative Commons Attribution-Share Alike 2.0 Generic *Contributors:* Oliver Dixon ... 29

Figure 4 *Source:* https://en.wikipedia.org/w/index.php?title=File:Gibraltar_Customs_side_of_the_Spain-Gibraltar_frontier,_Winston_Churchill_Avenue,_Gibraltar.jpg *License:* Creative Commons Attribution-Sharealike 2.0 *Contributors:* Paul ... 30

Figure 5 *Source:* https://en.wikipedia.org/w/index.php?title=File:Brexit-is-a-monstrosity-float-2017-10-01-in-manchester-photo-robert-mandel.jpg *Contributors:* 4nn1l2, Kaufkraft, LG02 ... 53

Figure 6 *Source:* https://en.wikipedia.org/w/index.php?title=File:DBG_22473_(26370830218).jpg *License:* Creative Commons Zero *Contributors:* @infozentrale ... 53

Image *Source:* https://en.wikipedia.org/w/index.php?title=File:Wiktionary-logo-en-v2.svg *Contributors:* User:Dan Polansky, User:Smurrayinchester 56

Figure 7 *Source:* https//en.wikipedia.org *Contributors:* User:Brythones, User:Mirrorme22, User:MrPenguin20, User:Nilfanion, User:RaviC, User:Sting, User:TUBS ... 64

Figure 8 *Source:* https://en.wikipedia.org/w/index.php?title=File:UK_EU_referendum_polling.svg *Contributors:* User:T.seppelt/UK EU referendum polling.csv, User:T.seppelt/UK EU referendum polling.csv ... 71

Image *Source:* https://en.wikipedia.org/w/index.php?title=File:Flag_of_France.svg *License:* Public Domain *Contributors:* Anomie, Fastily, Jo-Jo Eumerus ... 95

Image *Source:* https://en.wikipedia.org/w/index.php?title=File:Flag_of_Germany.svg *License:* Public Domain *Contributors:* Anomie, Jo-Jo Eumerus 95

Image *Source:* https://en.wikipedia.org/w/index.php?title=File:Flag_of_Austria.svg *License:* Public Domain *Contributors:* Alex Great, Andres gb.ldc, Bestiasonica, Camervan, Cycn, Denelson83, Doodledoo, Elisabeth59, Enbéká, Footyfanatic3000, Fry1989, Gabbe, Glaisher, Golden Bosnian Lily, Gryffindor, Gunnar.offel, Herbythyme, Homo lupus, Klemen Kocjancic, Kwj2772, MAXXX-309, Maire, Mattes, Mogelzahn, Nagy, Pixeltoo, Prev, Pumbaa80, Ricordisamoa, SKopp, Samah10, Sarang, Siebrand, Stiantoerst, Superzerocool, Tn4196, UV, UberHalogen, Ultratomio, VAIO HK, Xinunus, ZooFari, Zscout370, Ztga34z∼commonswiki, חיים 7, 13 anonymous edits ... 95

Image *Source:* https://en.wikipedia.org/w/index.php?title=File:Flag_of_Belgium_(civil).svg *License:* Public Domain *Contributors:* Allforrous, Andres gb.ldc, Bean49, Cathy Richards, David Descamps, Dbenbenn, Denelson83, Evanc0912, FreshCorp619, Fry1989, Gabriel trzy, Howcome, IvanOS, Jdx, Mimich, Ms2ger, Nightstallion, Oreo Priest, Pitke, Ricordisamoa, Rocket000, Rodejong, Sarang, SiBr4, Sir Iain, ThomasPusch, Warddr, Zscout370, ייהלייושמר, 15 anonymous edits ... 95

Image *Source:* https://en.wikipedia.org/w/index.php?title=File:Flag_of_Bulgaria.svg *License:* Public Domain *Contributors:* SKopp ... 95

Image *Source:* https://en.wikipedia.org/w/index.php?title=File:Flag_of_Croatia.svg *License:* Public Domain *Contributors:* Nightstallion, Elephantus, Neoneo13, Denelson83, Rainman, R-41, Minestrone, Lupo, Zscout370, MaGa (based on Decision of ... 95

Image *Source:* https://en.wikipedia.org/w/index.php?title=File:Flag_of_Cyprus.svg *License:* Public Domain *Contributors:* User:Vzb83 ... 96

Image *Source:* https://en.wikipedia.org/w/index.php?title=File:Flag_of_the_Czech_Republic.svg *License:* Public Domain *Contributors:* -xfi-, Alkari, Andres gb.ldc, AwOc, Benzoyl, Bjankuloski06en, C41n, Cycn, Denelson83, Denniss, Dzordzm, EZBELLA, Er Komandante, Fedor204, Fibonacci, FreshCorp619, Fry1989, Future Perfect at Sunrise, Gumruch, Homo lupus, JuTa, Klemen Kocjancic, Leyo, Li-sung, MAXXX-309, Madden, Miraceti, NeverDoING, Nightstallion, Pfctdayelise, Phlegmatic, Pseudomoi, Pumbaa80, Ratatosk, Ricordisamoa, Saibo, Sangjinhwa, Sarang, Shybird, SiBr4, Stephanie∼commonswiki, V-ball, Wiki-vr, علی المزارقه, 43 anonymous edits ... 96

Image *Source:* https://en.wikipedia.org/w/index.php?title=File:Flag_of_Denmark.svg *License:* Public Domain *Contributors:* Madden ... 96

Image *Source:* https://en.wikipedia.org/w/index.php?title=File:Flag_of_Estonia.svg *License:* Public Domain *Contributors:* Originally drawn by User:SKopp. Blue colour changed by User:PeepP to match the image at 96

Image *Source:* https://en.wikipedia.org/w/index.php?title=File:Flag_of_Finland.svg *License:* Public Domain *Contributors:* SVG drawn by Sebastian Koppehel ... 96

Image *Source:* https://en.wikipedia.org/w/index.php?title=File:Flag_of_Greece.svg *License:* Public Domain *Contributors:* (of code) cs:User:-xfi- (talk) ... 96

Image *Source:* https://en.wikipedia.org/w/index.php?title=File:Flag_of_Hungary.svg *License:* Public Domain *Contributors:* SKopp ... 96

Image *Source:* https://en.wikipedia.org/w/index.php?title=File:Flag_of_Ireland.svg *License:* Public Domain *Contributors:* User:SKopp ... 96

Image *Source:* https://en.wikipedia.org/w/index.php?title=File:Flag_of_Italy.svg *License:* Public Domain *Contributors:* Anomie, Jo-Jo Eumerus 96

Image *Source:* https://en.wikipedia.org/w/index.php?title=File:Flag_of_Latvia.svg *License:* Public Domain *Contributors:* Anime Addict AA, Cathy Richards, Ciervo258, Common Good, Cycn, Dark Eagle, David1010, Edgars2007, Editor at Large, Fred J, Fry1989, Homo lupus, IvanOS, Kalnroze, Klemen Kocjancic, Ludger1961, MAXXX-309, Mattes, Ninane, OAlexander∼commonswiki, RainbowSilver2ndBackup, Renessaince, Ricordisamoa, Rocket000, SKopp, Sarang, TFerenczy, V. Turchaninov, Wester, Zscout370, 12 anonymous edits ... 96

Image *Source:* https://en.wikipedia.org/w/index.php?title=File:Flag_of_Lithuania.svg *License:* Public Domain *Contributors:* Agente Rolf, CemDemirkartal, CrimsonViking, David1010, Fred J, Fry1989, GiW, Homo lupus, IvanOS, Juetho, Klemen Kocjancic, Ludger1961, Madden, Matasg, Nightstallion, Ninane, Ricordisamoa, Rodejong, SKopp, Sarang, TFerenczy, Telman Masliukou, ThomasPusch, Wizardist, Zscout370, Zzyzx11, חיים 7, 13 anonymous edits ... 96

Image *Source:* https://en.wikipedia.org/w/index.php?title=File:Flag_of_Luxembourg.svg *License:* Public Domain *Contributors:* User:SKopp ... 96

Image *Source:* https://en.wikipedia.org/w/index.php?title=File:Flag_of_Malta.svg *License:* Public Domain *Contributors:* Alkari, Allforrous, Cathy Richards, Cycn, File Upload Bot (Magnus Manske), Fry1989, Gabbe, GoldenRainbow, Hedwig in Washington, Herbythyme, Homo lupus, Klemen Kocjancic, Liftarn, Mattes, Meno25, Nightstallion, Peeperman, Prev, Pumbaa80, Ratatosk, Raymond1922A, Rodejong, Sangjinhwa, SiBr4, Xwejnusgozo, Yiyi, Zscout370, 7 anonymous edits ... 96

Image *Source:* https://en.wikipedia.org/w/index.php?title=File:Flag_of_the_Netherlands.svg *License:* Public Domain *Contributors:* Zscout370 96

Image *Source:* https://en.wikipedia.org/w/index.php?title=File:Flag_of_Poland.svg *License:* Public Domain *Contributors:* Anomie, Jo-Jo Eumerus, Mifter ... 96

Image *Source:* https://en.wikipedia.org/w/index.php?title=File:Flag_of_Portugal.svg *License:* Public Domain *Contributors:* Columbano Bordalo Pinheiro (1910; generic design); Vítor Luís Rodrigues; António Martins-Tuválkin (2004; this specific v ... 96

Image *Source:* https://en.wikipedia.org/w/index.php?title=File:Flag_of_Romania.svg *Contributors:* AdiJapan ... 96

Image *Source:* https://en.wikipedia.org/w/index.php?title=File:Flag_of_Slovakia.svg *License:* Public Domain *Contributors:* Achim1999, B1mbo, Cycn, Erlenmeyer, Fry1989, Herbythyme, Homo lupus, IP 84.5∼commonswiki, Illegitimate Barrister, J 1982, Justass, Klemen Kocjancic, Leyo, Madden, Mattes, Mogelzahn, Mxn, Nightstallion, Peter Zelizňák, Pmsyyz, Pumbaa80, Ricordisamoa, Ruwolf, SKopp, Samah10, Sangjinhwa, Sarang, SiBr4, Srtxg, Str4nd, TFCforever, Torsch, Tvdm, Wiki-vr, Zscout370, 11 anonymous edits ... 96

Image *Source:* https://en.wikipedia.org/w/index.php?title=File:Flag_of_Slovenia.svg *License:* Public Domain *Contributors:* User:Achim1999 . 96

License

Index

480

www.ingramcontent.com/pod-product-compliance
Lightning Source LLC
Chambersburg PA
CBHW020522270326
41927CB00006B/408

9 789352 979592